Peter Aguilar

The Little Mac Book

I know, I know—
the book's not so little anymore.
Neither is the Mac.

SEVENTH EDITION

Robin Williams

Peachpit Press
Berkeley ▾ California

The Little Mac Book seventh edition

Cover art illustration by Terry Widener; cover design and production by Ted Mader and Associates

Interior design and production by Robin Williams

Indexing by Robin Williams

Editing by Nancy Davis

Production management by Kate Reber

Back cover photo of Robin by John Tollett

The illustrations throughout the book are from the multi-talented pen/mouse of John Tollett.
www.UrlsInternetCafe.com

Peachpit Press
1249 Eighth Street
Berkeley, California 94710
800.283.9444
510.524.2178
510.524.2221 fax

Find us on the World Wide Web at **www.peachpit.com**
Peachpit Press is a division of Addison Wesley Longman

ISBN 0-201-74580-1

10 9 8 7 6 5 4 3 2

Printed and bound in the United States of America

To my mother, Patricia Williams,
who made it possible,
and to my father, Gerald Williams,
who would have been proud.

Acknowledgments

In 1989 I self-published the first printing of this book because not one of the ten computer-book publishers I queried would publish me. While I was at it, I also self-published *The Mac is not a typewriter.* A great deal has happened in the past twelve years, and these are some of the people who have meant a lot through it all:

Ted Nace, founder and first publisher of Peachpit Press, who believed in me and let me create the book the way my students needed it.

So many people from **BMUG,** who have always been so kind and supportive and were there from the very beginning.

Guy Kawasaki, who kindly took me under his wing.

Carmen Sheldon, Barbara Sikora, Kathy Thornley, Richard Abrahams, Max Hein, Shirley Davis, and **Bill in PR,** all at Santa Rosa Junior College, every one of whom I miss.

Mary Grady, who taught me to be a much better writer.

Everyone at Peachpit, especially **Nancy Davis** and **Kate Reber** who have worked on so many books with me; **Jim Norrena,** my dear friend and comrade; and **Nancy Ruenzel,** publisher, friend, and staunch believer.

Dave Rohr, Karen Rodney, Andrew Rodney, David Brownlow, Andrew Main, and **Lanis Loyd,** great friends from the Santa Fe Mac User Group who have given me great tech support.

Phil Russell and **Lew and Gloria Nelson** from the Corvallis Mac User Group; **Jim and Majie Alley** from the Savannah Mac User Group; **Lynette and Rick Redfern** from the Adobe Technology Exchange, all of whom have provided information, support, and warm friendship for years.

All of my students past, present, and future, from whom I have learned and continue to learn how to teach.

My family, who support me even though they don't read my books.

John Tollett, the one in the trenches with me, my knight in a muddy pickup.

When I first self-published this book, Scarlett was 3 years old, Jimmy was 7, Ryan was 11, and I was single. Now Scarlett is a teenager; Jimmy is 19; Ryan is 23, a Navy SEAL, and married; and I'm still single. It's funny how kids get older and we don't.

Contents

part two **beyond the basics**

part four — extra stuff

Read Me First

If you're intimidated or in a hurry, use theTutorial that starts on page 15, then shut the book and move on. Skip this part. Skip the rest of the book. Come back later if you get in trouble.

I hope you were warned that your Macintosh, like no other computer, is addictive. It pulls you in. It has you inventing work for yourself just so you can use it. It creates an attitude that makes you feel like you're having fun while being productive—what a concept.

This book is a direct path to the essentials of operating the computer so you can get straight to work without wasting too much time diddling around trying to figure it out. There's not much technical information here because most of us don't need it or want it; you don't have to know how to fly the plane to take a vacation in Rio.

This book used to be very little. It's gotten bigger because the Macintosh has gotten bigger. The Mac is still the easiest and most empowering computer to use, but it is a fact that there are some things that are now a little more confusing than they used to be. And everyone is in a rush and no one has time to do anything luxurious like spend time learning how to use a new computer, so these confusing features can be very frustrating. I know—you want to get straight to work.

So start with the Tutorial. It will walk you through just what you need to know to get up and running and on your way, telling you specifically which parts of the book to read. The rest of the book you can read another time—pick up the book while you're waiting for a document to come out the printer, open it when you realize there is something specific you don't quite understand, browse through it while waiting for the coffee to drip. You see, if you read this book all the way through, you won't absorb many of the tidbits of information the first time around. You need to let a certain amount of information sink in before you can absorb other bits. And many solutions just won't make sense until you've had the problem.

Skip over anything that doesn't make sense right away. That's one of the most wonderful things about the Mac—you can bumble along for a long time on a surprisingly small amount of information. When your brain is ready to absorb more, come back to the parts that didn't make sense the first time around.

Whenever you come across a term you are not familiar with, check the index. It will refer you to the page where that term is defined. Really—I spent an inordinate amount of time on the index so you would be able to find an explanation for every term in this book. After all, I want you to have fun and take advantage of this new concept in productivity as you, too, become addicted.

Quizzes

There are quizzes at the end of each chapter. As a teacher, I always give "open book, open mouth" quizzes. I do believe you are more likely to remember the right answer *if you write down the right answer,* no matter how you discovered it. And you're more likely to have fun discovering the answer if there is less stress involved in taking the quiz. So lighten up, relax, enjoy your new computer!

Mac OS 9.0 and up

This book is specifically for people who are using a Macintosh that is running some version of the "operating system" called Mac OS 9. If you're using system version 8.5 or 8.6, you'll still find 95 percent of this book appropriate. There will be several features mentioned that you don't have on your computer, but if you find them, just ignore them and understand it's not that you're doing anything wrong—those features are just missing.

If you want an edition of this book that is not specific to Mac OS 9, call Peachpit Press and request the Sixth Edition of this book, which covers Mac OS 8.5 and 8.6, or the Fifth Edition, which covers 8.0 and 8.1. If you have an older Mac that is using System 7.0 through 7.6, ask Peachpit for the Fourth Edition of *The Little Mac Book.*

Which System are you Running?

How can you tell exactly which system you have on your Mac? If you know how to use your mouse, first click once on the Desktop. Then go to the Apple menu and press on it—the first item in the drop-down menu will be either "About This Computer" or "About This Macintosh." Choose it to see which system you have.

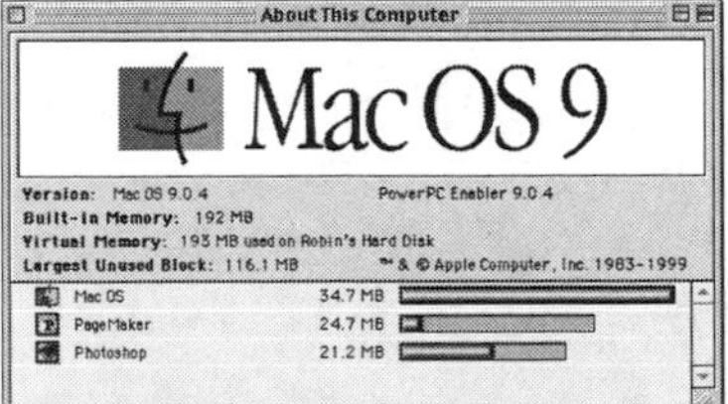

This is what you get from the Apple menu. It will tell you loud and clear exactly which operating system your Macintosh is running.

From the Publisher

This little book has enriched so many lives, mine included.

Long before I ever had the privilege of working with Robin Williams, I felt as though I knew her—as if I'd known her all my life. I worked my way through college as a typesetter, proofreader, and layout artist, and I took great pride in knowing how to create professional-quality publications. Then came the Mac, and I felt so incredibly stupid. All of us in publishing, type, and printing shops had to scramble to become Mac-literate, while watching our customers gleefully creating some of the worst-looking documents on the planet. But really, who could blame them? Almost overnight the Mac had democratized publishing tools. Suddenly, anyone who could type and owned a Mac could be a desktop publisher. We were all itching to learn how the tools could save us time and money. Most of all, we were all itching to stop feeling stupid and start being creative.

Then, out of the blue one day, someone handed us *The Little Mac Book*. I say "us" because to this day, over ten years after I was handed my first copy, people are still telling me—and with as much pride as I tell my story—how they were first introduced to Robin's *Little Mac Book*. Our stories are astonishingly similar: A friend helping us plug in our first Mac shared her copy; a work colleague slipped it to us over the cubicle wall; our boss gave us the first-day-on-the-job "read-this" routine. People not only recommend it, but they physically hand it to new users. We who were once nervous new users ourselves are confident, and pleased to reassure those who come after us, "Don't worry, everything will make sense once you read this little book"—just as Robin reassured her students back when she first got the idea to write this book. Little did she know that her self-published classroom textbook would turn into a million-plus bestseller that's still going strong more than ten years later! *The Little Mac Book* was the first book, and to this day still is the only book, to integrate commonsense, jargon-free teaching to show you how to get on friendly terms with your computer, with basic desktop-publishing do's and don't's.

It's not just the book that's still going strong. Robin's come a long way since the days when she was raising three young children and teaching graphics classes at Santa Rosa Junior College. She's become an icon in the Mac community. An internationally recognized expert on graphics, desktop publishing, and Web publishing, Robin has earned countless awards, attracted legions of fans, and launched several successful series of books, including *The Non-Designer's* series, the *Little Book* series, as well as desktop publishing classics such as *The Mac is not a typewriter, The Little iMac Book*, and one of her latest, *Robin Williams Design Workshop.*

If I know Robin, right about now she's starting to get embarrassed. She feels more comfortable teaching and nurturing others than fielding praise, which is why her readers come to view her as a friend. Her advice resonates as much for those who don't know an operating system from a sound system as for the folks who don't know a typeface from a smiley face. And when we learn it from Robin, we don't feel stupid or ashamed. As Robin's readers, we are a part of a much larger community—a community that has survived Apple's ups and downs, and a community that cares about quality and creativity. Nothing can ever diminish the community feeling among Mac users that Robin first sparked with this book.

Robin, I'm honored to speak on behalf of all your readers: Thank you for this little book. Thanks for your insights, your warmth, your wit, and your friendship. But above all, thanks for your hard work and commitment to your readers. Peachpit is honored to be your publisher and we want to congratulate you for ten amazing years of writing great books. We look forward to the next ten!

Nancy Aldrich-Ruenzel
Publisher, Peachpit Press
Robin Williams' biggest fan

P.S. Dear reader: Take my word for it—everything *will* make sense once you read this little book.

Tutorial

If you're new to your Mac, I suggest you start here. This tutorial follows a logical pattern that I have found to be successful in my classes (but it's not meant to be completed in one day!). These steps skip all over the book—I apologize for the hopping around you'll have to do, but you really shouldn't read *everything* about windows or the mouse or whatever at once. You need to know just enough to feel comfortable, then come back later for more. If you get overloaded, turn off the computer and have a cup of tea with me.

After you've finished the brief tutorial, spend a few weeks working on your Mac. Then come back to the book and read the rest of it. Not only will the tips and tricks make more sense to you, but you'll find you can actually absorb the rest of the information.

Don't Limit Yourself

You might think, in your eagerness to get right into a program and start creating something, that you want to skip all these dumb little exercises at the Desktop like making windows smaller and larger or copying blank folders onto disks. But trust me—it's too easy to turn on the computer, find the button for your program, and go right into it. But then you're limited. You won't have complete control over your computer. Some things will always confuse you. You'll never be a Power User (your Goal in Life, right?).

Quick Start

But for the person who wants to instantly create, save, print, and quit, the steps are quite easy:

- ▾ **Open** your word processing program
  (or other program of your choice): double-click on its icon.
- ▾ **Save** the new document:
  from the File menu, choose "Save As...."
  Name the file and click "Save."
- ▾ **Create** something: start typing.
  Save regularly as you work (from the File menu, choose "Save").
- ▾ **Print** the document:
  go up to the File menu
  and choose "Print...."
  Click "OK" in all the boxes.
- ▾ **Quit:** go back to the File menu
  and choose "Quit."

This is the same basic process you will go through in any application—it's really that easy. But to be truly powerful—ahhh, that takes a little more time.

Start Using the Tutorial Here

If you're using a Performa or any other Mac where the Launcher (shown below) is displayed, close the Launcher before you start this tutorial. Just click in the little close box, as shown below.

Read a few things first

So here are my recommendations on what you should spend time doing if your time is very limited. Actually, this is a good way to start even if you have lots of time; there is so much information to be absorbed that it works best to absorb a little now, then come back for more later. It also helps to run into a few problems, because then when you discover the solution, the solution makes much more sense.

I'll explain a task you need to know and tell you which pages have detailed information.

- Read the first chapter on Ks, megs, gigs, and disks. C'mon—it will only take a couple of minutes, and it will make everything else much clearer. And people will be impressed when you start tossing around terms like "30 gigabyte hard disk."
- You've probably already done this, but just in case you haven't, learn how to turn on your computer. Read the first several paragraphs of Chapter 2.
- What you see when you turn on the Macintosh is called the Desktop. It is also called the Finder because the software program that runs the Desktop is the Finder. The Desktop is kind of like home base. We'll talk more about it later.
- If you have never used a mouse before, read Chapter 3. Particularly take note of the pointer's "hot spot," and don't forget the part about how my terminology for "press" and "press-and-drag" differs from what you will commonly read in other documention. (My terms are more accurate, of course.) If you don't have a trackball, skip that section. And you can come back later to figure out how to clean the mouse. Now let's go practice using that mouse.

If the Launcher is showing, close it before continuing with the tutorial. Using the mouse, position the tip of the pointer right in the middle of this little box and click once to put the Launcher away. (Your Launcher doesn't look exactly like this—you have different buttons.)

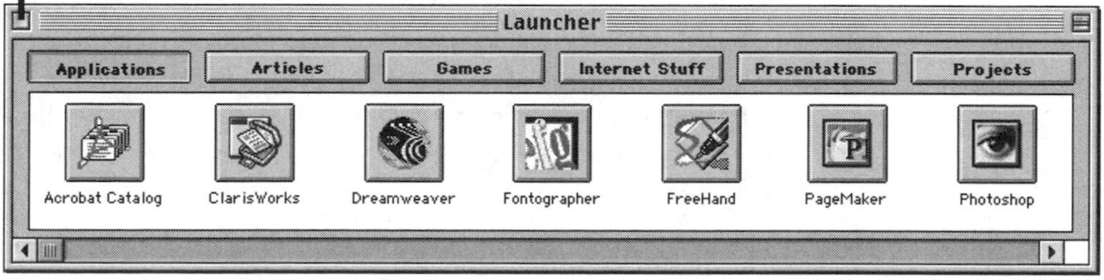

Using the Mouse

Your hard disk icon may look a little different from the one shown above, and your trash can might have garbage in it.

After you've read page 44, practice using your **mouse:**

- Click **once** on icons (the little pictures) you see on the screen, such as the hard disk icon at the top-right of your screen and the trash can icon in the lower-right. Notice the icons change color when you click once on them. (If the Launcher window is still open, *don't click once on any of its icons;* close the Launcher as described on the previous page.)
- **Double-click** the hard disk icon or the trash can. Notice that it takes a very quick click-click (double-click) or the computer thinks it is two single clicks. And you must hold the mouse very still between the clicks.
- Point to the menu bar across the top of the screen. **Click** on any name in the menu to see the list of menu commands. There are eight items in the menu bar (nine in Mac OS 9.1)—check out all of them! (Yes, the apple has a menu, as well as the tiny icon on the far right.) Don't choose any of the menu commands you see in any of the menu lists yet!

Using Menus and Menu Commands

Read the first two pages in Chapter 5 about **menus** and **how to choose commands.** You can read the rest of that chapter next week. Practice using your mouse to check out the menus, but be careful what you choose! You can choose menu commands in two ways:

1. **Click once** on a menu item and the menu list will drop down and stay there. **Click once again** on the menu command you want. (If the command is gray, that means you can't choose it right now.)

Optional information:

If you ever use a Macintosh that is running a version of the Mac OS before version 8.0, you will have do this in the menus:

Press on any menu item (hold the mouse button down) and slide down the list—this is a **press-and-drag.** Notice that some menu commands are black and some are gray. As you slide across the black items, the entire line highlights.

When choosing one of these menu commands using the press-and-drag method, don't click on the command! Just let go! Really. This is not just a suggestion, it is a rule that will prevent trouble later. Be conscious about it—make sure you are not *clicking* in any menu when you use this method. Press, drag, let go.

Using the Desk Accessories

Use some of the **desk accessories.** Read the pages mentioned below and follow the directions. This will help you feel more comfortable using the mouse, choosing menu items, and customizing your computer. If you press on the *name* of the open desk accessory, you can drag it around the screen. To put it away, click in the little box in the upper-left of the accessory.

- **Calculator** (page 214). Click the mouse to enter the numbers, or use the numeric keypad on the keyboard.
- **Note Pad** (page 218). Make some notes to yourself.
- **Jigsaw Puzzle** (page 219). This is really fun. Don't bother right now about customizing the puzzle.

Press-and-drag in this "title bar" to move the Calculator around your screen.

Also use one of the **Control Panels,** the Mouse control panel.

- From the Apple menu (where you got the desk accessories), click "Control Panels," then choose the "Mouse" control panel. Read about it on page 251 and choose the speed you like.

Manipulating Windows

Read Chapter 7 on *All Windows.* **Windows** are very important—every application you use will display itself in a window so you need to know how to control them. Chapter 7 is short, and everything you learn will apply every day in your work and play.

If you do not see a window on your screen at the moment, double-click on the icon (the picture) of your hard disk, the icon on the upper-right of your screen. Go through Chapter 7 and pick out all the parts to a window. Go through the list and use each part:

Your hard disk icon looks something like this, although it will have a different name.

- Resize the window.
- Move the window.
- Zoom the window large and small. Hold down the Option key (near the Spacebar) and click the zoom box. What's the difference?
- Open another folder; now you should see at least two windows. Which window is *active* (very important!)? How do you make another window active? What's the point of active windows anyway? *Be sure you can answer these questions!*
- Try all three methods of using the scroll bars when the window is sized small.
- Close the window using the close box.
- Open the folder again, using the menu command this time (*select* the folder first). Then close it using the menu. (Which menu is it in? You will always find the "Open" command in the same menu in every application).

Recognizing Icons

Read these pages about **icons** in Chapter 9: pages 92–93, the bottom half of 95, and page 97. Skip the rest for now! Even if you don't see too many icons at the moment, remember that icons tell you a lot; they are rich in visual clues that help you understand your computer.

Don't double-click on anything except folder icons at the moment. You can open the System Folder on your hard disk, and then open other folders that are inside the System Folder. Keep these things in mind:

- Folder icons always open to show you their contents in a window.
- Document icons always open the application they were created within and then display the document.
- Application icons always open to a clean, blank page, *or* to an *option* of opening a clean, blank page.

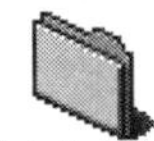

Web Sites

It's always safe to double-click on folders.

AppleWorks

Double-click on an application to open a new, blank page.

Care of Briards

If you double-click on a document, you will open the application it was created in.

(If you accidentally find yourself in an application, go up to the File menu and choose "Quit.")

Keyboard Commands

Use the keyboard commands to do some of those tasks you just used the mouse for. Read page 57, "Keyboard Shortcuts." Using the keyboard shortcuts is a sign of becoming a Power User.

The trick to making a keyboard shortcut work is that you must *first* select the item you want to affect. For instance, if you want to open a folder, *first* click once on the folder to select it, *then* press Command O to open it.

Do each of these things using a keyboard shortcut:

- Open a window.
- Close a window.
- Select every item in a window.
  (To deselect the items, click in any white space in the folder.)

Folders, Backing Up, and the Trash

This is a list of several basic Desktop tasks you need to learn because you will be doing them everyday:

- Read pages 105–106 about folders. Make a new folder. (What is the keyboard shortcut?!) Name your new folder.
- Make a duplicate of this new folder: click once on the folder to select it, then find the command for duplicating. Which menu is it in, and what is the keyboard shortcut? Change the name of this folder (page 107).
- Read pages 107–108. Put the second folder into the first folder. Take the second folder *out* of the first folder. You will constantly be putting things into and taking things out of folders. It's exactly the same as putting items into and taking items out of the manila folders in your office—you're just using a mouse and pointer to do it instead of your hands.
- If you have a Zip drive, insert a new Zip disk. (If you don't have a *new* disk, insert any one you do have). If the Zip disk is new, name it.
- Backup your work! You should do this to every document you want to keep. Read page 114. If you have a Zip drive, copy the first folder you created onto a Zip disk. *Now this Zip disk is your backup of that important file!* In case the file on your hard disk gets lost or trashed or your hard disk dies, you will have this extra copy.
- Use the trash can (read the top half of page 122). Throw away the first folder you made. Empty the trash (page 123, top half).
- Put your second practice folder in the trash. Oh no! That was a mistake! Open the trash can and put the folder back (read the last paragraph on page 122). Be way cool—use the "Put Away" keyboard shortcut.
- Read page 76. Change your window view to "as List." Then read pages 78 and 80 and "sort" your window in different ways.
- Change your window view to one of the lists, such as "by Name." Read page 109 about the *outline mode.* Practice expanding and compressing folders. This is just another way to look at the contents of folders, instead of opening each one to a window.
- Change the window view to "as Icons." Move the icons around: just press on them and drag. Use the View menu to arrange them.

Word Processing

Open a **word-processing** application (double-click on its icon). You surely have at least SimpleText, a tiny word processor, on your hard disk, and you probably have AppleWorks (previously known as ClarisWorks). Everything you learn in a word processor will apply to every other program you ever use. Any word processor is a great place to practice the most basic and valuable skills; once you feel comfortable here, you can bumble your way through any other sort of program.

- Read pages 132–137 in the Word Processing chapter. Type several paragraphs and practice using the menus, moving the insertion point, fixing typos, and selecting text and changing its font, style, and size. *Remember, all typing and backspacing starts wherever the* **insertion point** *is flashing, not where the I-beam or the pointer is pointing!*
- After you've finished several paragraphs and feel comfortable with the features you've been practicing, read pages 138–139 about the **Clipboard. Cut** some of your text. **Copy** some of your text. **Paste** the text somewhere else. Paste it in again. Make sure you can predict *what* will be pasted and *where* it will appear. Use the keyboard shortcuts for Cut, Copy, Paste, and Undo.
- *When you are feeling very confident,* try using some of the **special characters,** such as ¢ and • and ©, as described on page 141. If you're really feeling sassy, try typing "résumé" with the accent marks. See pages 216–217 for more about Key Caps.
- Read pages 143–145 and **save** your witty and intelligent report. Eventually you should return to pages 148 and 149 and study them, but right now just go ahead and save your document: From the File menu, choose "Save As...," type a title for your document, then click the Save button. (After you lose a few documents you will appreciate the information on pages 148 and 149.)

  If you are working on a Performa or an iMac, your document might be saved automatically into the Documents folder; see page 246.

Printing

You should just be able to get the Chooser from the Apple menu, click on the picture of your printer on the left, click on either the name of your printer or the printer port icon on the right, then close the Chooser and print. If it doesn't go this smoothly, you might want to have someone help you through this because it can be quite confusing.

Now you need **to print your document.**

- **If no one has ever printed from this computer before,** you need to read pages 152–153 and use the Chooser to tell your Mac which printer to use. Once the Mac has printed to a printer, you never need to go back to the Chooser again unless you have to switch printers. Skip over a bunch of pages, then . . .
- Read pages 160–161 and just follow steps 1 through 5. Basically all you're doing is choosing "Print" from the File menu and clicking the "OK" buttons.
- You need to **quit** the application if you are done for the day. Save the document again before you quit: just use the keyboard shortcut Command S. Then from the File menu, choose "Quit." The Quit command is always the very last item, and the keyboard shortcut is always Command Q. You really should read Chapter 17 on Closing and Quitting so you understand the difference between closing and quitting.

Other Very Important Features

After you quit an application, you will usually end up back at the Desktop. There are several **very important features** you can learn that will make you the life of any party. Here are suggestions for specific things you need to be in control of:

Sherlock

- Learn how to use **Sherlock.** Read pages 274–276 and experiment. Later, another day, read the rest of the chapter and learn how to do more complex searches (when you know what you're searching for) and search for things on the Internet.

Control panels

- Learn how to use some of your **control panels:** read Chapter 24. Check out only the control panels that interest you (ignore the others). Most of the ones you have are explained in Chapter 24.

Aliases

- Learn how to use **aliases.** Read pages 265–266 and pages 269–270. I guarantee you will find aliases to be one of the greatest features of organization and convenience on the Mac.

Visual clues

- Read Chapter 30 on **visual clues.** Absorb that information and keep your eyes open for other visual clues. Teach them to others. Find at least five more visual clues yourself.

Apple menu

- Learn why and how to take advantage of your **Apple menu.** Skim Chapter 23, even if customizing the menu doesn't quite make sense yet.

Saving and navigating

- To avoid having to use Sherlock twenty times a day to find lost files, learn how to **save** a document directly **into the folder** of your choice. It's critical that you have power over where your documents go when you save them. Read Chapter 28 on Navigating. Learning to navigate (getting yourself where you want to go and finding files through the dialog boxes) is one of the most important things to know and seems to be one of the most difficult concepts to grasp.

Very important information

- After you've gotten several "out of memory" messages or had applications "unexpectedly quit" or suddenly disappear, read Chapter 29, Very Important Information. It discusses the difference between hard disk space and memory and virtual memory, how to avoid running out of memory, and where to find those lost applications.

p.s.

- Read the book called *The Mac is not a typewriter.* It's little.

User Groups!

One of the best things you can do for yourself is join your local user group! Macintosh users have a history of joyfully sharing information, and a user group is an incredible source of help and support. To find the user group in your area, call this Apple number: **800-538-9696** and choose the User Group option. The automated system will automatically find the user group nearest you *based on the phone number you are calling from.* But often you want to find a user group in a town you will be visiting in the future to see if you can catch a meeting (we have lots of visitors to our Santa Fe group). If so, when the system asks you to confirm the town you are calling from, tell it that's wrong; you will get a chance to type in the zip code of the place you will be visiting. The system will find a user group within a hundred miles of that zip code.

If you're ever in Santa Fe on the first Wednesday of the month, visit the Santa Fe Mac User Group! I teach the beginners' session before the main meeting. Check the web site at www.santafemug.org, or call the hot line when you're in town: 505-474-SFMG (7364).

PART One
The Basics

This section describes the things you need to know to get up and running on your Macintosh, from starting up to shutting down. This section actually tells you more than you *need* to know there are lots of little tips and tricks embedded in these chapters, tips and tricks that may even impress your power user friends.

Remember, though, if you're in a hurry, start with the Tutorial. The Tutorial gets you up and running in the least amount of time. Then you can come back later and read all the parts you missed. If you come across terms you don't understand, look them up in the index!

Ks, Megs, Gigs, and Disks

People who've been working with the Mac for a while start tossing around jargon like, "It's a small file, only 230K," or "Hey, *my* Mac has a 20 gigabyte hard disk," and people who are not familiar with the Mac feel dumb because it all sounds so esoteric and we're sure we'll never be able to understand all this sophisticated computer stuff and besides we don't want to know all that technical stuff anyway, we just want to learn how to run the darn thing. Well, as far as technical stuff goes, all most of us need to know is the machine is magic. Pure, simple, magic. Like an airplane.

Knowing the difference between a bit and a byte, and between Ks and megs and gigabytes, though, will help you understand your computer, computer advertising, your applications and documents, memory and hard disk, and your friends.

Bits

0 1
Each one of these electronic messages is one bit.

Actually, the computer isn't that smart; it can only count to one. Remember in school when we learned the binary system which we have now completely forgotten except that for some reason we could only count from zero to one and we had to use exponential notation? Well, the Mac uses a binary system: it counts zero and one—zero means Off and one means On. It sends these little electronic messages, each a series of Off and On. And each one of those little individual messages (an on or off signal) is a **bit.**

Bytes

01000001
This byte represents the letter A.

Now, one little bit doesn't tell the computer a whole lot, so it strings together a bunch of bits to create a more important message: eight bits, such as **01000001,** make one **byte.** As you can see in the column to the left, one byte of information is still rather limited—it takes a lot of bytes to create a document.

Kilobytes

Approximately 1000 Bytes equals 1 Kilobyte.

So a bunch of bytes are grouped together and called a **kilobyte.** You would think that a kilobyte would be a thousand bytes, yes? No. Since the computer can only count to one, the closest it can get to 1000 in its binary system with exponential notation is 1024. But we generally round it off and say there are about 1000 bytes in a kilobyte. And kilobytes are the **K**s everyone talks about.

How do Ks figure in real life? Kilobytes are what file and document sizes are measured in; the larger and more complex the document or file, the greater the number of K it will occupy on the disk. Don't worry—we're going to get to **megabytes** and **gigabytes** in a minute, but first let's take a look at kilobytes in action.

Floppy Disks

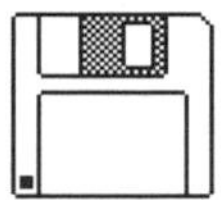

You've probably seen the nice little 3.5″ **floppy disks** that the Mac used to use. A disk can store some of the software you buy or the documents you create—it stores it in the form of bits and bytes and kilobytes.

For several years now, Macs have been built without floppy disk drives (the *drive* is the mechanism that reads the floppy). If you don't have a floppy disk drive (especially a new one that you added to your new Mac), skip to the next page and read about hard disks; if you ever need to know more about floppies, come back here.

Over the years floppy disks have become capable of storing more and more information. You still might run into older, double-sided floppy disks that hold about **800K** (kilobytes) of data: four pages of double-spaced typewritten text from your word processor take about 6K of disk space so you can get about *500 pages* of text on one double-sided disk (leaving some room for the messages the disk has to send to the computer). Spreadsheets, graphics, and other complex info take up a lot more space, of course.

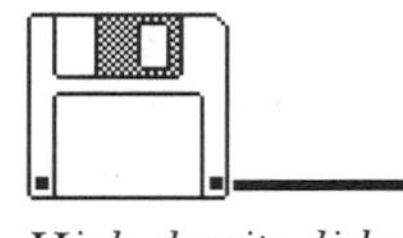

High-density disks have an extra hole on the right side of the disk.

Most common now, though, are the **high-density, double-sided disks,** which hold about **1,400K,** also written as **1.4MB** (megabytes, which are bigger than kilobytes; we'll get to megabytes in a minute) of data. These disks usually have the letters HD somewhere on them, and they have two holes, one hole with a tab that closes. The second, open hole tells the Macintosh that the disk is high-density. (Old Macs, like those made before 1989, can't read these high-density disks.) *Important note: if you attached a new floppy disk drive (probably connected with a USB cable) to your new Mac, it probably does not read any sort of floppy disk except the high-density, double-sided disks.*

Caring for Floppy Disks

Why is the disk called a floppy disk when it's not floppy? Actually, it *is* floppy. If you slide over that metal end you'll see the floppy disk inside. Don't touch it! It's full of tiny messages that your oily fingers or sharp nails can destroy. Keep your disks away from heat: they'll warp just like a record album when left in your hot car. And keep them away from magnets—a magnet will destroy all the data on the disk. So don't attach them to your refrigerator; don't store them near your telephone or stereo or any other electronic device; don't keep them in your purse with your automatic camera; and don't pile them on top of your magnetic paper clip holder. Also, don't keep disks in those little plastic bags they often come in; the plastic can build up static electricity which has the potential to destroy your precious data. Keep your disks in a box or disk drawer of some sort, someplace where they won't collect dust.

Initializing a New Disk

When you buy disks, they're already **initialized,** or *formatted.* That means the disks have already been prepared so a computer can "read" them. Make sure the box says they are formatted for a Macintosh! If they're formatted for a PC, you can still use them in a Mac—just reformat them first.

If you happen to buy **unformatted** disks, or disks that have already been initialized for PCs, you can easily initialize them for your Mac. When you first insert an uninitialized, or unformatted disk, the Mac will ask you to name the disk; if you insert a PC disk, from the Special menu choose "Erase Disk...." You may see a warning that you are about to erase all the information on the disk, but since it's blank, so what. When you finally click OK, the Mac will lay down the formatting it needs to store all the valuable info you will be giving it.

Locking and Unlocking a Floppy Disk

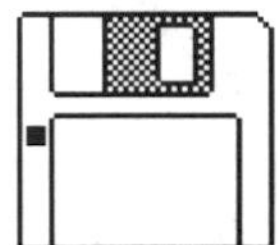

This disk is unlocked.

It is possible to **lock** a floppy disk. When a disk is locked, whoever is using it cannot change anything on it, nor can other files be saved onto it. To lock a disk, find the little black tab in the corner. You'll notice you can slide it up or down.

- When the tab covers the hole, the disk is unlocked.
- When you can see through the hole, the disk is locked.

Most disks have two holes, but only one of the holes has a tab that can be moved. The second hole indicates that the disk is a high-density disk (see the previous page) and has nothing to do with locking.

Hard Disks *(and thus megabytes)*

A **hard disk** is actually a large, *hard, disk,* a platter rather than a floppy piece of film. (Actually, it is several platters.) In principle it works the same as a floppy disk, but it can hold much more data. The hard disk itself may be installed inside your Mac, or it may be a separate unit encased in a sturdy plastic box. Or you might have both.

In any form, a hard disk is a storage container, like a filing cabinet, that holds all your software programs and documents. Hard disks allow you to store your files all on one disk instead of on a lot of separate floppies, which makes it *much* easier and faster to work. Your Macintosh probably has a pretty big hard disk inside of it because the storage space is essential—the bigger your hard disk, the more information and software you can store on it.

In fact, even a small hard disk holds so much data that it's not even measured in kilobytes—they are measured in **megabytes,** also known as **megs** or **MB.** You've already figured out that one megabyte is 1024 kilobytes, right? Right.

Megabytes

Approximately 1000K equals one megabyte (1MB).

Now, 1024 kilobytes (one megabyte) is about what *one* floppy disk can hold. Hard disks come in various sizes—a very small one might be able to store from 500 to 800 megs of information, and they're getting bigger all the time. So a very small hard disk, say 500 megs, has as much storage space as *500 floppy disks!* You can load all kinds of applications onto your hard disk and create all kinds of documents.

Gigabytes

Approximately 1000MB equals one gigabyte (1GB).

As the software applications get more and more sophisticated, they take up more and more space. In fact, **gigabytes** are commonplace—gigabyte hard disks, gigabyte graphic files. A gigabyte, as you might guess by now, is approximately 1,000 megabytes. If you bought a new Mac recently, it probably has a hard disk with 6 to 100 gigabytes of space.

Removable Storage Media, Cartridge Hard Disks

There are also hard disks on *cartridges* that you can insert into a "removable" disk drive (meaning you can take the hard disk out whenever you want), sort of like inserting a video into your VCR, so you can have a collection of cartridge hard disks. Zip disks, Jaz disks, Syquest disks, and others are examples of "removable storage media," removable hard disks, often called "cartridges." They're wonderful. You need a special "drive," or slot, to insert these hard disks; if your computer doesn't have the drive built in, you can always buy one and attach it to your Mac.

Specifications

Memory and hard disk capacity or . . .

You might see newspaper ads for Macs that describe the computer with numbers like these: **64/4GB** or **128/12GB.** The first number in these **specifications** is how much *memory* is in the computer (see page 322 for an explanation of memory). The second number indicates the size of the *hard disk,* in megabytes or gigabytes. So if you see a Mac advertised as "Mac 64/4GB," it means there are 64 megabytes of RAM (memory) and a 4-gigabyte hard disk. The bigger, the better, on both counts.

Model number and speed (megahertz)

You'll also see Macs labeled like **5300/400.** (Things get so complicated so quickly.) This kind of specification describes something completely different from memory and hard disk! In this case, the first number is the model of Macintosh, such as a PowerBook 5300. The second number is the speed of the computer, expressed in "megahertz." My second computer was a Mac IIcx, and it had a speed of 16 MHz (megahertz). The Mac I have now has a speed of 450, and the iMac I bought for my son is 400. The bigger the number, the faster the computer operates.

To find out the speed of your machine, go to the Apple menu and choose "Apple System Profiler." On the page that comes up, look for "Machine speed," as shown to the right.

Processor info:	PowerPC G3
Machine speed:	300 MHz
FPU:	Built-in

Making Backup Disks

A **backup** is an extra copy of your software or your document in case the original gets lost or destroyed. Make sure you store your original application CDs in a safe place. If the only copy you have of something is a file you "downloaded" (transferred from another computer to yours) from the Internet or a friend, make a copy of it onto a removable disk and store that disk in a safe place.

Backup any document that is important to you

Regularly backup all the documents you have so laboriously created because until you back them up, they don't exist anywhere else. A hard disk can "crash" and leave no survivors. Now, everything you ever read about the Mac will warn you to backup regularly, but I know you won't really do it until you have experienced your own catastrophe of considerable dimension. Experience is what you get when you don't get what you want.

At the end of each working day, or more often if it is really important, make copies (page 114) onto disks of everything you created or modified that day. Then label those disks! Never work longer without backing up than you could stand to re-do the work. That is, if you're working on a catalog and the last time you created a backup copy was three hours ago, would you mind recreating those three hours? Could you? Then back it up.

Backup Software

There are several software programs you can buy that perform overall hard disk backups onto a variety of media (hard disk, tape, CD, etc.). Ask at your local user group or ask your power-user friend what they recommend. Until you decide to invest in a full backup system (which you might never have a need to do), at least store copies of your work Zip disks or writable CDs or whatever you use. But I know you won't listen to me until you lose something important.

Rule Number 3

Backup Often. Like everyday. *(No, you didn't miss Rules 1 and 2—Rule 1 is on page 145; Rule 2 is on page 136.)*

Hardware and Software

You've probably heard the terms *hardware* and *software* a million times by now. Just in case it's still not quite clear in your mind what the difference is, here's a brief explanation: hardware is the stuff you can kick; software is the stuff you scream at.

Hardware is hard—you can drop it, break it, and throw it. If you can bump into it, it's hardware. Your computer is a piece of hardware, as well as external hard disks, scanners, modems, and printers. To send a piece of hardware to someone, you need a vehicle.

Software is invisible—it's the programming code written on the disks. You buy software—the programs, applications, utilities, and games you use—and it comes to you on some sort of disk, or you *download* it from another computer to yours. The disk it came on or the disk you are storing it on contains the software. You can accidentally destroy the software while the disk it's on remains perfectly hard and whole. To send a piece of software to someone, you can use your modem and send it over the phone lines.

Other Ware

Vaporware refers to software or hardware that has been promised for a while but hasn't yet appeared on the market. You might also hear the terms *wetware, liveware,* or *jellyware*—that means us, the humans.

1. An off-on signal, a 1 or 0, is an electronic signal called a:

2. Arrange these in order from smallest to largest:
   megabytes • bits • gigabytes • kilobytes • bytes

3. How much storage space is on a high-density floppy disk?

4. What is the most important item to keep away from floppy disks?

5. If you can see through both little holes on a high-density floppy disk, is the disk locked or unlocked?

6. The initial K stands for:

7. The initials MB stand for:

8. What do the initials MHz stand for, and what does it indicate?

9. If you see an ad that states "Macintosh for sale, G4/450," what does the 450 indicate?

10. Are you going to backup all of your important files every day?

Answers on page 423.

Starting Up 2

This is easy to do—so easy you will be tempted to skip this chapter. At least skim through it, though. The more information you can absorb about the Macintosh, the more power you will have over it.

Turning It On

A Macintosh usually **turns on** when you push the Power key or button at the top of the keyboard (usually on the right); on some machines, you have to press the button on the tower. The key or button has either a left-facing triangle on it or the power symbol: ⏻ . On most Macs, you can turn *off* the computer with the same key or button.

If you work in a large office or a computer lab at school, you might run across other Macs that turn on in different ways, or ones that have been set up to turn on differently—they might have buttons on the back, on the monitor, on a power strip, or somewhere else. But don't let any of it confuse you—even if you'll forget half the other stuff in this book, once you figure out how to turn on your computer you probably won't forget it.

Internal Hard Disk

Your new Mac has an **internal hard disk,** a hard disk built into the machine. As soon as you turn it on it will boot up from the System on the hard disk. The term "boot up" or "boot" comes from the idea of pulling itself up by its bootstraps, as the Mac is going into its own System and turning itself on.

External Hard Disk

If you have an **external hard disk,** which is an extra hard disk inside a plastic box that sits next to your computer, that piece of hardware should be turned on first, and then turn on your Mac.

Other Attached Devices

In general, if you have any **peripherals** (extra hardware parts that work with your computer, such as external hard disks or Zip drives, etc.) attached to your Mac, they sometimes need to be turned on before you turn on the Mac. But not always! You'll discover soon enough what needs to be turned on before your Mac boots.

Monitors

If you have a separate **monitor** (as opposed to an iMac), the monitor probably has its own power button on the front. Depending on how your Mac is set up, your monitor might turn on automatically when you start up your computer, or you might need to turn the monitor on and off separately. Whether you turn the monitor on before or after you start the Mac doesn't usually matter, although there are a few models that need the Mac to boot first before you turn on the monitor. If it's not working quite right, check the monitor manual.

System Folder

System Folder

System

Finder

System Resources

You must have a **System Folder** on your hard disk. The System Folder must have at least two icons in it: the **System** icon and the **Finder** icon (shown to the right). Without those two items in the machine, the Mac can't start itself up. Most machines now also need a file called System Resources or Enabler.

Your Macintosh arrived with the System Folder already installed on your computer, ready to run. This System Folder is such an extremely important item that there is an entire chapter dedicated to it (Chapter 20). Although you *can* rename the folder, I strongly suggest you don't, just to keep the concept clear. And don't go sticking things in it if you are not absolutely positive they belong there.

The **System** runs the computer, and the **Finder** runs the *Desktop*, which is the first thing you see when you boot your Mac (see Chapter 4).

Startup Disk

The disk icon that appears on your Desktop in the upper-right corner is the startup disk, the disk that holds the System Folder that booted (started) the Mac. It is sometimes called the *boot disk*. The icon for the startup disk, or boot disk, will always be the first icon in the upper-right corner of your Desktop. The examples to the right show you what several different sorts of hard disk icons look like—yours might look different and will surely be named differently.

Inserting a Disk into a Drive

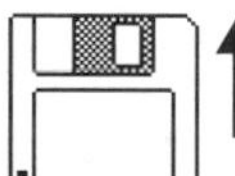

The term **drive** refers to the little slot on the front of your machine where you **insert a disk.** Each different sort of disk has its own drive. Zip disks and floppy disks go in their slots with the label-side up (the side that does *not* have the *round* metal piece on it), and the metal end goes in first.

Ejecting a disk

The easiest way to remove a disk is to drag its icon to the trash, and it will pop out. Don't worry—nothing will be trashed from your disk! See Chapter 18 for details about removing floppies, Zips, and other disks.

Inserting a CD into a CD-ROM Drive

You probably also have a **CD drive,** if your computer is fairly new, where you insert your CDs. Older CD drives use a holder—you have to put the CD into the holder, then slip the whole thing into the drive. *Your* CD drive probably just takes the CD itself. To open the drive door, press the little button right below it. You can gently push the door in, or press the button to make the CD go in. Some CD drives are slots, in which you just push the disk directly inside.

Ejecting a CD
Also see Chapter 18!

To **eject** a CD, you must first quit any programs that you opened from the disk, then drag the disk icon to the trash. Depending on your CD drive, the CD might pop out, or you might have to push the button.

Installing Your New Software

You may have had your software installed before you brought your computer home, in which case it is already on your hard disk waiting for you. But if not, or if you bought some new software, you may need to **install it yourself.** Piece o' cake. These instructions here, though, are very generic and thus very limited. I can't cover every piece of software, so really the best advice is: **RTFM.** That stands for "Read The Manual."

All software you buy today arrives on a CD, looking much like the music CDs you listen to. Put the CD in your CD drive and double-click its icon (if it didn't open automatically). You'll always see an "installer" icon, with the word "Install" somewhere in its name. Double-click the installer and it will put the software onto your hard disk—it will probably ask you where you want it stored. Not only does the installer put the actual program onto your hard disk, it usually adds a number of accessory utilities that the program needs in order to run.

This is the installer on this CD.

Keep in mind that many game CDs will install certain portions of the game on your computer, but when you play the game you need to insert the CD back into the drive so the game can use other files it left on the CD. Applications, such as word processors, page layout programs, etc., do not need the CD again after the software has been installed. Keep the CDs in a safe place in case you ever need to re-install.

Multiple disk software

If you have an old Mac with no CD drive, you can sometimes ask to have the software delivered on **floppy disks** (except for many games)—it will probably come on a lot of disks. Or the software might arrive on floppy disks anyway. The disks are labeled and one of the labels says something like "Program disk" or "Installer disk" or "Disk 1." Find the one that looks like the first in the series and insert it into the floppy drive. There should be an icon called "Installer." Double-click that icon and it will install the program for you. It will spit out the disks when ready and tell you which one to put in next. If there is an installer, *use it.* Many installers put various files in various folders in and around the System Folder, besides the main program where you can see it. If there is an installer, chances are great that the program won't even work if you try to just copy the files onto your disk.

Compressed software

MAD PlayBall.sea

These are examples of commonly found "compressed" files.

If you have any clue that the software has been *compressed*, then you usually need to first copy that compressed file from the floppy disk and into a new folder on your hard disk (see pages 106–107; the new folder actually has nothing to do with the process except to provide a contained place for the related files). Once the compressed file is on your hard disk, double-click on it. It will either open itself up and put files where they belong, or first ask you where you want to store the files. After you un-compress the software, the compressed version is usually still on your disk; you can throw the compressed file in the trash. You still have the original compressed file on the floppy disk.

ReadMe Files

ReadMe First! ReadMe

Kai's Power Goo™ ReadMe

You will often see a file called **ReadMe** on new software disks, or a ReadMe file might get installed onto your hard disk when you install new software. Guess what you should do with that file? Yes, Read It. Just double-click on the icon. The word processing utility called SimpleText is either on the disk also, or it's on your computer, and the ReadMe file opens in it. This file contains important information that was discovered too late to put into the manual. Yes, you should also read the manual.

If you have no version at all of SimpleText (which would be quite remarkable; it's more likely that you have several copies), you can open ReadMe files in almost any other word processor. Older Macs use a small program called TeachText instead of SimpleText.

Installing New Fonts

Installing new fonts (typefaces) is different from installing software applications. Please see Chapter 21 on Fonts.

System and Software Versions

All computer software is constantly being upgraded and updated, making it more efficient, powerful, magical. And sometimes they update software just to fix a *bug* (a minor problem that is not supposed to be there but supposedly they didn't know it was there when they sent it to you). The developers let you know which upgrade you have by labeling it with a **version number.**

How to pronounce version numbers

There is usually a period in the version number, which is pronounced "point." Thus the version 9.0 is pronounced "nine point oh." The version 9.1 is pronounced "nine point one" (or sometimes just "nine one"); 9.04 is "nine point oh four." And 9.0.2 is "nine point oh point two." The points give you a clue as to how important the upgrade is —9.1 is more important than 9.0.4.

How to pronounce document names

But when a file name for a *document* includes a period, the period is pronounced "dot." For instance, a compressed file may be labeled "brochure.sit" (the "sit" is a common file name *extension* that gives you a clue that the file is compressed). This is pronounced "brochure dot sit." You might name your file "Newsletter.March," which you would pronounce as "Newsletter dot March." The word "March" is an "extension" to the name; the extension makes the document name more precise.

You'll also find this "dot" in Internet addresses. When someone tells you their address is "AOL dot com," the dot means "period" and it's typed like this: aol.com (details in Part Three on *The Internet*).

Upgrade your System regularly!

As the System upgrades, the software programs are created to work with the particular nuances of the newer System, so it's a good idea (often it's critical) to keep up on both System upgrades and software application upgrades. If you never upgrade the System, eventually you will be severely limited as to the software you can use with your Mac. If you plan to share files with PCs (in general, a PC is any computer that's not a Mac; typically most PCs run some form of the Windows operating system), then it is even more important that you upgrade your system regularly; each new system adds more features to make the Mac the most cross-platform computer there is.

Power User

What is a **power user**? A power user is a person who knows more about computers than you do. Well, real power users know a lot. They can throw around terms like "32-bit addressing" and "clean ROMs" and "CPU" and actually have a clue as to what they mean. Power users use all the keyboard shortcuts instead of the mouse, and they load up their computers with all the extensions and shareware they can find. They get a thrill out of the speed of the SCSI-2 port and debate the advantages of RISC vs. CISC processing. Power users can even use ResEdit without quivering. Everyone should have a power user as a friend.

This is a power user. They also come in female form.

1. What is the "boot disk," or "startup disk"?

2. How do you know which icon is the startup disk?

3. Which two files (represented by icons, of course) must be on your hard disk so you can start your Mac?

4. What should you put into the System Folder?

5. Where do you insert a floppy or Zip disk?

6. What does RTFM stand for?

7. What should you do with ReadMe files?

8. How would you pronounce this System version: 9.1.2

9. How would you pronounce this file name: LoveLetters.sit

10. Who should be your best friend?

Answers on page 423.

3 The Mouse

The **mouse,** of course, is that handy little piece of hardware that controls the movement of the pointer on the screen. As you move the mouse across the desk, a *pointer,* sometimes called a *cursor,* moves across the screen in the same direction. In most Macintosh applications, you cannot fully utilize the program without the mouse. A few programs give you the option of doing absolutely everything from the keyboard if you choose; but why learn 450 keyboard commands—isn't that just what we're trying to avoid?

This short chapter helps you get familiar with the various ways of using your mouse.

The Pointer

The mouse moves the **pointer** around the screen. The *only* part of the pointer that does the trick is the *very* tip, called the "hot spot." So be sure that the extreme point of the arrow is positioned in the area you want to affect.

This is the hot spot . . . .

*The **tip** of the pointer does the trick.*

Using the Mouse

You'll use the **mouse** in several different ways. Always, the mouse sits on a flat surface and you roll it around with your hand on top of it, your index finger resting on the *mouse button* (the part that clicks—it really doesn't look like a "button"). Do not hold the mouse in the palm of your hand, and don't pick it up and point it at the screen.

Single Click

A **single click** is a quick, light touch on the button of the mouse, with the "cursor"—a pointer, an I-beam (page 132) or other shape—located at the spot of your choice on the screen.

Single-click with the *arrow* on an icon at your Desktop to *select* an icon; single-click with the *I-beam* to *set down an insertion point;* single-click to press a button.

Double Click

A **double click** is a quick click-click on the button, again with the pointer located at the appropriate spot on the screen. A double click has to be quick and the mouse must be still or the Mac will interpret it as two single clicks.

Double-click on a file to *open* that file; double-click on a folder to *open* the window for that folder; double-click on a word to *select* that word for editing.

Press

To **press** means to point to something and *hold* the mouse button down.

Press on the arrows in a scroll bar of a window to *scroll* through that window.

This is often misleadingly referred to as "click"—often directions tell you to "click" on things when they really mean "press." If clicking doesn't work, try pressing. Since Mac OS 8, we can *click* on things that we used to have to *press* on. That is, to drop down a menu you can either *click* on the menu item in the menu bar, **or** you can *press* and hold the mouse button down.

Press-and-Drag (also known, misleadingly, as click-and-drag)

Press-and-drag means to point to the object or the area of your choice, *hold/press the mouse button down, keep it down,* and *drag* somewhere, then *let go* when you reach your goal.

> Press-and-drag *to move icons* across the screen; press-and-drag to *select text.*

Shift-click
Command-click
Option-click
Control-click

You'll often see the terms **Shift-click, Command-click, Option-click,** and **Control-click.** This means to hold down that key (Shift, Command, Option, or Control) and then click the mouse button once. Different things happen when you do this.

> Shift-click individual icons on the Desktop *to select more than one,* or *to deselect* from a group of selected icons (see pages 116 and 117). Control-click on various items on the Desktop to get "contextual menus," which are menus that offer different choices depending on what you Control-click (see page 404).

Command-Option-drag, or Option-drag

You'll see terms like **Command-Option-drag** or **Option-drag,** which mean to hold down the Command and/or Option keys and drag the mouse.

> Command-Option-drag a file to make an alias of it (alias information is in Chapter 25).

Trackpads and Trackballs

Trackpad

Some people prefer to use a different "pointing device," such as a joy stick or a **trackball.** The Macintosh laptops use trackballs or **trackpads.**

A trackball is like an upside-down mouse—instead of moving the little mouse box around to make the ball roll underneath, you use your fingers to roll the little ball on top as it sits in the box. Trackballs have buttons to press that act like the button on the mouse. Depending on what kind of trackball you have, you may click the button with a finger or, as seems to be easier on the PowerBook, with your thumb.

The trackpad is a flat space and you use your finger to drag the pointer around the screen. It takes a little time to get used to it.

Trackballs and trackpads are particularly convenient for those people who have to use the mouse backwards. Yes, I have met several people who have to turn the mouse with the tail facing themselves. When they push the mouse to the right, the pointer on the screen moves to the left. If more than one person uses the same computer, each person has to turn the mouse around. With a trackball or pad, individual idiosyncrasies don't matter.

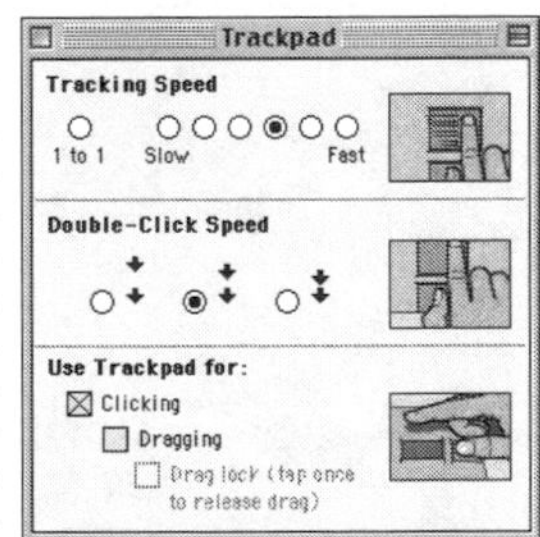

Use the control panel (see Chapter 24) to adjust your trackpad. Check "Clicking" so you can double-click by tapping your finger. Uncheck "Dragging" if you find you often drag files around accidentally.

Mouse Pad

You've probably seen or have a **mouse pad,** a small pad to put on your desk to roll the mouse across. The pad has nothing to do with the operation of the mouse, really—the mouse will work just fine without a pad. The purpose of a mouse pad is simply to provide better traction and a clear spot on your desk for the mouse. You can use a book, illustration board, a coaster, or even a piece of smooth paper.

Moving the Mouse ***when you've run out of space***

Sometimes you may be **moving the mouse** across the mouse pad or the desk and **run out of space** on the pad or desk before the pointer or the cursor gets where you want it to go. Just do this: Keep your finger on the mouse button, pressing it down. Pick up the mouse, keeping the button down, and move the mouse over to where you have more room. Then just continue on your path.

Mouse Control Panel

close box

The Mouse *control panel* is the first control panel you should change (if you have a laptop with a trackpad instead of a mouse, see the previous page). You'll read about control panels in Chapter 24, but this one is so important I think you should take a look at it as soon as you feel comfortable using the mouse and pulling down menus. *If you are brand-new to your Mac, come back to this page in a couple of days.*

- Click on the Apple menu and slide down to "Control Panels." A menu will pop out to the side: slide out to the side and down the menu to "Mouse"; click on "Mouse" to open the Mouse control panel (shown to the left).
- When the "Mouse Tracking" is set toward "Very Slow" or "Slow," you have to move the mouse a long way on your desk to move the pointer across the screen. If you drag the slider bar over toward "Fast," you only need to move the mouse a short distance to move the pointer across the screen. Try it—you'll notice the effects on the screen immediately.

  When you work in a drawing, painting, or image editing program, you may want to come back to this control panel and change the speed back to "Slow" so you have finer control over tiny details in your drawing. If you use a table with a stylus for drawing, try "Very Slow."
- Leave the "Double-Click Speed" set at the middle button.
- After you adjust the tracking speed, click in the *close box* (upper-left corner) to put the control panel away.

Connecting the Mouse

The mouse plugs into a port (socket). Newer Macs have what's called USB ports (see page 393 for details about USB) into which you plug the mouse. If you have a machine with USB ports (which includes all iMacs), you have two USB ports on the top sides of your keyboard; you can plug your mouse into either one. USB ports are rectangular, so of course the mouse cable has a rectangular connector.

This symbol indicates a USB port.

This symbol indicates an ADB port.

Older Macs have ADB ports (ADB for Apple Desktop Bus) for the mouse and keyboard. ADB ports and connectors are round. Really old Macs have two ADB ports on the backs of the machines, one for the keyboard and one for the mouse. Newer machines only have one ADB port on the back, so you plug your keyboard into that port, then plug your mouse into the keyboard.

Left-handed mousing

If you are **left-handed,** plug the mouse into the port on the left-hand side of the keyboard. If there is only one ADB port in the middle of the keyboard, then you'll just move the mouse to the left side.

Some monitors also have USB or ADB ports around their bases, making it even easier to connect keyboards and mice. Check your monitor.

> You can plug and unplug any USB device while the computer is up and running, although it's recommended that you quit any open applications first. If you have ADB ports, *always shut down first* before plugging and unplugging *anything* from your computer, including the mouse or the keyboard.

Cleaning the Mouse

Newer mouse models are "optical" and use light to communicate with the monitor. If your mouse has a little red glow in the middle, it's optical. If you have an older mouse with a ball on the bottom, it's important and easy to **keep your mouse clean**—cat hairs and dustballs get inside. Take it apart regularly and clean it, following these steps:

1. Take the mouse in your right hand and turn it upside-down.
2. With your thumbs, slide the round wheel to the left to open the lid.
3. Flip the mouse back over into your left hand so the lid and the ball fall out into your palm.
4. Clean the ball with a soft, dry cloth; clean the rollers inside with a cotton swab dipped in rubbing alcohol.
5. When clean, put the ball in your left hand; with your right hand place the mouse on top of the ball and flop your hands over. This places the ball safely into its little cubby.
6. Put the lid back on and twist it to the right, lining up the marker with the "L" for Lock (if you see one). That's it!

Did You Ask *Why?*

Why is it called a mouse? Well, if you grab the cord about four inches from the mouse and hold it at arm's length, squint your eyes and wrinkle your nose, it looks very much like a dead mouse.

Would you single-click (**S**), double-click (**D**), press (**P**), or press-and-drag (**P&D**) to accomplish each of the following tasks? Circle the appropriate abbreviation in the margin for each task.

S P D P&D

1. Select an icon (you always *select* something before you do something to it).

S P D P&D

2. Open a file, such as your word processing document, so you can type in it.

S P D P&D

3. Activate a button.

S P D P&D

4. Select a whole word for editing (to change it).

S P D P&D

5. Open a folder to see what's in it.

S P D P&D

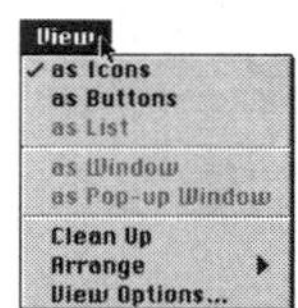

6. See what's in a menu.

S P D P&D

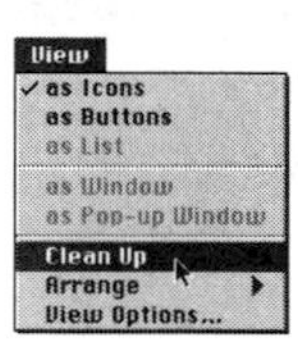

7. Choose something from a menu.

Choose one of the options in the left-hand column for the next three questions.

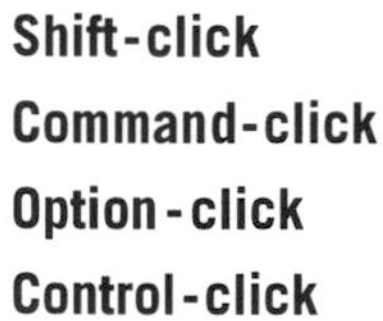

Shift-click
Command-click
Option-click
Control-click

8. Get a contextual menu on an item.

9. Select a group of items.

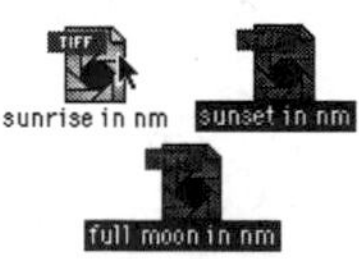

10. Deselect items from a selected group.

Answers on page 423.

4 Desktop and Finder

The **Desktop** is what you see on the screen when you first start up your Macintosh. This computer Desktop works much the same as your oak desktop at home or in your office: You have desk accessories (under the Apple menu) such as a calculator, sticky notes, and a note pad. You have a filing cabinet (the disk) that stores all your folders full of information. You have as many file folders as you could possibly want to organize it all. You can put folders inside of folders inside of folders almost *ad infinitum* just like you would organize your hanging files. You even have a trash can. This chapter helps you understand and manage your Desktop, which is critical since you will be using it often.

Finder

The **Finder** is the system software that manages the Desktop. The Finder keeps track of all the files you have stored on your Desktop, where you keep your applications, which disk you have stuck in the floppy drive, and other tasks. When you upgrade to a newer System (such as from Mac OS 8.6 to 9.1), you also get a new, upgraded Finder.

Well, What's It Called—the *Desktop* or the *Finder*?

The **Desktop** is the actual place you see, and the **Finder** is what controls and keeps track of the Desktop. But because the two are so closely related and you can't have one without the other, you will hear people interchange the terms as if they were the same thing. When you hear someone say, "Are you at the Finder?" you will understand that they mean, "Are you at the Desktop?" and vice versa.

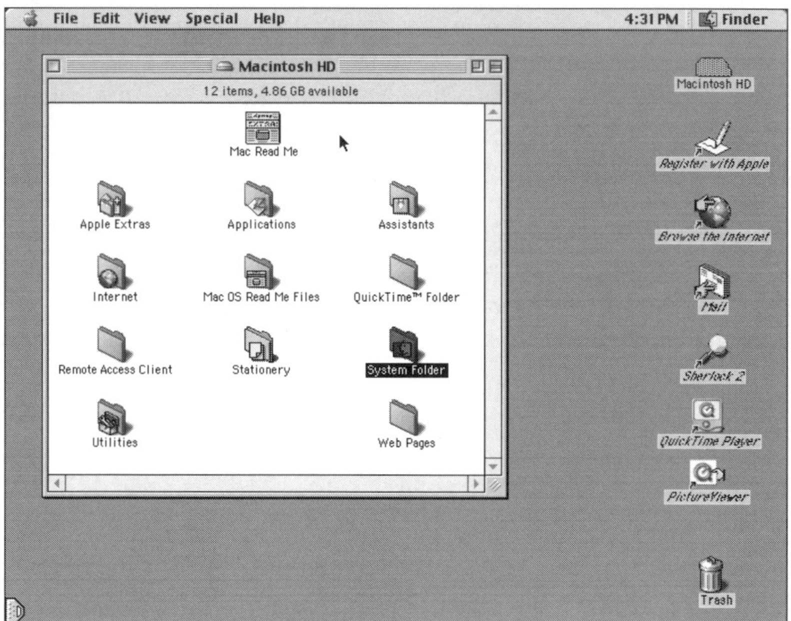

This is the Desktop. The background pattern on your Desktop may look different, and you'll probably have different icons (small pictures of files) on yours.

See page 382 for explanations of the icons on the right side of your Desktop (except for Trash; see page 121 for that one).

The Desktop as Home Base

Whenever you "Quit" working in an application, the Mac automatically takes you back to the **Desktop level,** which is kind of like home base. If you don't see "Special" in the menu bar across the top of the screen, as shown on the previous page, *then you are not at the Desktop.*

You might not be at the Desktop because you didn't actually "Quit" the application you were working in, but just "Closed" the current document and you are still in the application, or perhaps you're in some other application that is still open.

To actually get to your Desktop/Finder, click once on what you can see of the Desktop. As soon as you click, you'll notice that your menu includes "Special." If this does not make complete sense to you, then you really, really should read the chapter called "Very Important Information." It will make you a happier, more powerful person.

Organizing Your Desktop

It's a good idea to keep your Mac Desktop **organized,** just like you would your office desktop. Create new folders (from the File menu; also see page 106) for each category of information, and store all applicable files in the appropriate folders. You can create a new folder on the hard disk before you begin work in an application, then put your new document right into that folder when you *Save* (see page 148). Then when you come back to the Desktop after working, everything is organized and in its appropriate folder.

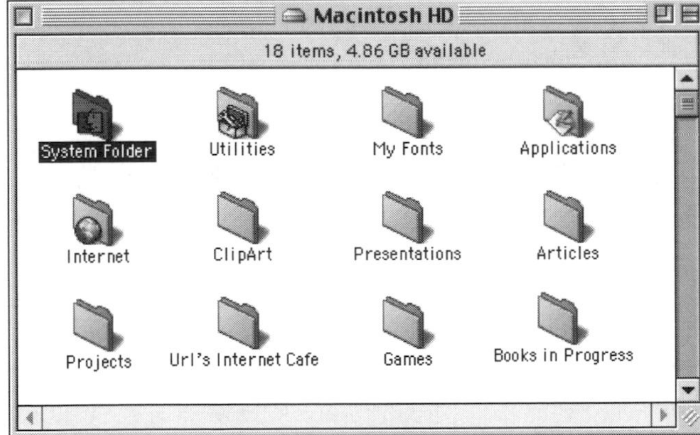

This is an example of a neatly organized hard disk, using folders inside of folders.

Each category of software or information has its own place, and inside these folders may be other folders, each storing other files.

It's much easier to keep things organized on a Macintosh Desktop than on an oak desktop.

Hide Others

Sometimes when you are working on the Desktop you can still see windows from other applications in the background. This can be very annoying, but it's easy to fix. Simply go up to the *Application menu,* which is the icon on the far-right corner of the menu bar (see the illustration below), and choose "Hide Others."

The applications listed in the bottom half of this menu are also open at this time. If you don't want to see any of their windows while working at the Finder/Desktop, choose "Hide Others."

Notice the checkmark on the bottom half, next to "Finder." That is a ***visual clue*** *that you are at the Finder, or Desktop.*

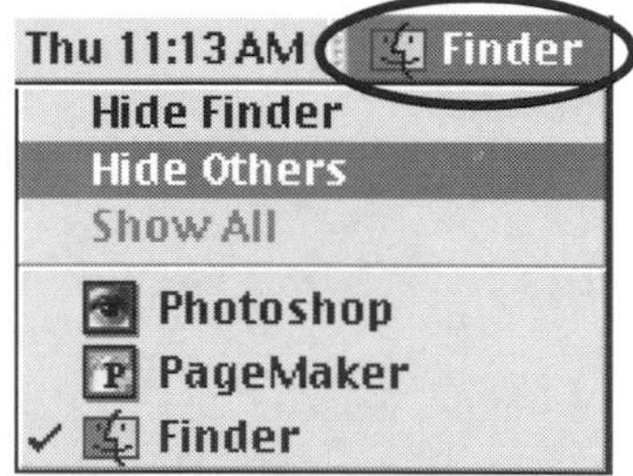

Hide the application window when you go to the Desktop

Often while you are working on something you'll find that you want to pop over to the Desktop (Finder). **To get to the Desktop and hide the window you're working in,** hold down the Option key when you go to the Application menu to choose "Finder"—the windows for the application you're working in will automatically hide. **Or** you can hold down the Option key and click on any part of the visible Desktop, and you will go to the Finder and the windows of the application will automatically hide. **To bring back the window you were working in,** use the Application menu and select that application again.

Clean Up the Desktop

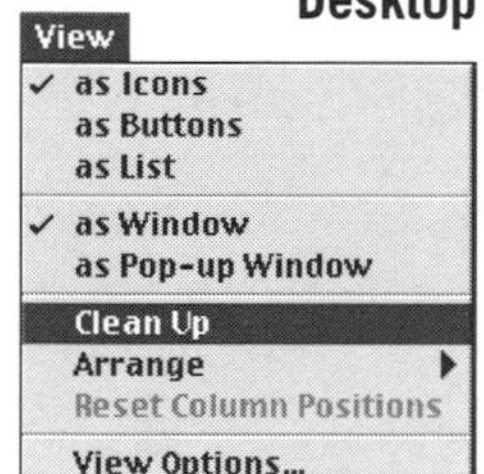

You can see that there are already files sitting on the Desktop, and you'll probably add more as time goes by. All the stuff hanging around the Desktop, like the disks and maybe a few *aliases* (icons that represent files, explained in Chapter 25) and a document or two and some email, starts looking a little messy. It's easy to **clean up the Desktop.**

- Click once on any *icon* on the Desktop, such as your hard disk icon or on the trash can.
- Press on the View menu, drag the mouse down to "Clean Up," then let go. This will make all the *icons* (not the open *windows*) snap to the nearest spot on an underlying invisible grid.
  - **Or** if you want the icons in a different sort of order: Press on the View menu and drag down to "Arrange." In the menu that appears, pick whichever order you want your icons to appear in (by name, size, kind, etc.), and you will see your icons magically snap to the far right and line up in the order you told them to. Wouldn't it be great if you could do this to your kitchen?

Shortcut to the View menu: *press the Control key and click anywhere on the Desktop.*

Desktop Colors or Patterns

You can change the color or pattern that appears on your Desktop. You have about fifty options built in. **To change the pattern:**

- Click the Apple menu, slide down to "Control Panels," then in the menu that pops out to the side, click "Appearance."

  Or hold down the Control key, click once with your mouse anywhere on the Desktop (not in a window), then choose "Change Desktop Background…" from the menu that pops up.
- In the dialog box that appears, click the tab labeled "Desktop."
- Press on the scroll arrows to see the list of choices; click on any choice in the list to see a preview on the left, as shown below. When you like one, click the button "Set Desktop." You will see the Desktop change instantly.
- The last pattern or color you choose with "Set Desktop" is the one that will stay on your screen when you close the dialog box.

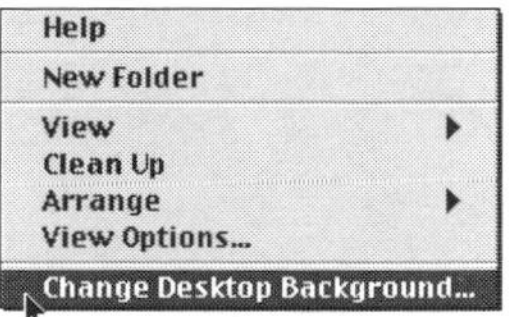

If you Control-click on the Desktop, this is the menu you will see.

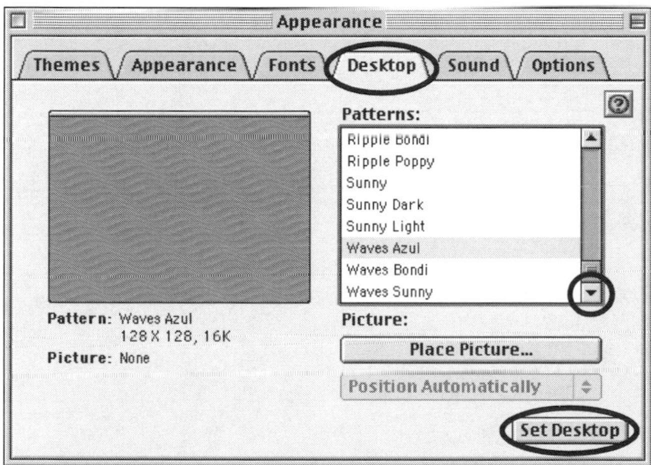

This is the Appearance control panel.

You also can place a picture on top of the pattern, if you want your Desktop to display scenery or alien spaceships. For this and other details (such as how to create your own pictures), see pages 240–242.

1. The Desktop level can be compared to:
   a) home base
   b) outer space
   c) the icing on the cake

2. What's the difference between the Desktop and the Finder?

3. What kind of icons do you use to organize your Desktop?

4. Can you store files directly on the Desktop, instead of keeping all of them in the windows?

5. Describe how to clean up your Desktop.

6. Which "control panel" do you use to change the pattern of the Desktop?

7. How can you tell if you are actually at the Desktop (or Finder) just by looking at the screen?

8. How can you temporarily get rid of (hide) the windows of the open applications you are not currently using?

9. What is the Power User tip by which you can click to get to the Desktop and have the windows of your current application disappear?

10. Are you going to keep your Desktop organized?

Answers on page 423.

Menus 5

Almost every program you'll ever use on the Mac has a **menu** across the top of the screen. This is called a **drop-down menu** (or sometimes a pull-down menu) because when you point to a menu item and click the mouse button, a list of menu commands drops down. This chapter discusses the various sorts of menus, the commands, and how to use them.

This is the Desktop menu bar (also known as the Finder menu bar).

This day-and-time feature shows up automatically.

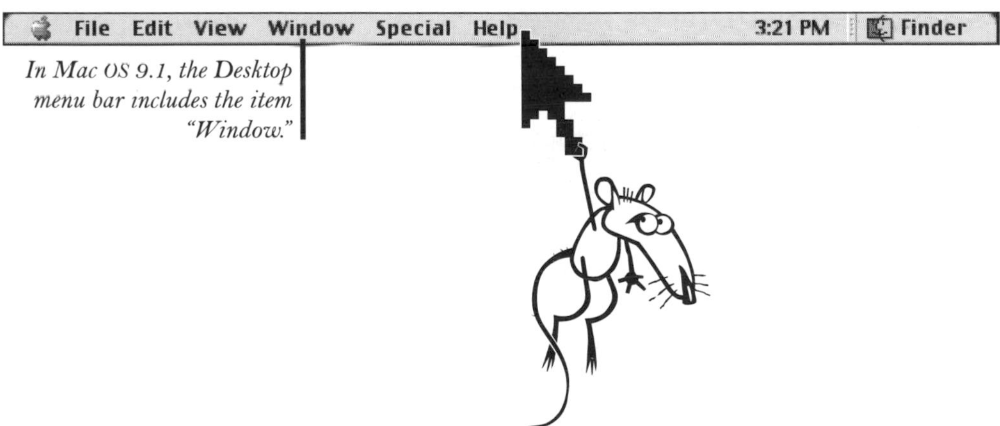

In Mac OS 9.1, the Desktop menu bar includes the item "Window."

Choosing a Menu Command

To choose a command from a menu, click once on any of the choices along the menu bar. The menu will pop open for you. As you move your mouse down the list of commands, the different choices *highlight,* or become *selected,* as you pass over them. When the one you want is highlighted, click on it.

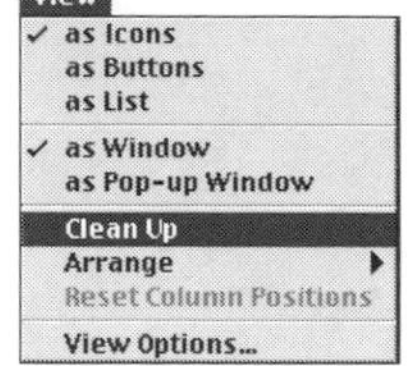

The command "Clean Up" is highlighted—click on it to select it.

Sticky menus

If you ever use an older Macintosh (one that is using an "operating system" older than Mac OS 8), you have to *press* the mouse button down on the menu bar to keep the menu visible, *drag* to the chosen command, and when it's highlighted, *let go.* But Mac OS 8 and above use **sticky menus,** where a single click drops the menu down and leaves it there until you click somewhere. Whether the Mac uses sticky menus or not, you can always press-and-drag to choose menu items.

Changing your mind

If you change your mind halfway through the menu list and don't want to choose anything, just move the pointer off of the list, then click (if you used the "sticky" method) or simply let go (if you used the press-and-drag method). The menu will disappear and nothing will be chosen.

Pop-Out, Pop-Up, and Contextual Menus

In some programs the pull-down menu itself contains a **pop-out menu** where you not only slide *down,* but also *out to the side,* usually in the direction of the arrow. These are also known as **hierarchical menus,** or **h-menus**.

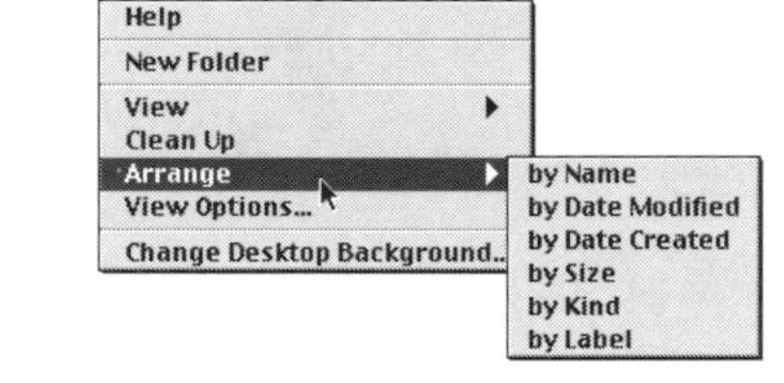

This is an example of a hierarchical menu.

You will also find **pop-up menus** where you press on an item toward the bottom of the screen and the list pops upward. And the Desktop has **contextual menus:** hold down the *Control key* (not the Command key), click anywhere, and a menu pops up. The choices in the menu depend on what you click.

For more details about contextual menus, see page 404.

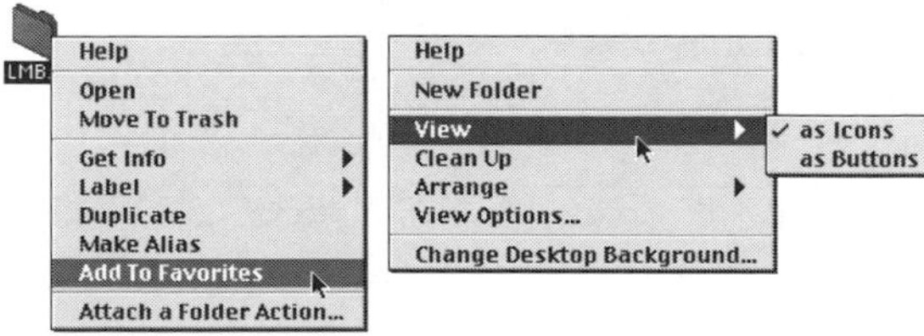

These are contextual menu examples—one for a folder (on the left), and one for the Desktop (on the right).

Gray *vs.* Black Commands

In a list of menu commands, some **commands** are in **black** letters and some commands are in **gray.** When a command is gray, it means *that particular command is not available at that moment.*

The most common reason a command is unavailable is that you did not *select* something before you went to the menu. For instance, you cannot choose "Open" from the File menu until you select a disk or file as the item to be opened. You cannot "Copy" text unless you first select the text you want to copy. (To select *text,* press-and-drag over it; to select an *object,* click *once* on it.)

Some commands are gray; some are black. In this example, "Empty Trash..." is gray because there is nothing in the trash can.

One rule of the Mac is: Select first, then do it to it.

Keyboard Shortcuts

To the right of the commands in the pull-down menus you often see a little code, such as **⌘ Nt** (pronounced "Command N"). This is a **keyboard shortcut** you can use *instead* of using the menu. Memorize the shortcut, then use it the next time you need that command *instead* of picking up your mouse.

Often the keyboard shortcut will include other symbols representing other keys; see the following chapter.

How to use a keyboard shortcut

To use a keyboard shortcut instead of the menu command, hold down the Command key (the one with the apple and/or the cloverleaf symbol, ⌘) and any other **modifier key** (any key that is not a letter or number, such as Shift) you saw in the menu. While you hold down this key or keys, type the **letter key** you saw in the menu—just *tap* the letter, *don't hold it down!* The computer reacts just as if you had chosen that command from the menu. For instance, if you click once on a file to select it and then press **⌘O,** the selected file will open just as if you had chosen that command from the File menu with the mouse. Thoughtfully, most of the keyboard shortcuts are alliterative: **⌘O o**pens files; **⌘P p**rints; **⌘E e**jects; **⌘ W** closes **w**indows; etc.

You'll often see keyboard shortcuts spelled out with a hyphen, a plus sign, or perhaps a comma between the keys. *Don't type the hyphen, plus sign, or comma!* Just press the keys! For instance, if you see a shortcut as "Command + Shift + B" ignore the plus signs—just hold down the Command and Shift keys, then tap the letter B.

Ellipses in the Menus

Anytime you see an **ellipsis** (the three dots, **...**) after a menu command (such as "Open**...**" or "Save as**...**"), it means you will get a **dialog box** when you choose that command. There are different varieties of dialog boxes, such as alert boxes or message boxes, but basically they all are meant to communicate with you.

Explore the dialog boxes!

Dialog boxes always give you an option to **Cancel,** so it is quite safe to go exploring menu commands. Just choose a command that is followed by an ellipsis, check out the dialog box, then click Cancel. Even if you click around on buttons or type in the dialog box, clicking the Cancel button will make sure none of your changes are put into effect.

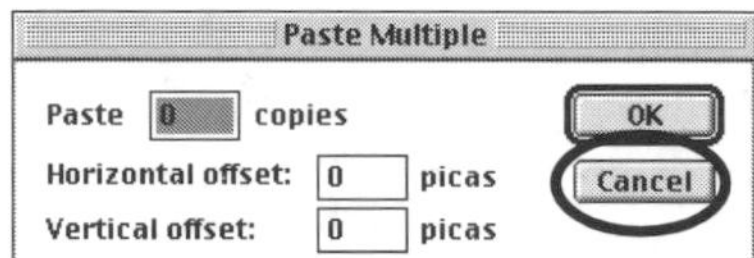

There is always a Cancel button. And you can almost always use the keyboard shortcut **Command Period** *instead of clicking on the Cancel button.*

Other Menus and their Visual Clues

You'll find other menus in all kinds of odd places. Well, they won't seem so odd once you become accustomed to the **visual clues** that indicate a menu is hiding. In the dialog box below, can you guess which boxes have menus hidden beneath them? Also, what do you think will happen if you click on either the "Rules…" or "Spacing…" buttons?

Which items are menus? (Notice also that both the "Rules…" and the "Spacing…" buttons have ellipses, indicating that if you click either button you will get another dialog box.)

Watch for shadows

Notice, in the illustration above, that the boxes next to "Alignment" and "Dictionary" each have a little **shadow** behind them. That little shadow is your **visual clue** that if you press or click on the word, you will get a pop-up menu, as shown below. Look for that shadow!

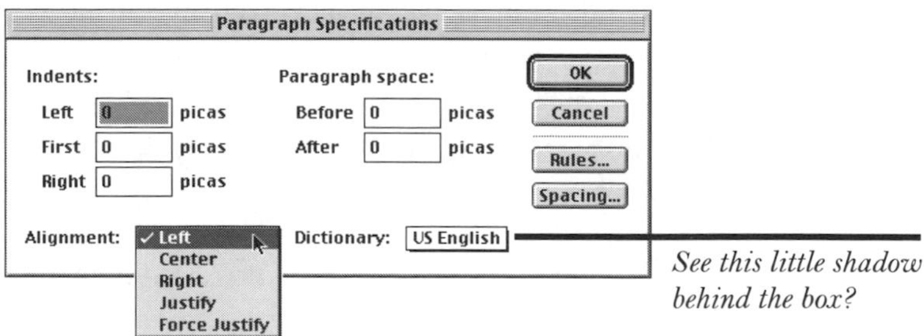

See this little shadow behind the box?

Edit boxes

The boxes that do *not* have a shadow behind them (as shown in the same dialog box below) are called **edit boxes.** You can type into these edit boxes to change the specifications.

These are called ***edit boxes.*** *You can type in them to change the values. There is no shadow behind them.*

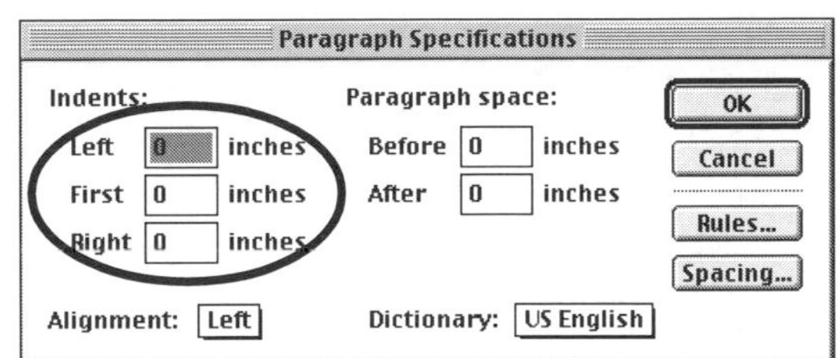

Arrows and edit boxes

Here is a closer look at the kinds of choices you have in dialog boxes. In the example below, the **edit box** for "Left Indent" has no shadow behind it, so you know you can type in it. "Label" has a shadow, *plus* it has an **arrow,** which is another **visual clue** indicating a hidden menu.

When you see an arrow in its own box (as in "li" and "Leading"), you can press on the arrow to get a menu of choices, **or** *sometimes you can type right in the edit box to change the information.*

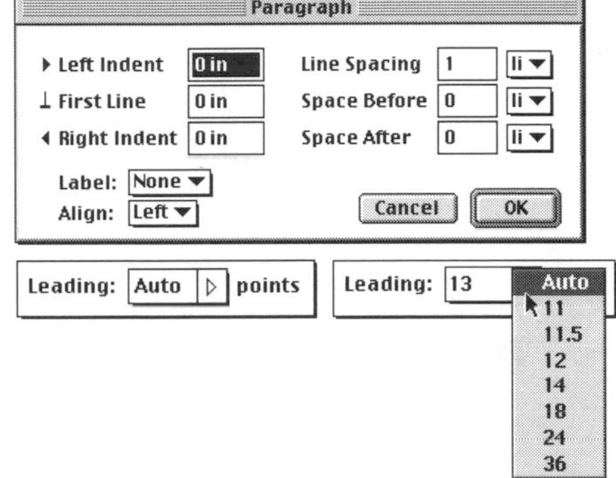

Double arrows

When you see **double arrows,** generally above a *list box* as shown below, you can press anywhere in that label to view and choose from the menu. You'll see the double arrows often.

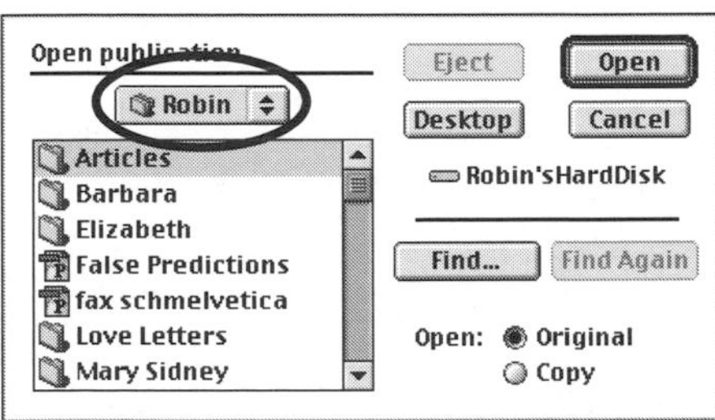

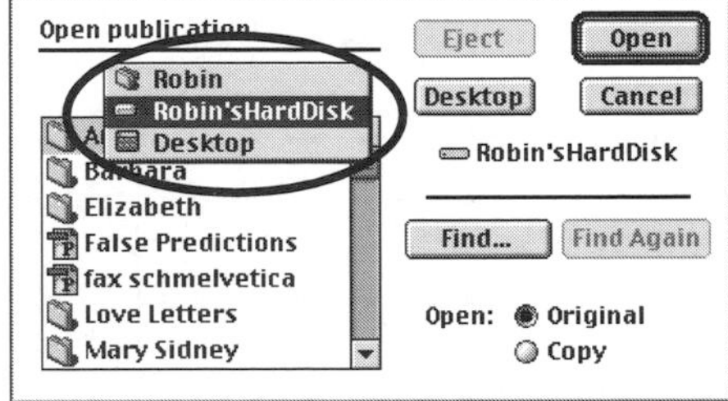

Press or click anywhere on the ***label*** *above the list box, shown circled on the left. You will get the* ***menu*** *shown circled on the right. Try it!*

Watch for those visual clues!

1. Which menu command is selected?

2. How many of these commands have h-menus (hierarchical menus that will pop-out to the side)?

3. How many of these commands will give you a dialog box when you choose them?

4. How many of these commands are not available at the moment?

5. How many of these commands have keyboard shortcuts?

6. What is the keyboard shortcut you could use to access this command instead of choosing it from the menu?

7. When you choose this item, what are you going to get?

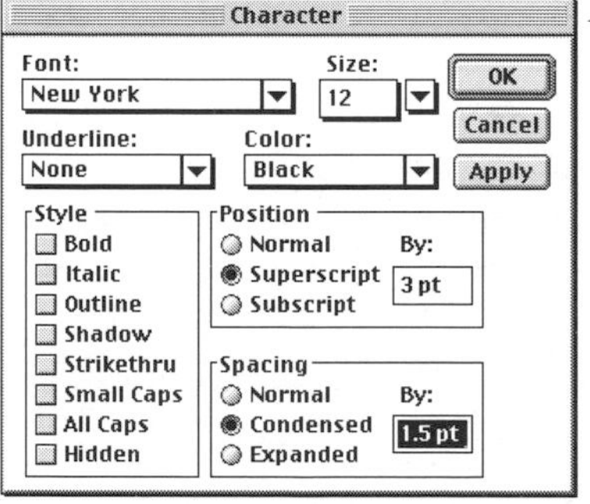

8. How many menus are there inside this dialog box?

9. How many edit boxes are there inside this dialog box?

10. What keyboard shortcut could you press to Cancel this dialog box?

Answers on page 423.

Important Keys

There are several **keys** on the Macintosh keyboard that are particularly important and useful. They come in handy for shortcuts, manipulating images, accessing alternate characters, and any number of things in specific applications.

Speaking of **keyboards,** there are several kinds for the Mac. Much older models use the *standard* keyboard with the keypad at the end, which is like a ten-key adding machine. You probably have an *extended* keyboard that has all the "function keys" (the keys with the Fs on them) and other little groups of keys.

Many of the Mac laptops have smaller keyboards where certain keys do double-duty; that is, you might see tiny letters or symbols in another color on a standard key. See page 65 for how to use those keys.

There are several fancy keyboards you can buy separately that bend in the middle or have special ergonomic features. All keyboards have standard characters, although they may appear in different places on different models. No matter where they are placed, though, all the keys perform the same function (although the function of some keys varies from program to program).

Modifier Keys

The symbols shown in the outer column under each of the following headings are the symbols that will appear in menus to indicate that key.

Some of the keys on the keyboard are called **modifier keys** because they don't do anything all by themselves, but are used in combination with regular keys to make something happen, like keyboard shortcuts (see "Keyboard Shortcuts" on page 57). The Shift key, for instance, is a modifier key you are already familiar with: the Shift key doesn't do anything when you press it by itself, but if you hold it down while you type an alphabetic character, you get the capital letter instead of the lowercase letter.

Sometimes a keyboard shortcut uses more than one modifier. Always *hold down all the modifier keys together* (Command, Shift, Option, etc.) while you give *one quick tap on the associated letter key.* For instance, to *paste* an item, the shortcut is **⌘ V**: hold down the Command key and type a quick V. If you *hold* the character key down (such as the V key) instead of tapping it once, you will usually end up repeating the command.

Any Key

There is no **Any key.** When a direction tells you to "PRESS ANY KEY," it means to press any key you want on the whole keyboard.

Caps Lock Key

The **Caps Lock key** does *not* act just like the Shift Lock on a typewriter. In Caps Lock you get capital letters, yes, but you do *not* get the characters above the numbers or above the punctuation. If you want the Shift-characters you must press the Shift key to get them, even if Caps Lock is down. (Some keyboard shortcuts will not work if the Caps Lock key is down, so check its position if you're having problems.)

Command Key

⌘

The **Command key** is on the bottom row, the key with the California freeway cloverleaf symbol on it: **⌘**. On most keyboards it also has an apple on it, and you may hear it referred to as the "Apple key" or "Open Apple." The correct term is Command key.

Most keyboard shortcuts use the Command key. Do not confuse it with the Control key!

Control Key

ctrl

^

The **Control key** is now standard on Macintosh keyboards—it's usually on the bottom far-left. Not only is it useful for people who are running DOS or Windows software on the Macintosh, but more and more Mac programs are taking advantage of this extra modifier key. For instance, contextual menus on the Mac (page 404) use the Control key. Be sure to read directions carefully and make sure you use the Command key when the directions call for Command and the Control key when they call for Control.

Delete Key/ Backspace Key

⌫

The **Delete key** (labeled **Backspace key** on older keyboards and typewriters), is located on the upper right. The name was changed to "Delete" long ago because that's really what it does—whatever is *selected* will be removed when the Delete key is hit; whatever letter is to the *left* of the "insertion point" will be deleted as you backspace over it. (There is another Delete key located in the little group of Edit keys that deletes the character to the *right* as you type; see page 67.)

Return Key

¶

The **Return key** is used for many things other than simply starting a new paragraph. For instance, any button in any dialog box that has the double border around it can be activated with the Return key instead of the mouse. Different programs use the Return key in different ways. Most things you do with the Return key you can also do with the Enter key, which is found in the numeric keypad.

Whenever you see buttons with a double border, like the ones in either "OK" or "Print" to the right, you can always press the Return key to make it happen instead of clicking on the button with the mouse.

Enter Key

⌅

The **Enter key** on the *numeric keypad* (the set of number keys on the right side of your keyboard) will also activate buttons with the double border, just the same as the Return key (above), and Enter will usually start a new paragraph as well. Different programs use the Enter key in many different ways.

Escape Key

esc

The **Escape key** (labeled **esc**) on the upper left of the keyboard is used in a few applications, but at the moment not too many programs make use of it.

If your screen freezes (that's when neither the keyboard nor the mouse has any effect), you can try holding down Command Option and then tapping the Escape key. This will often, but not always, unfreeze the screen.

This is a "force Quit." See page 411 before you try it.

Option Key (Alt Key)

⌥ or ⌥

Next to the Command Key is the **Option key.** (It sometimes also has the word "alt" on it because the Option key is often comparable to the Alt key when using Windows programs on the Mac; if not, try Shift.) The Option key is often used in combination with the Command key and/or the Shift key. It's through the Option key that you access the special characters, such as ¢ and ®, as well as accent marks, as in résumé and piñata (see pages 140–141).

Shift Key
⇧

The **Shift key** is one of the most commonly used keys in keyboard shortcuts, symbolized by an upward arrow.

Spacebar
␣

The **Spacebar** is represented in menus by the symbol shown to the left, or sometimes *as a blank space.* That blank space can really throw you. How long does it take to figure out that "⇧⌘ " means to press the Shift key, the Command key, and the Spacebar?

Tilde
~

The **Tilde** (~) is located on the upper left of the main set of keys on most keyboards and next to the Spacebar on others, especially older keyboards. This tilde was never used much until the World Wide Web was invented—now we see it all the time in web addresses so you had better know how to type it (press Shift, plus the tilde key).

Asterisk
*
(star)

The **asterisk** (*, Greek for "little star") is used as a multiplication symbol in calculators, spreadsheets, databases, etc. You can use the asterisk on the numeric keypad, or you can press Shift 8 to get the asterisk you see above the number 8 on the keyboard. Thank goodness this key is also known as the star key because so few people can spell or pronounce "asterisk."

Forward Slash
/

The **forward slash** (/) is used as a division symbol in calculators, spreadsheets, databases, etc. It's also used in World Wide Web addresses. You can use the slash on the numeric keypad or the one on the regular keyboard (usually on the same key as the question mark). Don't use the straight slash (|) or the backward slash (\, backslash) when you want to divide or when you type a web address.

Tab Key

The Tab key is not usually used in conjunction with other keys. You may see this symbol in word processing to indicate that a Tab has been pressed, or you may see just a right arrow.

The **Tab key** (upper left) acts like the Tab key on a typewriter in that when you press the Tab key you'll start typing at the next tab stop that's set. In most word processing programs, simply click in the ruler you see across the top of the screen to create a tab stop in the selected paragraph (to remove the tabs, press-and-drag the tab markers down off the ruler).

In spreadsheet and database programs, the Tab key will move the selection to the next cell or field *to the right,* just as it would move your typing to the right (the Return key will move the selection to the next cell or field *down*). Hold the Shift key down as you press Tab to move the selection backwards to the left (or Shift Return to move up).

When you are in a dialog box, **press the Tab key to select edit boxes.** Just try it: Open a dialog box, then press the Tab key to cycle you through the edit boxes. If there is something in an edit box already, the box will highlight; *anything you type will replace what is highlighted.* If the edit box is empty, the insertion point will flash to indicate you can now type something in it. It also works on most forms on web pages.

This is a little more advanced tip about the Tab key. Come back later if it confuses you now.

Fkeys
F1 – F15

The **Fkeys** are at the top of *extended* keyboards; it's that row of keys labeled F1, F2, F3, etc. If you don't see Fkeys, you don't have an extended keyboard (that's okay if you don't—you can live without it). But those Fkeys are handy for shortcuts. In most programs you can press F1 to *undo* your last action; press F2 to *cut* an item, F3 to *copy*, and F4 to *paste* (see pages 138–140 for explanations of undo, cut, copy, and paste). Some programs use the other Fkeys for other shortcuts particular to the application (check your manual). You can program the extra ones yourself; see the Keyboard control panel information in Chapter 24.

Numeric Keypad
Clear Key
Num Lock

On the far right of the keyboard is a **numeric keypad** that looks like calculator keys. In some applications, these keys will type numbers, and in other applications they will move the insertion point (see page 132 for a description of the insertion point). In some applications these keys can do both—they can type numbers or they can move the insertion point. That's why the Clear key is often also labeled "Num Lock" because when you press the Clear key (num lock), it locks the keypad into typing numbers instead of moving the insertion point.

When you use the Calculator desk accessory (see page 214), this numeric keypad operates the calculator. The asterisk (*) is the multiplication key, and the slash (/) is the division key.

fn Key
(Function Key)

On many laptops, there is a key with the tiny symbol **fn** in the bottom left, usually in a different color. You see other keys with tiny symbols or characters also in that color, such as num lock, clear, home, end, pg up, pg dn (page up or down), insert, or numbers. If you press the **fn** key, then the keys change their standard function to the symbols or characters in that matching color (the color that matches the **fn**). That is, press **fn** and you now have a numeric keypad to use in spreadsheets or calculators, you have a num lock, you can print a picture of the screen (prt screen), jump to the top or bottom of a web page, forward delete, etc. Experiment with it! Also see the Keyboard control panel in Chapter 24.

Arrow Keys

Depending on your keyboard, you may have **arrow keys** (keys with nothing but an arrow on each of them) tucked in with your letter keys, or you may have a separate little set of four arrow keys. Arrow keys are used for different things in different programs.

In word processing programs you can use the arrow keys to move the insertion point (the insertion point is that thin, flashing, vertical bar that moves along with the text as you type).

> Usually if you hold down the Shift key as you hit the arrow keys, the text will be *selected* as the insertion point moves along. Try it.

Some programs, such as page layout or graphics programs, may use the arrow keys to nudge objects around on the screen. In spreadsheets and databases, the arrow keys might be used to move the insertion point or they might be used to select other cells or fields.

In dialog boxes, the arrow keys will move the insertion point within the edit box.

RightArrow
LeftArrow
UpArrow
DownArrow

You'll notice when I write about commands that use **arrow keys** I write them out like this: RightArrow, LeftArrow, UpArrow, and DownArrow. For instance, I might tell you in this book to press Shift LeftArrow. I do this because I have seen beginners follow a command such as "Press Command + left arrow" by pressing the Command key and then looking for the key that says "left," plus an arrow key. (And many new users also try to press the + key.) So even though it may seem odd at first, combining the two words that describe the arrow keys makes it clearer that there is just one key.

Edit Keys

Help
Home
End
PageUp
PageDown
Del

If you have an extended keyboard, you have an extra little set of keys between the alphabet keyboard and the numeric keypad called the **edit keys.** These keys are primarily there to make the Macintosh compatible with PC programs. Not many Mac programs use these keys, although if you read your manual you may be surprised. Try them in your word processor. Or select a file in a Desktop window and try the PageUp and PageDown keys, as well as Home and End. The Help key in some programs gives you a question mark—you can then click on any menu item in your application and you will get the Help dialog box about that menu item.

In most browsers on the World Wide Web, you can hit End to take you to the bottom of the web page, and Home to take you to the top of the web page. PageUp and PageDown might take you up or down a window's length. Experiment.

Del Key (forward delete)

The **del key** (Delete), one of the edit keys mentioned above, deletes the character to its *right* (forward). This is just the opposite of the Delete key we usually use, which deletes the character to its *left* (backward). It's very handy. Unfortunately, some keyboards (like iMacs and some laptops) don't have this useful key.

Power Key

The **Power key** is the key, round button, or oblong button embossed or printed with a left-pointing triangle or the standard power symbol (both shown to the right), found at the top center of some keyboards and at the upper-right in others. This key turns on many of the newer models of Macintosh. The Power key makes it very easy for your cat or your small child to turn on your Mac when you least expect it. Some of the newest keyboards do not have a Power key (you have to use the button on the case)!

If you have a Power key on your keyboard, this key will also **shut down** your Mac. If you have cats and kids swarming around your house, you might find your computer turning on or off at odd times. Fortunately, you do get a warning beep asking if you really want to shut down, and even if the cat steps on the Return key (which chooses "Okay" to shut down), the Mac will save any files that were left open before it turns itself off. See Chapter 19 for more details about shutting down your computer.

Various models of iMacs also have a Power button on the monitor, which on some models turns off the computer and on some models puts the computer to sleep.

1. If you want to activate the OK button in this dialog box, but don't want to pick up the mouse, which key would you press?

Paragraph Specifications
Indents: Left [0] inches; First [0] inches; Right [0] inches
Paragraph space: Before [0] inches; After [0] inches
Alignment: [Left] Dictionary: [US English]
[OK] [Cancel] [Rules...] [Spacing...]

. . . .

2. If you want to select another edit box in the dialog box above ("Left" is currently selected), which key would move the selection from box to box?

. . . .

Tools
Spelling... ⌘L
Grammar... ⌘⇧G
Thesaurus...
Hyphenation... ⇧F15
Word Count... ⌥F15
Renumber... ⌘F15
Sort
Calculate ⌘=
Repaginate Now
Preferences...
Commands... ⌘⇧⌥C

Insert
Page Break ⇧⌅
Section Break ⌘⌅
Table...
Footnote... ⌘E
Voice Annotation

3. Which keys would you press to:

Check the grammar?

. . . .

Do a word count?

. . . .

Renumber?

. . . .

Insert a page break?

. . . .

Get the list of Commands?

. . . .

Insert a section break?

. . . .

4. Connect the name of the key with its symbol:

Escape key	**a)**	➡|
Option key	**b)**	⇧
Control key	**c)**	**esc**
Command key	**d)**	~
Tilde key	**e)**	/
Asterisk, or star	**f)**	^
Shift key	**g)**	⌃
Forward slash	**h)**	⌘
Backslash	**i)**	*
Tab key	**j)**	\
Enter key	**k)**	⌥ ⌥

Answers on page 423.

7 All Windows on the Mac

A **window** is a basic, fundamental element of the Macintosh.

> When you open any folder or disk, including your hard disk, the Mac displays the contents of the folder in a window. (Open the disk or folder by double-clicking on it.)
>
> When you open any application, such as your word processor, the Mac gives you a window in which to type your document. (Open the application by double-clicking on it.)

In this chapter I explain the details you will find in just about *every* window on the Mac, whether it is in your word processor, browser, spreadsheet, database, or whatever application you love to work with, *as well as* in the windows at the Desktop.

The chapter following this one is devoted to the features that you will find only in the windows on the Desktop, the ones that open to display the contents of folders and disks (not application windows).

Windows

Below is a typical window. You will find each of the items labeled below in just about every window on the Mac *(icons are only found in Desktop windows—you won't see icons in your application windows).*

Explanations for each of these items are found on the following pages.

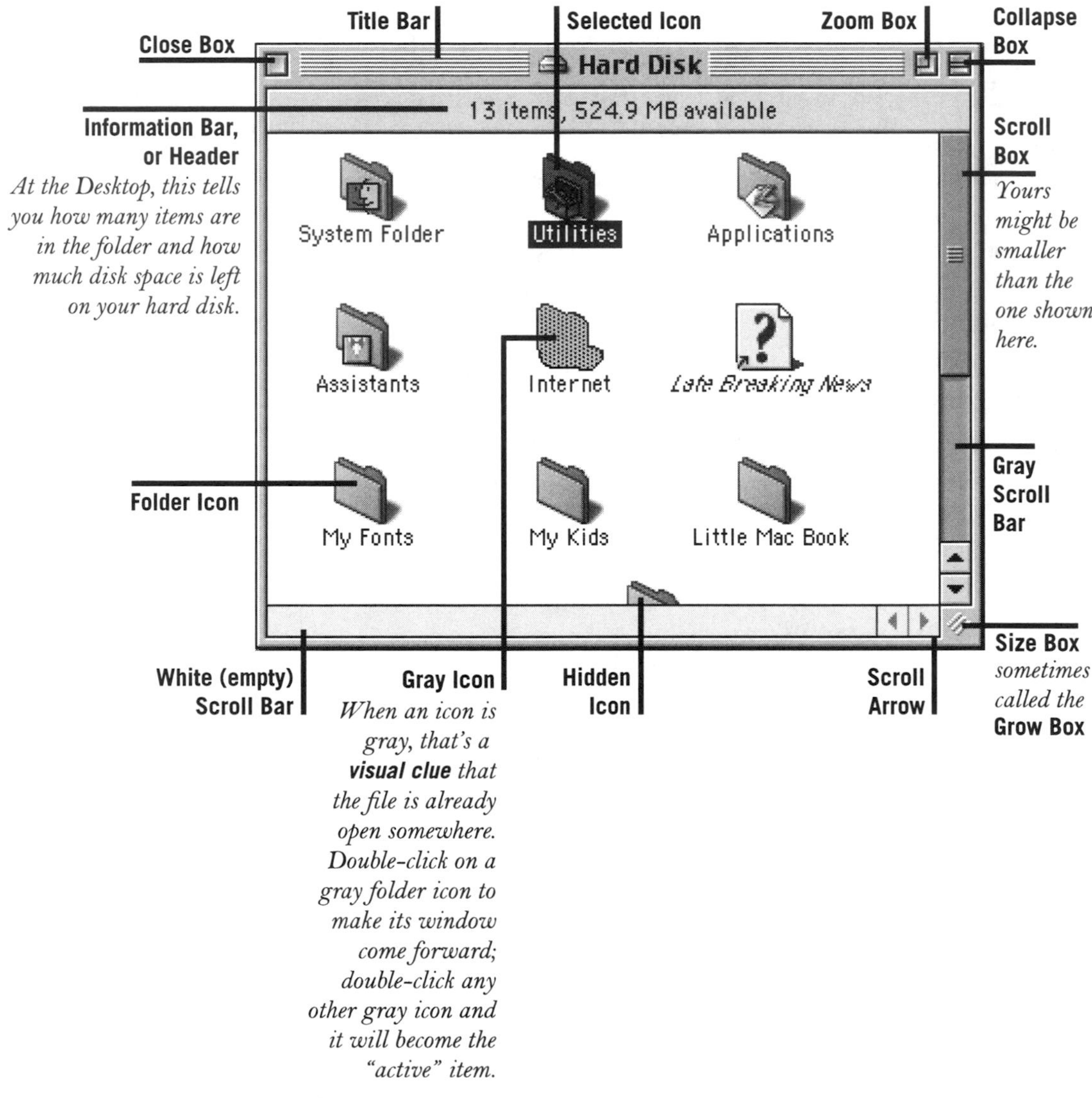

Title Bar

The **title bar** is the striped bar across the top of a window in which, logically, the title appears. This title is the name of the disk, folder, or document you have opened.

Moving the Window

Position the pointer in the title bar or on any edge of the window, then press-and-drag to **move** any window around the screen. As you drag, you will see the *outline* of the window. Just let go when you have the outline placed where you want, and the window will appear in that position.

Active Window

If you have more than one window open, only one will have lines, or stripes, in its title bar. The stripes are a **visual clue** that this window is the **active window.** If windows are overlapping, the active window is the one that is in front. Open several windows (folders) and check it out.

The **active window** is the window that the commands from the keyboard or the menu will affect. For instance, if you go to the File menu and choose "Close," it will close the *active* window. If you choose "New Folder," a new folder will appear in the *active* window. It's very important to be conscious of which window is active!

To make the window active

To make a window **active,** simply click on any visible part of it; this will also bring that window to the front of any others. You may have to move other windows to see the one that you want to make active.

> **Tip:** To move a window *without* making it active, hold down the Command key while you press-and-drag on any edge.

Size Box

On the bottom-right corner is the **size box,** or actually, the resize box. Press-and-drag in that box to make the window larger or smaller. If you have several windows open, you can resize and rearrange them so they all fit on your screen without overlapping. You can have several word processing documents on the screen, or perhaps a database file and two spreadsheet worksheets and a letter, and view them all at the same time.

Zoom Box

On the upper-right corner of the window are two little boxes. The box on the left of the two is the **zoom box.** If you click the zoom box, the window will enlarge just big enough to display everything inside. If you click the zoom box when the window is large, the window will zoom back down to the size it was *just before* you zoomed it larger.

> **Tip:** To open the window big enough to fill the screen, hold down the Option key and click the zoom box.

Collapse Box

The **collapse box** shrinks the window so all you see is the title bar. This is a great way to reduce the clutter on your Desktop or in any application. **To un-collapse the window,** click in the collapse box again.

Tip: *To collapse every open window on the Desktop, hold down the Option key when you click one collapse box.*

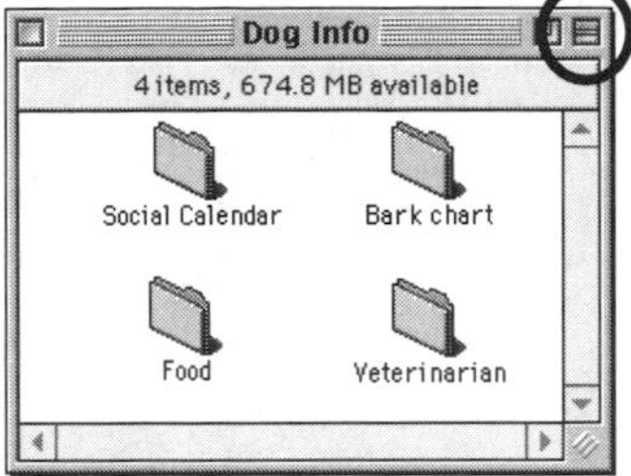

If you click once on the collapse box of any window (as shown to the left), it will shrink your window so just the title bar is visible (as shown above).

You can also double-click in the title bar to collapse a window, if that box has been checked in the "Options" section of the Appearance control panel (shown below; see page 243 for details on control panels). Of course, you can turn that feature off by unchecking it.

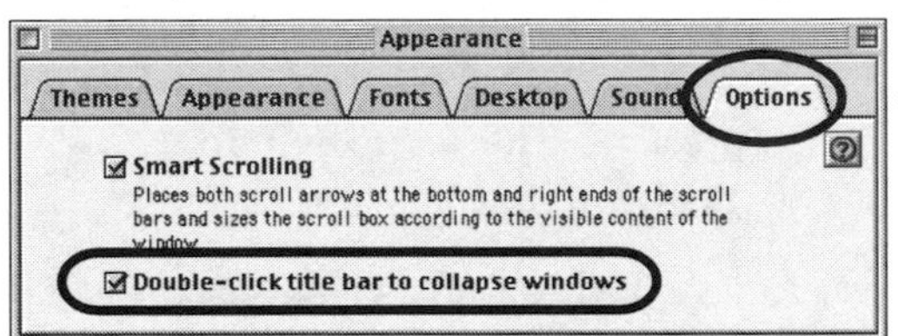

This is the section of the Appearance control panel where you can choose to collapse windows with a double-click in the title bar.

Close Box

And, of course, in the upper-left of the window is the **close box.** Click once in that little box to close the window, which sends the document or folder it was displaying back to the disk or folder it came from. On the Desktop and in many programs you can use the keyboard shortcut Command W to close the *active window.* That is, instead of clicking in the close box, you can press Command W to put the window away.

Tip: *To close all open windows on the Desktop, press Command Option W.*

Scroll Bars

Along the right and bottom edges of the window are the **scroll bars.** The scroll bars allow you to view everything in the window, even if it cannot all fit on the screen at once or if the window is sized too small. Notice the **visual clues** in the example on page 70: the scroll bar along the right side is *gray,* while the one along the bottom is *white.*

Gray Scroll Bar

When a **scroll bar is gray,** it's a **visual clue** that *there are other items in the window you can't see.* In the example on page 70, you can see a folder along the bottom edge that is barely visible so the scroll bar is gray, indicating something more is beyond its borders. When you see a gray scroll bar in a list of items, as in an "Open" dialog box, it means there are more items in the list than can be displayed. Scroll to see the others.

When the **scroll bar is white,** it indicates *there is nothing more in the direction of the arrows* (the horizontal direction in the example).

White Scroll Bar

At either end of the scroll bars are the **scroll arrows.** When the scroll bar is *gray,* press on a scroll arrow to make the contents of the window glide past, like the scenery outside a train window. Try it.

Scroll Arrows

Notice the little **scroll box** in the gray scroll bar (you will *only* see a scroll box if the scroll bar is gray). As you press on the arrows, this box moves so you can tell what portion of the window you are viewing. When the scroll box is all the way at one end, that's the end of the list or of the window. Some people call the scroll box an *elevator* because it goes up and down like one.

Scroll Box

This is the scroll box.

Press-and-drag the scroll box to move it to any position on the scroll bar, let go, and the window will immediately jump to that particular place rather than scroll through everything. This is very handy inside an application like a word processor where you have a long document and scrolling with the arrows would take too long. For instance, if your document is 50 pages long, dragging the scroll box to the middle of the scroll bar would take you to page 25. In some applications a number appears within the scroll box to indicate which page you're on.

Press-and-drag the Scroll Box

There's yet another way to use the scroll bars: simply **click** the pointer in any *gray* area of the bar, and the window will move up, down, or across, usually a full window view. Use this technique when you want to scroll through long windows quickly, like in your word processor or when you're browsing the web. Try it.

Click in the Scroll Bar

You can choose to turn on "Smart Scrolling": use the "Options" section of the Appearance control panel, as shown on the opposite page (it might already be turned on). This puts both of the scroll arrows at the bottom or the right side of the window, instead of one scroll arrow at either end, which allows you to scroll through a window in either direction without having to move your mouse to the other side of the window. Notice the different look of the scroll bars when Smart Scrolling is turned on. Experiment with this option!

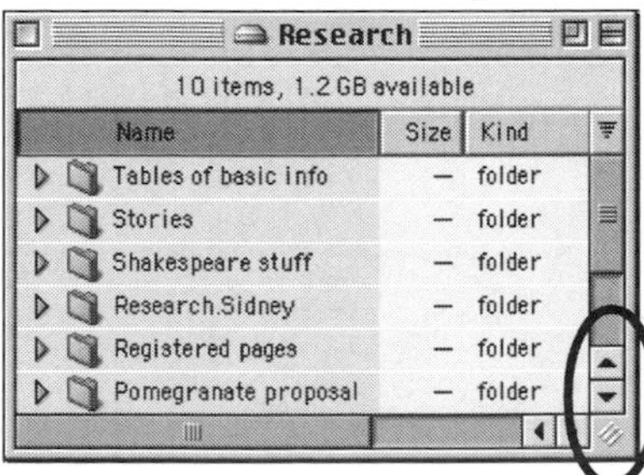

Notice both scroll arrows are here at the bottom of the window, instead of one at the top and one at the bottom.

"Smart Scrolling"

The size of the scroll box is a ***visual clue*** *that tells you how much of the window you can't see.*

1. Label the window below with the following parts:

Close box	**Size box**
Zoom box	**Title bar**
Scroll box	**Gray scroll bar**
Collapse box	**White scroll bar**
Folder icon	**Information bar, or header**
Scroll arrows (4 of them)	

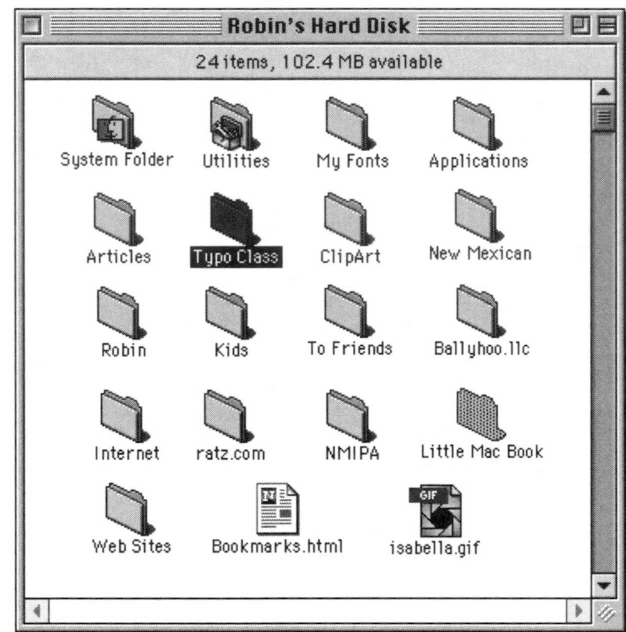

2. Which icon in the above window is ***selected?***

3. Which folder is already ***open?***

4. ***How many files*** are stored in this window (folder)?

5. What is the instant ***visual clue*** that tells you there are more files in this window than what you see?

6. Is "smart scrolling" turned on in this window? How can you tell?

Answers on page 423.

8 Desktop Windows

Desktop windows are those windows that open when you double-click a folder icon or a disk icon, including your hard disk icon.

The Macintosh allows you a great deal of control over the look and the feel of your computer and the options available so you can arrange your work and your working environment in a way that is most effective for *you.* The **Desktop windows** are a good example of the control you have on the Mac—you can choose to see what's in your window in a variety of ways, all appropriate for different purposes or styles; you can organize the windows any way you like; and you can create new icons for the files.

The techniques in this chapter apply only to the windows at the *Desktop* (also known as the *Finder*); they don't apply to the windows you use in your applications.

View the Contents of the Window

You can change how you **view the contents** of a Desktop window. Some people like to see their window's contents as icons, some like buttons, and others prefer to view a list. These different views are available from the View menu when you're at the Desktop.

To change the view of a window, first click anywhere in an open window to make that window *active* (because when you choose a view it applies to the *active window,* the one that has the lines in its title bar). The window will stay in the view you choose until you change it again. Below are the three different sorts of views, and the following pages explain how to work with them.

View as Icons

View as Icons (example 1, below) is what you typically see—icons are the pictures representing the files. Visually oriented people (like me) tend to prefer to view by icon. When viewed by icon, the files are in no specific order. You can organize them easily enough by pulling down to "Arrange" in the View menu (explained more fully on pages 78–80).

View as List

View as List (example 2, below) displays all your items as text names in a vertical list automatically arranged by various categories such as name, label, or size. When you view a window as a list, you can still manipulate the contents as if they were icons; that is, you can pick them up and put them in the trash or in another folder, you can rename them, copy them, open them, etc. (see Chapter 9 on *Icons and Files*). For information on what those little triangles are doing in your window when you view any folders in a list, see Chapter 10 on *Folders.*

View as Buttons

View as Buttons (example 3, below) turns the icons into squares that open with a **single mouse click.** As with lists and icons, you can rename, copy, open, and trash buttons. Because buttons are activated by a single click, you have to be careful when dragging them around—**drag a button by its name, not the button itself, or you'll open its folder or file.** *Select* a button by clicking once on its *name.*

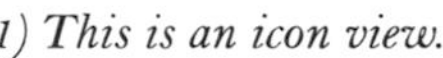
1) This is an icon view.

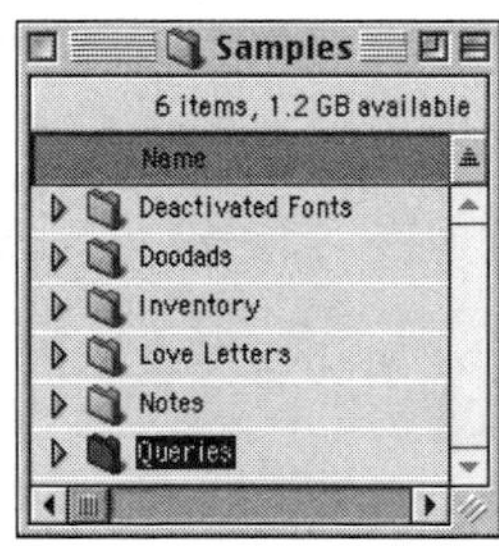

2) This is a list view.

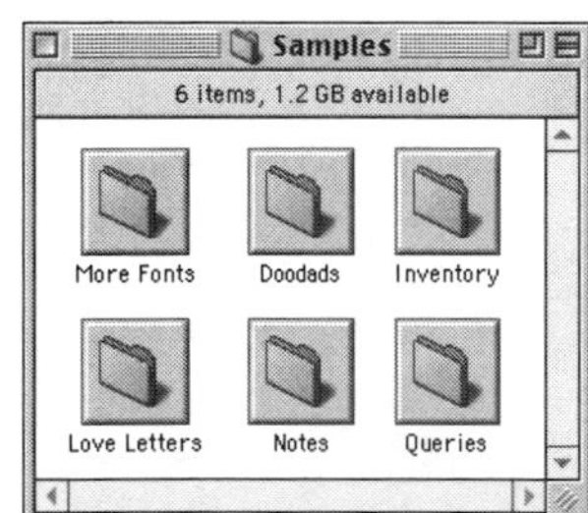

3) This is a button view.

Regular Windows vs. Pop-Up Windows

You can also choose to set up a window as a **regular** or a **pop-up** window. This won't affect your icons, buttons, or lists—**it just gives you different ways to work with the window itself.**

View as Window

This is the title bar in a regular window.

The view "as Window" is the way you're used to looking at windows. This is where you see the title bar, close box, zoom box, and collapse box that were explained in Chapter 7. When you want to view a regular window, as you know by now, you double-click on a folder or disk icon to open its window, and click the close box to close it.

View as Pop-up Window

This is the tab in a pop-up window.

When you choose to view "as Pop-up Window," a *tab* replaces the title bar, as shown to the right. As soon as you click on the tab or open anything from that window, the window collapses so all you see of it is the tab at the bottom of the screen showing the window's name. To open it again, just click on that tab and it pops up (hence the name).

To put files in a tabbed window, drag the files down to the tab and the window will pop open; drop them in the window. When you let go of the file, the window will pop back to its tab.

As soon as you click the tab or open any file in that window, it pops down to the bottom of your screen.

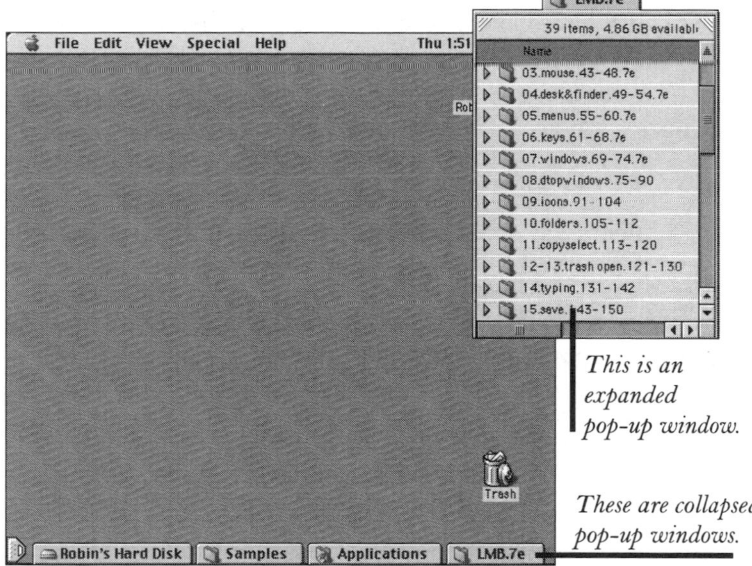

This is an expanded pop-up window.

These are collapsed pop-up windows.

Some people find the pop-up window feature to be a real space-saver and a convenience—store your most-used folders as tabs at the bottom of your screen and save time hunting around on the Desktop.

Create pop-up windows automatically

You can also create a pop-up window by dragging a window all the way to the bottom of the screen—it will automatically turn into a tab. To view it as a regular window again, either drag the tab up far enough until it turns into a window, or drag it part way up and then select "as Window" from your View menu.

Organizing Your Views

Tip: *You can also change views right from the window: Command-click on any empty spot in the window to get the menu.*

In any view, you can organize (sort) your window contents according to certain categories, such as by name, by size, or by version.

If you view your window as a *list* of names: From the View menu, slide down to "Sort List," then choose the heading you want your files organized as. Or arrange the list by simply clicking on the column headings at the top of the list window.

If you view your window as *buttons* or *icons:* From the View menu, slide down to "Arrange," then choose the heading according to how you want your files arranged.

View Options

You have a lot of control over how files are displayed in each individual window. Use the **View Options** dialog box (get it from the View menu). Here you can determine which headings you'll see in your list views, how icons will arrange themselves in the window, and how big the icons will appear. You can choose whether you want the computer to display the date of the files by relative dates ("Yesterday" and "Today") or by actual dates. If you have chosen to view as buttons or icons, "View Options" lets you choose how you want your items arranged: Do you want them to line up evenly along an invisible grid? (Choose "Always snap to grid.") Do you want them always arranged by name or size, even if you drop new files into the folder or resize the window? (Click "Keep arranged," and then pick your arrangement.)

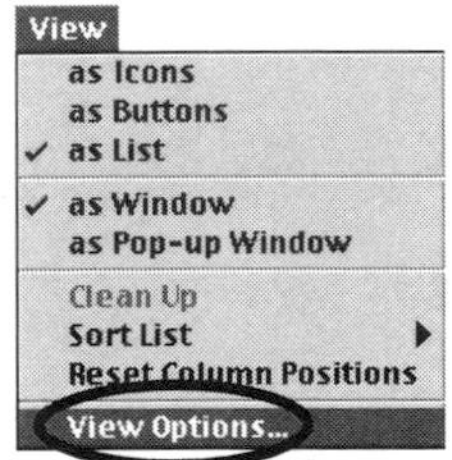

Get the "View Options" dialog box from this View menu. The choices you make will apply to the active window (the window in front with the lines in its title bar.)

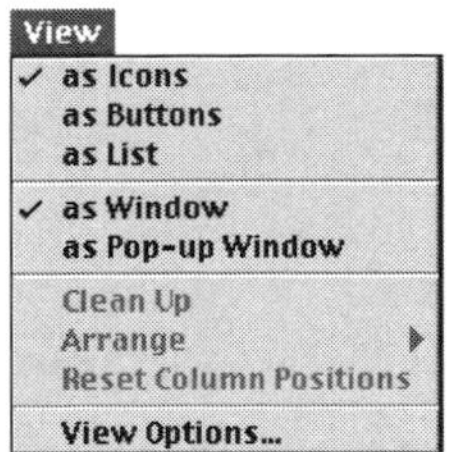

If the "Arrange" command is gray, it means the selected window has the "Keep arranged" button checked. If you want to change the arrangement, choose "View Options..." and click the button "None."

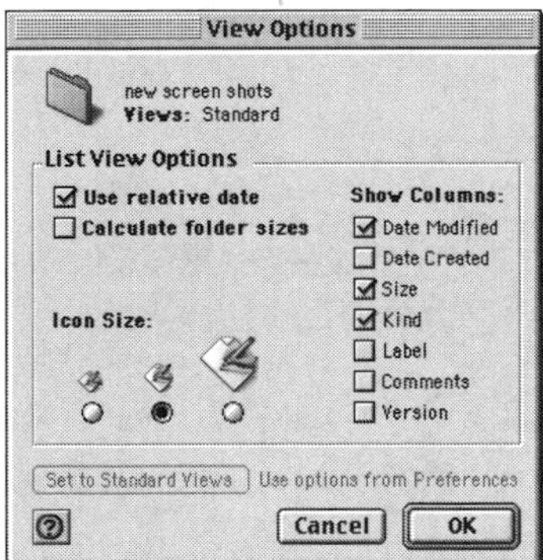

List view: *The column headings you choose in this dialog box will appear in the **selected window** as headings, and will also appear in the "Sort List" submenu.*

Experiment with the "Icon Size" options to see which you prefer.

Do not check the box "Calculate folder sizes"; it will slow down everything on your Mac.

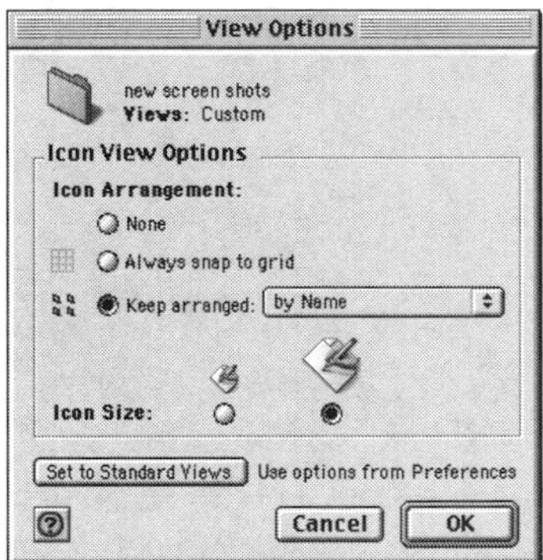

Icon or button view: *The option "Always snap to grid" works in conjunction with the grid spacing you choose in the Preferences dialog box (see page 87).*

If you choose "Keep arranged," then your icons or buttons will rearrange themselves in the chosen order even if you add or remove files from the window.

Experiment with the "Icon Size."

Standard and custom views

There are different sets of display options for the list view, the icon view, and the button view. Once you decide what you like, it can make you crazy to have to adjust every window to suit you. To make it easier, create your own "standard" view that you can apply to any window with the click of a button.

To create your own, customized "standard," go to the Edit menu and choose "Preferences...." You'll get this dialog box:

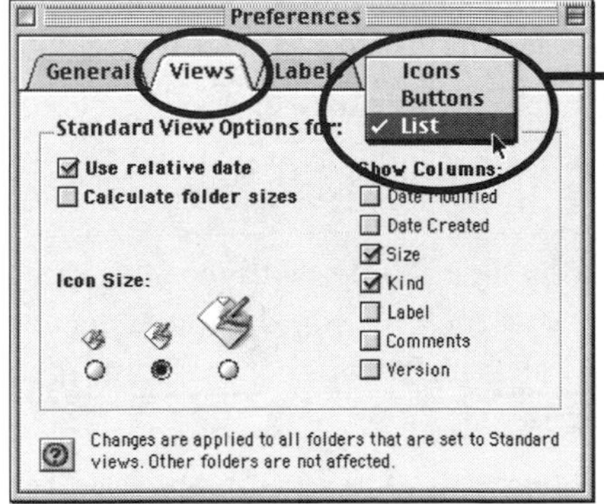

Click the "Views" tab.

Press on this little menu to choose one of the three possible views, such as "List," then set your own "standard" options.

Choose the other two views and set their standards as well.

Adjust the settings for each of the views, then close the dialog box (click in the little close box in the upper-left).

To apply your standards, open any window and get the "View Options" dialog box (either choose "View Options..." from the View menu, or Control-click in any window and choose "View Options..." from the pop-up menu). Click the button "Set to Standard Views," and your preferred settings will be applied to the selected window instantly. If the "Set to Standard Views" button is gray, that means the selected window already has the standard settings applied.

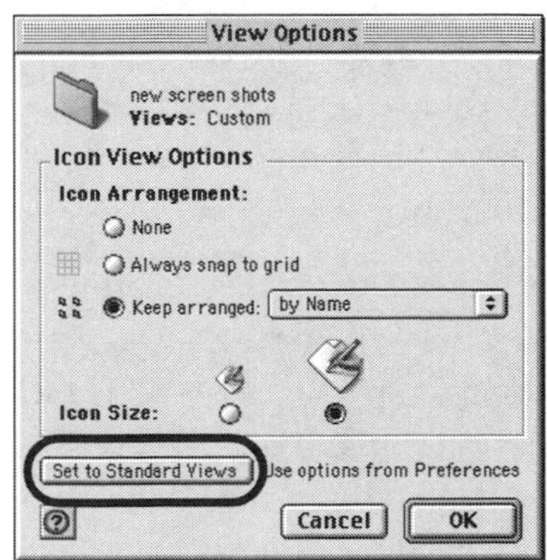

It's great to be able to apply your own arrangement with one click of the button.

Sort and Arrange Choices

So what do all those choices mean? What does it mean to arrange or sort something "by size" or "by version?" Here's a quick rundown:

by Name

By Name organizes your icons alphabetically. Names that start with empty spaces or punctuation are alphabetized first. **Never begin a file name with a period—it can cause internal problems.** (How do you think I know that?)

by Date Modified

By Date Modified lists files in chronological order, with the most recently **modified** files first. The last time you opened a file or folder and did something to it is the date it was last modified.

Arranging folders by either date modified or date created can come in handy when, for instance, you have several budget documents and you want to see the most recent edition.

by Date Created

By Date Created lists the files in chronological order with the most recently **created** files first. The Mac looks at the creation date as determined by the date and time you've set in the Date & Time control panel (details for that control panel are on page 247).

by Size

By Size lists the files in order of size beginning with the largest. If you are viewing by list, you may notice that your folders show no size, and that choosing the "Size" column heading doesn't rearrange the folders. If you want to see folder sizes, you have to choose "Calculate folder sizes" in the "View Options" dialog box (see page 78). It can be quite time consuming for the computer to figure out folder sizes, and it can even cause problems on some machines!

by Kind

By Kind lists the files in groups: applications, documents, and folders. This is handy if you want to see a list of all your applications or all the documents you've stored in your budget folder, etc.

> **Tip:** "Arrange by Kind" is particularly useful for a folder that holds an application (or a game) plus all of its accessories—the dictionaries, tutorials, technical files, samples, etc. The view "by Kind" will always put the application (or game) at the top of the list so it's easy to find.

by Label

By Label groups files according to their "label." A label is something you make up and apply to a file (see page 100–101). For instance, you can create a label called Love Letters and apply it appropriately. Then when you choose the "Arrange" or "Sort List" command and choose Label, all the love letters in that window are grouped together. You can also search by label, so you could search your hard disk for all Love Letters.

by Comments

By Comments will display the first 31 characters of any text that was typed into the Comments box in the Get Info window (see page 102).

by Version

By Version lists the files in alphabetical order, with applications listed first. Each application has its version number displayed. How many copies of SimpleText do you have on your Mac? Well, you can use Sherlock (Chapter 26) to find them all, then gather them into one folder and arrange that folder "by Version." Throw out all but the newest version of SimpleText, the one with the highest version number.

Resize and Rearrange the Columns

You can **resize and rearrange the columns** of information that are displayed in your window when you view items in some sort of list. First choose a list view of some sort.

To resize the columns, just position the pointer on the line right between two column headings. The pointer will turn into a two-headed arrow, shown below, which is your **visual clue** that you can resize the columns —just press that two-headed arrow and drag to the left or right.

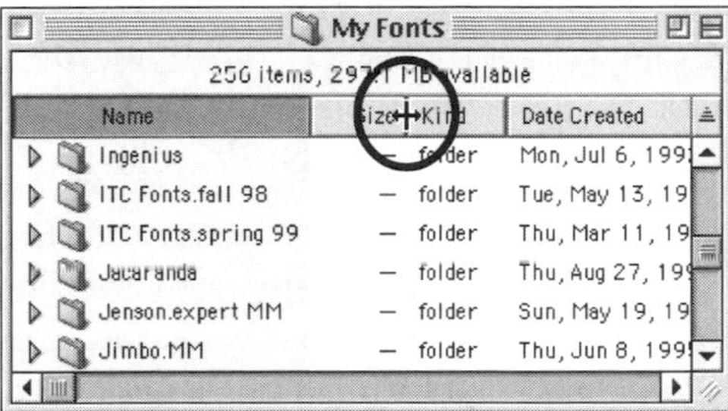

If you see a one-headed arrow, that's a **visual clue** *that you can only resize that particular column in the direction the arrow is pointing.*

To rearrange the columns, press directly on any column heading and drag to the left or right. As soon as you start to drag, the pointer tool turns into the grabber hand, which is your **visual clue** that you are about to rearrange the columns. The only column you cannot move out of position is "Name."

Sort Order Button

When you view the contents of a window as a list, there is a little triangle above the scroll bars on the right side. If you click it, the items in the list sort themselves *in the opposite order.* For instance, if they are sorted by name, as shown below, they will sort alphabetically in order backward or forward when you click the sort order button. If you select the column "Date Created" (click once on the column heading to sort the list by that feature), then the sort order button will rearrange the list from the oldest to newest files, or from the newest to oldest.

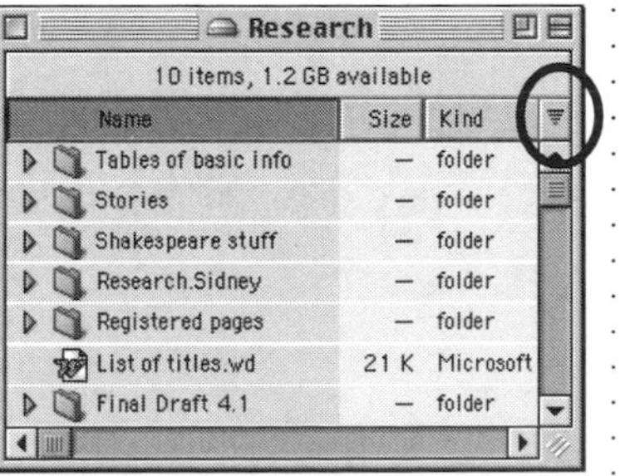

How can you tell by looking at this window that the files are arranged by name? (The **visual clue** *is in the heading column.)*

The Window Menu
(Mac OS 9.1 only)

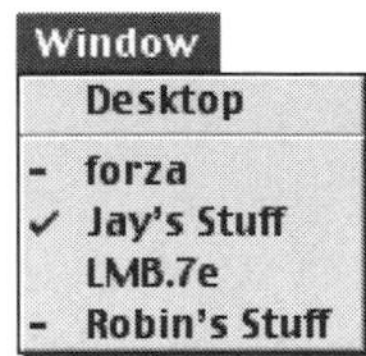

In Mac OS 9.1, there is a new menu item between View and Special, called **Window.** In it you will find a list of the titles of every window that is currently open on your Desktop.

- A checkmark next to a window title indicates the active window.
- A hyphen indicates that the window is collapsed.
- Choose any title to bring that window to the front.
- Hold down the Command key when you choose a title and that window will close.
- Hold down the Command and Option keys, choose "Desktop," and *all* the windows will close.

Clean Up and Arrange

These are the buttons I want in my house—to make the dishes jump to their shelves, the laundry put itself away in the drawers, and all the papers fly back into the filing cabinet.

When you're viewing icons or buttons in your windows, they often get all scrambled up and the place looks like a mess. This can also happen to your Desktop if you tend to keep lots of icons right on the Desktop. There are several ways to organize your icons so everything lines up neatly: The **Clean Up** command under the View menu is one simple way—this forces all the icons into the nearest little cubby on the underlying invisible grid.

However, Clean Up doesn't keep things in the arrangement you chose, so this command might not be what you want. If not, you can organize with the **Arrange** command, also in the View menu (see pages 78–80).

Organize your Desktop

If you want to **organize a messy Desktop,** there is a shortcut to get to the Arrange command: Hold down the Control Key and click on the Desktop, and you will get a special menu. This menu, in addition to several other useful commands not usually found in the View menu (such as Help, New Folder, and Change Desktop Background), includes View, Clean Up, Arrange, and View Options.

Outline View

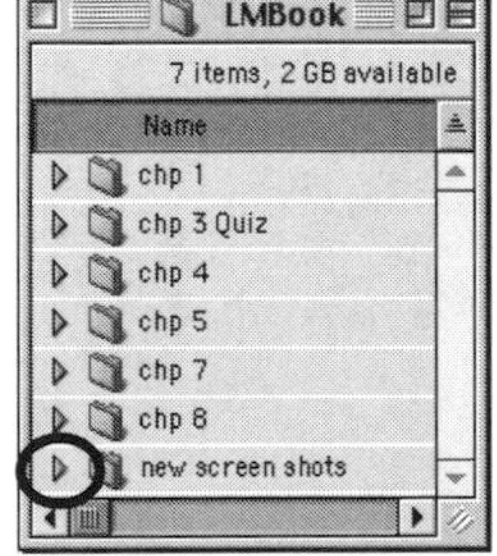

See Chapter 10 for details on the outline view.

If you are wondering about those little triangles to the left of folders in a list view, please see Chapter 10 on *Folders,* page 109 in particular. These triangles in the **outline view** collapse and expand the folders so you can see what's inside each one without having to open a new window. There are some great tricks to working with these, all of which are explained in Chapter 10.

Close *all* of the Windows

To simultaneously **close every window** that is open on your Desktop, hold down the Option key while you click in the active window's close box; all the windows will go away one after another!

. . . and other window-closing tricks

- You'll notice in the File menu a keyboard command to close the active window: Command W. **To close all the windows at once,** don't go to the file menu, but press Command Option W and *all* of the windows will fly home. You don't need to click anywhere.
- If you are running Mac OS 9.1 and want **to close all the windows at once,** hold down the Command and Option keys, go to the Window menu, and choose "Desktop."
- **To collapse all the windows at once,** hold down the Option key and click the Collapse box in the upper-right corner. This also works in applications when you have more than one window open.
- Often the file you want to open is buried within several folders. Hold the Option key down while you double-click to open those folders to get to your file. **The windows will close up behind you** as you go along.
- When you eject a disk or turn off the computer, the Macintosh remembers which windows were open when you left. When you insert the same disk or when you turn the computer back on, those windows will re-open in the same position in which you left them. You can take advantage of this fact and arrange your windows before you Shut Down.

  Or you might find it irritating to open a disk and have windows pop up all over the place. If you hold down the Option key when you insert a disk or start the computer, **any windows that had been left open will be closed** when you get to the Desktop.

Scroll Through the Window without using the Scroll Bars

There is a nice little trick for scrolling through the contents of any Desktop window without using scroll bars. Hold down the Command key, then *press* in any blank spot in the window and *drag* the mouse around: As soon as you *press* the mouse button down, the pointer changes to a little grabber hand; *drag* that grabber hand and the contents of your window will move around any which way, not just vertically or horizontally as they do when you use the scroll bars. Try it.

Spring-Loaded Folders

If you're using a system older than OS 8, such as System 7 or 6, you won't find these spring-loaded folders or pop-up windows.

Desktop windows can be **spring-loaded.** You may have accidentally discovered this feature already—if you drag a file icon onto a folder and hold it there, the folder window springs open in front of you. It can be quite a surprise if you're not expecting it.

The spring-loaded feature allows you to burrow down through folders-inside-of-folders without cluttering up your Desktop with open windows. On your way to the folder you want, each one you dig down through will automatically close up when the next window springs open.

To move an icon using spring-loaded folders, take an icon and hold it over a folder. That folder will spring open. Still holding that icon (don't let go!), drag it over another folder. If you don't see the other folder you want in the window, drag to the sides or up or down to make the window scroll. When you find the folder you want, hold the icon over that one and it will spring open. You can keep digging deeper this way. When you come to the folder you want, let go of the icon, either before or after the folder springs open. After you let go of the icon, you'll notice that every other folder along the way has put itself back where it belongs instead of hanging around open on the Desktop.

The magnifying glass is a **visual clue** *that you did the click-and-a-half correctly.*

To dig through nested folders to find a file, double-click on a folder *but don't let go after the second click* (this is called a **click-and-a-half**). Hold the mouse button down and in a second or two the pointer turns into a magnifying glass and the folder will spring open. Keep holding the mouse button down and any other folders you pause over will spring open. All the windows that popped up for you (except for the last one) will snap shut when you let go of the mouse! Try it.

Turn spring-loaded folders on or off

To use the spring-loaded feature, make sure it's **turned on:** From the Edit menu at the Desktop, choose "Preferences...," click the "General" tab, and check the box for "Spring-loaded folders." Drag the slider to set the amount of delay: If you set a long delay, you have to wait several seconds for the folder to open; with a short delay, windows spring open in your face when you don't expect it.

Tip: *Set a long delay or even uncheck the box to turn it off, then use the Spacebar when you want the folder to open faster: that is, hold a file over a folder, then tap the Spacebar; that folder will open instantly.*

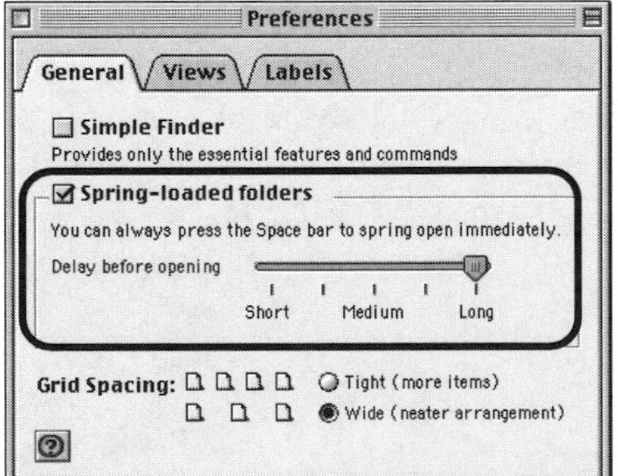

If the spring-loaded feature drives you nuts, ***turn it off*** *completely by unchecking the box.*

Gray Icons

Sometimes you can't see the window itself but you *can* see the **gray icon** of a folder or disk, which indicates *its window is open somewhere, you just can't see it.* In that case, double-click the gray icon to bring its window forward and make it active.

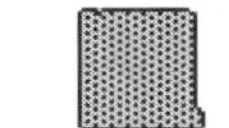

Double-click a gray disk or folder icon to make its window come forward.

Hierarchy of a Folder (Window)

To view the hierarchy of a nested folder (to see the folders that a particular folder is contained within), hold the Command key down and click or press on the **title** of the window (not the stripes in the title bar, but on the actual title or word itself). This displays a drop-down menu, as shown below, right. You can choose any other folder in that drop-down menu to open its window and bring it to the front.

Hold down the Command key and press right here.

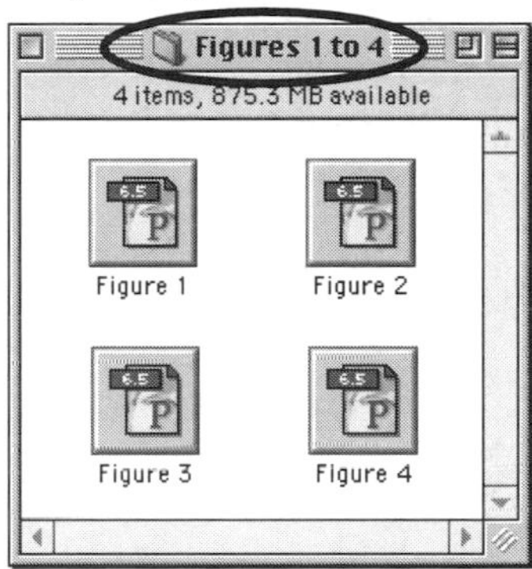

You will see the list of folders that contain this window.

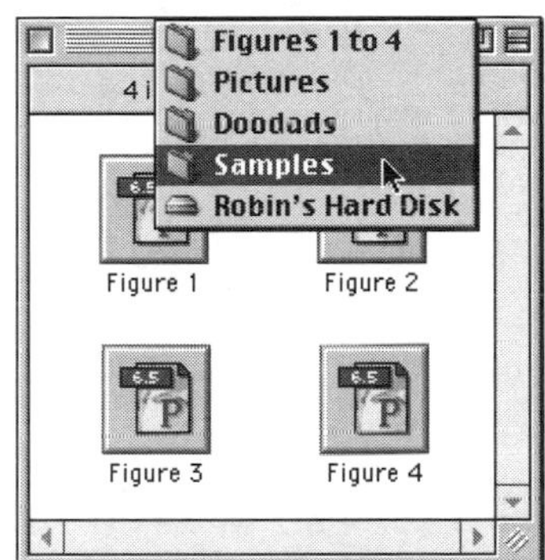

You can see from the title bar menu that the folder "Figures 1 to 4" is inside a folder called Pictures, which is inside the Doodads folder, which is inside the Samples folder, which is in my hard disk window (which is named "Robin's Hard Disk").

Preferences Dialog Box

The **Preferences** dialog box (get it from the Edit menu at the Desktop), is *another* place where you can fine-tune the appearance of your Desktop. The "View Options" command we talked about on page 78 changes the appearance of each *individual* window: the choices you make in the Preferences dialog box affect *all* windows on your Desktop.

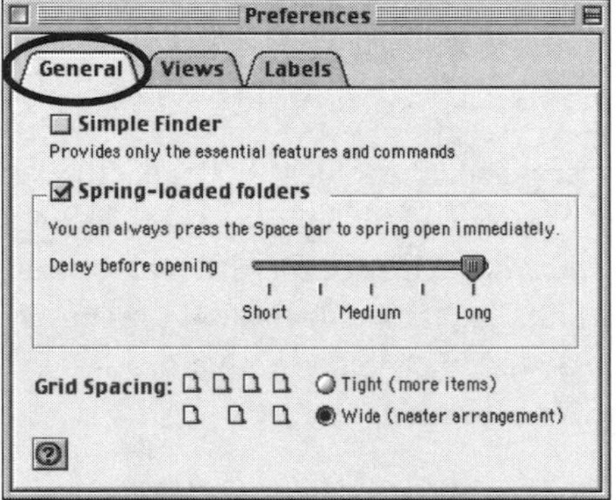

See the opposite page for an explanation of each of these items.

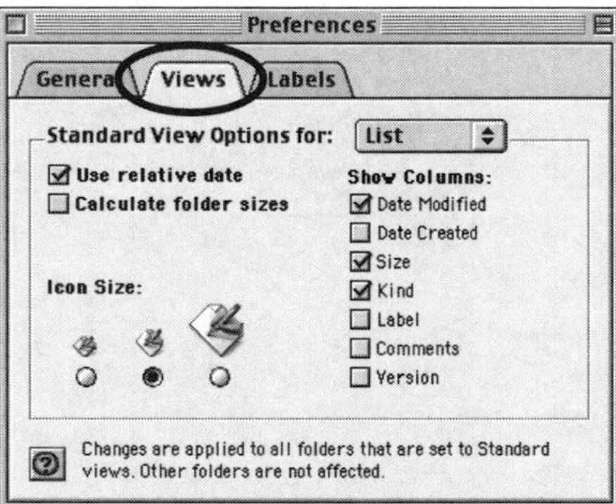

See pages 78–81 for explanations of each of these items, and to understand the difference between these same items in the "Preferences" dialog box and in the "View Options" dialog box.

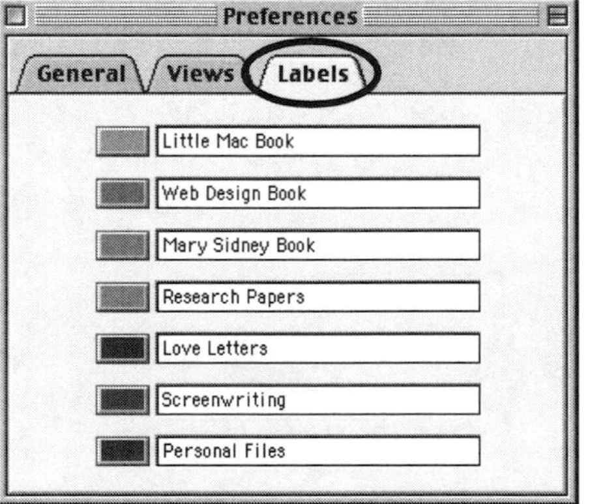

Labels are discussed in Chapter 9 on Icons and Files, *pages 100–101.*

Simple Finder

The **Simple Finder** was designed to prevent beginners from feeling overwhelmed when they look at their menu options. If you check this box, you will have only the very basic Finder menu choices available to you, as shown below. Check it out.

File
New Folder ⌘N
Open ⌘O
Print ⌘P
Move To Trash ⌘⌫
Close Window ⌘W
Get Info ▸
Label ▸
Duplicate ⌘D
Make Alias ⌘M
Add To Favorites
Put Away ⌘Y
Find... ⌘F
Show Original ⌘R
Page Setup...
Print Window...

This is the regular File menu.

This is the File menu you see when you choose Simple Finder. As you can see, Simple Finder narrows your choices considerably.

Spring-loaded folders

Spring-loaded folders are discussed on page 84.

Grid Spacing

Grid Spacing controls the size of the underlying invisible grid upon which your icons sit, should you choose to force your icons to align upon it (see "View Options" on page 78). A tight grid means you can fit more icons into the space, a wide grid means your icons will line up farther apart from each other. If you have long file names, wide spacing prevents the names from overlapping.

As with everything else in the "Preferences" dialog box, the choice you make here **applies to every window on your computer.** The "View Options" dialog box, on the other hand, **applies to individual windows.** So for each individual window, you can choose from "View Options" whether or not the icons in the window will "Always snap to grid," but the grid spacing they snap to is determined in the Preferences dialog box, and the same grid spacing applies to every window.

Fonts in the Windows

You can choose the **font** (typeface) and **size** in which the names of your files and folders appear. From the Apple menu, slide down to "Control Panels," then click "Appearance." Click the "Fonts" tab, and use "Views Font" (for more control panel details, see pages 240–241).

Generally, **city-named fonts** are easier to read on your computer screen, so choose a font with the name of a city, such as Geneva, Chicago, or New York. If you have a hard time seeing the tiny file names, make the size of the type bigger.

Borders Interview

A playful font that is easy enough to read can make your Desktop more fun.

Print the Window

Occasionally you might need to **print** the information you find in a particular **window.** For instance, you might want to make a list of all the documents that are on a Zip disk or all the dated budget files in the Budget folder.

This technique only works with the windows on the Desktop. If you want to print a "picture" of a window or a screen within an application, or any dialog box, see the next page, "Print Other Windows."

To print the info in the active window:

1. Turn on your printer.
2. Make sure the window that contains the data you want is the active window (click once on it).
3. From the File menu, choose Print Window... (it's the very last item; if you see "Print Desktop..." instead, that means you don't have an active window—click on the open window that you want to print).
4. In the Print dialog box, change any of the options to suit your fancy, then click OK (or hit the Return key).

Print the Desktop

The above procedure prints only the contents of the *active window.* While you are at the *Desktop* (this will only work at the Desktop level), you can print all of the icons.

To print all of the icons that are visible on the Desktop:

1. Turn on your printer.
2. Make sure the Desktop is active: click on any icon on the Desktop, such as the trash can or hard disk, **or** press Command Shift UpArrow.
3. Your computer monitor is probably too large to print onto an 8.5 x 11 piece of paper, so first reduce the printed size: From the File menu, choose **Page Setup....** In the "Reduce or Enlarge" edit box, type in something like 75 or 50 percent, depending on the size of your monitor. Click OK.
4. From the File menu, choose **Print Desktop...** (it's the very last item; if the command you see is "Print Window...," then you are not at the Desktop level—repeat Step 2).
5. In the Print dialog box, change any of the options to suit your fancy, then click OK **or** hit the Return key.

Print Other Windows or the Screen

If you want to print a "picture" of a whole window in an *application* (as opposed to printing the *text* of your document normally), see if there is a command called "Print Window" in one of the menus. If not, you can create and print a *screen shot,* also called a *screen dump* or *screen capture,* of the entire screen.

1. **a) To take a picture of the entire screen,** press Command Shift 3. You'll hear a nerve-wracking little sound as if a tiny fuse is breaking inside your computer and your screen will freeze for a moment. Don't worry—the computer is taking a picture of the screen.

   b) To capture just a *selected portion* of the screen, press Command Shift 4—you'll get a crosshair cursor, shown to the right. Use that cursor to drag a box around what you want a picture of. Let go.

   This is the crosshair cursor. Use it to select a portion of the screen.

   c) To capture the *active window,* press the Caps Lock key down, then press Command Shift 4—you'll get a target cursor, as shown to the right. Click on the active window.

   This is the target cursor. Use it to capture the active window.

2. Now go to your Desktop and look in the window belonging to the hard disk. You will see a new item called "Picture 1."

Picture 1

This is what will appear on your hard disk when you take a screen shot.

3. Double-click on "Picture 1." It will open in the application called SimpleText, a small word processor.
4. From the File menu, choose "Print...," then click OK. (If it looks like it's too big to fit on one piece of paper, go to the File menu, choose "Page Setup...," and reduce the printed size.)
5. After it prints, choose "Quit" from the File menu, ***or*** press Command Q.

> **Tip:** It's possible to take a screen shot of the active window (or any individual icon on your screen, message, or portion of the screen) and paste it directly into any open document (see pages 138–139 for details about the Clipboard and pasting). Do this:
>
> Use the technique in either Step 1b or 1c above; when you get the crosshair or the target cursor, hold down the Control key and *then* select a portion of the screen or click the target cursor on a window. You won't get a file called Picture 1; instead, the screen shot is sent to the Clipboard, which means you can open any blank document in just about any application and then paste (from the Edit menu, choose "Paste") to put the image you captured directly into your document. Try it.

1. How would you arrange a Desktop window to see how large your files are?

2. How would you arrange a Desktop window to alphabetize your list of files?

3. What is the shortcut for changing views from one list to another?

4. How do you print a picture of the active window?

5. How can you move a window without making it active?

6. What is the shortcut that makes a window enlarge (zoom open) to fill almost the entire screen?

7. How can you organize a window full of icons alphabetically?

8. How can you close all the Desktop windows at once without touching the mouse?

9. How can you see a list of *all* the folders in which a folder/window is nested?

10. If a folder icon is gray, what does it mean? What will happen if you double-click on a gray folder icon?

11. How can you "spring open" a folder even if the spring-loaded feature is off?

12. What is a click-and-a-half good for?

Answers on page 423.

9 Icons and Files

Icons—the little pictures you see on the screen—are an intrinsic part of the look and feel of the Macintosh. Instead of having to type a code to open an application or document (which you had to do before the Mac was invented), you simply click on the icon representing it.

The icons offer rich **visual clues.** At first they may look like an odd collection of junk, and many people instantly change their view to a text list so they're not overwhelmed by all the pictures. But once you really look at them you'll see how much information icons instantly provide. This information is valuable to you, and that's the purpose of this chapter—to help you take advantage of these clues. I suggest you leave your windows in the icon view for a while in the beginning. After you start seeing the patterns and noticing the clues, after you are comfortable with copying and moving and organizing your icons, go ahead and view your windows in whatever sort of list is useful to you (as explained on pages 76 and 80).

An icon can represent any kind of **file**—a file is any form of information you see on your computer. The term "file" might refer to an application, document, control panel, extension, clip art, folder, email, web page, or anything else. As you've learned by now, files can also be represented as buttons or as a list, not just as icons. Most of the techniques in this chapter, such as moving an icon or changing its name, also apply to files represented by buttons or items in a list.

Disk Icons

When you're at the Desktop (as on page 50), you'll always see icons of any **disks** you're using. Your hard disk icon may look different from the ones shown below.

- Single-click on a disk icon to select it.
- Double-click on a disk icon to open it and show you a window displaying all the files.

  Note: If a **disk** icon is gray, it is already open—double-click on it anyway and its window will come forward.

Robin's Hard Disk   Power HD

Hard disk icons

Scarlett's Font

Floppy disk icon

Mac OS 9   Graphics   Art Parts

CD-ROM icons often look like the one on the left, but they **can** *look like anything else, as shown here.*

LMB.7e

Typical Zip disk icon

Folder Icons

Whenever you have a Desktop window open, most likely you'll see **folder icons.** They act just like folders in your filing cabinet in that you store items in them for organization, and you can open them to see what's inside. Be sure to read the following chapter on folders since they are an incredibly important tool that you will be using constantly.

- Single-click a folder to select it.
- Double-click to open the folder to display a window with all the files that are stored in that folder.
- Click-and-a-half to spring the window open temporarily (see page 84).

If you see any folders such as the ones shown below, with wires coming out of the folder, happy faces, or dark tabs, it indicates they are sharing files with another computer. See Chapter 27 on *Sharing Files* for details.

To Share   To Share   Samples   Samples   images for web book

(Notice the dark tab.)

These folders are sharing (or are ready to share) their contents.

Application Icons

SimpleText

Quicken Deluxe 2000

Application icons are typically rather fancy, although lots of other icons are fancy as well.

Application (or **program**) **icons** are the fancy ones. These belong to the actual applications (the software programs that you work in). Each application has its own design so they all look different, but what they have in common is that many try to give some sort of **visual clue** as to what they do. For instance, to the right you can see that the SimpleText icon represents a word processing program; the Quicken icon represents a financial program.

- Single-click an application icon to select it.
- Double-click an application icon to open to either a new, blank page within that program, or at least to a dialog box where you can choose to create a new, blank page.

Document Icons

Article

Robin's Account

Document icons almost always have the top-right corner turned down.

Document icons represent documents, or files, that **you** (or someone like you) have created in any particular application. Whenever you are working in an application and you save your document with a name, a document icon is created for you somewhere on your Mac.

Document icons almost always look like a piece of paper with the top-right corner folded down, or perhaps like a sheaf of papers or a stack of cards. Typically they have some resemblance to the application they were created in, as you can see by the SimpleText and the Quicken icons on the right, which match their corresponding programs as shown above.

- Single-click a document icon to **select** it.
- Double-click a document icon to open the application **in which the document was created,** with that particular document on the screen. (If you get an error message, check page 412, "Can't open a file.")

Blank Document Icons

The fact that this file is blank is a ***visual clue*** *that the program it was created in is probably not installed in the computer.*

Occasionally you will see a **blank document icon.** This usually means that the application in which this document was created is not in the computer. For instance, the blank document shown to the left is the same as the Quicken Accounts file on the previous page. When this file is in a computer that has Quicken installed, it looks like it belongs to Quicken. But if I copy the same file to a computer that does **not** have the application Quicken installed, the icon is blank.

(If the blank document icon has the **bottom-right corner** turned up, that's a visual clue that the document is actually a **stationery pad;** see page 103.)

(If the blank document icon has an **upper-left corner** turned down, that's a clue that the document is actually a **font,** and it probably has a problem; replace it.)

If you double-click a blank document icon, you will usually see this message:

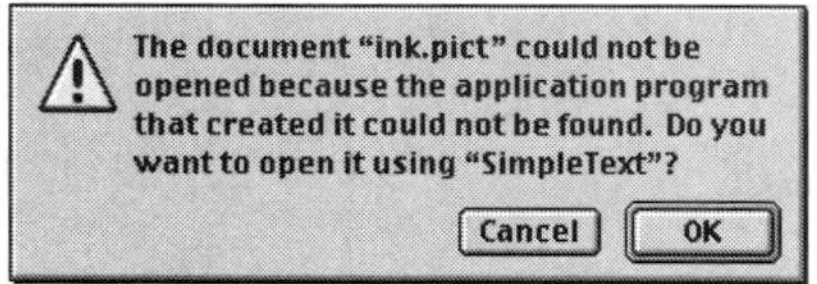

If you have the File Exchange control panel turned on (details on page 256), then you will see this sort of message:

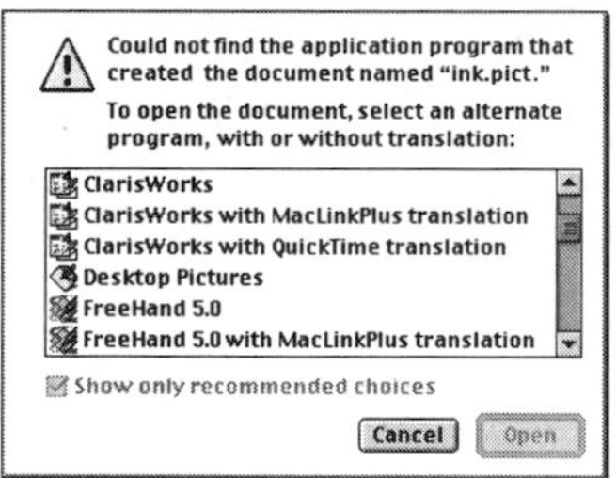

You can choose an application from this list that you think might open the file.

Or try the tip below.

Advanced tip! Try dragging the **document** icon on top of various **application** icons. If an application can open a file of this type (AppleWorks, for instance, can open almost any text file), the application icon will become highlighted (as shown below). This is your clue that this application can open this file; let go of the document and it will open in that program.

Drag the blank icon on top of various application icons and see if any of them will open the file. If the application icon highlights, let go. Sometimes, though, an application thinks it can open the file and it tries, but at the last minute gives up.

System Icons

Inside the folder named System Folder are **system icons** that help run the Macintosh, as well as a variety of icons that are for extra or fancy options. System icons represent programming that performs essential operations. You'll see a variety of types of system icons. You'll see one called System and one called Finder—if those two are not inside the System Folder, you won't even be able to use your machine.

- Single-click a system icon to select it.
- Double-clicking on most system icons will give you a message that "This file is used by the system software. It cannot be opened." That's because most system icons are just visual representations of the data on your disk that makes them work—there's really nothing to look at besides the cute little icon. (Although you *can* open the System file itself and the control panels.)

Your System Folder has quite a grand collection of icons, doesn't it? The System Folder is so important that it earns its own special chapter, Chapter 20, and you should probably actually read it. And I'll remind you once again—don't go stickin' things in the System Folder unless you *know* they are really supposed to be there.

Icons that are part of the operating system appear in several sizes and shapes.

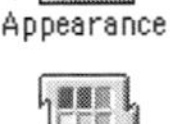

Control panels, such as Appearance and General Controls, have little slider bars in the icons. Extensions, such as Color Picker and Speech Manager, look like puzzle pieces.

Highlighted, or Selected, (dark) Icons

When an **icon is dark,** like the one shown to the right, it is **highlighted,** or **selected**—it got selected because you clicked once on it, or perhaps you typed the first letter or two of its name. When an icon is selected, you can press-and-drag it somewhere. Menu commands, such as "Open" or "Put Away," affect highlighted (selected) icons.

- Single-clicking is what selected this icon in the first place.
- Double-clicking a selected icon will open it just like any other icon.

Button icons

If you view your files as **buttons,** however, it's a little different. You cannot select a button with a single click because that single click will open the file! If you need to *select* a button, click once on its *name*, not on the button itself. Or you can use the pointer tool and drag around the outside of the button to select it, as shown below.

Press-and-drag around any portion of the button to select it.

Gray Icons

An open folder icon.

An open disk icon.

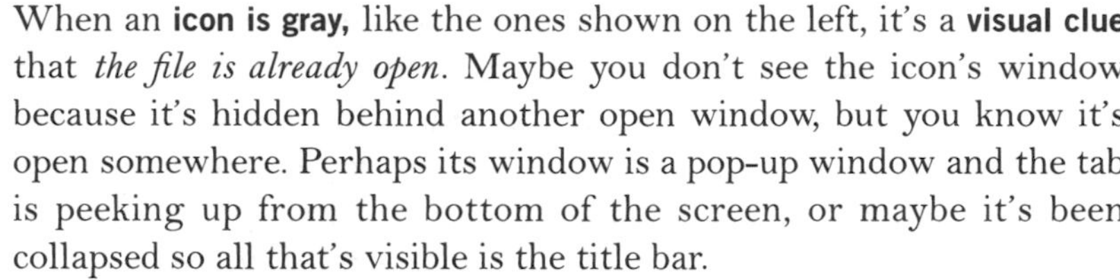

When an **icon is gray,** like the ones shown on the left, it's a **visual clue** that *the file is already open.* Maybe you don't see the icon's window because it's hidden behind another open window, but you know it's open somewhere. Perhaps its window is a pop-up window and the tab is peeking up from the bottom of the screen, or maybe it's been collapsed so all that's visible is the title bar.

- Single-click a gray **icon** to select it.
- Double-click a gray icon to bring its window to the front as the *active* window.

SimpleText
An open application icon.

If the gray icon is an **application icon,** it means the application is still open. If you double-click on its gray icon, the application will become active. So you double-click on it, and you say nothing happened? But it did. Look at your menu bar: When you are at the Finder (Desktop), your menu bar will have the item "Special" in it, and the File menu will not have "Quit" at the bottom. Read Chapter 29 about *Very Important Information*—you need that information to have control over your Mac. And that control will make you happy and powerful.

Putting Away Wayward Icons

Have you ever dragged a file out of its folder, left it on the Desktop, then forgotten where it came from? Or perhaps someone else pulled it out and forgot to put it away and you don't know where it belongs. Or maybe you're just too lazy to do it yourself. Simply select the icon (click once on it), then from the File menu, choose **Put Away** (or press Command Y). A little invisible assistant grabs the file and puts it right back where it last came from.

You can also ask this little assistant to put away a file that you stuck in the trash can and then changed your mind about: Double-click the trash can to open it, select one or more files (hold down the Shift key to click on more than one file), then press Command Y.

Moving Icons

To move icons, simply press-and-drag them. You can put any icon into or drag any icon out of any *folder* icon. When you drag an icon (or any file, no matter what it looks like) from one place to another **on the same disk,** the computer **moves** it to the other place. When you drag a file **from one disk to another disk,** the computer **copies** it to the other disk. For details, see Chapter 11 on *Copying and Selecting Files.*

Renaming Icons

When an icon, button, or list item is ready to be renamed, you'll see a border around its name.

To rename any icon—a folder, a document, a program, a disk—just click once on the icon's *name* (not on the icon's *graphic*); then simply type the new name. A box appears around the name so you know you're changing it. **Or** instead of clicking on the name, select the icon and press Return to get that box around it.

Use standard word processing procedures, as detailed in Chapter 14, to set an "insertion point" (the flashing vertical bar, your **visual clue** that you are in typing mode). Double-click a *word* to select it, backspace to delete characters, etc. You can use your arrow keys to move the insertion point. In fact, press the UpArrow or DownArrow to move the insertion point to the very beginning or the very end of the name. As soon as you click somewhere else, or hit the Return or Enter keys, the name is set.

Undoing a Name Change

If you do **accidentally change the name** of an icon (which is very easy to do—files have been known to mysteriously change their names to \\\\\\\\\\\\ or `````` while you weren't doing anything but leaning on the keyboard), you do have one chance to restore the name to its original form: **Undo.** As soon as you see the mistake has been made, from the Edit menu choose "Undo." *If you haven't done anything* since this minor catastrophe (and things could be worse), Undo will restore the original name, even if you forgot it. If you are too late to catch Undo, you'll just have to rename it yourself (if you know what it was). Remember, the keyboard shortcut for Undo is Command Z.

If the computer doesn't let you change the name, see the following page.

If You Can't Change the Name

You **cannot change the name** of a folder, disk, or application that is being **shared** (see Chapter 27 on *Sharing Files*) or that is **locked:**

images for web book

The little black bar on the tab indicates that this folder is being shared.

A shared folder is indicated by a little black bar along the top of the tab, as shown to the left. **A shared disk** has no visual clue that it is being shared; the clue will be the fact that you don't get a border around the name when you click on it. If you really need to change the name of a shared item, you need to first turn off sharing (page 305). Even though a disk or folder may be shared, you can still change the name of any of their *contents* that are not being shared.

To unlock a file (folder, application, document, etc.), see page 103. **To unlock a floppy disk,** see page 30.

Creating Your Own Icons

Scarlett

Robin

Although this can be a wonderful trick, I don't like to encourage beginners to change all their icons because that original icon tells you so much information. If you start changing icons, how do you know what will happen when you double-click? Is this object a folder that will open to a window, or is it an application, a document, a system icon, or what? Just be sensible.

You can **create your own icons** and apply them to any existing icons.

- Open a graphic program like AppleWorks (paint or draw) or Photoshop. Or use any clip art or Scrapbook image instead.
- In the graphic program, create the little picture that you want as your icon. No matter what size you make the art, the Mac will reduce it to an appropriate size as it becomes the new icon. But if you make it too large, it will be unrecognizable when reduced.
- Select the image you created or found; copy it (from the Edit menu).
- Go back to the Finder (press the Application menu in the far-right corner of the menu bar; choose "Finder").
- Click once on the icon you want to replace. From the File menu, choose "Get Info" (**or** press Command I).
- Click once on the icon that appears in the upper-left of the Get Info window (see below, circled).
- From the Edit menu, choose "Paste" (**or** press Command V).
- Close the Get Info window (press Command W).
- **To change an icon back to the original,** select its tiny icon in the Get Info window; from the Edit menu, choose "Clear" or "Cut."

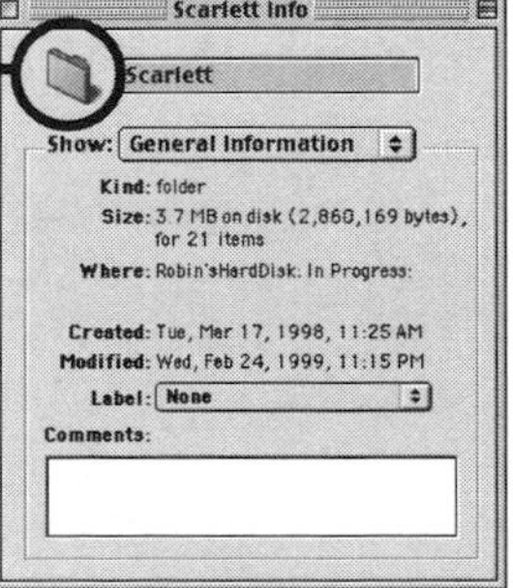

Click here to select the icon's image, either to paste in a new one or to clear out an existing one.

Occasionally you will see or create an icon named Picture 1 or Picture 2, etc.; this is a **screen shot,** also known as a "screen dump" or "screen capture." A screen shot is a picture of the computer screen at the time you pressed a special key combination.

To take a screen shot, press Command Shift 3. You will hear an unsettling noise, like a tiny fuse shattering, and your screen may freeze for a moment. Don't worry—the computer is just taking a picture of the screen. (**To capture just a selected portion of the screen,** press Command Shift 4 to get a crosshair cursor. Use that cursor to drag a box around what you want a picture of.) In the window for your hard disk you will see the Picture 1 icon as shown above, right. Every time you take a shot, the icon will have another number. You should rename the icons so you'll know what they are.

You can open a screen shot to see what it looks like in SimpleText; in fact, double-click on the Picture 1 icon and it will open SimpleText and put itself there. You can open the Picture 1 screen shot in most paint or draw programs and view/change the image just like you would any other graphic image.

You can **print a screen shot** from the paint or draw program, or you can paste it into another document, such as a letter or a newsletter. Or you can print it "as is," just the Picture 1.

To print a screen shot as is:

- Drag the Picture 1 icon over to your printer icon on the Desktop. Just drop it right on the printer icon and it will print.

If that doesn't work for any reason:

- Double-click on the Picture icon at your Desktop. It will open in the utility called SimpleText, which is a tiny, limited word processor that you probably have a dozen copies of.
- To print the screen shot, from the File menu, choose "Print...," **or** press Command P. Click OK in the print dialog box.

If you get a message when you double-click on a Picture icon that "SimpleText cannot open this kind of file" or that you should "Try opening the document within the application," then:

- First open SimpleText (find it and double-click on it).
- An open window appears; press Command W to close it.
- From the File menu, choose "Open...," **or** press Command O.
- Find the name of the Picture icon you want to open and double-click on its name. Now it should open and you should be able to print the image.

Screen Shots

These icons represent screen shots. These are in the PICT format.

You can open a screen shot in SimpleText.

How to print a screen shot

This is a Desktop printer icon. While a document is printing, the icon changes to look like this:

Color Your Icons with Labels

Labels allow you to set up a labeling and **coloring** system for the files on your Mac, which you can apply from the Label menu (under "File") at the Desktop. Applying a label applies its corresponding color. The label and color are *in addition* to the icon's name. They're just attached to the file; the label itself does not appear in the name.

In your Desktop windows, you can choose to display the "Label" as another column of information (use the "View Options" dialog box; see page 78).

Using labels

You can do this just for the heck of it, or to make your dull life more colorful, or you can use the color as an organizational tool. For instance, you may want to apply a passionate red color to all the love letters you have written and received. That way no matter what folder they are stored in or what sort of file they are (maybe you keep a database of all your lovers and letters, a stationery pad for creating multiple copies, a faxable version, and a graphic file of your photograph to send over the modem), you can instantly recognize any file belonging to the passionate red classification. Or you may have a series of lectures you present in different fields. You can store each of the lectures in the folders for their respective fields, but apply a "Lecture" label to them so you can search for and group them together when necessary. Perhaps you have a folder with lots of files in it from a variety of topics. You can label some or all of them, then when you view by "Label," all the files from each topic will be grouped together.

Change the name of the label

To change the name of any of the existing labels:

- At the Desktop, go to the Edit menu and choose "Preferences…."
- In the "Preferences" dialog box, click the tab "Labels."
- Select an existing label name. Press the Tab key to select each one, or press-and-drag over an existing name to select it.
- Type the name of the new label.
- The revised label will instantly appear in the Labels menu, under File, as soon as you close this dialog box.

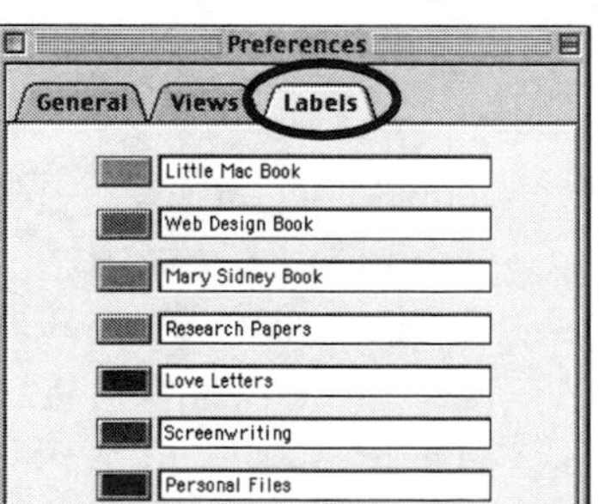

This is the Labels section of the Preferences dialog box. Select an existing label and change its name.

Change the color of any label

To change the color of any of the existing labels:

- Open the Preferences dialog box from the Edit menu.
- Click once on the colored box next to any label. The Color Picker will appear (shown below). Don't worry about how complicated it looks—just play with it. Try the color model called Crayon Picker (click its icon on the left), and click on a crayon. Or if you choose another color model, you might see little arrows, a slider bar, or a color wheel—play with them. You'll see the new color you are creating in the box in the upper-right called "New." If you want the original color back, click "Original," or just Cancel.

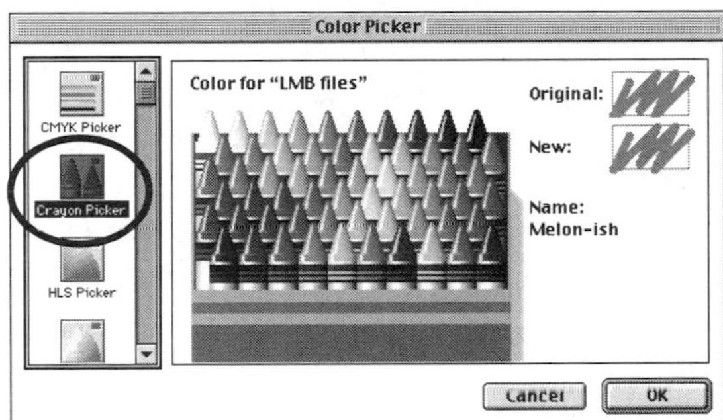

Apply a label and color

To apply a label and color to an icon:

- At the Desktop, select the icon or group of icons.
- From the File menu, slide down to "Label" and choose the label or color of your choice. **Or** hold down the Control key and click on a file or selection of files; from the menu that pops up, choose the label you want to apply.

  Note: If you apply a label one day and then later change the name of that particular label, all icons with the original label attached will change to the new label! For instance, say I label eight documents as "Love Letters." If I go to the dialog box and change "Love Letters" to "Dog Food," every document that had the label "Love Letters" will now have the label "Dog Food."

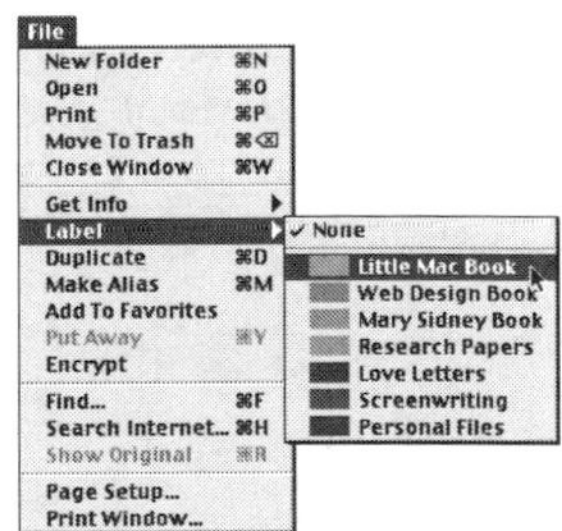

The labels you create in the Preferences dialog box will appear in the Label menu under File.

Use Sherlock to Find Labeled Files

Use **Sherlock** to search for items of a certain label or color. Some applications apply colors (which also applies a label) to certain files. In Sherlock, click the "Edit..." button, then check the "Label" box and choose your label. See Chapter 26 for details.

Get Info

Click this menu; there might be more information.

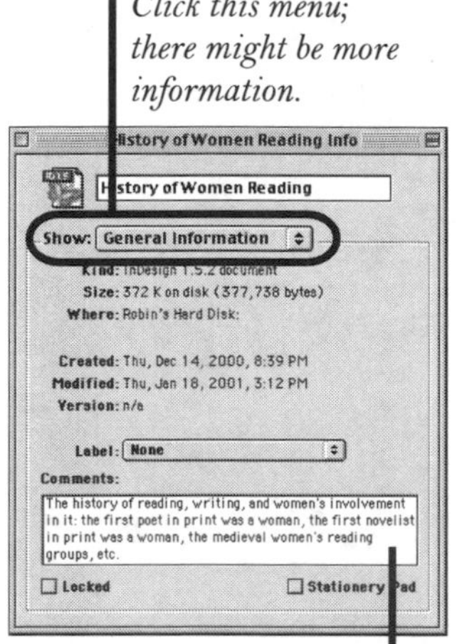

This is the box into which you can type your own notes.

Get Info is not an icon, but a menu item that can give you important information about any file represented by an icon on your Desktop, such as an application, document, system, folder, or any file at all.

Select an icon (or any file name in a list) by clicking once on it; then from the File menu choose "Get Info." (If you are viewing buttons, remember, you must select a button by clicking once on its *name*, not on the button itself.) You'll get a little information window that tells you interesting things about the file, such as how big it is, when it was created, which software program it was created in (if appropriate), which software version you have.

Another nice thing about this window is that you can type your own information in the Comments box at the bottom (the "insertion point" flashes, waiting for you to type). This comes in very handy: you can write notes to yourself about that particular file and what it contains, briefly detail this budget file from that budget file, make note of further changes you want to employ, leave notes for your lover, etc. The information is automatically saved.

Use Sherlock to search comments

You can also take advantage of the fact that Sherlock can search through these comments. Perhaps you have a habit of making notes in this box about which files need to be updated. You can then search for all the files that need to be updated. See Chapter 26 on Sherlock.

View comments in your Desktop windows

You can also choose to view your Desktop window with these comments displayed (as shown below). Use the Views section of the Finder Preferences (from the Edit menu on the Desktop) to set this up (details on page 78).

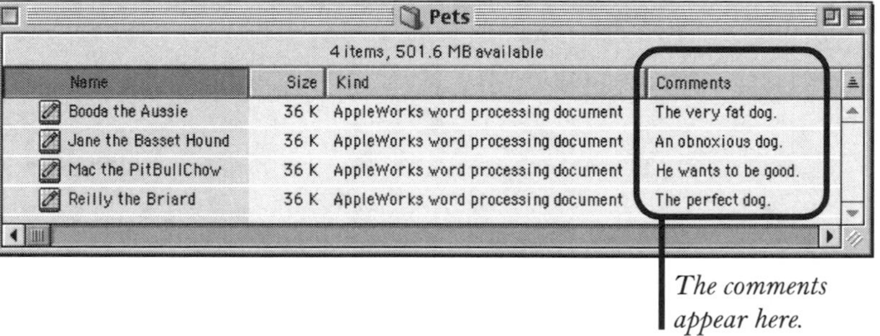

The comments appear here.

Locking the File

There is a **Locked** checkbox in the lower-left corner of the **Get Info** window (see previous page for Get Info details). If you check this box (click once on it), this file cannot be renamed or inadvertently thrown away—as soon as it hits the trash, a dialog box comes up telling you a locked file cannot be thrown away. It also becomes a **read-only** file: anyone can open and read the file, but no one can save any changes to it. You can't even change the Get Info notes. This is handy for sending around copies of a document and ensuring no one accidentally changes anything.

> **Tip:** If you hold down the Option key, you *can* throw away a locked file. Uh oh.

To **unlock the file,** click in the checkbox again. If there is no ✔, it is unlocked. (To unlock a *disk,* see page 30.)

☑ **Locked**

This file is now locked.

☐ **Locked**

This file is now unlocked.

Stationery Pad

Also through the **Get Info** box you can make a "template" out of any document, which is sometimes called a **stationery pad.** This is like a reusable "pattern" of a document. For instance, you could create your own personal letterhead by setting up and arranging your typefaces, margins, indents, graphics, etc. Then make a template, or stationery pad, of the document. When you next open that template, you'll actually open an *untitled copy* of the file (you may get a little dialog box telling you to name it before it opens all the way). You can write the body of the letter, save it, and print it. The *original* template, or stationery pad, remains unchanged so you always have a clean master copy. The icon for a stationery pad looks like a sheaf of papers with the *bottom-right* corner turned up, as shown to the right.

To make a stationery pad, go to the Desktop:

- Select a **document** icon by clicking once on it (this doesn't work on any sort of file except a *document*).
- Press Command I to get the Get Info box.
- Click the checkbox at the bottom called "Stationery Pad." If you don't see that checkbox, that's your **visual clue** that you can't make a template out of that file.

On the left is the original document. On the right is the stationery pad created from the document. The **visual clue** *is the turned-up corner on the* **bottom**-*right instead of the top-right.*

☑ **Stationery Pad**

This is a typical icon for a stationery pad.

If you see this little "Stationery" button (above) in your software, clicking it will ***also*** *make a stationery pad, or template. It creates the same kind of file as the Get Info box does.*

Draw lines to match the description with the icon! Carefully read through the list first—although there are several similar icons, each has a different visual clue.

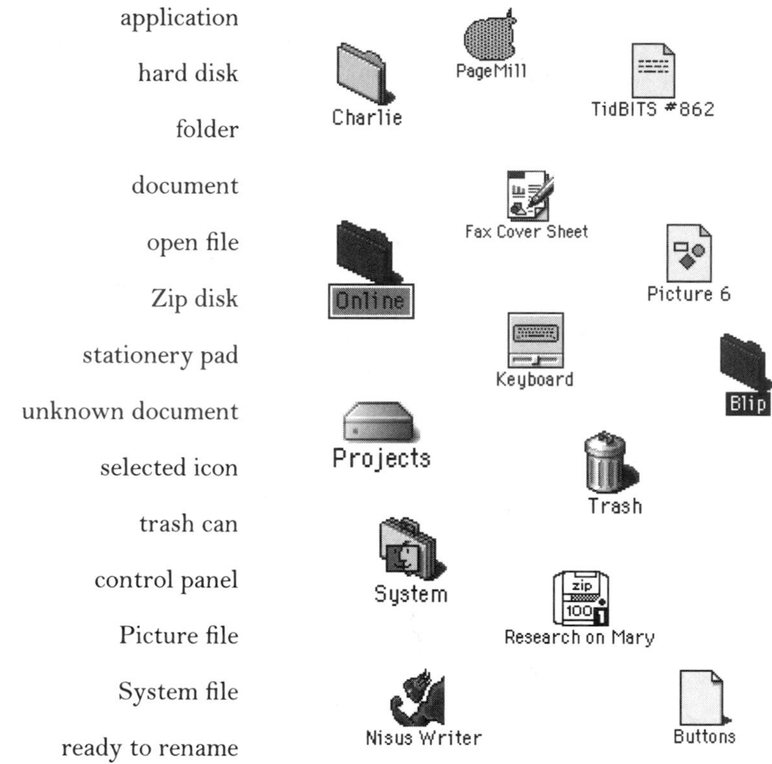

Match the application with a document created in that application:

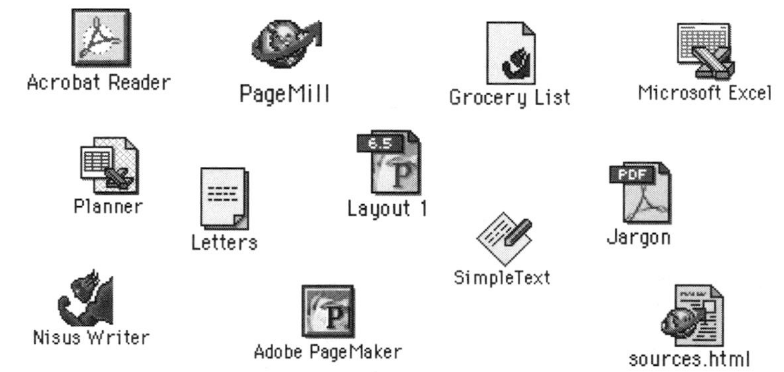

Answers on page 423.

Folders 10

Folders are essential to organizing your work on the Mac. Folders are, of course, visual representations of our office and home environments, and they function in much the same way.

You can consider your disk to be the main filing cabinet. When you store items in a filing cabinet, you don't just toss them in the drawer, do you? Can you imagine what a mess your filing cabinet would be without folders? A Macintosh can become just as messy and just as difficult to find work in if you don't have some sort of organizational system. It's very important to learn to take advantage of the folders.

Creating a New Folder

It's easy **to create your own** new, empty folder.

- Make sure the window in which you want a new folder is *active* (click on it). If you want the new folder to sit directly on the Desktop (not in another window), first click on the Desktop.
- From the File menu, choose "New Folder," or use the keyboard shortcut, Command N. A new, "untitled folder" will appear in the active window.

Naming the New Folder

These are what new folders might look like, depending on the view you have chosen for the window:

When the new folder appears in the active window, it's already *highlighted*, or *selected* (the **visual clue** is that it's dark), and it has the name "untitled folder." The Mac assumes you want to **change the name,** so while the folder is highlighted with a white border around the title, **just type the name you want it to have and the new name will appear.** Yes, really, all you do is type. If you type an error, just backspace over the error (use the Delete key in the upper right of the main keys) and continue typing. (See the next page if you blew it already.)

You can type up to 31 characters in a folder name, but you can't type a colon. If you *try* to type a colon, the Mac will substitute a hyphen. And don't ever start a folder name (or any file name) with a period.

After you name the new folder, the border disappears as soon as you click anywhere else, or when you hit the Return or Enter key. When the border disappears, you are no longer in the naming mode.

Where did your new folder go?

How you have your window arranged or sorted, such as by name or by size, will affect where your new, *untitled* folder will appear. For instance, if you view your window as a list which you have sorted "By Name," the untitled folder will appear near the bottom of the list, alphabetized as "untitled." If you sort "By Date," the untitled folder will appear first in the list because it is the most recent.

After you name the untitled folder and click anywhere or hit the Enter key, *the new folder gets arranged in the list according to the view you have chosen.* That is, if the list is sorted By Name, the folder instantly gets alphabetized into the existing list, *which means it may disappear from your sight.* You can use the scroll bars to go find it, or just type the first letter or two of its name and it will pop up again right in front of your face.

Changing the Name of a Folder

If you accidentally un-highlight the new folder before you change its name, or if you want to change the name of any other folder (or any icon of any sort), it is still very easy to do: simply click once on the *name* and the icon will turn dark with a border around the name. The border is a **visual clue** that whatever you type will *replace* the current title. So go ahead and type the new name while you see the border.

> **Tip:** Once you click on the name, it seems to take a "long time" (like a whole second or two) for the border to appear. If you want faster service, click on the icon or the name, then hit the Return key to get the border.

> **Tip:** Use standard word processing procedures (Chapter 14) to type the new name: press-and-drag to select text; click to insert an insertion point; backspace to delete characters, etc. Hit the UpArrow to move the insertion point to the beginning of the name, and hit the DownArrow to move it to the end of the name.

Putting Something inside a Folder

To put something inside a folder, press-and-drag any icon over to it; when the folder turns black or changes color, let go and the icon will drop inside. Remember, it is the *very tip* of the pointer that selects the folder, *not* the shadow of the icon that goes inside.

You can have folders inside of folders inside of folders, which is technically called the *Hierarchical File System* (HFS). You can drag an item from one window and put it into a folder in another window.

A folder does not have to be closed to place an item inside of it, and the folder can be gray. The folder window can be displaying icons, a list, or buttons. The only trick to putting something inside a folder is that you have to be able to see both the item you want to drop in *and* the folder you want to drop into. Sometimes this requires moving your windows around the screen so you can see both items at once.

Opening a Folder

Double-click any folder to **open** it to a window that displays all the valuable files stored inside. You can also, of course, select a folder (click once on it) and then choose "Open" from the File menu. Or select the folder and press Command O as a shortcut.

The cursor turns into this little magnifying glass when you click-and-a-half on a folder icon.

Yet another option to open a folder (when it's in icon or list view) is with a "click-and-a-half"—this is sort of like a double click, but **don't release the mouse after the second click.** The folder will spring open for you. If you keep the mouse held down, you can position the magnifying glass over any other folder and that one will also spring open, without even a click. Once you let go of the mouse button, all open folders except the last one will close up behind you.

Removing Something from a Folder

To **remove** something from a folder, you have to *open* the folder first (double-click it) so you can see its window and the icons inside. Then simply press-and-drag the icon(s) out of the folder; drag them either to the Desktop or to another folder or window.

"Moving" as opposed to "Copying"

If you drag the file to someplace else **on the same disk,** the file will just pop out of that one folder and **move** into the other.

BUT if you drag the file **to a different disk,** the original file will stay put in the original folder and the Mac will put a **copy** of the file on the other disk. (See tips on pages 114–117.)

Organizing Your Disk Using Folders

Below is an example of a well-organized hard disk; there isn't a bunch of junk lying around making it difficult to find things. *(I wish it was this easy to keep a house organized.)* The hard disk is basically arranged the same way a filing cabinet would be. Some folders have folders inside of folders.

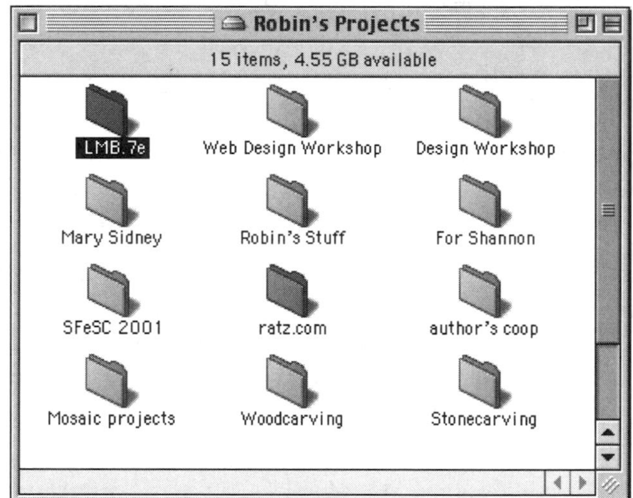

Everything on this hard disk (the "filing cabinet") is tucked into a folder. The folders may each contain more folders to further organize their contents.

Outline Mode

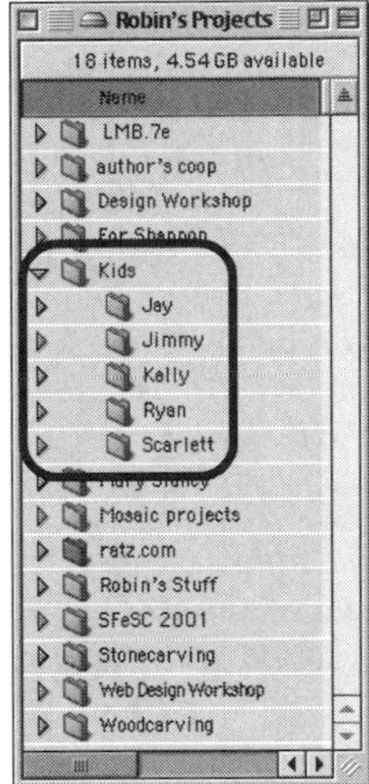

You may prefer to view your window as a list, as described in Chapter 8 on Desktop Windows (page 76). The list view is also known as the **outline mode.** There's a tiny triangle next to each folder's name, and if you click on that triangle you can see what's in that folder without opening another window—as in the folder "Kids" shown to the right. The items contained within a folder are indented just a little from the left, which is your **visual clue** that the items are inside the folder.

In the outline mode, you can keep opening folders within folders until you are all the way to the bottom level of your filing system, *with everything displayed in the same window.*

One benefit to this view is that you can see at a glance exactly how your files are organized and what's in them. You can move items from one folder to another, even if the folders are several levels apart. You can Shift-click (page 117) to select items from any number of different folders, which is impossible to do if the folders are opened as windows. (These techniques are explained in detail in Chapter 11 on Copying and Selecting Files.)

Expanding a folder

- To **expand,** or *open* a folder, single-click on the little sideways-pointing triangle (or select the folder icon and press Command RightArrow).

Compressing a folder

- To **compress,** or *close* a folder, single-click on the downward-pointing triangle (or select the folder icon and press Command LeftArrow).

Compressing all folders

- To simultaneously **compress all the folders** that are expanded, press Command A to select everything in the window.
Then press Command LeftArrow.

Moving an Item to a "Buried" Folder

And don't forget about the **spring-loaded folders** feature you read about in Chapter 8 (page 84). If you want to drop an item inside a folder that's within a folder, just drag the file icon over to a folder and hold the icon over it—the folder you hold the file over will spring open for you, displaying its contents. Keep holding down the mouse button and dig through as many folders as you need to this way, until you see your destination folder—position the file over that last folder and let go of the mouse to place the item. All of the folders that opened along the way will spring close.

Creating a New Folder for a Specific Project

You don't have to read this yet!
Don't read this until you are comfortable with your Mac and until you have experienced frustration over losing files through disorganization.

The solution will make more sense if you've had the problem first.

One of the best ways to keep windows tidy is to **create a specific new folder** for a new project *before* you create the documents for the project, and then *save the documents right into their own folder.* For instance, if you are about to create a newsletter in which there will be ten to twelve separate stories, it's best to store all these files in one folder with a recognizable name, right?

1. **At your Desktop, before you open the application** to start creating the reports, make your new folder and name it (let's name this one *Budget News*). This new folder can be inside of another folder, of course.

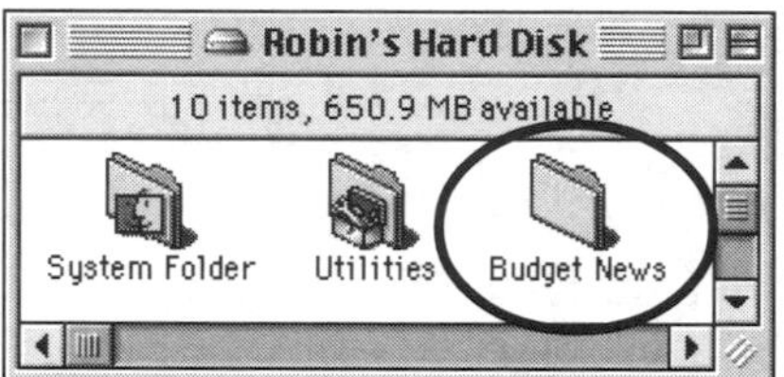

This is the new folder in the hard disk window, waiting for you to save new stories inside.

2. Open your application and create the first report.
3. Choose "Save As…" and name the document. Find the folder *Budget News* in the Save As dialog box (as shown below). *If you have trouble finding the folder, read Chapter 28 about navigating, or pages 148–149 about saving documents.*
4. In the *list box*, or *directory*, you'll see the name of the folder you created earlier. Double-click the name ("Budget News" in this example) to open the folder in the directory.

In this example, here in the list box is the folder Budget News; double-click its name to open it.

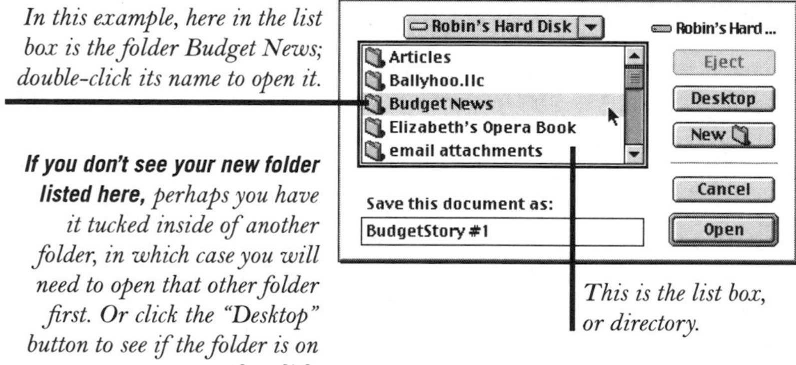

***If you don't see your new folder listed here,** perhaps you have it tucked inside of another folder, in which case you will need to open that other folder first. Or click the "Desktop" button to see if the folder is on another disk.*

This is the list box, or directory.

5. After you double-click on the name of the folder, you'll see its name and an open folder icon in the *label* above the list box, as shown below. If you choose to "Save" right now, your document will be saved into *that* folder whose name is in the label.

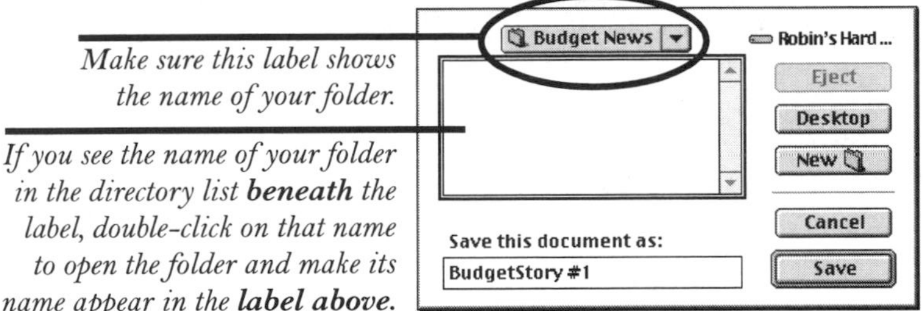

Make sure this label shows the name of your folder.

If you see the name of your folder in the directory list ***beneath*** *the label, double-click on that name to open the folder and make its name appear in the* ***label above.***

Whenever you save a file, it is ALWAYS saved into whichever folder or onto whichever disk appears in that label at the top of the list!!

6. When you go back to your Desktop you'll find that your new document is tucked away right where it belongs, right into its own folder, and nothing will have been misplaced.

Saving directly into a new folder

There's another way to save work into a new folder: Do you see the "New" button in the "Save As" dialog box above, below "Desktop"? If you click that "New" button, the Mac will make a new folder for you. (Sometimes this button says "New Folder.") You will get another dialog box asking you to name the new folder you are creating. **The new folder will then be placed into whichever folder is shown in the label above the directory.** When you click "Save," your document will be saved into that new folder you just made.

Your new folder will appear inside whichever folder or disk name appears here—take note of this so you know where your work is going!

Enter the name of your new folder here.

If you lose your files anyway

If you refuse to read and follow these directions and have lost files because *you don't know where you saved them,* do read about Sherlock in Chapter 26. And when you really get frustrated with losing files all the time, read the special chapter on navigating (finding your way around these dialog boxes), Chapter 28.

1. What is the purpose of a folder?

2. At the Desktop, when you go to the File menu and choose "New Folder," how do you know where that new folder will appear?

3. What is the keyboard shortcut to create a new folder?

4. How do you rename a folder, and what is the **visual clue** that tells you a folder is ready to be renamed?

5. How do you open a folder?

6. What happens when you open a folder, and what do you see?

7. What are the keyboard shortcuts for expanding and compressing folders in outline mode?

8. How can you close all of the expanded folders at once?

9. What are two big advantages to outline mode?

10. Are you going to create folders to organize your Macintosh work, just like you would make folders for your filing cabinet?

Answers on page 424.

11 Copying and Selecting Files

Copying files is an everyday task. You may need to copy an application from its original disk onto your hard disk; copy a report to give to a coworker; copy a document and its graphics to take to a service bureau for high-resolution printing; create the ever-necessary backup copy; etc., etc., etc. Before you copy any file, though, you must first **select** it.

Apple has made it as easy as possible to copy files on the Mac (which is why *pirating*, or copying software without paying for it, has always been such a problem). Copying files has no effect on the *original file*, nor is there any loss of quality in the new version—there is absolutely no difference from the original to the copy.

Copying from the Hard Disk to another Disk

Actually, the copying process only works when you copy a file *from one disk to another disk.* When you drag an icon into another position on the *same* disk, such as into another folder on the *same* disk, you are simply *moving* the file, not *copying* it.

The cursor with a plus sign is your ***visual clue*** *that you are copying something.*

To COPY a file from one disk to another disk (such as from your hard disk to a Zip disk):

- At the Desktop, click once on the file you want to copy.
- Press-and-drag the selected file to the icon of the disk that you want to copy it onto. A little message comes up telling you it's being copied.

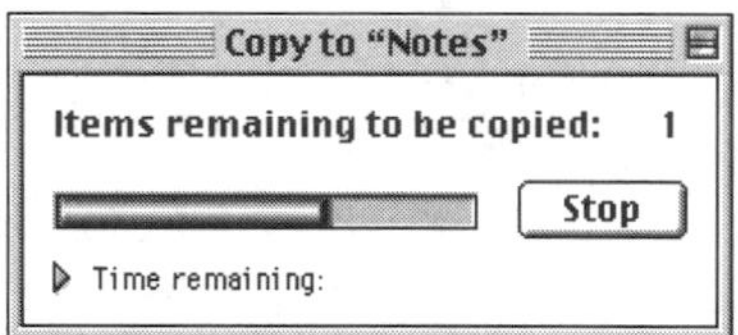

This message will appear when you copy. The lines in the title bar are a ***visual clue*** *that you can drag this box around on the screen. For instance, you might want to move it away so you can do something else while the item is copying.*

Copying from a Removable Disk to the Hard Disk

There are a couple of ways to copy files from your removable disk (such as a floppy, a Zip disk, or a CD) to your internal hard disk. Read the rest of this page before you copy.

To COPY from a removable disk to your internal hard disk (one way):

- Insert the removable disk.
- Double-click the removable disk icon to open its window.
- Take a look at the files on the removable disk, then *selectively* choose the ones you need to copy. Press-and-drag the chosen files to the hard disk icon, or drag them directly into a folder on the hard disk.

To COPY from a removable disk to your hard disk (another way):

This method copies *every single item* from the removable disk to your hard disk. If you want to *selectively* copy files from the removable disk, use the method above.

- Insert the removable disk.
- Drag the icon of the removable disk onto the icon of your hard disk. The Mac will make a new folder on the hard disk, name it with the name of the removable disk, and copy all the contents of the removable disk into the new folder. Too cool.

Don't ever copy another System Folder onto your hard disk (unless you really know what you are doing and why).

Make sure the disk or folder you are copying to is selected!

You can copy from your hard disk onto a removable disk, from a removable disk onto your hard disk, or directly into a specific folder on any other disk. In every case, make sure the icon of the disk or folder you are copying *into* becomes *highlighted* (highlighting is usually darker), which is your **visual clue** that the disk or folder is *selected* as the place to copy to. When the icon is highlighted, that means it's ready to accept the file(s). If the icon is not highlighted, you'll end up just placing the file *next* to the disk or folder, not *inside* of it. The *tip of the pointer* is what highlights/selects any icon.

When you copy straight into an open *window*, the window will not highlight by turning dark; if you look closely at the window, you'll see an extra gray or blue border line appear around the inside of the window, which is your **visual clue** that the window is selected.

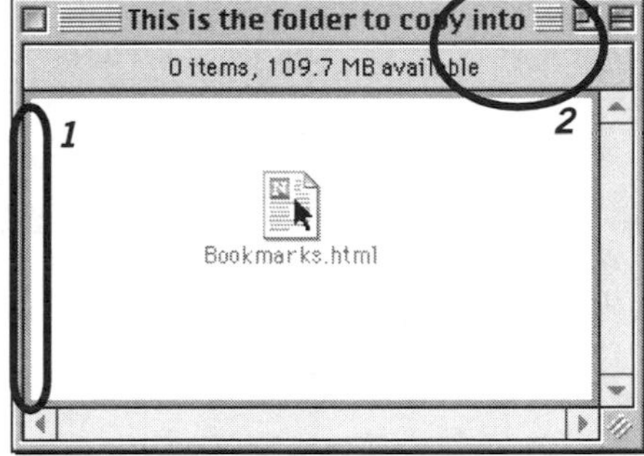

A border appears inside the window (1) when you drag an icon into a window. You can also drop an icon onto the title bar or information bar (2) and it will land in the window (folder); this is handy when the items are displayed in list view.

Duplicate/Copy a File on the Same Disk

Sometimes you want to make another copy of a file on the same disk. But the *copying* process, remember, only takes place if you drag the file to *another disk*. So here's how to make a duplicate.

To make a copy (duplicate) of the file on the *same* disk:

- ▾ First click *once* on the file icon to select it.
- ▾ From the File menu choose "Duplicate" (*or* press Command D). This creates a second version in the same folder named "______ copy." If you make more copies of the same file, they will be named "_____ copy 1," "_____ copy 2," etc.

When you duplicate or copy *folders*, every item contained within that folder is also copied.

> **Great tip:** To *put a* **copy** *of a file into another folder* **on the same disk,** hold down the Option key and drag the file to the other folder. This puts a copy of the file into the other folder but does *not* rename the file "______ copy."

Go back to work while the computer is copying

If you have a large file to copy, you can **go back to work** on something else while the computer is going through its copying process. You can copy multiple files simultaneously, browse through your windows, empty the Trash, or do other Finder tasks. Don't copy *too* many large files at once, though, as you may run up against memory problems.

Copying More Than One File at a Time

To copy more than one file at a time, *select* more than one file (detailed in the next paragraph). When more than one file is selected, dragging *one* file will drag them *all together*, either to the trash can, into another folder, onto another disk, or simply to clean up the joint. Just make sure when you drag that you press on one of the *highlighted* items; if you click anywhere else, all of the items will be deselected!

You may have noticed in the Desktop that when you *press in an empty space and drag the pointer*, a dotted rectangle comes out of the tip—this is the **selection marquee** (sometimes called *marching ants*), found in many Mac programs. On the Desktop, any file that is even partially enclosed in this marquee will be selected.

This is the selection marquee—just press-and-drag with the pointer.

Selecting all the icons this way will highlight them all.

- When you press-and-drag on the *highlighted* area of one of the selected items, they will all drag together.
- Click in any *white* space or on any unselected icon or on the Desktop to *deselect* all the files.

Selecting more than one file in a list view

You can also drag to select files that are next to each other when you are in a list view. Press in a white space in the window next to a file name and start to drag. The selection marquee will appear when you drag, and any item that is even partially enclosed within the marquee will be added to the selection.

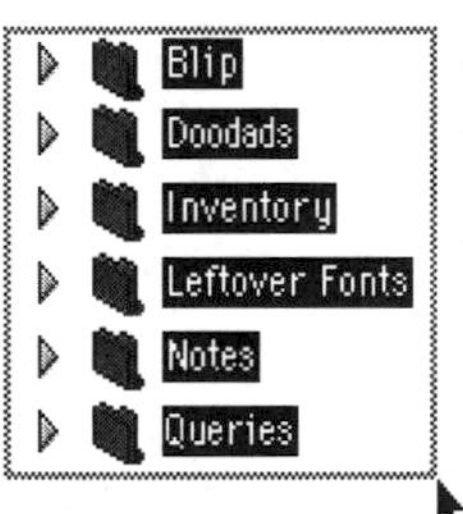

Press-and-drag to select adjacent items in a list view. Click anywhere else to deselect all of the items in the group.

Shift-Click to Select More Than One File

Another method of selecting more than one item at a time is to **Shift-click.** You may have noticed that once a file is selected, it gets deselected the instant you click somewhere else.

> *But hold down the Shift key while you click* and every one of the files you click will be selected. You can select several files in different corners of your window, or even from different folders when they are *expanded* (see next page) in the list view.

Shift-Click to Deselect

In the same manner, you can **deselect** one file at a time. For instance, if you group a bunch of files within the selection marquee but you don't want the one in the middle, simply hold down the Shift key and click once on that one in the middle—it will be the only one deselected.

Hold the Shift key down and click once on a selected file to deselect it.

Selection Shortcuts

To select any single file (no matter how you are viewing the window), **type the first letter** of the name of the file and it will be instantly selected. If there are several files with the same first letter, quickly type the first two or three letters. This technique makes it a lot easier to find your folder named "Waldo" in an alphabetized list, for instance, or a file that starts with Z, or any icon in a crowded folder. *This technique also works in any dialog box with a list of files, such as in "Open" or "Save As" dialog boxes.*

Arrow keys

You can also use the **arrow keys** to select files. *Once you have a file selected,* either by clicking on it or typing its first letter, the arrow keys will select the next icon or file name in the window. In a list, the UpArrow and the DownArrow select, of course, the next file in the list. In an icon view, the four arrows select the icon to the left, right, up, or down, unless there is nothing else in that direction.

Select the next file alphabetically

- To select the icon that would be *alphabetically after* the currently selected icon, press the **Tab key.**
- To select the icon that would be *alphabetically before* the currently selected icon, press **Shift Tab.**

Edit keys

You can also use the **edit keys** on an extended keyboard to scroll through a window, although this does not *select* anything. The edit keys (that little set between the alphabet keys and the numeric keypad) come in handy, though, if you instantly want to get to the top or the bottom of a list where you might want to select something, or if you want to move the window past in a hurry.

Home rolls the window straight to the top.

End rolls the window straight to the bottom.

PageUp and **PageDown** roll the window one window-sized section up or down.

Selected file name at the top of the list

You really must have had the problem first before you will appreciate this solution! If you haven't had the problem, ignore this until later!

A common complaint about selecting a file name in a list by typing the first letter or two is that the name appears at the *bottom* of the window. It is much more convenient (really—you'll soon discover this) if the file name shows up toward the *top* of the window. You can take advantage of the edit keys to solve this problem:

Tip: If you have an extended keyboard, press the **End** key before you type the first letter or two of the file name. This will make your selected file appear near the *top* of the window!

Selecting from Expanded Views

If you view your window "as Icons" or "as Buttons," you can select items *from only one window at a time.* But if you view your window "as List," then you can **expand** the folders and **select** *any number of files from any number of expanded folders within that one window.*

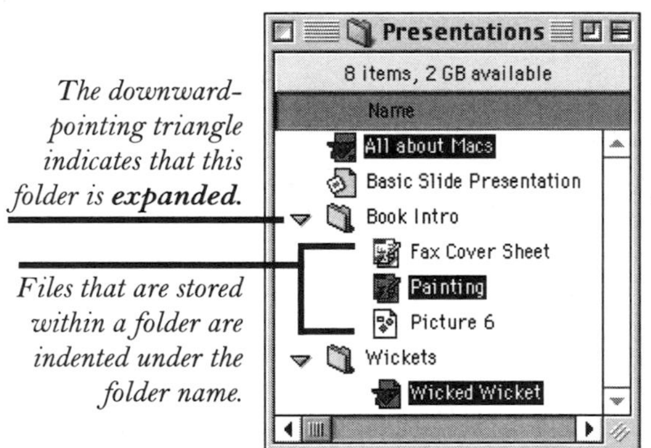

The downward-pointing triangle indicates that this folder is ***expanded.***

Files that are stored within a folder are indented under the folder name.

The three highlighted files you see in this window are ***selected.*** *Press on any one of them to drag them all together, to open them all at once, to print them all, etc.*

Notice there are two files in the above folder window just sitting loose. There are also two folders, both of which have been *expanded* (I clicked on their triangles) to show the contents. By Shift-clicking I selected three separate items from three separate folders. If I press-and-drag any one of these three items, all three of them will move. I can copy, trash, print, open, or move them, all at once.

Using Sherlock to Select Files

You can also **use Sherlock to select files** from all over your hard disk (see Chapter 26 on *Sherlock* for all the intimate details).

All of the found files will be shown in one window, and you can select their icons from that "found" window and drag them to the trash, open them, move them, etc. (remember, press on *one* selected item and *all* selected items will follow). Make it a point to learn to use Find File—you'll discover it comes in handy in a number of ways.

I often use Find File to select a file even when I know where it is because it's so much faster than digging through levels of folders. If I need a document, I hit Command F, type in a few letters, hit the Return key, then lo and behold there is my file in front of my face. I double-click the file name to open it and off I go.

Circle the correct choice in the following multiple choice and true/false questions.

1. **When you drag a file from your hard disk to a removable disk, you are:**
   a. making a copy of the file onto the removable disk.
   b. making a copy of the file onto the hard disk.
   c. simply moving the file from one place to another.
2. **When you drag a file from one window on your hard disk to another window on your hard disk, you are:**
   a. making a copy of the file onto the removable disk.
   b. making a copy of the file onto the hard disk.
   c. simply moving the file from one place to another.
3. **When you drag a file from a removable disk to your hard disk, you are:**
   a. making a copy of the file onto the removable disk.
   b. making a copy of the file onto the hard disk.
   c. simply moving the file from one place to another.
4. **If you want to make a copy of a file on the same disk, the fastest and most efficient way is to:**
   a. make a copy onto a removable disk, then drag that copy back onto the hard disk.
   b. select the file, then from the File menu, choose "Duplicate." *Or* press Command D.
   c. hold down the Option key as you drag the file into another folder or window.
5. **In outline mode, you can select multiple files:**
   a. by dragging around them with the pointer tool.
   b. that are in different folders.
   c. both a and b.

T F **6.** It's always okay to drag the icon of the removable disk onto the icon of the hard disk when you want to copy something onto your hard disk.

T F **7.** To select more than one file at a time, hold down the Option key as you click each one.

T F **8.** You can press-and-drag the pointer around any number of files to select them all.

T F **9.** The quickest (and coolest) way to select a file is to type the first letter or couple of letters of its name.

T F **10.** Once a file is selected, the Tab key will select the next largest file.

Answers on page 424.

12 Trash Can

The **trash can** on the Mac works just like the trash can in your yard—you put things in it you don't want anymore and the garbage collector comes and takes it away and you never see it again. The trash can doesn't have to stay in the bottom-right corner of the screen—you can move it around on your Desktop, and it will stay where you last left it. You can also make aliases (Chapter 25) of the trash can and store the aliases wherever they might be handy to have. Since the trash is such an important part of working on the Mac, it gets its own chapter with tips about using it.

Putting Something in the Trash

The overflowing trash is an obvious **visual clue** *that there is something in the garbage.*

To put something in the trash, press-and-drag a file icon over to the can. *When the can becomes black,* let go and the file will drop inside. Don't let go of the file before the can turns black! If you find a bunch of garbage hanging around outside the trash, *it's because you didn't wait for the can to turn black*—you just set the trash down next to the can. Try again.

The trick here is that the **tip of the pointer** must touch the can! Whether you are putting one file in the trash or whether you have selected fifteen icons and are dragging them all together to the trash, **the tip of the pointer** is the thing that opens the lid (figuratively, of course). The shadows of the objects *have nothing to do with it*—forget those shadows trailing along behind—just make sure the tip of the *pointer* touches the can and turns it black. *Then* let go.

It's the tip of the pointer, not the shadow of the icon, that opens the trash.

More Ways to Trash Files

This is called a contextual menu.

There are several other ways to move an item to the trash.

- Select the item. From the File menu, choose "Move To Trash."
- **Or** select the item. Press Command Delete.
- **Or** hold down the Control key and click on a file you want to throw away. A tiny little menu (called a "contextual menu") pops up and gives you, among other things, the option to move that item to the trash (shown to the left). Choose it.

Taking Something out of the Trash

To remove something from the trash, double-click on the trash can and you'll find that it opens up to a window, just like any other window. So if you decide you want that item you just threw away, you can go get it. To put the file right back where it came from, click once on the file in the trash window to select it, then from the File menu choose **Put Away** (or press Command Y). **Or** you can always just drag the icon back to the disk/folder it came from.

The trash can opens to a window.

Emptying the Trash

You can also use the contextual menu to empty the trash: hold down the Control key, click on the can, and choose "Empty Trash" from the little menu that pops up.

Anything you put in the trash can will stay there, even if you turn off the computer, until you consciously empty the trash: from the Special menu, choose "Empty Trash." (In Mac OS 9.1, you can press Command Shift Delete to empty the trash.) Once you do that, everything in the trash can is gone forever. No amount of crying or pleading will bring it back. Believe me. *(Well, there is software and there are technicians who can often bring back your information, so if you lose something important call your local guru, power user, or user group. In the meantime, don't turn off your computer or create new files. But in general, to be safe, when you toss something in the trash, consider it gone.)*

The Warning Box

When you empty the trash, you'll get a **warning box** asking if you really want to throw the files away:

The Trash contains 7 items, which use 231 K of disk space. Are you sure you want to remove these items permanently?

Cancel | OK

- **If you don't want to see the warning box,** hold down the Option key when you choose "Empty Trash."
- **If you want to throw away a locked item,** hold down the Option key when you choose "Empty Trash."
- When tossing items to make more space on a disk, the trash must be emptied before the space will open up; watch the numbers in the information bar of the window when you *empty* the trash. Until you actually empty the trash, the files continue to take up space on your hard disk or any other disk.

Disabling the Warning Box

Uncheck this box to avoid the warning.

If you find this warning box to be a nuisance (yes), you can easily **disable** it permanently (permanently until you choose to turn it back on again). Perhaps if you have kids working on your machine, you might want to leave the warning on.

- Select the trash can icon (click *once* on it).
- From the File menu, choose "Get Info."
- Click the checkbox "Warn before emptying" to uncheck it.
- Close the Get Info window (click in the little close box in the upper-left).

1. What does it indicate when the trash can is overflowing?

2. When does the stuff in the trash disappear?

3. What happens if you double-click on the trash can?

4. What are the four ways you can move an item to the trash can?

5. If you decided a file should *not* be in the trash after all, how do you get it out? What is the keyboard shortcut that makes it easy to put an item in the trash back where it came from?

6. If you have emptied the trash, can you get your file back?

7. How can you throw away a locked item?

8. What key do you hold down to avoid seeing the trash warning?

9. How can you disable the trash warning?

10. Does the trash can have to stay in the bottom-right corner?

Answers on page 424.

13 Opening Files

What is a **file?** It's a rather generic term referring to just about any icon on your computer. A file might be an "application," which is the program you use to create things, or a "document," which is the thing you created in your application, or a "font," which is a typeface, or a number of other sorts of digitized pieces of information. The files you will work with the most are applications and documents. This chapter gives you some basic guidelines so you can understand and work with your files.

What is an Application?

The term **application** is often used synonymously with **program** (although an *application* is only one form of programming). *Application* refers to the software package you use to create your documents, such as AppleWorks, Adobe PageMaker, Macromedia FreeHand, etc. They all do something different; they all have a particular function. Sometimes it takes a little research to find the software applications that meet your specific needs.

Opening an Application

Kai's Power SHOW

This is an application icon.

To open an application, or software program, you need to find its icon, button, or file name on your hard disk. Application icons, as noted in Chapter 9 on icons, typically look fancier than anything else.

- From the Desktop, double-click on an application's icon or name.
- This usually opens to a blank page, ready for you to create a new document. Some applications, however, open to a commercial, and you need to go to the File menu and choose **"New"** to create a **new,** blank page, or **"Open"** to find a document you previously created that you want to **open** again. Some applications ask what sort of document you want, or how you want your pages set up.

Tip: If you sort your window "by Kind," as shown below, the applications will be at the top of the list. Simply click on the heading "Kind" to change views!

All the files in this folder relate to PageMaker. The window is organized "by Name," so you really have to look for the actual PageMaker application. Do you see it?

*Notice the heading "Kind" is now highlighted, which is a **visual clue** that this list is organized "by Kind." Do you see that the application is now listed first?*

Opening a Document from the Desktop

This is a document icon.

To **open a document** that has already been created and saved in an application, find its icon, button, or file name. (A document icon, remember, typically looks like a page with the upper-right corner turned down.)

Double-click on a document icon; most of the time this will also open the *application,* placing your *document* on the screen as you last saved it.

Important Note!

Now, just because you have an icon representing a document you created in a certain software application *doesn't mean you can open up that document on just any other computer.* Double-clicking on a document icon will only open it **IF** *the application itself is also in the computer,* either on the hard disk or on another disk that is inserted into one of the drives. If the application isn't there, then the document doesn't have anywhere to put itself! Generally, you must have the same *version* (see page 40) of the application as the one in which it was created.

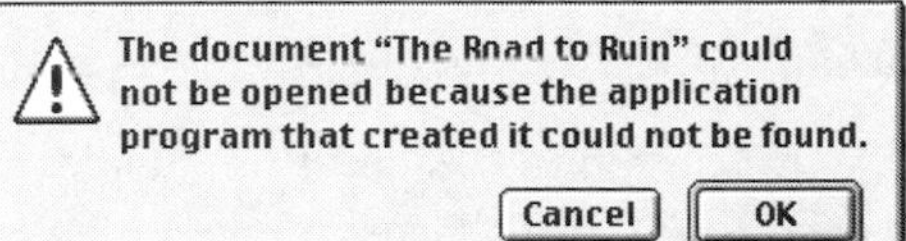

Don't give up if you see this! Try the tip below, and read the next page.

And then again, some programs won't *allow* you to open their documents from the Desktop. If you know the software program is really installed *in* the computer on the hard disk, and you still get a message telling you an application can't be found, there is a possible solution. Also try this if your document was created in an older version of the application:

- *First open the application.*
- From the application's File menu, choose "Open." This will display the "Open" dialog box, as shown to the right (tips for getting around in this dialog box are on page 129).
- In the Open dialog box, find the name of the file you want to open. If the name is visible and is black, the application can probably open it; if the name doesn't appear at all, the application can't open it. **Note:** The Open dialog box in your application might have a little menu, like the one shown circled to the right, that gives you options for what sorts of files you can open. If it does, choose something like "All files" and see if your document appears in the list. If the document's name does appear, it will probably open.

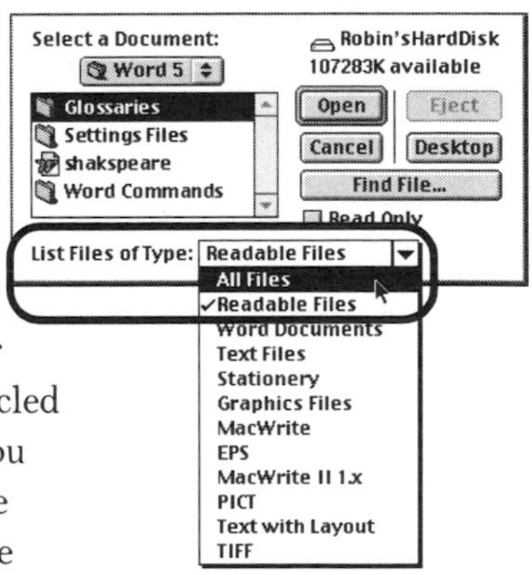

(See the section on the following pages for tips on using the Open dialog box and also on opening documents for which you don't have the application.)

Drag-and-Drop to Open a Document

You can also open a document by **dragging the icon** and **dropping it** on top of its application icon. You'll notice that the application icon will turn dark (highlight), which is the **visual clue** that if you let go your document will open. (Usually.)

Now, a great thing about this trick is that you can open a document in an application other than the one it was created in! For instance, the application AppleWorks (previously known as ClarisWorks) is able to open documents created in many other programs. If you have a word processing document someone gave you but you don't have the program they wrote it in, you can drag the foreign document on top of the AppleWorks application icon. If AppleWorks highlights, let go of the document and the program will open the file for you.

So if you ever get a blank document icon with no clue where it came from or even whether it's a paint file, a text file, or a spreadsheet, drag the icon over every application program you own. Whichever application turns black will (usually) open the document.

Check Chapter 25 on *Aliases* for directions on creating an alias of each application you own. You can store these aliases in one folder on your Desktop (or even directly on your Desktop, not in a folder) and thus make them easily accessible for opening all files, strange or not.

Drag a file onto application icons to see if that program can open that file. (Sometimes the application tries to open the file, but then decides it can't.)

New vs. Open

Once an application is up and running, in the File menu you see two choices: **New** and **Open.** This confused me at first because I thought, "Well, I want to *open* a *new* one." The difference is this:

- **New** creates a clean, blank page on which you can begin a *new* document.
- **Open** takes you to a dialog box (shown on the next page) where you can choose to *open* a document that was previously created and saved.

An "Open" Dialog Box

See Chapter 28 for full details on navigating and for examples of another type of Open and Save As dialog box.

Finding your way around an **"Open" dialog box** is called "navigating." It's one of the most important skills you can learn, and you'll need this skill in other dialog boxes, like when you save documents or when you import or export text. Try to take the time to understand and absorb what each part of the dialog box is telling you.

*The name in the **label** shown here is the specific folder or disk that contains the files you see in the list box.*

*When the icon to the left of the **title** or **label** here is a **folder** (as opposed to a disk) this is a **menu.** Press on the label to see the hierarchy. As shown here, this menu indicates that the folder **EyeWire** is in another folder called **Articles,** which is on **Robin's Hard Disk,** which is on the **Desktop.***

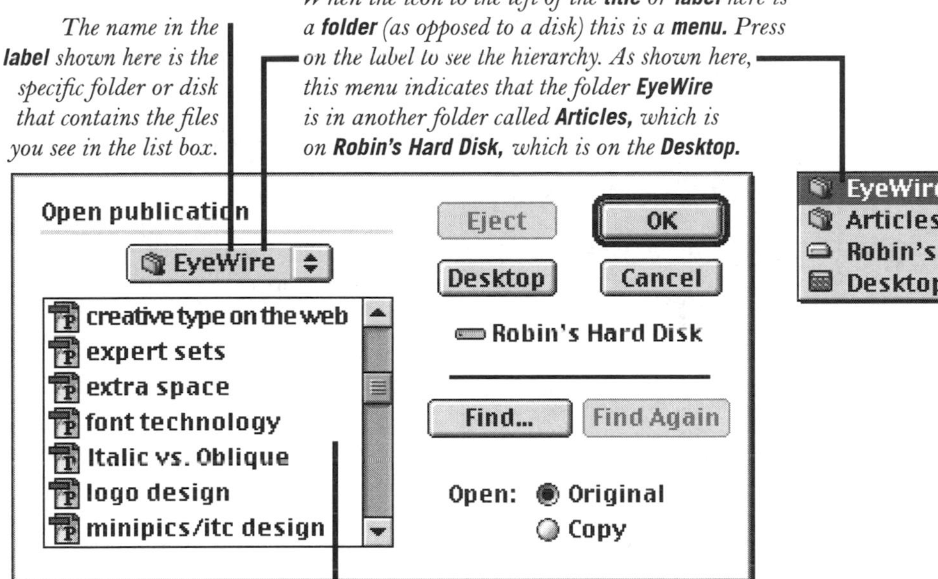

*The only **documents** you will see in this list (directory) are documents that the current application can open.*

*Single-click any name to **select** that file.*

*Double-click the name to **open** the file.*

*When you **double-click a document,** it opens that document on your screen.*

*When you **double-click a folder or a disk,** it opens here to show you a list of the files inside that folder or on that disk, and that title of that new folder or disk will be displayed in the label above the list (where it now says "EyeWire" in the example shown above).*

*Click **Eject** to eject a disk so you can insert another.*

*Click **Desktop** to see what's on the Desktop level, including disks in other drives.*

*Click **Cancel** to take you back to where you were before you chose "Open" from the File menu.*

*Click **OK** (the button might say **Open**) to open the **selected** file; **or** double-click directly on the file name in the list.*

1. Is this file an application or a document?

2. What will happen when you double-click on it?

3. Is this file an application or a document?

4. What will happen when you double-click on it?

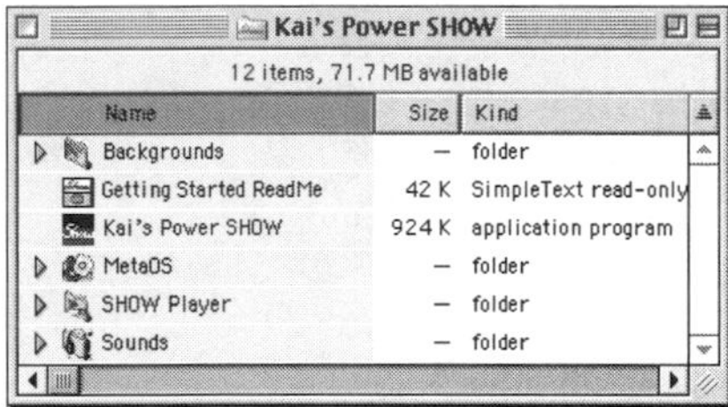

5. What would be the fastest way to view this window "By Kind" so you can tell which file is the application?

6. In the File menu in an application, what is the difference between "New" and "Open"?

7. Label these parts on the Open dialog box, below:
   a. the **directory,** or **list** of files and folders you can open.
   b. a **document** that can be opened.
   c. the **name of the folder** that contains the files you see in the list.
   d. the hidden **menu.**

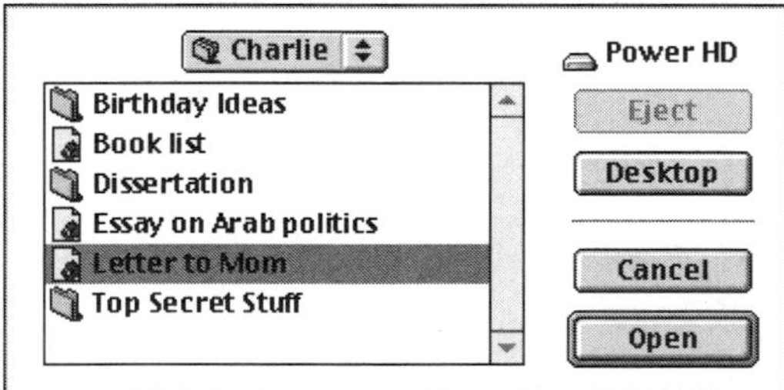

Answers on page 424.

14 Word Processing

also known as "typing"

You may have grown up **typing** on a typewriter or you may have grown up **word processing** on a computer of some sort. Typing and word processing are very similar, of course, in that they use a similar keyboard. The difference is that word processing is much more fun.

You're going to be typing in some manner everywhere on your Mac. In some applications typing is the main point, as in word processors. In others, it is the way to input the data whose purpose is to be manipulated, as in databases or spreadsheets. In others, typing is a sideline that is occasionally necessary, as in paint programs. And everywhere you find dialog boxes where you type some answer or other, and even on your Desktop you type the names of files and folders. Fortunately, in the consistent Mac environment, typing follows the same patterns and features everywhere.

I-Beam

I I

These are two variations of an I-beam.

You may already be familiar with the Macintosh word processing **I-beam** (pronounced eye-beam). It looks like this: I

On the Mac, the I-beam is a **visual clue** that you are now in a typing mode, as opposed to having an arrow or a cross-hair or any number of other "cursors" that appear in various programs.

The I-beam is simply another pointer. And just like the pointer, it doesn't do anything until you *click it* or *press-and-drag it.*

Insertion Point

When you move the I-beam pointer to a spot within text and *click,* it sets down a flashing **insertion point** that looks like this: | (but it flashes).

After you click the mouse to set the insertion point, then you can move the I-beam out of the way (using the mouse)—**the insertion point is what you need to begin typing,** *not the I-beam!!* The I-beam just positions the insertion point.

With the insertion point flashing, anything you type will start at that point and move out to the right. This is true whether the insertion point is at the beginning or the end of a paragraph, in the middle of a word, in a field of a dialog box, under an icon at your Desktop, or anywhere else. (The only time the words will not move to the right is if the text is flush right or centered, or if you've set a tab other than left-aligned.)

At any time you can take the mouse, move the I-beam pointer somewhere else, click it, and start typing from the new insertion point.

Delete (or Backspace)

Also from that insertion point, press the **Delete** key (found in the upper right, called the **Backspace** key on older keyboards) to backspace over text and remove any letters along the way. So you can backspace/delete to **correct typos** as you go, or you can click to set the insertion point down anywhere else in your text and backspace/delete from there.

One Space After Periods

What?! One space after a period? If you grew up on a typewriter, this is not an easy habit to change, I know. Or if you were taught keyboarding skills by someone who grew up on a typewriter, they taught you typewriter rules. But characters on a Macintosh are not *monospaced* as they are on a typewriter (except for Monaco and Courier), so there is no need to use two spaces to separate two sentences. Check any book or magazine on your shelf; you will never find two spaces after periods (except publications produced on a computer typed by someone still using typewriter rules). If you find this hard to accept, read *The Mac is not a typewriter.* If you're interested in creating fine typography, read *The Non-Designer's Type Book.* Yes, I wrote them.

Highlighting (Selecting) Text

When you **select text,** it becomes **highlighted.** Once it is selected, you can do things to it, such as change its size, the typeface, delete it, etc.

If you double-click on a word with the I-beam anywhere on the Mac, the entire word is selected, indicated by the highlighting.

This **word** is highlighted.

If you want to select more than one word, press-and-drag over the entire area you wish to highlight.

Part of this line is highlighted.

Replacing highlighted text

Once a word is highlighted (selected), anything you type will *entirely replace* the highlighted text. Or you can now change the font (typeface) or style or size of the text using your menu commands. Or you can copy or cut or delete that text. Or you can paste something in to replace it. In fact, you *cannot* do any of these things *unless* the text is first highlighted. (Each of these procedures is explained in this chapter.)

Tip: To **un-highlight** (deselect), click once anywhere, even in the highlighted space.

Several selection tips

Very few applications (almost none) let you select "discontiguous" text—that is, it's not possible to select one line from the first paragraph, plus a line from the third paragraph. The selected text must all be contiguous, or connected together.

Try these shortcuts for selecting text anywhere on the Mac:

- Double-click in the middle of a word to select the whole word.
- Triple-click in the middle of a sentence to select either the whole line or the entire paragraph (depending on the program).
- The arrow keys move the insertion point backward and forward, up and down. Hold down the Shift key as you use the arrow keys, and the text will be selected along the way.
- If you have a lot of text to select, **click** at the beginning. Scroll, if necessary, to the end of the text you want to select, even if it's on another page. Hold down the **Shift** key and **click.** Everything between **click and Shift-click** will be selected. This also works in spreadsheets and database lists.
- In many applications, the numeric keypad will either type numbers (when the Num Lock key is down) or it will move the insertion point (when Num Lock is not down). Experiment with it. For instance, in Microsoft Word or Adobe PageMaker, the number 1 will bounce the insertion point to the beginning of a line, and the number 7 will bounce it to the end. Other keys move the insertion point up or down a paragraph, a page, a word, etc. And if you hold the Shift key down, the text will be selected as the insertion point moves.

When to Use the Return Key

A word wrap is sometimes called a soft Return (although technically it isn't, really).

Word wrap: In a word processor, you should *never* hit the Return key at the end of your line *unless* it is the end of the paragraph or unless you *really do* want the line to end there, as in an address. This is because word processors *word wrap*—the words just wrap themselves around onto the next line when they get to the right margin. Why is that? Well . . .

Hard Return: When you press the Return key you insert what is called a *hard return* that tells the computer to always stop the line at that point. Then when you change your margins, your line will *always* break at that hard return, even if there are only two words on the line. So, just keep those nimble fingers moving along and only hit the Return key when you really want a new paragraph.

> On the Mac, a **paragraph** is created every time you hit the Return key. So a return address of three lines is really three paragraphs.

Double-Return: Hitting the Return key twice is like pushing the carriage return on a typewriter twice—you get a double space between the lines. This is for extra space between paragraphs (although in word processors you can ask for an automatic increase of space between paragraphs). If you want the entire document, or even just a piece of it, double-spaced—that's different: there is always an instant way to change your spacing to double-spaced, usually just a button to click *after you select all the text.* Check your manual for the method for your particular application.

Most word processing programs have a command for showing invisible characters such as Returns and spaces, which makes it easier to get rid of unnecessary ones. The command might be something like "Show invisibles," "Show ¶" or "Display ¶."

Removing a Return: The computer sees a Return as just another character, which means to remove a Return you simply *backspace over it,* just as you would to remove an unwanted character. The problem is, in most programs you can't *see* the Return character. So you must set the insertion point just to the left of the first character on the line and backspace/delete, like so:

> |Set the insertion point at the beginning of the line (as shown here) and backspace to *remove the empty line* above this one. Backspace/delete *again* to *wrap the sentence back up* to the one above.

Blank Spaces

The computer thinks a **blank space** is just the same as any other character you can see. Every Tab, Return, Spacebar space, etc., is a character on the Mac. This means you can select blank spaces, blank lines, blank tabbed spaces, or Returns to delete them. Select and delete them just like you would any other character.

```
The space between these words is highlighted.

        This tabbed space is highlighted.

If you hit double Returns, you can also
select the blank space between

the lines and delete it.
```

Also, since these blank spaces are characters, you can actually change the size of them (font size, that is), as well as the *leading* (space between the lines), the style, the paragraph spacing, etc.

Centering Text

And a most important thing: when you **center** a word or line, the Mac takes all those blank spaces into consideration, so any Spacebar spaces or any first-line indents or any tabs you've inserted will be used to calculate the center of the line, making the line not *appear* centered!

```
This line is centered.
This line is also centered
but it includes a tab.
The invisible tab character
that is disrupting the alignment
must be highlighted
and removed, like so:
        This line is also centered.
Then it will be centered just fine:
This line is also centered.
```

I hit the Tab key before I typed the first word in this centered line. Thus the line appears not to be centered.

I selected the tab space and deleted it.

After I deleted the invisible space, the line centered just fine.

Changing Fonts (typefaces) and Rule #2

Throughout the entire Mac environment, to make any changes to anything you must follow this rule, Rule #2:

Select First, Then Do It To It.

For instance, **to change to a different font,** or typeface: first *select* the characters you want to change (press-and-drag over the text), then *choose* the font name you want to change it into. The font list is found in your menu under various labels, depending on your program.

Formatting the insertion point

Notice that the insertion point picks up whatever font and style and size and alignment *is directly to its left.* No matter where you set the insertion point, you will type in the font, etc., of that character, even if that character is an empty space.

Advanced tip!

Now, let's say you know that the next thing you're going to type is going to be in a different font. Do you need to type the text first and then select those characters and change the font? No!

- Make sure your insertion point is positioned where you are going to type with the new font.
- *With no text selected,* go up to the menu and choose the font (and style and size, if you like); *when there is no text selected, all the formatting gets poured into the insertion point*—whatever you type next will be in the font you just chose.

  As soon as you place the insertion point elsewhere, though, it will again pick up all the formatting of the character to its left.

Changing Style

Style refers to whether the type is plain, **bold,** outline, *italic,* etc. To change the style of the type, you need to follow Rule #2: *select first, then do it to it.* **Select** the type you want to change (highlight it), then **choose** the style you want from the menu. You can choose more than one of these; for instance, you can have a face that is ***bold-italic-outlined-shadowed-underlined.*** Gag.

To remove all of the style choices at once, simply *select* the text and *choose* Plain or Normal.

Changing Styles Mid-Sentence—Without Using the Menu

As mentioned in that last section about changing *fonts*, you can choose the style you want from the menu *before* you type it (as long as you don't move the insertion point after choosing). But even that's a pain if you just want to italicize the next word and then return to normal text. This is an easier method:

Notice the keyboard shortcuts in the style menu? They're almost always Command **B** for Bold, Command **I** for Italic, etc. (Some programs may use Command Shift B and Command Shift I, etc.)

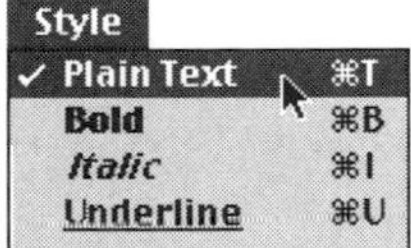

Learn these keyboard shortcuts!

- As you're typing along, simply press Command **B** and the next word you type will be **bold!**
- When you want the next word to be *not* bold, press Command **B** again and it will take *off* the bold (that's called a *toggle switch*—when choosing the same command turns that command off).
- Logically, you can press Command **B I** to create a word that is (guess!) *bold italic.*
- If you want to take all the extra formatting off at once (for instance, you want to remove the shadow, the outline, and the bold), select the text and apply the shortcut for Plain, Normal, or Regular style (whatever your application calls it).

Changing Type Size

8 point

48 pt.

Size in type is measured in *points.* There are 72 points in one inch. In your menu you see different numbers referring to the size of type; logically, the bigger the number, the bigger the type. Again, to change the size of characters: *select first, then do it to it*: select the text, then go to the Size menu and choose a point size. Or set your insertion point down and choose the size from the menu *before* you type (see the last two sections on changing fonts and styles). For more information on type sizes, see Chapter 21.

Alignment

Alignment refers to where the text is lined up: *align left* text is lined up on the left margin; *align right* is on the right, obviously; *align center* is centered on a vertical axis *between your margins; justified* is lined up on both the left *and* right margins. To change your alignment, you know what to do! That's right: *select first, then do it to it*—highlight the text, *then* choose the alignment from the menu or the buttons.

Cut, Copy, and the Clipboard

Almost anywhere you can type, you can cut or copy text. When you **cut** text (or graphics), it is *removed* from your document and placed on the "Clipboard." When you **copy** text (or graphics), the original text *is left in your document* and a *copy* of it is placed on the Clipboard. Well, what the heck is a Clipboard?

Clipboard

This is the Clipboard icon that is stored in the System Folder. If you double-click on it, you'll see what is currently being stored in it.

The **Clipboard** is an invisible "container" somewhere in the depths of the Mac. It holds whatever you have *cut* or *copied*, be it text, spreadsheet data, graphics, etc. Once something is on the Clipboard, it waits there until you paste it in somewhere (we'll get to that in a minute).

The most important thing to remember about the Clipboard is that it holds *only one thing at a time;* that is, as soon as you cut or copy something else, whatever was in the Clipboard to begin with is *replaced* with the new selection.

In some programs, including the Finder, you'll find a menu command called *Show Clipboard,* in which case it appears as a window with its contents displayed. In most programs, though, you never see the actual Clipboard—simply trust that it's there.

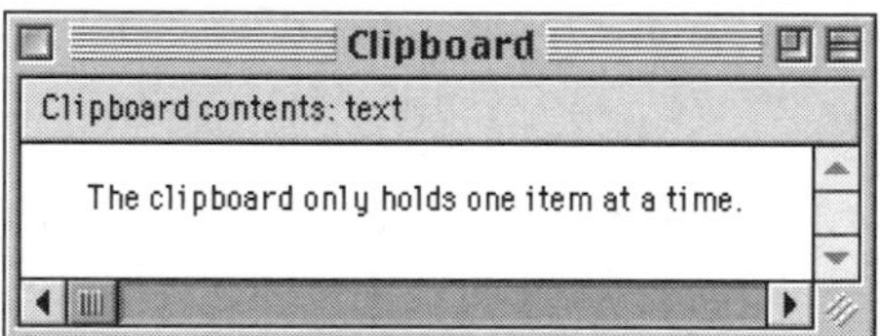

The Clipboard appears as a window (if it's available for looking at in your program).

Items will stay on the Clipboard even when you change applications: you can put a paint image on the Clipboard in a paint program, then open up a word processing program and paste the paint image into a new text document.

Items will leave the Clipboard all by themselves if the computer is turned off or if there is a power failure—the contents are stored in RAM, so anytime RAM gets wiped out, so do the contents of the Clipboard. (There's an explanation of RAM on page 322 in Chapter 29.)

Cut

How to Cut: Simply select, then do it to it. For instance, select the text you wish to remove from the document (press-and-drag over it). Then from the Edit menu choose "Cut." The text will be *eliminated* from your document and placed on the Clipboard. (Be sure to read about "Delete" further on in this section.)

Copy

How to Copy: Simply select, then do it to it. For instance, select the text you wish to copy (press-and-drag over it), then from the Edit menu choose "Copy." The text will *remain* in your document and a *copy* will be placed on the Clipboard.

OK, it's on the Clipboard. Now what? Well, the Clipboard holds objects for *pasting*. You can take text or a graphic out of one place and paste it into your document somewhere else, just as if you had a little glue pot.

Paste

How to Paste: From the Edit menu choose "Paste." If you are working with text, whatever was on the Clipboard will be inserted in your document *beginning at the flashing insertion point*. If you have a range of text selected, the pasted item will *replace* what was selected. Spreadsheet data, graphics, etc., can be pasted in as well. In some programs, especially graphic programs, the pasted object will just land in the middle of the page.

As long as something is on the Clipboard, you can paste it in a million times in many different applications.

Delete *or* Clear and the Clipboard

Now, the **Delete** key (found on the upper-right of the main group of keys, called **Backspace** on older keyboards) works a little differently: if you hit this key while something is selected, whatever is selected is *deleted* and is *not* placed on the Clipboard. This means if you are holding something in the Clipboard to paste in again, whatever you *delete* from your document will not replace what is currently being held in the Clipboard. But it also means that you don't have that deleted item anymore—whatever you delete is really gone. **Clear,** in the Edit menu, does the same thing as Delete.

Undo

Undo can sometimes save your boompah (no, that's not computer jargon—it's Grandma's euphemism). When you do something that makes you scream, "Aack! Oh no!" then try Undo. It's always the first command in the Edit menu (or press Command Z).

> **Note:** What Undo can undo is *only the last action that occurred.* For instance, if you selected two paragraphs of brilliantly witty text that you spent three hours composing and then the cat walked across your keyboard and obliterated the entire work, Undo could give it back to you **IF** you Undo before you touch *anything*. If you start fiddling around with the keys and the mouse, then what you will undo is that fiddling around. So if something goes wrong, don't scream—**UNDO.** Then scream.
>
> (Some applications, such as illustration programs, can Undo multiple times. Check your manual.)

Commands Z, X, C, V

Thoughtfully, the keyboard shortcuts for the undo/cut/copy/paste commands are very handy. Notice on your keyboard the letters **Z, X, C,** and **V,** all lined up in a row right above the Command key. Remember, select first (*except to Undo*); then hold down the Command key and lightly tap the letter.

Command **Z** will Undo	(very close to the ⌘ key).
Command **X** will Cut	(X like eXiting or Xing it out).
Command **C** will Copy	(C for Copy, easy mnemonic).
Command **V** will Paste	(V because it is next to C; it's sort of like the caret symbol ^ for inserting).

Using Real Accent Marks

Here is a list of common accent marks:

- ´ (Option e)
- ` (Option ~)
- ¨ (Option u)
- ~ (Option n)
- ^ (Option i)

The Mac lets you type **accent marks,** as in résumé and piñata. You can find them in Key Caps (next page), but it's easy to remember that you use the Option key, and they are hiding beneath the keyboard characters that would usually be under them. For example, the acute accent over the **e** is **Option e;** the tilde over the **n** is **Option n.**

To type accent marks, follow these steps (using the word résumé):

- Type the word until you come to the letter that will be *under* the accent mark; e.g., **r**
- *Before* you type that next letter (the letter **e** in this case), type the Option combination (**Option e** in this case, which means hold down the Option key and tap the **e** once)—*it will look like nothing happened.* That's okay.
- Now type the character that is to be *under* the accent mark, and both the mark and the letter will appear together; e.g., **r é s u m é**

Accessing Special Characters

Special characters are the symbols you have access to on the Macintosh that aren't available on a typewriter, such as upside-down question marks for Spanish (¿), the pound symbol for English money (£), the cents sign (¢), the registration or trademark symbols (® ™), etc. You can view all these with your **Key Caps** desk accessory (greater details are found on pages 216–217).

To get special characters into your document, follow these steps:

- While working in your document, pull down the desk accessory Key Caps from the Apple menu (far left; press on the apple).
- From the Key Caps menu (a new item that appears in your menu bar!), choose the font you wish to view.
- Find the character you want by pressing Shift **or** Option **or** Shift-Option together; press the character key. Notice which combination of keystrokes produces the character you want. For instance, Shift Option K in the font Times will produce an apple.
- So *remember* that keystroke combination. Close Key Caps and go back to your document (remember, you can access desk accessories in any program).
- In your document, click to set your insertion point. Choose the font Times and press Shift Option K. The apple will appear!

Using Key Caps

Here are some special characters and the keys to access them in any font:

Option 8	•
Option g	©
Option 2	™
Option r	®
Option $	¢
Option Shift 8	°
Option ;	…
Option hyphen	–
Option Shift hyphen	—

There is also a handy chart at the end of this book.

Using Characters from a Different Font

If the character you need is in a different font than you are using, such as a ❤ in Zapf Dingbats, you can also do this: Through Key Caps, find the keystroke combination for the character (Option 6 in this case). Press Option 6 in whatever font you are currently using; some strange character will appear. Select the strange character and change it into Zapf Dingbats; it will turn into a ❤.

> **Tip:** Remember, the insertion point picks up the *formatting of any character immediately to its left, even if it's a blank space,* so anything else you type will be in that character's font, style, etc. To continue in your *original* font, leave your insertion point right where it is; from the menu just choose the font specifications you were originally using.

1. What is Rule #Two on the Mac?

2. Draw an I-beam, an insertion point, and a pointer.

3. Which of the three items mentioned above do you use to select text?

4. When you press the Delete key, which of the three items above backs up?

5. Name the two ways that an insertion point knows which typeface, size, and style to type in.

6. What is the keyboard shortcut to make selected text bold? Italic? Underlined?

7. How can you make the next word you type appear in bold, without going to the menu? After you type it in bold, how do you make the next word you type appear in plain text?

8. If you decide you really want the last paragraph in your document to be the first paragraph, what are the four steps you must take to make that happen?

9. What are the keyboard shortcuts for cut, copy, and paste?

10. What is the difference between "cut" and "clear"?

Extra Credit (50 points): How many spaces should you type after a period?

Answers on page 424.

15 Saving Documents

While you are in the process of creating a document of any sort within any program, the information you put into that document is floating around in the depths of the computer. If you were to turn off the computer, that document would disappear. In fact, if there was a power flicker, the document would disappear. If your computer crashed, the document would disappear. You probably want to keep a permanent copy of it, right? So you need to **save the document** onto your hard disk. Later you can save a backup copy onto removable disk such as a Zip or Jaz cartridge or a CD.

RAM: Random Access Memory

Until you actually go through the process of naming a document and saving it, the document hangs around in **RAM,** which stands for **Random Access Memory.** RAM is sort of like the top of the desk in your office, and you can consider your *hard disk* as a filing cabinet where you keep all your folders of information.

When you are working on a project, you don't keep running to the filing cabinet every time you need a little piece of information, do you? No, you take out all the applicable info and put it on your desk, then when you're finished you put it all away again and take out something else. RAM is sort of like that: when you open an application the computer puts a copy of that application into RAM, also called *memory.* When you quit that application and open another one, the Mac puts the first one back where it came from and puts the new application into RAM. That way the computer doesn't have to keep going into the filing cabinet to do its work and it can operate much more efficiently.

When you create a document, it sits in RAM, too, until you put it in the filing cabinet—your disk. You put the document on your disk by **saving** it. Once it's on a disk, it will stay there until you trash it yourself.

Danger!

All that time your document is in RAM, it is in **danger.** At any moment, if there is a power failure, even for a split second, or you accidentally hit the wrong button, have a system crash, the screen freezes, your child pulls out the power cord, or any other catastrophe of considerable dimension happens to befall, then everything in RAM *(memory)* is gone. Just plain gone. No way on earth for a mortal person to get it back.

Rule #1: Save Often!

The prevention? **SOS:** Save Often, Sweetie. Save Save Save. Every few minutes, when you're just sitting there thinking about your next marvelous move, Save. In every application it's this easy: just press Command S. Then if there *is* a catastrophe you will have lost only the last few minutes of your work. Of course you won't listen to me until you have experienced your own catastrophe.

Save As... *vs.* Save

To save a document for the first time, it must be given a name. Under the File menu are the commands **Save As...** and **Save.** At first the subtle difference can be confusing.

Save As...

Save As... is the command you must use *first* to give the document a name (many applications will not let you save a file without a name). "Save As..." gives you a dialog box such as the one shown on page 148 (they're slightly different from program to program).

Save

Save is the command to use *after* you have named the document and you want to save the new changes onto that same document. *Save* just goes ahead and does it—you won't get a dialog box, but you will see the Edit menu flash for a quick second. Get in the habit of typing Command S (the keyboard shortcut to save) regularly.

> **Tip:** Often there is no keyboard shortcut listed in the menu for "Save As...." But if you have not yet given the document a name, then choosing *Save* (Command S) will usually give you the *Save As...* dialog box because the file must have a name. Many programs will not allow you to name a document with the default of "Untitled"—they insist that you apply a real name.

Making Several Versions

Sometimes you might want to create changes in a document, but you still want to keep a **copy of the original without the changes.** For instance, you write a witty letter to Uncle Jeff, then decide you also want to write to Uncle Cliff. You have a few things to tell Cliff that Jeff isn't interested in, but you don't want to retype the entire letter. That's when you'll use *Save As...* a *second* time to give the document a *new* name.

- ▼ Save the letter to Uncle Jeff. You've probably named it "Witty letter to Uncle Jeff."
- ▼ Now from the File menu, choose "Save As...."
- ▼ Change the name from "Witty letter to Uncle Jeff" to "Witty letter to Uncle Cliff."

This puts the original document (to Uncle Jeff) safely away on your disk and opens a new one (the copy to Uncle Cliff) right on the screen. You'll notice the name in the window title bar of your document will change to what you renamed it. Any changes you make to *this* document (Uncle Cliff's) will not affect the original (Uncle Jeff's).

Witty Letter to Uncle Jeff

Witty Letter to Uncle Cliff

Witty Letter to Uncle Lloyd

Witty Letter to Uncle Floyd

All of these letters are based on the original letter to Uncle Jeff. I just kept choosing "Save As" and giving the new ones new names. The information, layout, type choices, etc., all stayed the same, but now each letter is separate and I can add or delete the details in each.

Templates and Stationery

Another way to make several versions of the same letter, or to keep a master copy of your newsletter or budget report, etc., is to make a **template** or **stationery** copy of the document. One of the easiest ways to do this is to select the document at the Desktop (click once on it). Then from the File menu, choose "Get Info." Click the box at the bottom for "Stationery Pad" (circled, below) Now the original document is what the Mac calls a "stationery pad," otherwise known as a template. It contains all the fonts, formatting, information, etc. When you double-click a stationery pad, the original does not open—a ***copy*** of the original opens. The original stays on your Desktop, intact, so any changes you make to the copy do not affect the original.

Witty Letter

This is the original document. Notice it has the ***upper-right*** *corner turned down. Click once on it to select it, then choose "Get Info" from the File menu.*

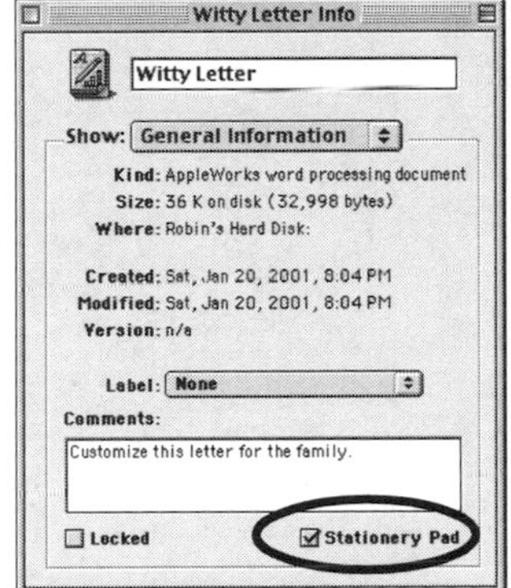

In the Get Info box, click this checkbox.

Witty Letter

The original is now a stationery pad, also known as a template. Notice it has the ***lower-right*** *corner turned up. Open this (it will open to an untitled copy), and move on with your letter.*

Reverting to a Previously Saved Version

Sometimes you might make a bunch of changes to a document and then decide you don't like the changes. In that case, check the File menu to see if your application has a command called **Revert.** If so, choose it and the document will revert *to exactly how it was the last time you saved it.*

If there is no Revert command, then *close* the document. When you see the box that asks if you want to save the changes (shown below), click the button that says "No" or "Don't Save." Reopen the document and everything will be exactly the way it was *the last time you saved it.* This means, of course, that anything you did since you last saved it, *the good stuff as well as the bad,* will be gone.

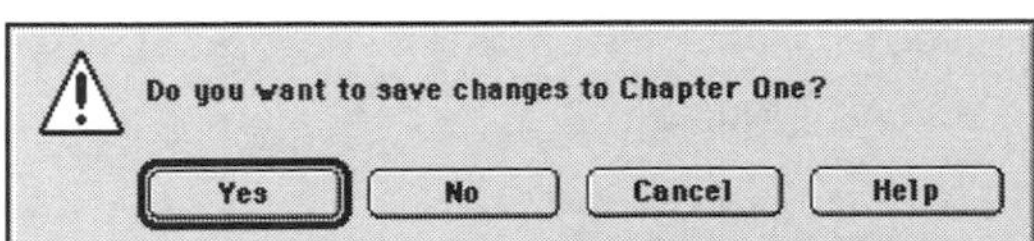

If you click "No," your document will revert back to how it was the last time you saved it.

The "Save As" Dialog Box

Below and opposite are illustrations of a typical **"Save As..." dialog box.** This is a very important box for you to understand because you will be using it every time you start a new document. **I know all this information looks intimidating, but it's actually not that bad and it's very important.** If you spend a few minutes here, *you* will be in control instead of being at the mercy of the computer system.

*This **label** shows which **folder** (notice the folder icon) you are saving your document into. Also notice the double arrows—remember, these mean there is a **menu** here!*

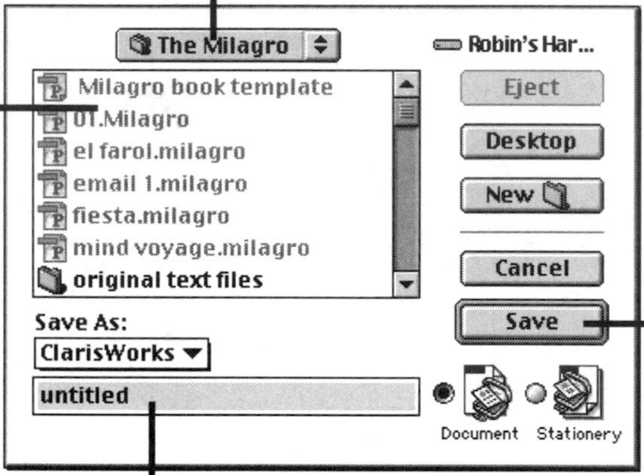

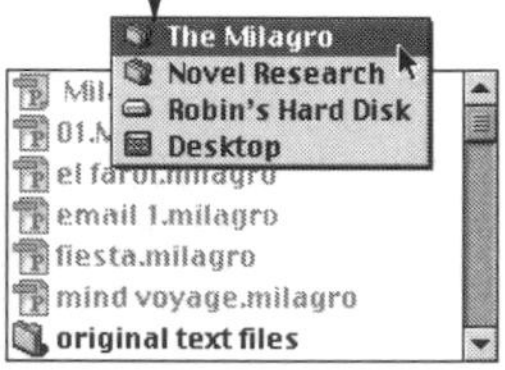

The Milagro
Robin's Har...
Milagro book template
01.Milagro
el farol.milagro
email 1.milagro
fiesta.milagro
mind voyage.milagro
original text files
Eject
Desktop
New
Cancel
Save As:
ClarisWorks
untitled
Save
Document
Stationery

The Milagro
Novel Research
Robin's Hard Disk
Desktop
email 1.milagro
fiesta.milagro
mind voyage.milagro
original text files

*This is a **list,** or **directory,** of all the folders and documents in the folder or disk named in the **label.** Folder names are black because you can double-click to open them and store something inside. Other documents are gray because you can't open them, but you can see they are there.*

*Type here to name the document. The highlight is a **visual clue** telling you that this current name, "Untitled," is **selected**—if you just type, this highlighted text will be replaced (that is, you don't have to delete the existing text first).*

*Click the **Save** button after you name the document. Sometimes this button is not active until you have given the document a name.*

Sometimes this button says "OK" instead of "Save."

If you have selected a folder icon, this button says "Open" so you can open the folder to save it inside.

Visual Clues in the Dialog Box

As is typical on the Mac, the dialog box has many **visual clues** that tell you what to do or what to expect. These are just a couple of them. See Chapter 28 for details on "navigating," *which is a critical skill!* It will teach you how to save a document into exactly the folder you need it saved into.

Look very carefully at the dialog box below. What are the two differences between this picture and the one on the opposite page? The differences, the ***visual clues,*** *are important!*

A double border around this list is a* ***visual clue,*** *indicating that* ***this list is selected.*** *If you type a character, you will select the file in this list box that begins with that letter.*

When a file name is gray, it is a ***visual clue*** *that the file itself is in the folder, but you can't do anything with it.*

Folder names are black, which is a ***visual clue*** *that you can open them (double-click) to store documents inside.*

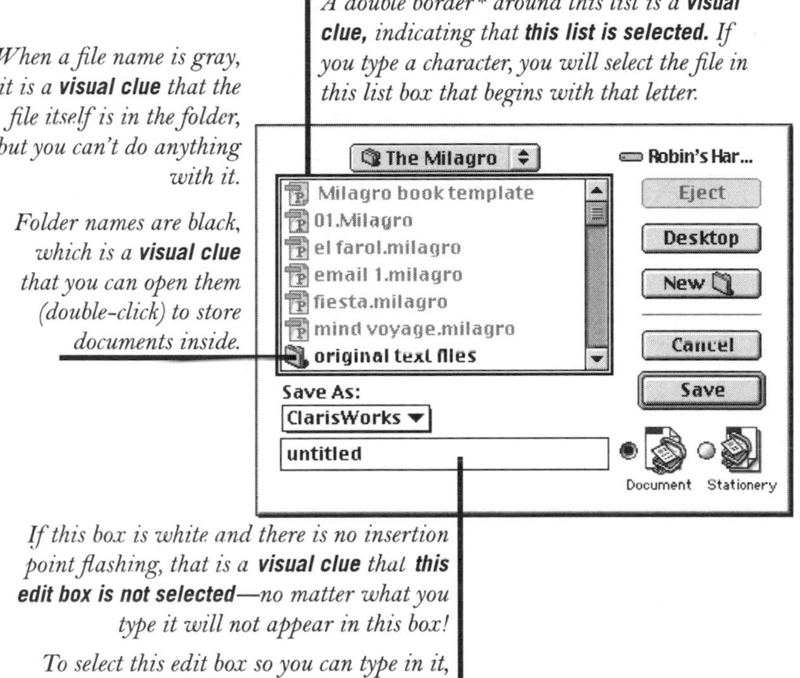

If this box is white and there is no insertion point flashing, that is a ***visual clue*** *that* ***this edit box is not selected****—no matter what you type it will not appear in this box!*

To select this edit box so you can type in it, click in it or press the ***Tab key.***

* Why does this list have a border around it sometimes and not others? If you click in the **list,** it becomes selected, which **deselects** the edit box where you type in the name!

Try this: Open any application, then choose "Save As…." Notice the edit box is highlighted (selected). Press the Tab key. Notice the list box is now selected. Press the Tab key several more times to see how Tabbing moves the selection back and forth from the list to the edit box.

Quiz

Use the dialog boxes shown (A or B) to answer the questions.

1. Which dialog box has the list, or directory, selected?

2. Which dialog box is ready for you to name the document?

3. If you were in dialog box A and you typed the letter "F," what would happen?

4. What would happen if you were to double-click on the folder named "Notes"?

5. If you were in dialog box A and you wanted to name the document, which key would you press to select the edit box (name box)?

6. What would you press to get the little menu shown to the left?

7. What would happen if you were to choose "Power HD" from this little menu shown to the left?

8. Briefly describe two ways to avoid saving your changes.

9. Where does the document hang out before you save it?

10. Which command would you use to save another copy of a document, but with a new name?

Answers on page 424.

Printing Documents

16

Printing is usually the point, right? It's well and good to create all these great things on the computer, but most of the time we need to actually print our creations to make them useful. In this chapter I'll walk you through the printing process, but keep in mind that each of the hundreds of printers for the Macintosh has its own software, so details might look different from what I show here. Please read the documentation that came with your printer!

Also, different applications often create their own Page Setup and Print dialog boxes, so the ones you use might not exactly match the ones I show in this chapter—but they're all similar.

Quick Start

Here are the briefest of directions for **printing your pages.** If it works, *then just skip the rest of this chapter!* For this very brief quick start, I have to assume you have the printer plugged in to both the wall and the computer with the appropriate cables, there is paper in the printer, and that someone has installed the printer software.

- ▼ Turn on the printer and let it warm up.
- ▼ Open the document that you want to print.
- ▼ From the File menu, choose "Print...."
- ▼ Click the "OK" or "Print" button (or hit the Return key).
- ▼ That's all.

OR: First Time Ever Printing to this Printer

If this is the **very first time** you have ever printed to your printer, you will have to make a brief stop at the Chooser before you print. You only need to do this the very first time, *or* if you are printing to a different printer than usual! After this initial process, you only need to follow the steps above.

- ▼ Turn on the printer and let it warm up.
- ▼ Open the document that you want to print.
- ▼ From the Apple menu, choose "Chooser."

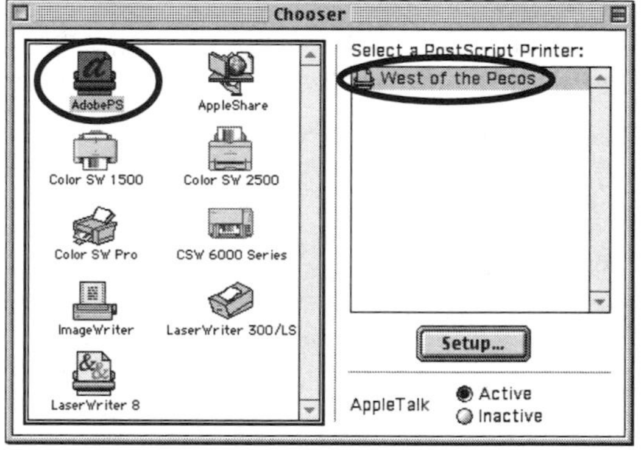

This is the Chooser. Details about it are on the following pages.

- ▼ Click on the icon on the **left side** of the Chooser that has the brand name of your printer. Or if you have a PostScript printer (see page 154) and you see an icon that looks like a printer with a page of ampersands (&) like "LaserWriter 8" above, click on it. Chances are you have the same icon.
- ▼ On the **right side** of the Chooser, click on the name of the printer (if your printer is not turned on and warmed up, you won't see any names listed yet!), or click on the printer "port" icon (it will either be the "USB Port" or the "serial" port).

- You might get a message telling you AppleTalk must be on or off. The Mac will turn it on or off for you.
    - If you are printing to a PostScript printer for the first time, click the "Setup…" button.
    - Click "Auto setup." Click OK.
- After you have chosen the printer info on the **left** and the **right,** close the Chooser (press Command W, Command Q, or click in the close box in the upper-left corner of the window).
- You will probably get a message telling you that you have changed printers, and to go to "Page Setup." Do that: in your document, go to the File menu and choose "Page Setup." Don't change anything—just click OK.
- From the File menu, choose "Print…."
- Click the OK or "Print" button.

Did it Work?

Now, if that didn't work, read the rest of this chapter more carefully. It may be that you did not choose the proper printer "driver" in the Chooser, or that you're not sure whether your printer is PostScript or not and so you clicked the wrong button.

Do This Before Moving On!

Okay. If you are going to move on through this chapter, make sure your printer is plugged into the socket in the wall. You also need the correct cable to connect your printer to your Mac. Most printers don't automatically come with a cable to connect it to the Mac (you have to buy it separately), so if you brought your printer home without one you will have to go back to the computer store and get one before you can print. This cable plugs into the printer and connects to the Mac. (I'm assuming that if you bought a printer, you made sure it was compatible with your Macintosh; for instance, if your computer uses USB ports, you must get a USB-compatible printer and a USB cable. See Chapter 34 for some information on ports and the things that plug into them.)

Also with your printer you got a disk with software on it. Follow the directions in the manual to install the software.

Turn on your printer. It takes most printers several minutes to warm up and get the connection established between it and the Mac, so give it enough time.

Printers

There are basically two types of printers: **PostScript printers** and **QuickDraw printers** (also called "non-PostScript printers"). These two types have nothing to do with describing printers that are *compatible* with your particular Macintosh; see Chapter 34 if you are confused about USB and serial in reference to printers.

QuickDraw printers
Also known as non-PostScript printers

QuickDraw is a computer programming language that your *Macintosh* uses—it creates what you see on the screen. A printer that can only reproduce what is on the screen is usually called a QuickDraw printer (although there is really nothing "QuickDraw" in the printer itself). The old ImageWriter, the HP DeskWriter, the Apple StyleWriter, and just about any printer with the word "inkjet" or "deskjet" are examples of QuickDraw printers, with *resolutions* ranging from about 75 to 600 dots per inch (the higher the resolution, the smoother the printed image). If your color printer cost less than several thousand dollars, it's not a PostScript printer.

PostScript printers

PostScript is a "page description language," a programming language, that a *PostScript printer* can interpret. A PostScript printer doesn't care what the heck you have on your screen. If the font or the graphic image is created with PostScript, it can look dreadful on the screen but will print beautifully on the page. Personal PostScript printers are the expensive desktop models, typically around $1,000 to $3,000, with color printers often above $4,000. They're expensive because they have a powerful computer inside, complete with memory and a specialized CPU (central processing unit, the tiny chip that runs the entire process).

Imagesetters

There are also *very* expensive (like $100,000), very high-end PostScript printers with resolutions of around 1270 or 2540 dots per inch, such as the Linotronic. These machines, called **imagesetters,** output (print) onto resin-coated film, not plain paper, and the hard copy looks virtually like traditional phototypesetting, limited only by the professional expertise of the person who input (typed in) the text. This book was output on an imagesetter, and I input the text.

Service bureaus

Since the high resolution machines are so expensive, you only find them in **service bureaus**—shops where they offer the output (the hard copy, the printed pages) as a service. You take the disk containing your document to them, leave it there, and they print it up for you. It usually costs from $4 to $10 a page, but it's beautiful.

Chooser

The very first time you print from your Mac, *or* if you are hooked up to more than one printer, *or* sometimes if you go somewhere else and print, *or* if you have difficulty printing, you need to go to the **Chooser** to direct the computer to the printer. If none of these situations apply to you, you can skip this information, go right to the section "OK, OK, Let's Print" (page 160), and remember these details are here if you ever need them.

Select the Chooser from the Apple menu.

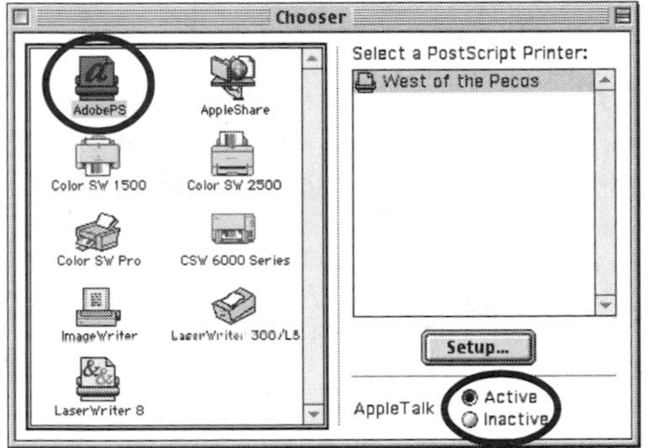

This is the Chooser with one of the PostScript printer drivers selected. AppleTalk must be active.

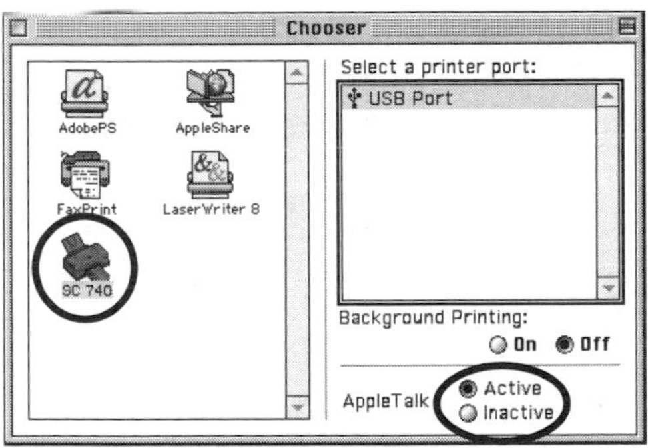

This is the Chooser with a USB printer driver selected. AppleTalk must be active.

See page 158 for information about "Background Printing."

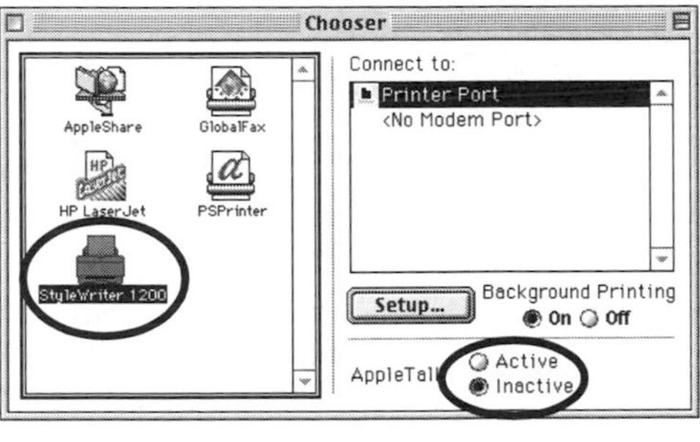

In this case, a non-Postscript serial printer, the StyleWriter, is selected. Notice that AppleTalk is inactive. If AppleTalk was previously active when you chose a QuickDraw printer, the computer will flash a message letting you know it is making AppleTalk inactive.

—continued

Printer drivers

This is the printer driver for one of the Apple Color StyleWriters.

On the **left** side of the Chooser window you see various icons. These icons represent the **printer drivers** that are installed in your System Folder (a printer driver is the program that tells the printer what to do; it *drives* the printer). For every printer driver that's checked in the Extensions Manager (see pages 258–259), there is a matching icon in your Chooser. *Even if you have a printer hooked up right next to you, you won't be able to print to it unless its driver is installed in your System Folder.*

- In the Chooser, click on the icon representing the printer to which you want to print.

If you need to install a printer driver

If you don't see an icon for your printer, you must close the Chooser for now (click in its close box) and **go install the driver:**

Find the disk that came with your printer. You should see an icon named something like "Installer"; double-click it and follow the directions.

If you selected a non-PostScript printer icon, then on the **right** side of the Chooser you will see a *port* icon, asking which port (sort of like a plug) the cable connected to the printer is plugged into. The picture on the screen should be the same as the one your cable is connected to on the back of the Mac.

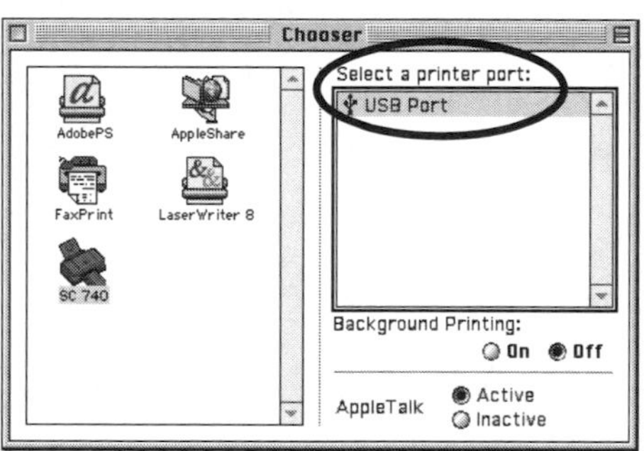

If you have a Mac with USB connections, you are probably using a USB printer, in which case you will see an icon for the USB port in the right side of the Chooser window.

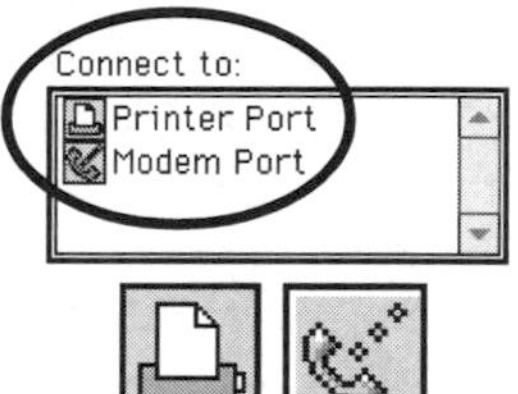

These are the printer port icons you'll see on an older Mac, one that does not have USB connections. The cable to your printer is plugged into one of these ports on the back of your Mac, usually the printer port (check the little pictures on the back of your Mac).

[If you have a modem, its cable should be plugged into the port with the little telephone picture on it.]

If you selected a PostScript printer icon or a network server icon, then on the **right side** of the Chooser you should see the names of all printers that are connected to your Mac **and that are turned on.**

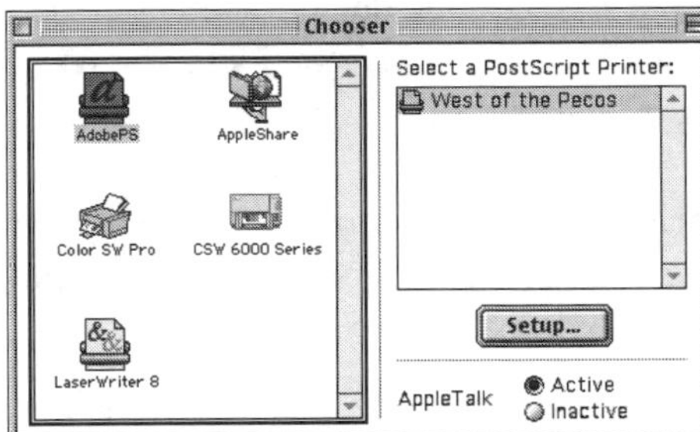

If you don't see a name here, it means either the printer is not turned on, the printer is not warmed up enough, the connections are loose (plug them in tightly), or the cable is bad (try another one).

- Click on the port or printer name that your computer is connected to.
- **If you are on a network** (which you would be if more than one computer is going to the same printer) or **if you are connected to a PostScript printer or USB printer,** then make sure the AppleTalk button is clicked **Active.**

  If you are the only one connected to a QuickDraw (non-PostScript) serial printer, AppleTalk should be **Inactive.**

  Don't worry if you don't know either of the above things—the Mac will tell you if AppleTalk needs to be active or not and will actually switch the buttons for you.

- Notice in the illustration above that **two** items are *highlighted:* the icon representing your printer (on the left), and the name or the port of your printer (on the right). These two items must both be highlighted! Highlight (select) each one by clicking once on each.
- It feels like the Chooser should have an OK button, but it doesn't. I have always wondered why not. So now that you've told the Mac which printer to print to, just close the Chooser window (click its close box or press Command W or Command Q) and proceed with printing your work.

  Yes, you'll probably get the message telling you that you have changed printers and you should choose "Page Setup." You should do it. See the next page if you want more info on that.

Background Printing

Also see "Desktop Printer Dialog Box" on page 166.

Background Printing, if you have that option, allows the Mac to print to a printer while you go on with your work. **If you do not** check this button, then you have to wait until the printer has finished all the pages before you can work on the computer again. **If you do** check this button, the computer sends the information into a "buffer," then lets you use your screen. The buffer sends the information to the printer at the slower rate the printer requires, while you continue with your work. You will notice, during background printing, that occasionally your cursor may twitch, freeze, or your typing may stop. This is normal behavior because the computer is trying to do two things at once.

Background printing can also be turned on in your printer software. Keep in mind that it takes longer to print in the background and it uses hard disk space. If you have a complex, color job to print, Apple recommends you turn off background printing.

Page Setup

Just about every program that prints documents has a **Page Setup** dialog box where you can set specifications for the document. Before you print, always check this Page Setup feature. Shown on the next page are sample Page Setup boxes, but your particular application may have added other features of its own. They are generally self-explanatory, and if you need information, click the "Help" button—it provides short explanations for each option.

Remember when you went to the Chooser and selected a printer driver and you got this message:

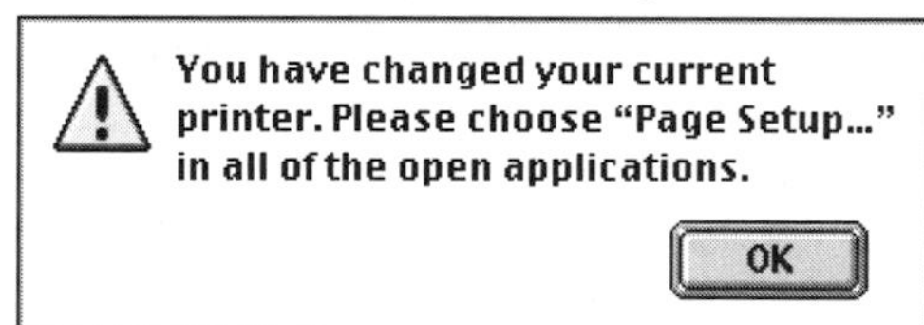

This is because there are different options and features in Page Setup depending on the printer driver you chose.

If you got this message, click OK, then go to your document. From the File menu, choose "Page Setup..." and click OK. Then your application knows which specifications are allowed in the document and printing process.

Various Page Setup dialog boxes

Here are samples of several Page Setups, but remember that you probably won't see exactly what is here because of a variety of factors. All of the Page Setups say about the same thing, and you really can't click any buttons that will hurt anything—feel free to experiment. Some of the most common features are explained here.

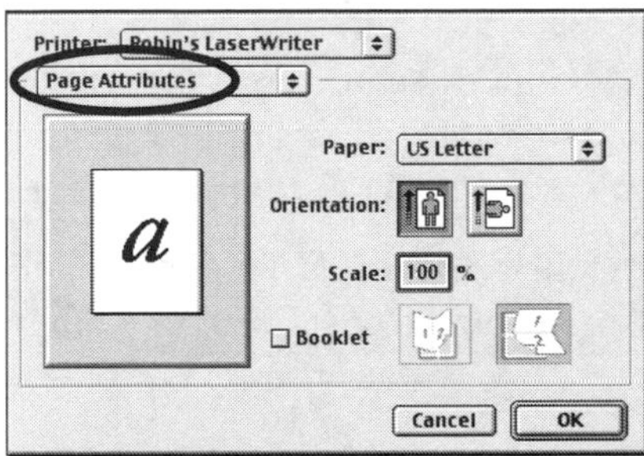

Choose "Attributes" such as the paper size, whether it prints regular or sideways, how much to enlarge or reduce the image, and whether to create a booklet.

Notice when you choose certain options, the image on the left gives you a ***visual clue*** *as to what to expect.*

Printer: Robin's LaserWriter
PostScript™ Options
Visual Effects:
☐ Flip Horizontal
☐ Flip Vertical
☐ Invert Image
Image & Text:
☑ Substitute Fonts
☑ Smooth Text
☑ Smooth Graphics
☐ Precision Bitmap Alignment
☐ Unlimited Downloadable Fonts
Cancel
OK

From the little menu (circled, left), choose to see the Options to get a dialog box similar to this.

Here is the button that turns New York into Times, Geneva into Helvetica, and Monaco into Courier. If you are printing to a PostScript printer, ***uncheck this box.***

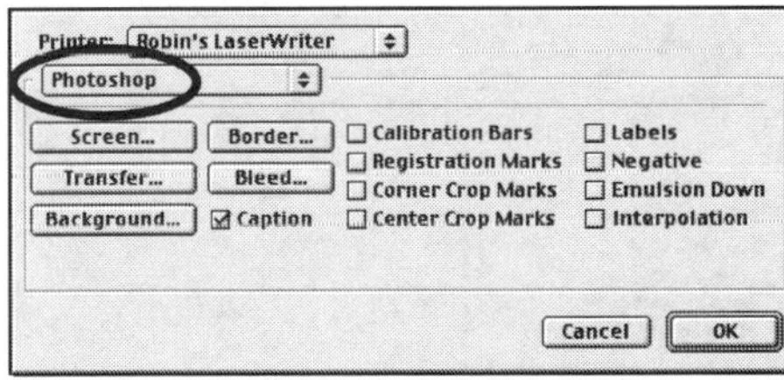

Different applications will have different specifications here (some may have none). If you get something like this, click each button to see what the options are (remember, the ellipsis tells you that if you click the button, you'll get another dialog box).

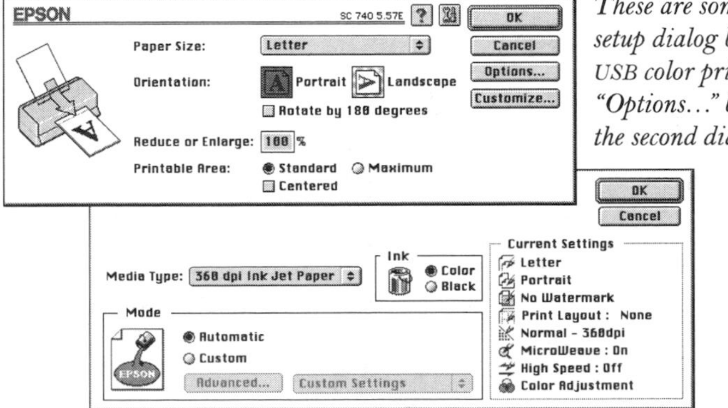

These are some of the page setup dialog boxes for a USB color printer. Click the "Options..." button to get the second dialog box.

Visual clues

Remember, whenever you see a downward arrow and/or a shadow behind a box, it is a ***visual clue*** *that there is a menu if you press.*

Checkboxes are for clicking in to choose options.

Edit boxes are for typing changes in.

Help!

Click the Help button in these boxes! They really are helpful!

OK, OK, Let's Print!

This is the longer, more detailed version of the **printing** process, as opposed to the quick start directions in the beginning of this chapter. You may see different print dialog boxes depending on which printer you are connected to, and the dialog boxes within different applications may look slightly different from what you see here, but basically all you need to do is answer the questions they ask.

1. Save again

The first thing to do is **Save** your document again—as a preventive measure always save just before you print. Also, make sure the printer is turned on (an ImageWriter must have its "Select" button on as well).

2. Go to Chooser if necessary

If you haven't printed to this printer before, go the the **Chooser** and select both a printer driver and the name or the port for your printer (see the previous pages).

3. Check the Page Setup

Check the **Page Setup** command under the File menu. This sets certain parameters for printing. Because this dialog box and any of its Options boxes may vary from printer to printer and from application to application, you should check your manual for specific details on all the buttons. Click OK when you're done.

4. Choose "Print"

If you get a message telling you it's not possible to print, check the previous section on Chooser, and make sure your printer is on.

Now go to the File menu and choose **Print....** Depending on which application and which printer you are using, you'll get a dialog box (an example below) asking you questions.

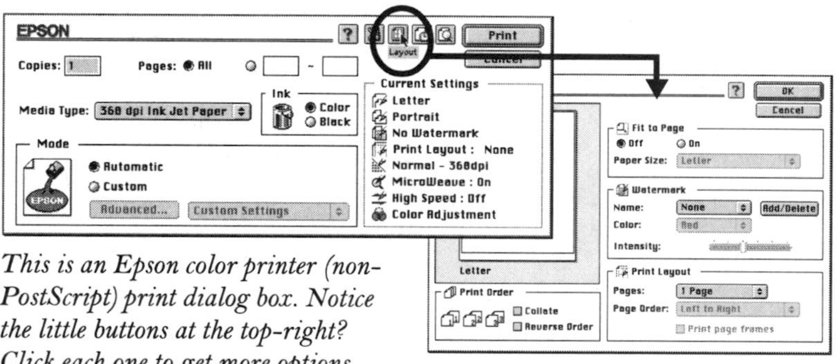

This is an Epson color printer (non-PostScript) print dialog box. Notice the little buttons at the top-right? Click each one to get more options.

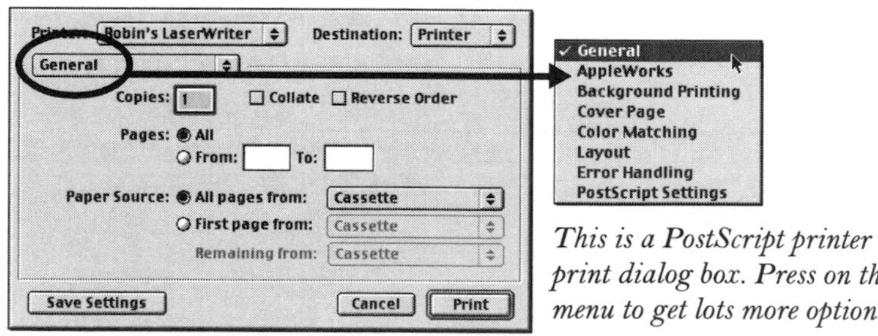

This is a PostScript printer print dialog box. Press on the menu to get lots more options.

5. Click the "OK" or "Print" button

When you click the last **OK** or **Print** button in the last dialog box (sometimes there are three or four dialog boxes), the messages will be sent to the printer and your brilliant document shall come rolling forth.

A few details

There are many variations on the Page Setup and Print dialog boxes. Here are explanations of the more common features:

Orientation: Your application may use another term for it, but what the Mac wants to know is if it should print upside right or sideways (8.5 x 11 or 11 x 8.5); also known as **Tall** or **Wide, Portrait** or **Landscape.**

Reduce or Enlarge; Scale: Regardless of the precise term your printer driver uses, you can enter a number or press the arrows here to enlarge or reduce the printed page. For instance, enter 50% to print your work at half size. Remember, half of an 8.5 x 11 is 4.25 x 5.5—you must halve *both* directions. On paper, this looks like the image is ¼ the original size; it isn't—it's half of *both* the horizontal *and* the vertical.

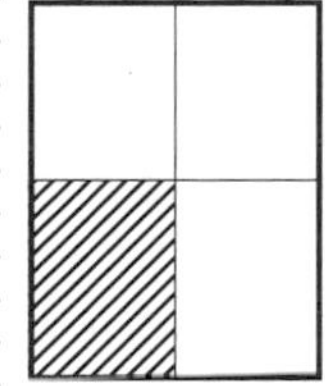

The shaded portion is 50% of the larger size—half of both the width **and** *the length.*

Copies: Type in the number of copies you want to print. If you're printing more than one copy and you have a **Collate** button to check, the printer will print all the pages in order, then print the next set all in order. If you *don't* click collate, you will get, for instance, 5 copies of page 1, 5 copies of page 2, 5 copies of page 3, etc. But keep in mind that it's faster for the printer *not* to collate than to print all the pages in order and then go back again and print the next set.

Pages: All or **From __ To __:** You can choose to print *all* of the pages contained in your document, or just pages 3 through 12 (or whatever your choice is, of course). Choose **All** to override any numbers in the **From/To** boxes.

Computer Paper: *This does not refer to pin-fed paper!* Computer paper is 11 x 13 inches. The pin-fed paper that fits through a printer with the holes along the side is 8.5 x 11—pin-fed paper is usually letter-size; it's just all strung together. Computer paper is a special size.

Paper Source: If you have more than one paper tray, you can tell the printer which tray to choose paper from. This is one of the details the printer driver tells the computer and printer.

Cover Page: If you ask for a cover page, then before or after your document prints (depending on which button you click) you will get a very useful and handy page with details of this job, like this:

User:	**Robin Williams**
Application:	**AppleWorks 6.0**
Document:	**Resignation Letter to the Boss**
Date:	**Saturday, May 6, 2001**
Time:	**12:49 A.M.**
Printer:	**Toad Hall**
Pages:	**3**

If you find this cover page to be a valuable item for you, make sure you also check into date and time stamping within your appl-cation—many word processors can add those important details directly into a header or footer that appears in small type at the top or bottom of each page.

Making a PostScript file

Destination: Ahh, this is an interesting one. It tells the computer whether to send the document to the **printer** as usual, or to create a PostScript **file** on a disk. If you choose to save as a PostScript file, the Mac will save a *copy* of your document in a long and large text file that is nothing but PostScript command codes. If you open this PostScript file in a word processor, it will look like a bunch of gibberish: **gsave @2 load stopped not { @1 0gt { PointsAvailable @1ge / @3 @3 2 mul dup setflat store . . .**

If you need to print your document on another computer or have someone else print your document, be sure to go to Adobe's web site and read the information about Acrobat PDF, Portable Document Format.

www.adobe.com

But, you can use a "downloader" utility to send this file directly to a PostScript printer to print your pages! Why would you want to do this? Well, do you ever take your documents to a public computer, like to a copy center, to print? Do you ever take or send your documents to another computer that does not have the same fonts? Do you need to print from another computer that doesn't even have the same application you use? Does your service bureau request a PostScript file? Then make a PostScript file, take that file plus a downloader utility to the other computer and PostScript printer, and download it straight to the printer. It doesn't matter if that other computer has your application or your fonts. Too cool. You also need to make a PostScript file if you want to distill it as an Acrobat PDF file (see sidebar).

PostScript files are huge, though, especially if you choose to include all the fonts. That's your main consideration—whether you can fit it on a disk to take it somewhere else. For instance, a six-paragraph page of text in SimpleText that was 33K turned into a 439K PostScript file (including fonts).

To print a PostScript file, you need a utility like one of those shown to the right. You probably have one on your hard disk, or sometimes when you buy fonts a downloader utility comes on the disk. Just double-click it, go to the File or Utilities menu, and choose "Download PostScript file...." Find your file and click OK to send it to the printer.

Downloader utilities

Print the Window

When you are at the Finder (Desktop), you can also **print the contents of the active window** (the active window is the one with the horizontal lines in its title bar). Just click once on the window whose contents you want to print. Then from the File menu, choose "Print Window...," which is the very last item in the list (if your menu says "Print Desktop...," then you forgot to click on the window that you want to print).

If your window is showing icons, then the Mac will print the icons. Even if all the icons are not visible on the screen, all of them will print. If your window is in a list, the entire list and all the details will print, even if all the details are not visible on the screen. This comes in very handy for keeping track of what's on your removable disks—just print up a picture of the window and file it away with the disk.

Print the Desktop

You can also **print the contents of the Desktop.** Click once on any icon on the Desktop level, such as the trash can. From the File menu, choose "Print Desktop...." (It's the very last item in the list—if this item still says "Print Window...," then you have not selected the Desktop level. Try again.) The Mac will print up as many pages as necessary to display everything that is on your Desktop, excluding any open windows.

Printing from the Desktop (Finder)

Desktop printer icons: If you have a bunch of these sitting on your Desktop and you never use most of them, open your Extensions Manager (see pages 258–259) and uncheck the boxes for those printers. Then drag all their matching icons on your Desktop to the trash. Don't worry, the Mac can always make those icons again if you want them back; see page 166.

You can select one or more **documents** from the **Desktop** (Finder) and choose to **print** them, using "drag-and-drop printing." You don't have to go to the Chooser to change printers or open the file. For most items, the Mac opens the application in which the document was created, prints the files, then quits the application and returns to the Desktop. Some items, like certain types of graphics, will print without any application opening at all.

- Select the file you want to print by clicking once on it. You can select more than one file—just make sure you don't select too many files from so many *different* programs that the Mac cannot open all these applications all at once. You can usually, however, open several documents that all belong to *one* application without experiencing difficulty.
- Once the file is selected, drag it over to the printer icon on your Desktop. The icon should turn dark (highlight) as you drag it across the printer icon—if it doesn't highlight, that printer is not available for printing. Maybe your printer isn't turned on.
- The application that created the document will open and the print dialog box for that application will pop up. Set whatever print parameters you want and click on the "Print" button.

Desktop Printer Utility

Desktop Printer Utility

You can get special information about your printer through the Get Info box, such as how much memory the printer has, which fonts are installed in its ROM if it's a PostScript printer, what the status of currently printing jobs are, and more. Once your Desktop printer has been set up (see below), the Get Info box will give you a couple of extra menu options to choose from.

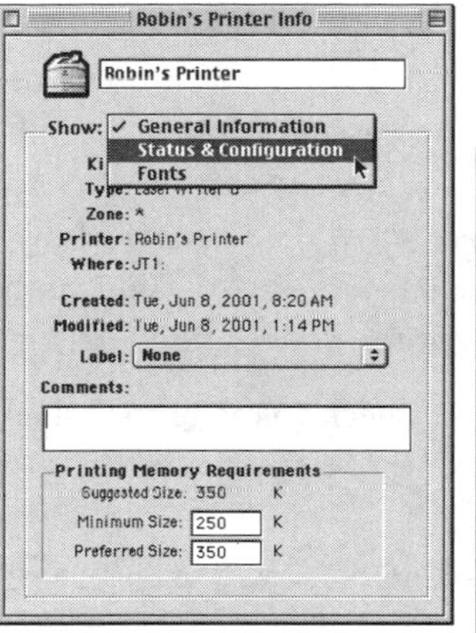

You will only see these options for your Desktop printer if it's been set up first, as explained below.

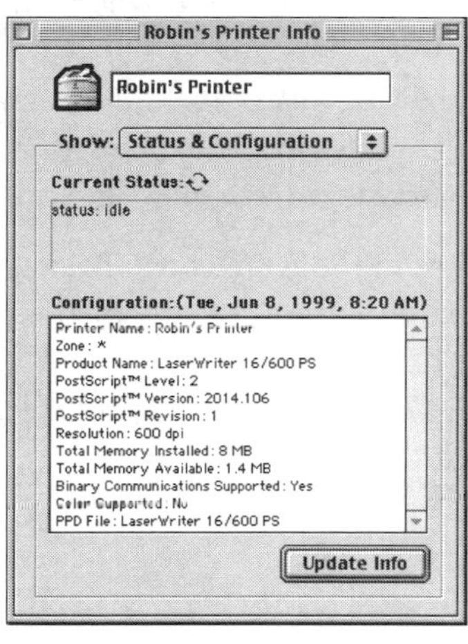

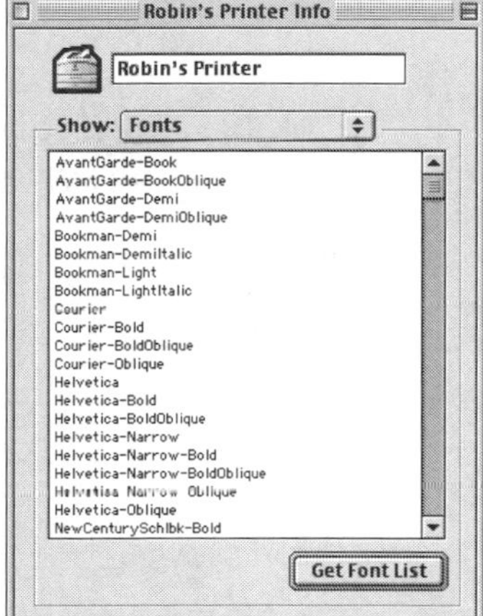

You must have version 1.2 (at least) of the Desktop Printer Utility (its icon is shown above, right). Use Sherlock's Find File to find the utility, and use Get Info (select the icon, press Command I) to see which version it is.

Double-click the utility, then from the File menu, choose "New." Click "Change" to choose a printer and a description file (if you have a PostScript printer). Then go to your Chooser, choose your printer, and click the "Setup" button. *Then* Get Info can provide the information.

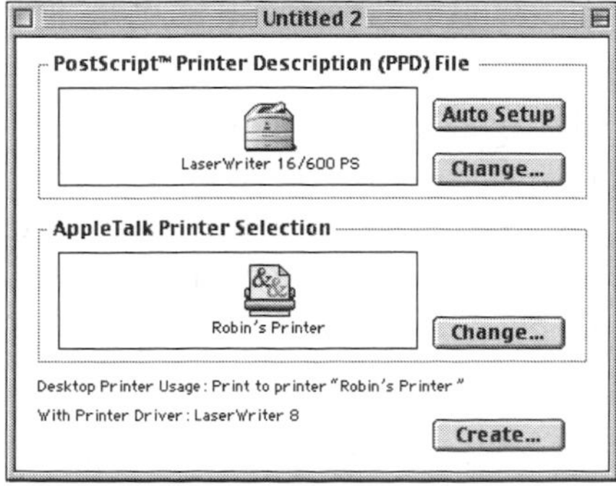

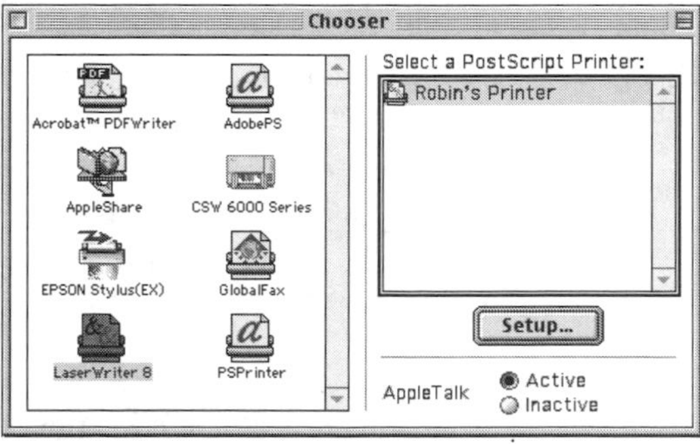

Desktop Printer Dialog Box

When you double-click on a Desktop Printer icon, the **Desktop Printer dialog box** pops up to let you control background printing (the printing that goes on in the background while you work on something else—see page 158). Desktop printing is always done in the background. Through this dialog box you can check on the status of any printing job, postpone or cancel a printing job, or set a time (the hour and the date) that you want a document to print.

Extensions you need

These two extensions must be loaded if you want to use Desktop printing.

There are two extensions that must be loaded for Desktop printing to work: the **Desktop Printer Spooler** and the **Desktop PrintMonitor.** Check the Extensions Manager to see if they are loaded: from the Apple menu, slide down to Control Panels and out to Extensions Manager. Find those two files in the list under "Extensions" and make sure there is a checkmark next to them. If not, check the boxes and restart.

While you're in the Extensions Manager, check to make sure there is a checkmark next to the name of the printer driver you want to use. Every printer driver you check will appear in the Chooser and you can make a Desktop Printer icon for it. Of course, it's usually silly to check printer drivers for printers you don't have.

Creating a Desktop Printer icon

You can have more than one Desktop Printer icon. In fact, you can have one for every printer driver you have loaded: go to the Chooser and pick a printer, then close the Chooser. The icons act like any other icons on your Desktop: you can move them around, trash them (although you do have to have at least one—the Mac won't let you trash the last one), rename them, make aliases, etc.

Opening the Desktop Printer Dialog Box

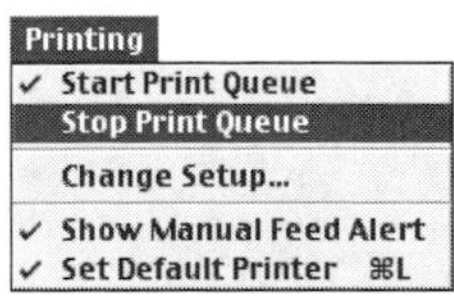

After you have started printing a document, go back to the Desktop and double-click on the Desktop Printer icon. The file(s) you sent to print will be listed in the dialog box in order of scheduled printing, with the one in progress listed in the top portion. You can close the Desktop Printer dialog box anytime without affecting your printing job.

While the dialog box is open, a new menu, "Printing," appears on the Desktop. It allows you to "Stop Print Queue" (which doesn't permanently cancel jobs—it just puts all the printing jobs on hold) and "Start Print Queue." These two commands affect *all* of the print jobs listed in the queue. The choice "Set Default Printer" allows you to select a Desktop Printer icon as the default printer without having to go to the Chooser.

You can also get a similar menu by holding down the Control key and clicking on the Desktop Printer icon, as shown to the left.

Flashing Application menu

If you see the **Application menu** start flashing during a print job, or a diamond next to any name in the Application menu, or if a warning sign appears over your Desktop Printer icon, that's a **visual clue** that there's a problem with the printing process. Click on the Application menu and select the Finder—often this will give you a message letting you know what the problem is. Double-clicking on the Desktop Printer icon also may tell you what's going on.

Desktop Printer visual clues

A dark border means this is the default Desktop Printer.

*This Desktop Printer is **not** chosen for printing.*

A document is being printed on this printer.

This printer is no longer available.

The print queue has been stopped.

There is a problem with the print job.

Example of a Desktop Printer Dialog Box

*These four little print buttons affect whichever print job is **selected**, whether it is in progress or in the queue. See below for what they do.*

This print job is currently in progress.

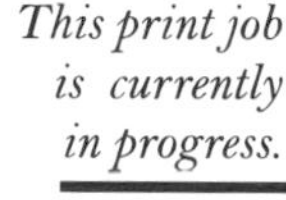

*I clicked on this print job to select it, so now **it** is the one that will be affected by any commands to hold, resume, remove, etc.*

*Click on these column headers to arrange your list accordingly. This will **not** change the order in which the documents print.*

These two print jobs are in the queue—they have to wait until after the one in progress finishes before they can go. You can rearrange the order of this list—and the order in which documents print— by dragging the icons up and down the queue.

Print Buttons

Hold: *Puts the selected job on hold until you click the Resume button.*

Resume: *Select a job on hold and click this button to restart the printing process.*

Remove: *Moves a job to the trash, canceling it. It does not trash your original file!*

Set Time: *Lets you set the time a print job should start, as well as designate an "urgent" job.*

1. Put the tasks below in the proper order for printing to a new printer for the first time:

   A. From the File menu, choose "Page Setup...," then click OK.
   B. Choose the name of the printer.
   C. Customize any specifications necessary in the Print dialog box, such as the number of copies or the range of pages. Click OK.
   D. Open the document you want to print.
   E. Turn on the printer.
   F. Choose the printer driver.
   G. From the File menu, choose "Print...."
   H. Close the Chooser.
   I. From the File menu, choose "Chooser."
   J. Click the Setup button, if there is one, choose Auto Setup, click OK.

2. Why would the cursor and typing sometimes get jumpy and fidgety while your pages are printing?

3. Is it the QuickDraw or the PostScript printer that is actually a specialized computer?

4. What size is "computer paper"?

5. At the Desktop, when you choose to "Print Window...," which window gets printed?

6. How do you open the Desktop Printer dialog box to monitor a print job in progress?

7. What's the difference between clicking the "Hold" button and choosing "Stop Print Queue"?

Answers on page 424.

17 Closing and Quitting

There is a big and important difference between **closing** and **quitting.** You *close* a *document*, but you *quit* an *application*. This is an extremely vital concept to get, so don't skip this short chapter.

Quit vs. Close

At first it seems a bit confusing—what's the big deal, **quitting** or **closing.** Either way, you're finished, right? Wrong.

Essentially, this is what happens: Say you open your word processing application— that is comparable to putting a typewriter on your desk. Then you start a new document—that is comparable to putting a piece of paper in the typewriter.

When you choose "Close" from the File menu, that is comparable to taking the piece of paper out of the typewriter. The typewriter, though, is still on the desk! And on the Mac, both the desk and the "typewriter" are rather invisible. You might *think* the typewriter is gone.

But the typewriter—the word processor—stays on the desk (in the computer's *memory,* called *RAM*) until you physically put the word processor away. When you choose "Quit" from the File menu, that is comparable to putting the typewriter away.

If you leave too many applications open without quitting, the memory on your Mac gets full and you'll get "out of memory" errors, you might not be able to print or copy files, and your computer will crash.

Closing a Document

When you are finished working on a document, you can **close that document** window by clicking in its close box or by choosing "Close" from the File menu. Either way, you are just *closing the document* (putting away the paper) and *the application (the software program) is still open and taking up memory.* You still see the menu belonging to the application, even though the rest of your screen may look just like your Desktop, and even if you see windows that belong to other programs or to the Desktop!

> **Tip:** If you just *closed* a document window and now you see "Special" in your menu, it does not necessarily mean you *quit* the program—you have just *closed,* but not *quit.* If you click anywhere on your screen, you will pop into the Finder/Desktop, deluding you into thinking you have quit the application!

Choose to close when you are finished with a document and want to start another, or perhaps when you know you are going to come back to this application later.

> **Tip:** Usually the keyboard shortcut to close a document is **Command W,** just like closing a Desktop window.

Quitting an Application

To **quit an application,** you must choose the Quit command. This is always done from the File menu, and "Quit" is always the very last item. In every program you can use the keyboard shortcut: **Command Q.**

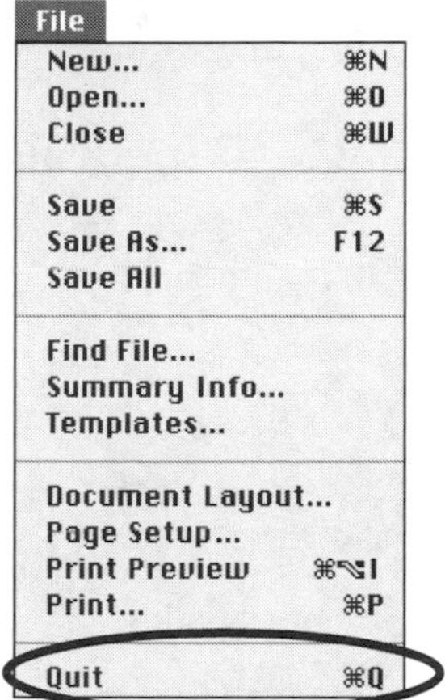

The item "Quit" is always the last command in the File menu. If you don't see Quit in the File menu, you are probably at the Desktop/Finder.

If you haven't saved all of your changes in any of the open documents, the Mac will politely ask if you want to save them at this point, whether you are closing or quitting. Thank goodness.

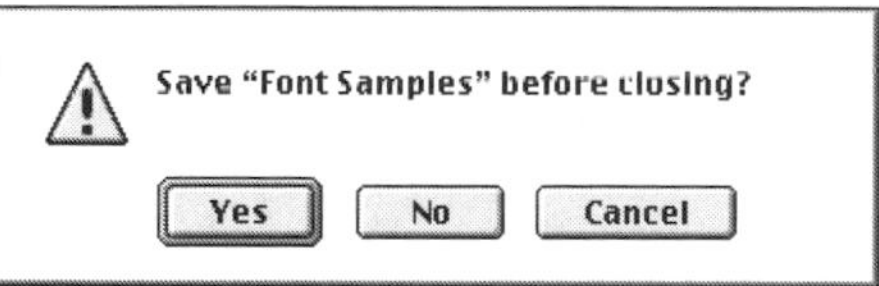

If you click **Yes** and you haven't yet even saved the document with a name, you'll usually get the "Save As..." dialog box (page 148) to name the document before quitting, because nothing can be saved without a name. You can hit the Return or Enter key to hit the Yes button.

Click the **No** button if you decide at this point you don't want the changes (or the document, if you've never named it). Often you can type the letter N instead of actually clicking the No button.

Click **Cancel** to return to your document without saving any changes. You can always press Command Period to cancel.

Once you have quit, the application is removed from the computer's memory. **Quit when you are finished working in the application for the day** (or if you are running out of memory—see page 322).

If you're not sure if you have quit your applications or not:

Check the Application menu, the tiny icon and/or the name on the far right of the menu bar. Any application name that appears in the list (besides "Finder") *is still open in memory.* Choose that name, then press Command Q to quit, even if you don't see the application anywhere! Trust me. For more details, read Chapter 19.

This Application menu tells me PageMaker is open.

Circle the correct answer to these questions:

close	**quit**	**1.** To put away a document.
close	**quit**	**2.** To put away an application.
close	**quit**	**3.** Press Command W.
close	**quit**	**4.** Press Command Q.
close	**quit**	**5.** Take the "paper" out of the "typewriter."
close	**quit**	**6.** Put the "typewriter" away.

Use this illustration to answer the rest of these questions:

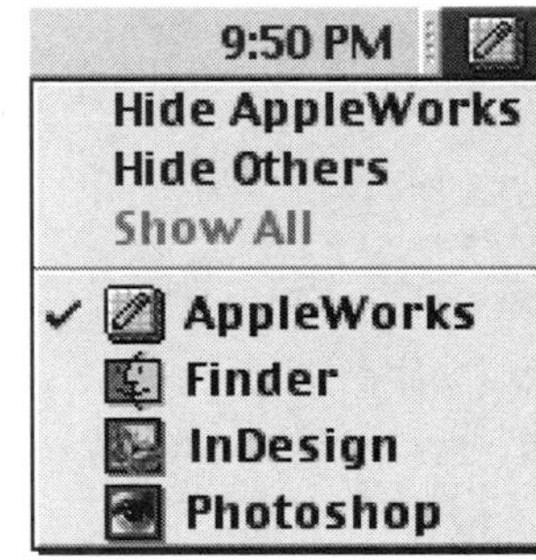

7. What is this menu called, and where do you find it?

. . . .

8. How many applications (besides the Finder) are open at the moment?

. . . .

9. Which application is "active" at the moment?

. . . .

10. Describe how to quit Photoshop.

. . . .

. . . .

Answers on page 425.

18 Ejecting Disks

Disks go in and disks come out. Sometimes they don't come out. Sometimes they get stuck. Sometimes they won't "mount," which means their icon doesn't show up on the Desktop This short section covers all the tricks to getting floppy disks, removable hard disks, and CDs in and out of your Macintosh.

Ejecting a Removable Disk

There are actually several ways to **eject a removable disk**, some of which are preferable to others. These techniques work for ejecting any removable disks you might use, such as floppies, Zip, Jaz, or Syquest disks, or CDs. Also check page 177 for extra notes.

Shut Down

Also see page 169.

If you are done for the day and are planning to **shut down** the whole system, then close up all your windows (a quick shortcut is to press Command Option W). From the Special menu choose "Shut Down." This will close any open applications, eject any floppy disks and most removable hard disks and CDs, and turn off the computer.

Ejecting from the menu or the keyboard shortcut

Even if you're not ready to shut down, you may sometimes need to eject a floppy disk or removable hard disk to trade it with another, or simply to take your disk and go away. One way is to select the disk (click once on it) and choose "Eject" from the Special menu (or use the shortcut **Command E**). This will spit out the disk.

Ejecting a disk through the trash

Another simple and effective method—and more frequently used—is to eject your disk through the trash.

Aack, you say! Yes, that's a frightening thought, but calm down; it's quite all right. *The trash can doesn't erase anything off your disk.* First make sure you have closed any documents and quit any applications that you used on that disk. Then simply **press on the disk icon, drag it down to the trash, and put it in.** Floppy disks and removable hard disks will safely pop out. Here is the shortcut:

- Select the disk (click once on it).
- From the File menu, choose "Put Away,"
  or use the keyboard shortcut **Command Y.**

Ejecting a disk using a contextual menu

The third easy method of ejecting a disk is to hold down the **Control key and click** on the disk. A contextual menu will pop up—one of the choices is to eject the disk.

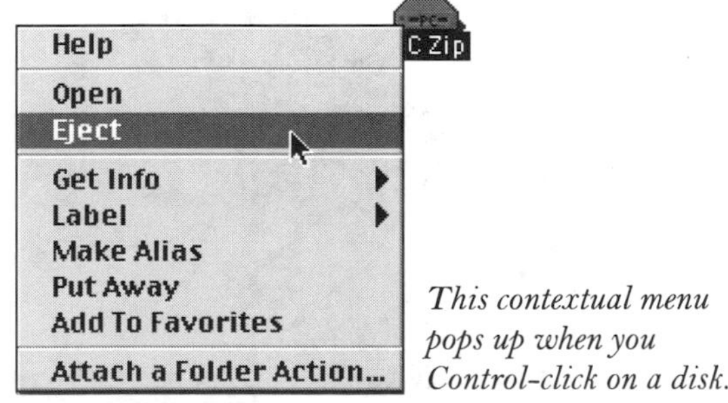

This contextual menu pops up when you Control-click on a disk.

“Save As…” and “Open” **dialog boxes** give you options to eject a disk. When you’re working in an application and want to eject a disk, just choose “Open…” even though you don’t really want to open a new document. Then:

- Click the Desktop button.
- Click once on the name of the disk you want to eject, then click on “Eject.”
- After you take it out, click the Cancel button to get back to your document.

Ejecting a disk through dialog boxes

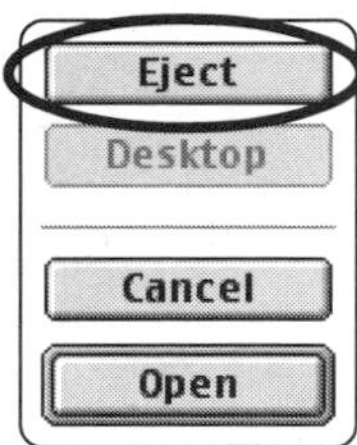

Click on Eject to kick out the disk you have selected.

After ejecting a disk through this dialog box, you can of course insert a new disk if you like. If something from the ejected disk is still open on the computer, though, the Mac will ask for the ejected disk again so it can put it away; after you replace the disk, the Mac will do what it needs and the disk will pop out again so you can put the new one in.

You may notice when you eject a disk with this method that a gray version of the icon stays on the screen. That’s because the memory of this disk is still in RAM (in *memory,* see page 144). If someone else comes along to use this machine while the gray icon is still showing, when they insert their disk the Mac will very often kick theirs out and ask for the one that just left. That’s not a problem if the disk is sitting on the desk, but if Mary took that disk and left for a meeting in Chicago, then you may have a problem.

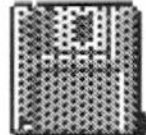

Gray disk icon left on the screen after being ejected through a dialog box.

Try this!

If the computer asks you to insert a disk and you don’t have it, try pressing **Command Period.** This will often force that rude question to disappear. You may need to do it a few times, along with clicking OK to a dialog box or two. You can try dragging that gray disk icon to the trash, but sometimes even then you’ll get that dialog box asking for it to be inserted.

If the message won’t go away with Command Period and you don’t have the disk (the disk must be named exactly the same and have exactly the same data on it—you can’t fool the System), *then the only thing you can do is restart the computer!* (See next page.)

Restart When you restart the computer, it usually ejects any disk in any drive.

- ▼ Try this: hold down the Command and Control keys, then while those two keys are down, push the Power button (the button you turned the computer on with).
- ▼ If you have a **Restart button** on the front, side, or back of your computer (it's the button on your computer *box*—not your monitor or keyboard) with a tiny triangle on it, push that.
- ▼ If you have an **iMac,** you'll have to push the little button on the side of the machine, the tiny button marked with a tiny triangle inside that little door where you plug things in. On older iMacs, you have to straighten a paper clip and push it in that tiny hole marked with the triangle.

If you cannot restart (which is rare), then you have to turn off the computer. There is a button on either the back (usually) or the front (sometimes) of the Macintosh, or on some iMac monitors (on some iMacs, the button on the monitor will put the computer to sleep; on others it will shut down). When you find the power button, just push it; on certain Mac models you have to hold the button down to the count of five before it shuts down the computer. Wait a minute before you turn it back on. (See page 418 for more details.)

Mounting and Unmounting You may hear talk of **mounting** and **unmounting** disks, rather than inserting and ejecting them. The terms *mount* and *unmount* refer to hard disks (internal or external), floppy disks, removable hard disks, and CDs. It is possible and very common to have more than one hard disk attached to your computer. You probably have removable hard disks that you insert into a cartridge drive sort of like inserting a video tape into a VCR (Zip or Jaz). But even though the hard disk is attached to the computer or you have inserted a disk into a drive, that does not guarantee that its icon will show up on the screen. If the icon does not appear (which means the computer cannot "read" the disk), we say that the disk did not *mount.* (You can sometimes hear power users muttering under their bated breath as they wait that suspenseful moment for the computer to find and read the disk, "Mount, baby, mount." Why is it suspenseful? Because sometimes they don't.)

Removing CDs and removable hard disks

Removable hard disks do not always eject like floppy disks. Most removable hard disks and CDs must be *unmounted* before they can be removed from their drives.

To remove a CD:

- Drag the icon to the trash to unmount it. Your CD will most likely pop out. With some older drives, you might have to push the button near the CD slot to eject the disk after it is unmounted.

To remove a cartridge hard disk:

- Drag the icon to the trash to unmount it—for **Zip disks,** this is all you need to do. Press the button to eject an unmounted **Jaz disk.**
- **Syquest disks** will not pop out by themselves. After it's unmounted, push the button on the drive to stop the disk from spinning. **Wait** until it stops spinning completely. Push the little lever to the side; hold your hand in front of the drive slot to catch the cartridge as it comes flying out.

Something is Still in Use?

If, when you eject a disk, you get a message telling you something is still in use and you don't think it's true, check this: did you read a ReadMe File or something similar? Did you open fonts directly from the disk? Check the Application menu to see which applications are still open (click on the tiny icon in the far-right of your menu bar); select any application listed, then quit. If you loaded fonts, close them.

The Mouse Trick

If for some reason, perhaps because of a power outage or a system error, when you turn off the computer your floppy disk is still inside, do this:

> Hold down the mouse button. *Keep holding it down* and turn the computer back on; your disk(s) should pop out like toast.

The Paperclip Trick

If all else fails, notice that tiny hole next to the floppy drive, the Zip drive, or the CD slot? That's paperclip size. Unbend a paperclip and push it in. It's pretty safe, as all you're doing is releasing the mechanism that holds the disk in place—push firmly.

1. When you shut down your System, what happens to removable disks that are still in your drives?

2. What are three easy ways (other than shutting down) to eject a disk?

3. Say you inserted a floppy disk and read the ReadMe file on it. You closed the ReadMe file, but now when you eject the disk you get a message telling you the disk cannot be put away because something is still in use. What do you do?

4. What does it mean to say a disk or CD didn't "mount"?

5. What are two keyboard shortcuts to eject a floppy disk or unmount a hard disk or CD?

6. If you eject a disk by going to a Save As dialog box, selecting the name of the disk, and clicking "Eject," what happens?

7. If someone ejected a disk and then left the room, but they left a gray icon of the disk on the computer, what are the steps to take to get rid of the gray icon?

   First, I would:

   If that didn't work, I would:

   If that didn't work, I would:

   If that didn't work, I would:

Answers on page 425.

19 Shutting Down

Shutting down is the computer's process of tying up all the loose ends inside of itself and "parking" the hard disk before it's turned off. It is certainly possible to turn the computer off without going through the **Shut Down** process, but you run the risk of losing data and possibly damaging mysterious but important elements. At the very least, turning off your Mac without choosing Shut Down leaves your computer in an unstable state. So follow this simple ritual when you are finished for the day!

Good Housekeeping

When you're done with the Macintosh, it's good housekeeping to close up all your windows on the Desktop. Press Command Option W (or Option-click on a close box) and every open Desktop window will fly away home. This is an especially nice thing to do if more than one person uses the machine, because any windows left open when you shut down will reopen the next time the computer is turned on.

However, if you don't have to share your computer with anyone, you can take advantage of these windows staying where you left them and perhaps leave your nice, neatly organized hard disk window open so when you return to the Mac you can skip the step of double-clicking the hard disk icon to get to your files. Or leave open the folder that contains the project you will be working on for the next several days (remember, you can also change that folder into a pop-up window and store it at the bottom of your screen).

Quitting All Applications

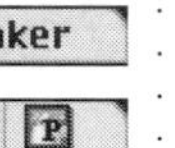

The tiny icon on the upper, far-right of the menu bar changes, providing a **visual clue** *as to which application you are currently using. The name of the application might also be showing (if it isn't, drag that little dividing bar to the left).*

Before you shut down, check to make sure you have quit from all your *applications:*

- Press on the Application menu, which is the icon in the far upper-right of the menu bar (the *menu bar,* not the Desktop; look *above* the icon of your hard disk).
- Look at the bottom portion of that menu. If there is any name at all listed besides "Finder," it means *that application is still open.* There is a checkmark next to the application that is currently active.
- To quit any other open application, select it from this Application menu. It may seem that nothing whatsoever happened and you are thinking, "So what?" *But something did happen!* Trust me. Look at your menu bar. I'll bet it's different than it was a few seconds ago. And in the far right of the menu bar, the tiny icon has changed. *Even though you may see no other indication of your application*—no window, no document, in fact, you may see windows from *other* applications—*the application you chose from the Application menu is open and ready.* Really.

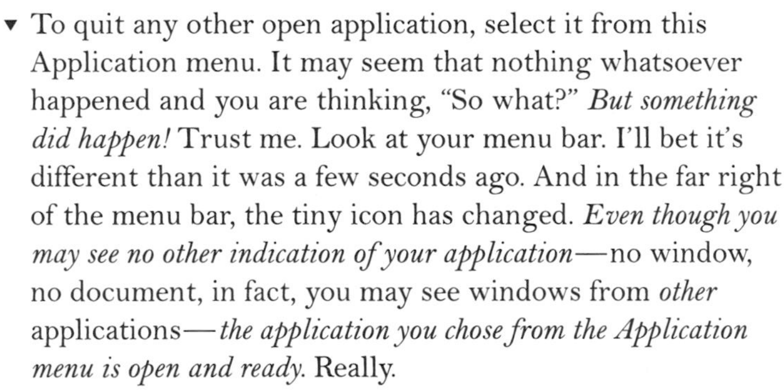

  If this confuses you, be sure to read Chapter 29. For now, though, proceed to the next step.

Notice there is a checkmark next to AppleWorks, and there's a AppleWorks icon in the upper-right, both **visual clues** *telling you what is still open.*

- So now you're in the open application. From the File menu choose "Quit," which should be the very last item. (If the File menu does not have "Quit," then you probably clicked on the Desktop which popped you back to the Finder. *Don't scream.* Check the Application menu again.)
- Repeat this process for each program listed in the Application menu (except the Finder).

Shut Down

Now from the Special menu choose **Shut Down.** Actually, to tell the honest truth, if you leave any applications or documents open, the Mac takes care of putting them away, asking if you want to save any unsaved documents. But I do believe that you need to know what is going on so you can be in control.

When you shut down, any disks will pop out and any extra hard disks will unmount. On most Macs, "Shut Down" will automatically turn off the computer. If you are using an older Mac, you'll get a reassuring dialog box that says you can now turn off your computer safely. In that case, turn it off with the same button you turned it on with.

The **Power key** (the key you pushed to turn the computer on) will also Shut Down your Mac. Fortunately for those with small children and cats, the Mac will ask if you want to save any documents before it turns everything off. Click "Cancel" if hitting this button was a mistake. On some Macs, the Power key can be turned into a Sleep button to it just puts the computer to sleep instead of shutting it down. See page 262 for details.

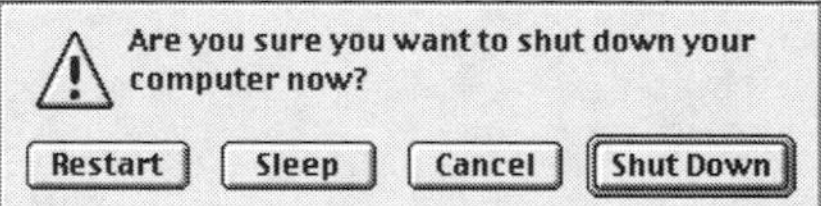

When you press the Power key to shut down, this message usually pops up, depending on which Mac you have. You can hit the Return or the Enter key instead of clicking the "Shut Down" button.

Improper Shut Down

If you turn off your computer without shutting down, for whatever reason, you will get a reprimand when you turn it back on. You can disable this announcement through the General Controls control panel—uncheck the box for "Warn me if computer was shut down improperly" (see page 245 for more info on the control panel).

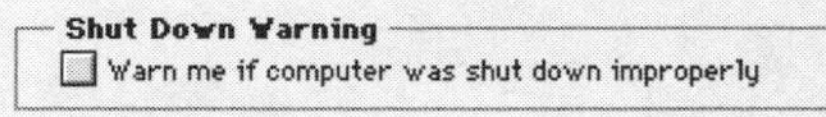

This is the box to uncheck if you don't want to see that warning.

1. In the illustration above, how many applications are still open (not including the Finder)?

2. Describe how to quit each of the open applications you see in the Application menu, above.

3. What will happen if you choose "Shut Down" from the Special menu before you have quit each application?

4. What is the keyboard shortcut to close all of your Desktop windows?

5. What happens when you press the Power key when your computer is already on?

Answers on page 425.

PART TWO

Beyond the Basics

This section explains features of the Macintosh beyond the basic things you need to know just to get your work done. Many of the items in this section are for customizing your Mac, making your work much easier, and helping you to be more efficient. Everything in this section is important for you to understand, but you may want to take it in small chunks. For instance, read through the Desk Accessories chapter and play with each of the desk accessories. Then in a couple of days read about the Apple menu and aliases, and make some aliases to put into your Apple menu. Next week spend some time with Sherlock. Oh, you have many treasures to discover!

20 System Folder

The **System Folder** is a powerful thing. It's in charge of running your Mac, and a great number of items work simply because they are inside the System Folder. Many things will *not* work if they are *not* stored in your System Folder.

The blessed System Folder.

This folder is so special because it contains the System file and the Finder file, as we talked about in Chapter 2. If either the System or the Finder are not in the System Folder, the folder's icon changes, as shown to the right. We affectionately refer to the System Folder with the icon as the "blessed" (two syllables) System Folder.

Oh no—this System Folder is not blessed! This is a ***visual clue*** *that either the System or the Finder is missing.*

Important: The System Folder is a critical part of the functioning of your Macintosh, and you should never put anything inside of this folder unless you know for absolutely, positively, certain that it really truly belongs there. And if you are a student in a school computer lab: **don't touch the System Folder.**

What's in the System Folder?

If you take a look inside the **System Folder,** you'll see other important folders; each folder takes care of some detail of working on the computer.

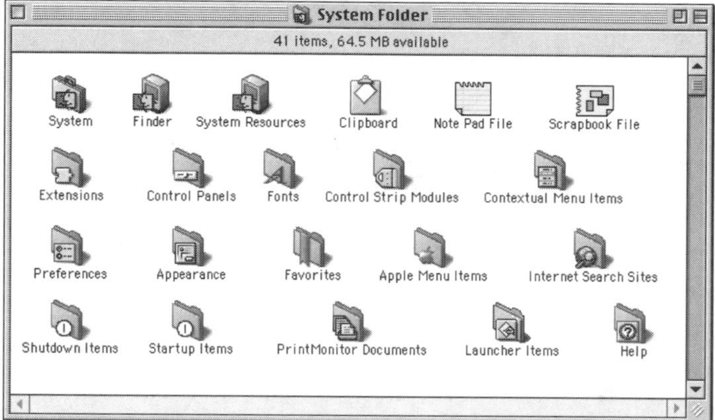

Notice the information bar tells us there are 41 items in this folder, plus the vertical scroll bar is gray. Both of these **visual clues** *indicate that at the moment there is a lot more stuff in here than you're seeing, like items from applications or other utilities.*

(I tend to hide what I don't need or don't understand—I "shove it under the bed" by rolling the window up. This way when I look at this window I feel like I know what I'm doing.)

You can read this chapter later!

You can live a long time without knowing much about every folder and file inside the System Folder. Eventually you will need to know just what some of these folders are and what they do so you can be in control, but if you are feeling the least bit overwhelmed, let go of this and come back some other day.

On the following pages are some of the icons and folders you will see in your System Folder:

System File

The **System file** (the *file* that actually runs your Mac, as opposed to the System *Folder*, in which the System *file* is stored) opens up to a window when you double-click on it, just like any other folder or suitcase on your hard disk. Inside you'll see icons for sounds and probably for various keyboard layouts. Double-click on any sound icon to hear it.

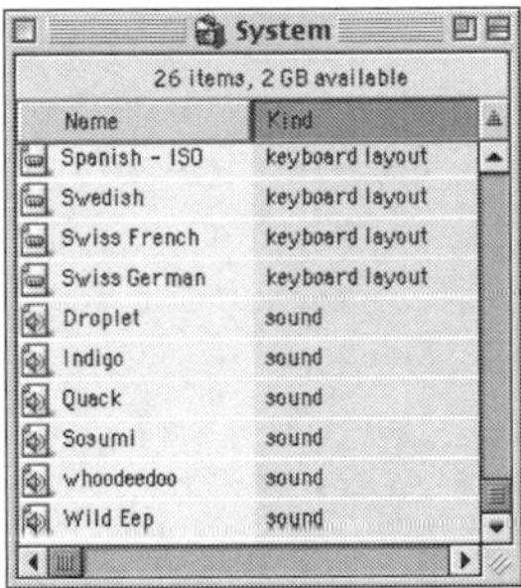

You can safely toss any of the keyboard layouts for languages you think you will never use, such as Flemish or Swiss German.

When you make new sounds through your Sound control panel (page 252), the Mac puts the sound in this System file. (That's why you don't have "whoodeedoo" in your System file—I made it myself.)

Don't let those simple icons fool you into thinking this is all the System file does—those sounds and keyboard layouts may take up a total of about 200 kilobytes of space, but if you check the Get Info window for the System file, you'll find it weighs around 12 to 20 megabytes! All the rest of the invisible stuff is for the inner magic that makes the machine work. The System *file* must remain inside the System *Folder* or you will not be able to start the computer!

Finder

The **Finder** is the program that runs the Desktop and keeps track of all your files. This icon is just as important as the System file, and it must stay in the System Folder or you won't be able to start the Mac! If you try to open the Finder icon, you'll just get a message telling you it's none of your business. (Well, not exactly those words.)

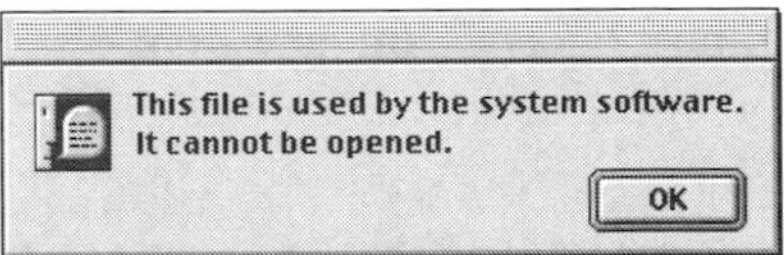

This is the message you'll get if you double-click the Finder icon to try to see what's inside.

System Resources

You probably have a file called **Enabler** or **System Resources** in your System Folder, one or the other depending on exactly which operating system you have running in your Mac. Whichever one you have, it helps the System do its job. There's nothing you can personally do with these files, but definitely do not ever try to throw either one away.

Clipboard and Scrapbook File

Clipboard

Scrapbook File

The **Clipboard** and the **Scrapbook File** are stored in your System Folder. The Clipboard *temporarily* stores text, graphics, or sounds that you "cut" or "copy" so you can "paste" them somewhere else. The Scrapbook *permanently* holds text, graphics, or sounds so you can paste them somewhere else. Although you see these files here in your System Folder and you can double-click on either icon to see what is stored within each file, you don't actually use them from here. See pages 220–221 for details on exactly how to use the Scrapbook, and pages 138–139 for how to use the Clipboard.

Note Pad File

Note Pad File

The **Note Pad File** appears after the first time you use the Note Pad "desk accessory" from the Apple menu. The chapter on *Desk Accessories,* page 218, describes in detail how to use the Note Pad. You don't actually use this file here in the System Folder; you *can* open this Note Pad and type messages into it, but typically you will actually get and use it from the Apple menu without going into the System Folder.

Control Panels

Control Panels

The **Control Panels folder** holds the tiny programs called "control panels" that let you customize your Mac and the features of many utilities. With the control panels you can alter your Desktop pattern, set the mouse speed, control the repeat rate of the keys on your keyboard, change the number of colors displayed on your monitor, and many other things. Because control panels are so important and you will eventually be getting into this folder often, you should read Chapter 24 (after you're feeling comfortable with your Mac).

Control Panels (Disabled)

You can choose which control panels to use through the Extensions Manager (also explained in Chapter 24). When you choose not to use one, that control panel is automatically sent to this folder named **Control Panels (Disabled)** where it stays until you want it again.

Apple Menu Items Folder

Apple Menu Items

The **Apple Menu Items folder** contains the icons of every item on your Apple menu (the menu on the far left of the menu bar). The Apple menu is a key to organizing your work and making your life simpler and happier. You can put documents, programs, folders, desk accessories, web addresses—anything you like—in your Apple menu by dragging icons or aliases to this folder. See Chapter 23 for details on how to customize your Apple menu, and see Chapter 22 for details on desk accessories.

Startup Items Folder

The **Startup Items folder** can be very handy. Any document, program, or folder that you store in the Startup Items folder will automatically open each time you start your Mac. (Use "aliases," though—see Chapter 25 on Aliases.) This is great, for instance, if you are busy for weeks on the same project—every time you turn on your computer, you can have that particular project open automatically for you, or at least the folder that contains all the files. Or put an alias of your hard disk icon in here and then every time you turn on your Mac your hard disk window will open.

You can also put sound files in the Startup Items folder, and when the startup process gets to the Desktop, this sound will play. If your Mac arrived with a microphone, it is extraordinarily easy to make your own sounds (see page 255). You could leave sweet messages for your lover or reminders to your kids, but of course you would never leave a nasty sound to surprise and terrify that boss you don't like.

In Chapter 24 on Control Panels (pages 258–259) you'll learn how to use the Extensions Manager to turn things on and off. If you choose to turn off a Startup Item, that item gets sent to the folder named **Startup Items (Disabled).** The item waits there until you turn it back on again, so don't throw this folder away!

Shutdown Items Folder

The **Shutdown Items folder** is just like the Startup Items folder mentioned above in that anything in this folder will activate when you Shutdown. There aren't a whole lot of things that you want to start when you're shutting down. It's a good place for personalized goodbye sounds. My machine says, "Ooooh, baby baby, goodbyyyye!" You can add any sound you create or capture using the Sound control panel (see page 254). When you make a sound, the Mac creates an icon for it. Put that icon into the Shutdown Items folder and it will play when you shut down.

In Chapter 24 on Control Panels, you'll learn how to use the Extensions Manager to turn things on and off. If you choose to turn off a Shutdown Item, that item gets sent to the folder named **Shutdown Items (Disabled).** The item waits there until you turn it back on again, so don't throw this folder away!

Extensions Folder

The **Extensions folder** holds certain System-related files that help run your Mac or your peripheral equipment. These "system extensions" must be stored in the Extensions folder or they won't work. This folder also contains utilities that let you share files on a network. See page 193, "Installing Files into the System Folder," for details on how to tell if something belongs in the Extensions folder.

In Chapter 24 on Control Panels (pages 258–259) you'll learn how to use the Extensions Manager to turn things on and off. If you choose to turn off an extension, that item gets sent to the folder named **Extensions (Disabled).** The item waits there until you turn it back on again, so don't throw this folder away!

Preferences Folder

The **Preferences folder** contains files that have settings about how your programs think you want them to work. You can't open the files in this folder because they're created by your programs. You don't have to put anything in here yourself—your application program and the Mac will take care of that.

Appearance Folder

The **Appearance folder** is where the Mac stores the files that customize the look of your Desktop, the sounds things make (like the sounds of windows "rolling" up, items dragging and dropping, or buttons being clicked), the background pictures, the themes you create, etc. When you get to know your Mac really well you can add items, such as background pictures, to this folder to customize its look even further.

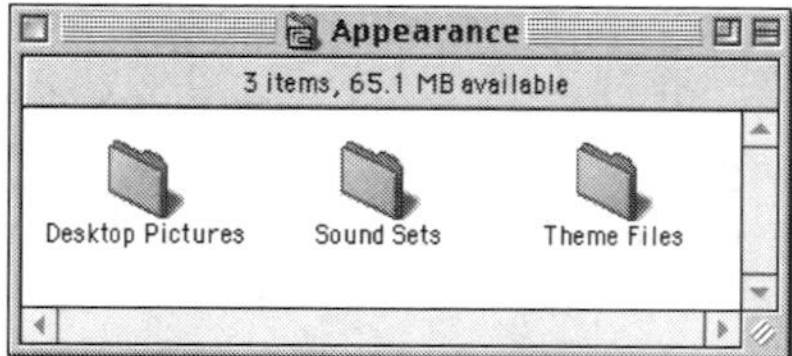

If you have your own photographs you want to use as background pictures, open the "Desktop Pictures" folder you see here, and put your photos in the "Photos" folder. Then use the Appearance control panel as described in Chapter 24.

Contextual Menu Items Folder

This is a contextual menu plug-in that's stored in the folder.

The **Contextual Menu Items folder** contains small files, some called "plug-ins," that provide useful and fun options in the contextual menus, as described on page 56. A certain number of these come with your System. Some applications install plug-ins into this folder so you have special options for that application. You can find more contextual menu plug-ins online, download them, drop them into this folder, restart, and your contextual menus will have more to offer.

Help Folder

The **Help folder** contains files that provide the answers to just about any questions you have about your Mac. See Chapter 36 for details on how to use Help. Don't throw this folder away!

Favorites Folder

The **Favorites folder** stores all of your "favorite" files, web addresses, applications, folders, etc., that you have chosen as favorites. Each of the items in the Favorites folder is an alias (a pointer to the actual file). When you want to remove items from the list of favorites, you can always open this folder and delete anything you see; since everything is an alias, you will not be deleting the original file or folder! See page 228 for more details about this folder and its purpose.

Internet Search Sites Folder

The **Internet Search Sites folder** works with Sherlock, the Mac's robust file-searching program that can find items not only on your disks, but also on the Internet. If you've used Sherlock (Chapter 26), you've probably noticed that Sherlock finds a lot of web site addresses from a variety of different search engines. That's because it keeps track of the database files from those particular search engines, as shown in this folder. See Chapter 26 for details on how to update these files so you can search more efficiently.

While you're browsing the web you might see buttons or links on search engines that refer to Sherlock—these are usually files you can download, drop into the appropriate folder in this Internet Search Sites folder, and thus expand Sherlock's capability to find things on the Internet. Sherlock can also go to the Internet and find updates for itself. See Chapter 26 for details.

This is what's inside the folder. The different "channels" are organized by folder. To the right you see the contents of the Shopping folder.

PrintMonitor Documents Folder

The **PrintMonitor Documents folder** holds files waiting to be printed. You never put a document in here yourself—under certain conditions, the Mac will try to send a file to the printer but for some reason it can't make it at the moment, or you might tell the Mac to print it at a later, specified time. If so, the computer stores a temporary copy of the file in the PrintMonitor Documents folder until it can complete the job. You can ignore this folder completely (but don't throw it away).

Fonts Folder

The **Fonts folder** is where all fonts, including TrueType and both parts of PostScript fonts, are stored. If you're interested, the next chapter tells more than you ever wanted to know about fonts on the Macintosh.

Launcher Items Folder

The **Launcher Items folder** is where you put aliases of the files and applications that you want to show up in the Launcher, if you use it. You can also rearrange existing Launcher items from here, or delete those you don't need. For full details on how to work with and customize the Launcher, see pages 248–249.

Control Strip Modules Folder

The **Control Strip Modules folder** is where you place any Control Strip modules (duh) that you want to appear in your Control Strip, that little retractable strip that might appear in the bottom-left corner of your screen. For details, see page 260.

All Other Folders

As you've surely noticed, there is a lot more stuff in that System Folder. Most of it is important for one thing or another, so it is very difficult to know what you can toss and what must stay. If you don't absolutely positively know you can toss it, then leave it.

Easier Access to Folders You Use Often

If you find you are using your Apple Menu Items folder regularly, or the Startup Items, Launcher Items, Appearance, or the Favorites folders, or that you often use certain desk accessories, you can create aliases, or substitutes, of these files and put the aliases someplace where they are easier to access instead of digging into the System Folder. You could put an alias of the Favorites folder on the Desktop, for instance, so you can easily organize the items you designate as Favorites. The files you put into the alias folder will actually drop into the real folder. See Chapter 25 on *Aliases* for details.

Installing Files into the System Folder

When you're ready to add or **install** something to your Mac's system, like a font, desk accessory, new control panel, contextual menu plug-in, Internet search site update, or an extension,* don't worry about which folder it is supposed to be stored in. Here's what to do:

- Select the file or files you want to install. (To select more than one file in the same folder, click once on the first icon, then hold the Shift key down and click on other icons.)
- Press-and-drag the icon(s) to your *closed* System Folder (as shown to the right).
- The Mac will ask if it's OK to put the item in the appropriate folder. Yes, it's OK. Let the Mac figure out which folder it belongs in. If you have several different sorts of files, the Mac will put each one where it belongs, then tell you where they were placed. How thoughtful. Thank you very much.

*Drag the files and drop them on top of this **closed** folder icon, **not** to the open window of the System Folder.*

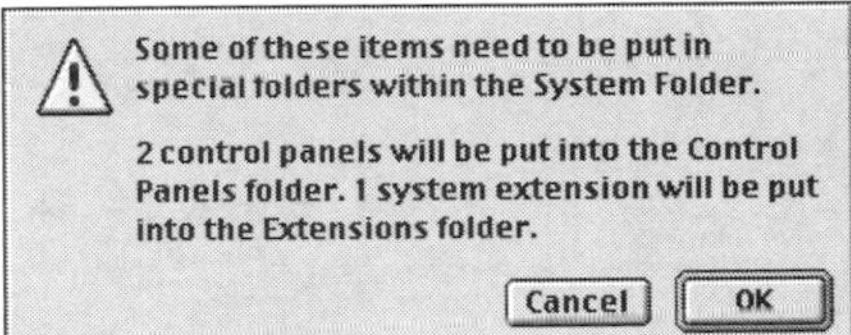

This is the message you will see when you drop something on top of the System Folder and the Mac knows where to put it.

Important Note: When installing items, drag the new item to the *closed* folder icon (even if it's gray) of your System Folder, *not* to the open window of the System Folder. If you drag files to the open window, they will be placed inside the System Folder, yes, but *not* in the specific folders in which they belong.

***Another Important Note:** This method of installing files does not work for any files that you want to store in the **Apple Menu Items, Startup Items, Preferences, Launcher, Favorites,** or in the **Shutdown Items folder.** If you want anything to go into any of these folders, you must drag it there directly.

1. If you are a student in a computer lab at school, what should you put in the System Folder?

2. If you are a student in a computer lab at school, what should you take out of the System Folder?

3. If you are working at home or at your business, should you mess around with the System Folder without knowing what you are doing?

4. Which two files must be in the System Folder so your Mac will work?

5. Do you need to worry about most of the stuff in the System Folder?

6. How do you install fonts, control panels, or extensions?

7. Name four folders in which you might want to put items yourself.

8. If you want a sound to play when you start your computer, where should you put the sound file?

9. Which folder inside the System Folder will you probably use the most, once you are familiar with your Mac?

10. If you are a student in a lab, will you ever touch the System Folder?

Answers on page 425.

Fonts 21

It used to be so easy. Now font technology and font management have become so complex that I have written a separate book on the subject, called *How to Boss Your Fonts Around, second edition.* In this chapter I'm going to tell you only the very basic things you need to know. And maybe you don't even need to know these things. **If your fonts are working fine and this information bores you or makes you quiver, just skip this chapter.** My sister, Shannon, calls font technology "the F word."

I'm serious—ignore this chapter unless you **really** *want to know the technology of fonts!*

Fonts

In the computerized world, the term **fonts** refers to **typefaces.** Technically and traditionally, that's not exactly what "font" means, but we'll let it pass for now rather than confuse the issue.

Font technologies

At the moment there are two basic font technologies on the Macintosh: PostScript and TrueType. First I must explain a little about PostScript printers and non-PostScript printers so the font information makes more sense. Find out whether you have a PostScript or a non-PostScript printer before you read the rest of the font chapter (see below).

PostScript Printers

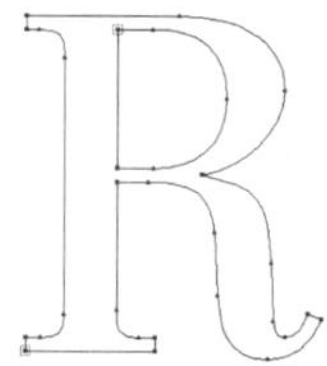

This is an example of a PostScript outline character.

PostScript is a "page description language" from Adobe Systems, Inc., that allows a printer to draw certain fonts and graphics. See, certain fonts and graphics are created in the computer using mathematical formulas and outlines. To the left is an example of the outline for the letter "R" in a particular font.

Printers print dots, though, not outlines or math formula descriptions. They print tiny dots in "resolutions" of, for instance, 600 or 1200 dots per inch. The more dots per inch, the smoother the edge of the object because the dots are smaller and closer together. Very high-end PostScript printers, called **imagesetters,** print 1270 or 2540 dots per inch so the edges of the type look very smooth (the type you are reading right now was set by an imagesetter).

Anyway, when PostScript fonts or graphics come down the cable from the computer to the printer, the printer freaks out at these outlines. The PostScript interpreter takes over and translates, or *rasterizes,* the outlines into dots so they can be printed. PostScript printers are the expensive ones because they have a computer inside of them—***if your printer cost around $1000 or so, it's probably PostScript. If it cost $200 or $300, it's definitely not PostScript.***

So a PostScript printer, then, is a printer that has a computer inside of it, and it can interpret the PostScript page description language for complex drawing of fonts and certain types of graphics.

Non-PostScript Printers

also called QuickDraw printers

Printers that are not PostScript are called **non-PostScript printers,** or sometimes **QuickDraw printers.** This is not because there is anything called QuickDraw inside the printer!

The images you see on the Macintosh screen are displayed using the QuickDraw programming language. A QuickDraw, or non-PostScript printer, has no computer inside of it, and so it can only reproduce what it sees on the Macintosh screen—that's why it's sometimes called a QuickDraw printer. The Epson Stylus, HP DeskWriter, and the Apple StyleWriter are all QuickDraw, or non-PostScript, printers. If it's a color printer and it cost significantly less than $4,000, it's non-PostScript.

OK. Got that? Do you know what kind of printer you have on your desk? Now for the F information.

As I mentioned, there are two types of font technologies you will run into on the Mac: **PostScript** and **TrueType.** We'll talk about each one separately, then I'll suggest which one you might prefer to use. Remember, you can skip all this stuff until the day you really think you want and need to know it, which might be never.

PostScript Fonts

Screen fonts are usually stored in "suitcases." Screen fonts appear on your screen and their names appear in the font menus.

A **PostScript font** has two parts to each font. There is a **screen, bitmapped** part which is what appears on your **screen:** little electronic bits of information are "mapped" to the pixels (dots) on the screen, turning the dots on or off so you can see the shape of the letters. The name of the screen font is what shows up in your menu. Screen fonts (bitmapped fonts, same thing) are usually stored in little suitcase icons, although they can actually be kept almost anywhere. You might also hear bitmapped fonts referred to as "fixed-size fonts."

The outline portion, or printer font, of a PostScript font is what a PostScript printer reads and prints with.

The second part of a PostScript font is the **outline** part, which is what a PostScript **printer** reads. This outline portion is actually a mathematically derived outline of the shape of the letter. See, it's like this: On your screen you're viewing the bitmapped font. When the page goes to the PostScript printer, the printer says, "Oh, I don't understand bitmap information. I'll go find the outline of that font." It finds the outline, which is sometimes called the **printer font** because that's what the printer needs. The PostScript interpreter "rasterizes" that outline into dots, then fills the outline in with black dots so it looks solid.

Printer font icons (as shown above) may look different, depending on which vendor they are from.

If you have a PostScript printer and you use PostScript fonts, then it doesn't matter what your type looks like on the screen.

The type can look like this on the screen: 

but it will print like this: Q

That's because the bitmapped font displays on the screen, but the printer creates the type from the outline font.

(If you have a non-PostScript printer, though, also known as a QuickDraw printer, then if it looks crummy on your screen it will look crummy when it prints. Don't worry—there are a couple of wonderful and easy ways around this. We'll get to them.)

PostScript fonts
Outline fonts
Scalable fonts
Type 1 fonts

You'll hear these terms in reference to PostScript fonts:

- All *PostScript fonts* are also known as *outline fonts.*
- All PostScript fonts are *scalable,* meaning they can be scaled, or resized, to any size you like and they will still print nicely.
- Almost all PostScript fonts are *Type 1* (some are *Type 3*). All Type 1 fonts are PostScript.

What Do You Get When You Acquire a New Font?

When you buy PostScript fonts, you will get both parts: you will get a suitcase file that contains the screen fonts, plus you will get a printer font for each style of screen font. For instance, if you have Centennial Light, Centennial Light Italic, Centennial Bold, and Centennial Bold Italic screen fonts in the suitcase, you will need four printer fonts, one for each of those styles. To install them, see page 204–205.

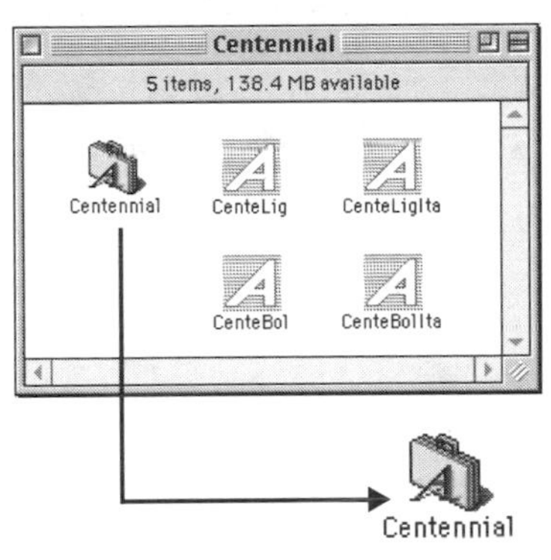

This disk contains both the screen fonts (inside the suitcase icon) and the printer fonts.

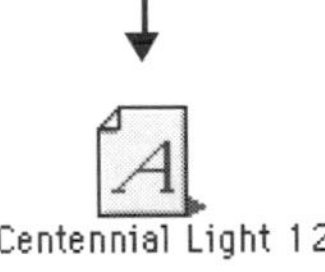

Inside the suitcase icon are the four screen fonts, as shown here, below.

Occasionally you may have screen fonts on a disk that are not contained in a suitcase file. That's okay, too.

Screen fonts always have a number (the point size) at the end of their names. That's a **visual clue** *that the icon represents a screen font (also known as a fixed-size font).*

TrueType Fonts

This is a TrueType font icon.

Geneva

This is what TrueType Geneva looks like right on the screen. This is 19.3-point type.

TrueType fonts, created by Apple, are also outline fonts, although their outline uses a different mathematical system from PostScript's. TrueType fonts are also scalable, in that they can be resized to any size. TrueType is not PostScript, and TrueType is not Type 1.

The TrueType screen information and the printer information are built into one file so you don't have two separate icons for each font (like you do for PostScript fonts). This means the screen can use the same information the printer uses, and the screen can simulate the look of the printed type on the screen. TrueType fonts, at any size, will look smoother than you thought your monitor would allow. TrueType fonts, when printed to either a PostScript printer or to a non-PostScript (QuickDraw) printer, will print at the resolution of the printer. That is, if you use an Epson Stylus with a resolution of 400 dots per inch, your type will print at 400 dots per inch. It's beautiful on the screen and it's beautiful on the page.

This makes it sound like TrueType is better than PostScript, yes? Well, in some cases it is and in some it isn't. Let me explain Adobe Type Manager first and then suggest a couple of optimal combinations of font technology and printers.

Adobe Type Manager (ATM)

Adobe Type Manager is a small program, a "utility" from Adobe. It makes PostScript fonts appear smooth on the screen, and makes them print smooth even to a non-PostScript printer.

Adobe Type Manager, usually called **ATM,** uses the printer font portion (the outline) of the PostScript fonts. It rasterizes this outline (turns the outline into dots) and displays it on the screen. Basically, ATM does the same thing the PostScript printer does, but instead of outputting it to paper like the printer would, ATM outputs it to the monitor. So your PostScript fonts look as beautiful on the screen as they do on paper.

In fact, ATM will also rasterize the outlines and output them to a non-PostScript printer at the resolution of the printer. This means that with ATM, your Epson Stylus will create smooth type at 400 dots per inch, which looks as good as type from a PostScript Apple LaserWriter!

If "~ATM" is not in your control panel list (it's usually the last item in the list), use Sherlock to see if you have ATM somewhere on your Mac. If you find it, put it into the Control Panels folder and restart your Mac.

ATM is usually installed when you install just about any Adobe product, or you can order it for the price of shipping. See their web site at www.adobe.com.

On the screen without ATM

On the screen with ATM

ATM makes an incredible difference in the way type looks on your screen and in the way type looks when you print it to a non-PostScript printer. These examples are actual screen shots showing the difference in the way PostScript fonts look on your monitor without and with ATM.

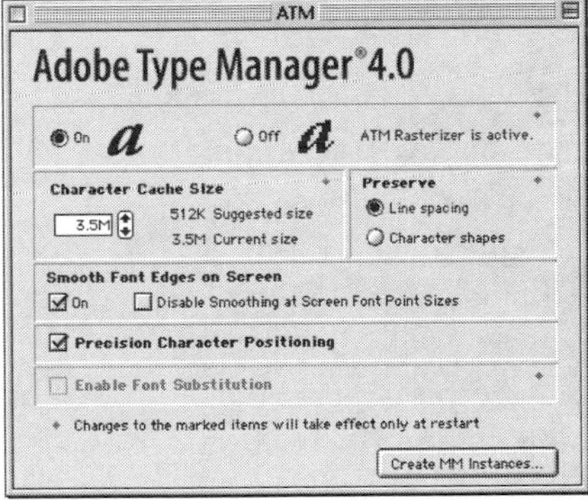

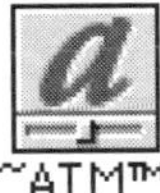

ATM is a control panel. It just sits in your Control Panels folder and does what it is supposed to do.

But if you ever have trouble printing lots of fonts in a document or printing very large sizes of a font, go to the control panel and increase the Character Cache Size to about 2.5M.

If you have trouble with the bottoms of letters getting chopped off on the screen, like in Photoshop, open ATM and change the "Preserve" option to "Character shapes."

Which Font Technology for You?

With **TrueType** you get nice smooth type on the screen and nice smooth type on both PostScript and non-PostScript printers. With **PostScript** (Type 1) fonts *combined with ATM,* you get the same thing. So which font technology should you use?

It's possible to use both TrueType fonts and PostScript fonts on the same machine and in the same document, minding this one rule:

> Don't keep two fonts with the same name from the two different technologies in your computer! That is, don't keep both TrueType Times and PostScript Times in your Mac. I'll come back to this later (page 207).

Here are suggestions for optimal combinations of font technology and printers.

Non-PostScript printer: one option

If you have a non-PostScript printer (DeskWriter, DeskJet, StyleWriter, Stylus, etc.), you will be able to see beautiful type on your screen and create beautifully typeset pages using **TrueType.** If you already have TrueType fonts that came with your machine, then when you begin to invest in more fonts you may want to continue to invest in TrueType.

Non-PostScript printer: another option

If you have a non-PostScript printer, you will be able to see beautiful type on your screen and create beautifully typeset pages using **ATM and PostScript fonts.** If you already have PostScript fonts, you may want to continue investing in PostScript. There are currently many more typefaces available in PostScript than in TrueType.

> Keep in mind that both TrueType and ATM technologies are centered around type, not graphics. Many graphics use PostScript, and if you have a QuickDraw (non-PostScript) printer, neither TrueType nor ATM can help create those graphics on the printed page. You will not be able to get high-end, smooth PostScript graphics on a QuickDraw printer, but then if you are in the market for high-end graphics you would not have bought a non-PostScript printer.
>
> *(There are a couple of software solutions, however. One is StyleScript from Strydent Software, and the other is BirmyRIP. They do the same thing to PostScript graphics [EPS files] that ATM does to PostScript type. Check them out at www.strydent.com or www.birmy.com.)*

PostScript printer

If you have a PostScript printer, the general consensus is to ignore TrueType. Use **ATM and PostScript fonts.** One of the reasons for this is that the PostScript interpreter perfectly understands the PostScript fonts; they speak the same language. But the PostScript interpreter has to figure out what to do with TrueType; files take longer to print, and often a file won't print at all. Also, the larger the point size of the type and the higher the resolution of the printer, the more trouble TrueType causes. Which means:

Imagesetters

If you plan to have your **pages printed on an imagesetter** (which is very high resolution), **don't use TrueType.** Imagesetters really don't like to deal with TrueType fonts—they create many problems in the output. TrueType slows down the machines incredibly, and sometimes they simply clog it up and won't print at all. Those $100,000 PostScript imagesetters are even fussier than our $1000 laser printers. Check with your service bureau before you show up with a document containing TrueType.

How to Install Fonts

Fonts, PostScript or TrueType, must be loaded into your System before you can use them. I'm going to tell you **how to install fonts,** but then you really must read the ***Important Note*** after the directions.

If the Application menu shows any other applications open besides "Finder," you must close each one first.

- With the newest operating systems, you can install fonts while an application (like your word processor) is running, but the fonts will not appear in the menu (in most programs) until the next time you open the application. So it's good practice to just quit all the applications before you install any fonts: Check the Application menu (on the far-right of the menu bar) and make sure there is no other application listed except the "Finder." If there is, select the application from that menu, then press Command Q. Follow this step even if you don't know what I'm talking about and even if, when you choose the application, you don't see any change on your screen. Trust me.
- Make sure your System Folder is closed.
- Make sure you can see both the closed System Folder and the fonts you want to install at the same time.
- Whether you have a suitcase or a series of bitmapped fonts (PostScript or TrueType), select them and drag them over to the closed System Folder. When the System Folder is highlighted, let go of the fonts. You'll get a message asking if you want the Mac to put them where they belong. Of course you do.
- If you are installing PostScript fonts, next find the printer font icons and drag them, all of them, over to the System Folder and drop them inside also. The Mac will put them in the Fonts folder.

This is the closed System Folder.

When you drop your fonts on the closed System Folder, the Mac puts the fonts in this Fonts folder. If you like, you can put your fonts directly into this folder yourself. You'll find it in the System Folder.

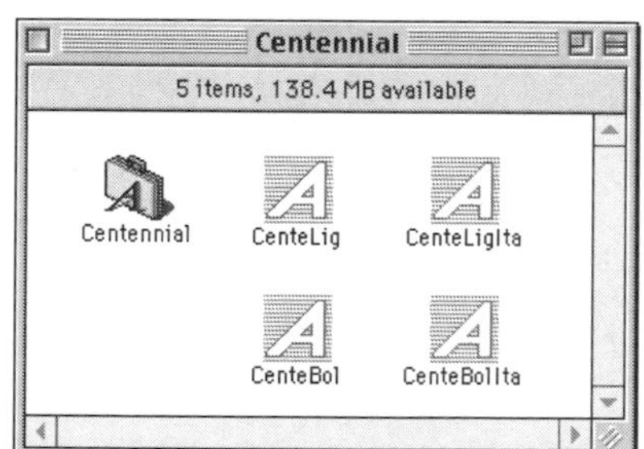

If the fonts are PostScript, you need to drag all of these items to the System Folder to install the fonts—one printer font for each bitmap in the suitcase.

If the fonts are TrueType, you only need to install one icon for each font. For instance, Times Roman, Bold, Italic, and Bold Italic would be four separate fonts, four separate icons.

You can drop a combination of screen, printer, and TrueType fonts onto the System Folder simultaneously and the Mac will place each one where it belongs.

Ignore the AFM files.

- If you have an AFM file (Adobe Font Metrics), ignore it. Do not install it anywhere on your Mac. Store the AFM file on a disk on the *very* off chance you may ever need it. If you do need it, the application you are using will tell you so.

Even if you don't know what to do with it yet, keep a recent version of a font downloader on your hard disk.

- You might find some sort of "font downloader" utility also on a disk of fonts. If you don't already have a downloader in a folder somewhere, copy it onto your hard disk (but not into the System Folder!) so when the day comes that you know what to do with it and need it, you'll have it.

Important Note

Important Note: What I just described is the standard, typical way of installing fonts, the way you read about in all the magazines and books about the Mac. "Oh, just drag those fonts and drop them into the System Folder." The truth is, though, once you start adding fonts to your collection you need to become responsible and knowledgeable about how to manage those critters. Once you acquire a font addiction and start adding massive quantities of fonts, you must buy and use a font management utility because all those fonts really should not be kept in the System Folder! If you buy maybe five or ten or even twelve font families, you'll be safe enough with all of them in the System. But any more than that and you're going to need help. You need to manage them. You need to buy either Adobe Type Manager Deluxe (which is different from the regular ATM), Font Reserve, Suitcase, or MasterJuggler, and you need to learn how to use it. All of this is the topic of another book of mine, *How to Boss Your Fonts Around.*

This following bit of information will pertain to you if you use PostScript fonts and ATM, no matter what kind of printer you have.

Resident Fonts

PostScript printers have RAM (random-access memory) and ROM (read-only memory) inside, just like your computer. Permanently built into the ROM chips is the printer font information for the standard laser printer fonts: Avant Garde, Bookman, Courier, Helvetica, Palatino, New Century Schoolbook, Times, Zapf Chancery, Symbol, and Zapf Dingbats. These fonts are considered **resident** in the printer. When you buy a PostScript printer, you are given a disk with the corresponding screen fonts to install in your Mac. Whenever you print using one of these fonts, the printer looks in its own ROM first, finds the printer font information, and prints.

If you use PostScript fonts and ATM, you may notice that ATM does not affect these standard, resident laser fonts on the screen—they still appear rough and jaggy on the screen (although they will print smooth on a PostScript printer, they will print jaggy on a QuickDraw printer). Well, remember, ATM uses the printer (outline) font to produce the smooth shapes on the screen. But ATM cannot find the printer fonts for these standard laser faces because the printer fonts live in the ROM of the PostScript printer! If you want to see these fonts rendered beautifully on your screen or if you want to print them to a non-PostScript printer, then you need to buy the printer fonts from Adobe. (Personally, I would rather take that money and buy some different fonts.)

When you install ATM using the installer utility, it installs printer fonts for Helvetica, Times, Symbol, and Courier. The others you must buy.

Now, this following bit of information will only pertain to you if you use a ***PostScript printer.***

Fonts of the Same Name

Just about all Macintosh operating systems automatically install **TrueType** Times, Courier, Helvetica, Palatino, and Symbol. It is not possible, though, to print TrueType Times, Helvetica, Courier, or Symbol to a PostScript printer. Most applications call on a font by name. If a document goes down to the PostScript printer and asks for Times, the printer looks in its own ROM first for an outline called Times. It finds one there, of course (see the information on the previous page).

So you may see TrueType Times on your screen, but you will print PostScript Times. They are not exactly the same face. You may end up with different spacing, different line endings, or even different page breaks. If you have a PostScript printer, then you also have the Post-Script versions of these fonts. Remove the TrueType versions of any fonts with the same names as your PostScript printer's resident fonts, and reinstall the PostScript fonts. The downloader utility usually has a menu item that tells you exactly which fonts are resident in your printer.

Is It TrueType or PostScript?

How do you know if you are using **TrueType** or **PostScript**? Well, you can always look at the icons in the System Folder, as explained on the next page. If it's got three "A"s on it, it's TrueType. If it has matching bitmaps and printer fonts, it's a matched set of PostScript. But let's assume you are working in an application and you want to know right then and there.

Type size

Unless you are in Microsoft Word, you can tell whether the font you are using is TrueType or not through a **visual clue** in the type size menu.

Have you noticed how some of the sizes listed in the Size menu are in outline style (which has nothing to do with outline fonts), and some are not (see below, left)? This can be different for each font. (Unfortunately, Word ignores this important visual clue.)

If just about all (all except for maybe the 6- and 8-point sizes) are displayed in the outline style (see below, right), then the currently selected font is TrueType.

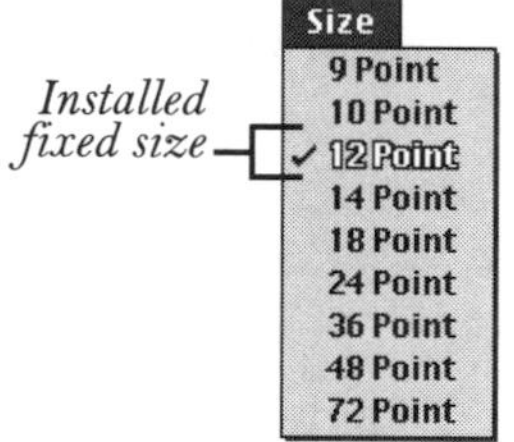

If there are only one or two installed sizes indicated (or you might see installed sizes for 10, 12, 14, 18, and 24), the selected text is probably a PostScript font.

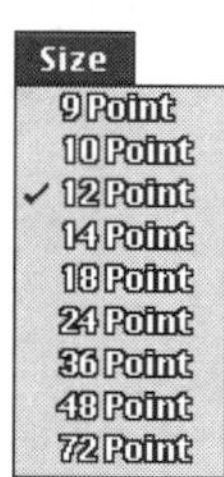

*If **ALL** of the sizes are displayed in the Size menu in the outline style, then the **selected text** is TrueType.*

In the example above left, what the outlined number indicates is that this particular size for this particular PostScript font has been installed in the System. Remember the numbers you saw at the ends of the names of the screen font icons on page 199? Generally, type will look its best on the screen in the outlined size and will print best on a QuickDraw printer in the outlined size. You can ask for any other size and in some programs you can choose "Other…" and type in a point size up to 127 point or even up to 650 point, but if you are not using TrueType or ATM, it'll look funky on the screen because the computer has to fake that size. The bigger the size, the funkier it looks. And if it looks funky on the screen, it will look funky on a QuickDraw printer because that printer can only reproduce what it sees on the screen.

Check the icons

You can also look in your Fonts folder within the System Folder to determine whether the fonts are TrueType, and also to determine which sizes of screen fonts are installed. Just double-click on the Fonts folder (found inside the System Folder). You can open any font suitcase, no matter where you find it, to check fonts, also.

TrueType font icons have three "A"s; screen fonts have only one A.

> **If the icon has three "A"s on it, it is TrueType.**
>
> **If the icon has only one "A," it is a bitmapped font.**
> The icons with a single A will have a number after the name, such as "Zapf Dingbats 12." This means it is the 12-point screen size. Now, just to keep things confusing, these bitmaps might belong to TrueType fonts or to PostScript fonts. How can you tell? You can't. All you can do is assume that any bitmaps in the folder belong with the matching outline font in the same folder.

Why Do You See Both Icons?

Well, now, I bet you might be wondering why, if you have TrueType Geneva, you also see **screen fonts** (bitmaps) for Geneva 10, Geneva 12, and even perhaps Geneva 18 in your System. Yes, I did say earlier that TrueType combines screen and printer font information into one icon. These screen fonts for TrueType Geneva (and any others you find that match your other TrueType fonts) are simply there because supposedly it is faster for the Mac to create the font on the screen if it can use the already-created screen font in that size, rather than having to use the TrueType technology to create that size. Since most people use 10- and 12-point type sizes most of the time, the screen fonts are merely to speed the process. You can remove these screen versions from your System and never notice any loss of speed, although some TrueType fonts do *look* better at the fixed sizes.

You Can See What Any Font Looks Like

Anywhere you find a TrueType icon or a screen font icon, double-click on it to see what the font looks like. If it's TrueType, you'll see the font in three sizes. If it's a screen font, you'll see it in that size screen font.

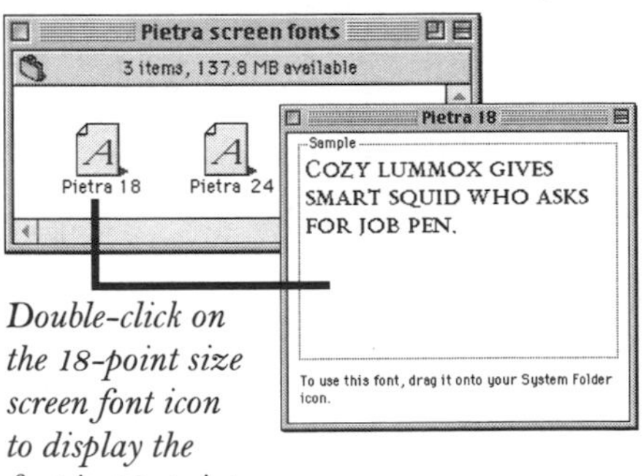

Double-click on the 18-point size screen font icon to display the font in 18-point.

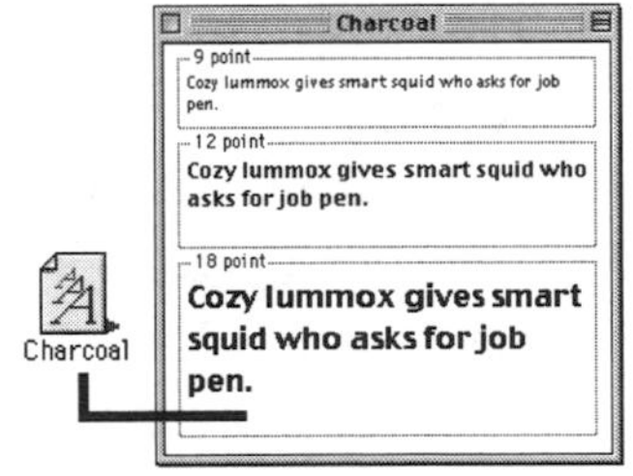

Double-click a TrueType icon to display the font in three sizes.

Font Substitution

When you are printing to a PostScript printer and you use the city-named fonts New York, Geneva, or Monaco, many applications will automatically **substitute fonts.** This is true even if you are using TrueType city-named fonts. This is why and what happens:

While in your favorite application, choose "Page Setup" from the File menu. Most applications will display these dialog boxes:

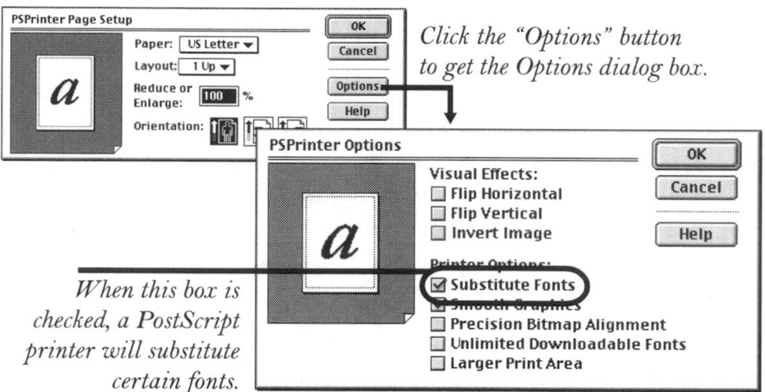

Click the "Options" button to get the Options dialog box.

When this box is checked, a PostScript printer will substitute certain fonts.

Notice the first checkbox button, "Substitute Fonts"? This box is checked as a "default" (an automatic selection). Unless you consciously uncheck it, this box makes the printer substitute certain fonts. It will substitute Times when it finds New York, Helvetica when it finds Geneva, and Courier when it finds Monaco. Because the city-named fonts are designed for a lower resolution, the words take up more space. The PostScript substitution tries to keep the line of text as long as it was in the city-named font, but to do that it must add more space to fill out the line. Have you ever noticed printed pages with too much space between the words? Or numbers that look like they're supposed to align but don't? Or an underline that's dashed? That's the result of trying to print a font with a city name to a PostScript printer.

Try this yourself. Type a page using the fonts Geneva, New York, and Monaco in different paragraphs. Print the page to a PostScript printer once with "Substitute Fonts" checked, then print it again without "Substitute Fonts" checked. Put the two pages together and look at them.

TrueType Chicago, however, prints very nicely on a PostScript printer, because there is no corresponding substitute or similarly named printer font living in the printer.

Samples of Installed Fonts

An asterisk (*) indicates fonts that are on both Macs and PCs.

Below are examples of the TrueType fonts installed in Mac OS9. Some fonts have an italic version, plus a bold and a bold italic. The only way to know if a font has these other versions is to look in its suitcase.

The razor-edged fox backed over the dog's lazy green hide.	Andale Mondo
The razor-edged fox backed over the dog's lazy green hide.	*Apple Chancery*
The razor-edged fox backed over the dog' s lazy green hide.	*Arial**
The razor-edged fox backed over the dog's lazy green hide.	**Arial Black***
THE RAZOR-EDGED FOX BACKED OVER THE DOG'S LAZY GREEN HIDE.	CAPITALS
The razor-edged fox backed over the dog's lazy green hide.	**Charcoal**
The razor-edged fox backed over the dog's lazy green hide.	**Chicago**
The razor-edged fox backed over the dog's lazy green hide.	Comic Sans*
The razor-edged fox backed over the dog's lazy green hide.	Courier
The razor-edged fox backed over the dog' s lazy green hide.	Courier New*
The razor-edged fox backed over the dog's lazy green hide.	**Gadget**
The razor-edged fox backed over the dog's lazy green hide.	Geneva
The razor-edged fox backed over the dog's *lazy green hide.*	Georgia
The razor-edged fox backed **over the dog's** *lazy green hide.*	Helvetica
The razor-edged fox backed over the dog's lazy green hide.	Hoefler Text
	Hoefler Ornaments
The razor-edged fox backed over the dog's lazy green hide.	**Impact***
The razor-edged fox backed over the dog's lazy green hide.	Monaco
The razor-edged fox backed over the dog's lazy green hide.	New York
The razor-edged fox backed over the dog's lazy green hide.	Palatino
The razor-edged fox backed over the dog's lazy green hide.	**Sand**
The razor-edged fox backed over the dog's lazy green hide.	Skia
Τηε ραζορ–εδγεδ φοξ βαχκεδ οϖερ τηε δογΠσ λαζψ γρεεν ηιδε.	Symbol
The razor-edged fox backed over the dog's lazy green hide.	**Techno**
The razor-edged fox backed over the dog's lazy green hide.	***Textile***
The razor-edged fox backed **over the dog's** *lazy green hide.*	Times
The razor-edged fox backed over the dog' s lazy green hide.	Times New Roman*
The razor-edged fox backed over the dog' s lazy green hide.	Trebuchet
The razor-edged fox backed over the dog's *lazy green hide.*	Verdana*
	Webdings*

Do you care? If you don't, skip this! Go take a nap! Do something useful!

1. Which sort of printer is actually a computer: PostScript or QuickDraw?

2. Which technology uses "outlines," PostScript or TrueType?

3. PostScript screen fonts are usually stored in little suitcase icons. Do they have to be?

4. If you use PostScript fonts, what other software utility should you also use?

5. Label the icons below with **A, B,** or **C:** **A)** TrueType font **B)** PostScript printer font **C)** bitmapped screen font

6. If you will be printing to a high-resolution imagesetter, which font technology is the only choice?

7. Describe the easy way to install fonts.

8. Why does ATM not work on Avant Garde?

9. Make two appropriate groups out of the icons below, and . . .

10. State why you grouped them together.

Answers on page 425.

22 Desk Accessories

Desk accessories, commonly called **DA**s, are handy little tools found in your menu under the apple, on the far left of the menu bar. The purpose of desk accessories is to make life easier—you'll find a handy calculator, a CD player, a note pad, and other things you might find on your office desk. Access a desk accessory like any other menu item—slide down the list until the name of the DA is highlighted, then let go. Desk accessories appear in windows, so you can move them around the screen with their title bars and close them with their little close boxes. You can open any DA while you are in any application. You can buy an amazing number of additional desk accessories, many for very low prices. They do all manner of useful and useless things.

The Apple menu used to hold nothing *except* desk accessories so it was very clear what was a DA and what wasn't. But now the Apple menu can hold anything you want to put in it so not everything you see in the menu is a DA. In fact, it is now difficult to tell which items *are* desk accessories, so don't worry if it's not clear what is and what isn't—it doesn't really matter. The following information explains just the desk accessories that come standard with every Mac—you might have others.

Calculator

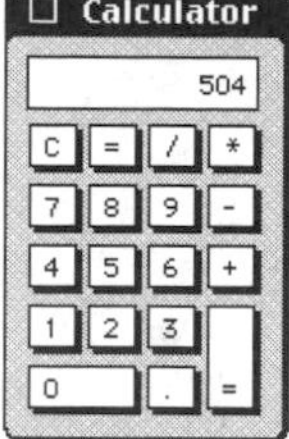

The **Calculator** is a very handy item. It operates just like your hand-held calculator, although it has only the four basic functions. Remember, this calculator is a window so you can drag it around like any other window and put it away with its close box. Access it within any application.

- Operate the calculator with the mouse (click on the numbers on the screen), the numbers on the main keyboard, or use the numeric keypad (the little set of numbers on the right side of most keyboards).
- If using the main keyboard (as opposed to the numeric keypad), make sure you use the real numeral 1 (one) and not a lowercase l (el).
- The division sign is the slash: /.
  The multiplication sign is the asterisk: *.
- You can copy and paste the results into your document using Copy and Paste from the Edit menu. You don't need to select the numbers first—if the Calculator is the active window, the Copy command knows what to copy. You can also copy numbers from your document and paste them into the Calculator.

This calculator is extremely limited, though. It won't even add the percent to the sum. If you find you use this little calculator a lot but would like more features, you might want to check with your local user group or friendly power user for one of the many commercial or shareware (meaning almost free) versions available.

Graphing Calculator

The **Graphing Calculator** is not installed in the Apple menu in Mac OS 9 (instead, it's in the Applications folder), but you might have it in your Apple menu as a leftover from a previous system. It is a serious tool that, among other things, can actually graph equations, create 3D examples of the equation, and then rotate them. If you do the sort of work that needs a graphing calculator, then you can probably figure out how to use this one. Open it and run the demo—it's amazing.

Chooser

The **Chooser** is where you choose which printer you wish to use. If you are working at home or at work and are hooked up to only one printer, you need to use the Chooser only the very first time you print. If you have the option of printing to more than one printer, you can set up a Desktop printer icon for each one. For all the gory details on using the Chooser, please see Chapter 16 on Printing.

CD Player

AppleCD Audio Player

If you have a CD drive, you can play audio CDs (yes, music CDs). You can listen to Gregorian chants while balancing your electronic checkbook. Shown below is the **AppleCD Audio Player.** It's very self-explanatory—it works just like the one in your living room, except you can change its color (check out the "Options" menu after you open the CD Player). In Mac OS 9, this item is not in the Apple menu—it's in the Applications folder.

Click here to repeat the CD.

This is what a music CD looks like on your Mac.

To listen to music CDs, you might have to also change a couple of settings in the Sound control panel. First, try the CD:

Put the CD in the drive, double-click the CD icon, then double-click any track you see. The control panel shown above should appear and you should hear music. If it doesn't work, do this:

- ▾ From the Apple menu, slide down to Control Panels, slide out to the right, and choose "Sound" to get the Sound control panel.
- ▾ Click the "Input" tab.
- ▾ In the list, click "CD."
- ▾ (In the OS 9 version of this dialog box, choose "Input" on the left, "Internal CD" on the right, and choose "CD" as the "Input Source" on the bottom-right.)
- ▾ Click in the close box (upper-left) to put the control panel away. Now you can play your music.
- ▾ If it still doesn't work, check your Extensions Manager (details on pages 258–259) to make sure you have the extension called **Foreign File Access** turned on. If it was off, check the box to turn it on, restart your Mac, and try the CD again.
- ▾ If it still doesn't work, open the CD Player and choose "AppleCD Audio Player Guide" from the Help menu. There are several variables and this guide can give you specifics for your setup.

In any version of Mac OS 8, use the Monitors & Sound control panel.

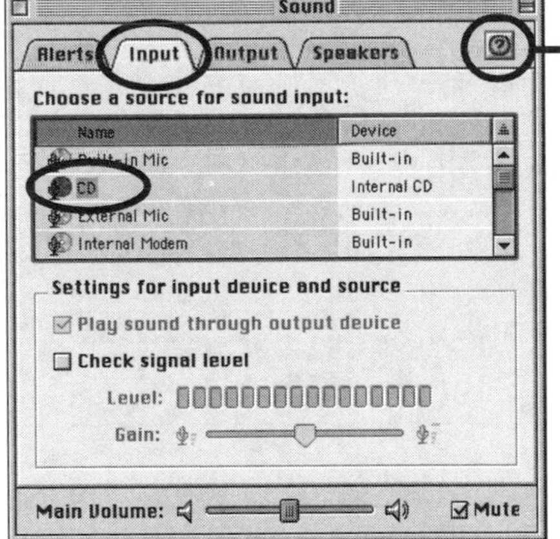

Click the Help button (top-right in this dialog box; bottom-left in the dialog box in Mac OS 9) for the answers to any questions.

Foreign File Access

Key Caps

Key Caps can show you the keyboard layout for every font that is loaded in your System. On a Macintosh keyboard you actually have four separate sets of keys, two of which you know already and two of which only a few people know about. You are about to become In The Know.

- After you open up Key Caps, you have a new menu item called "Fonts," as shown to the right.
- Pull down the Fonts menu—this is a list of the typefaces that are installed on your System.
- Select the font you want; the characters of that font will appear on the keyboard (these are the characters everybody knows about).
- To see the Shift characters, press the Shift key (everybody knows these, too).
- To see the Option characters, press the Option key (Ha! You are now In The Know).
- To see the Shift Option characters, press the Shift and Option keys simultaneously.

Fonts

Andale Mono
Apple Chancery
Arial ▸
Capitals
Charcoal
Chicago
Comic Sans MS
Courier
Courier New PS MT
Gadget
Geneva
Georgia
Helvetica
Hoefler Text ▸
Impact
Monaco
New York
Palatino
Sand
Skia
Symbol
Techno
Textile
Times Roman
Trebuchet MS
✓ Verdana
Webdings
Zapf Dingbats

Once you open Key Caps, you'll find a menu called "Fonts" in the menu bar.

Different fonts have different characters in the Option and Shift Option keyboards—some have more, some have less. Most of the Option key characters are consistent in every font, so you can always find characters like the accent marks or copyright, trademark, and monetary symbols, etc., in the same place.

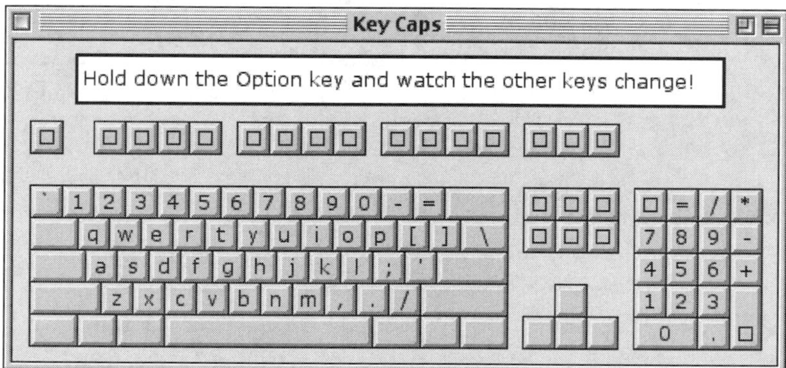

This is the Key Caps desk accessory.

How to Use Key Caps

Key Caps is only for finding the *placement* of all the available characters on the keyboard. Hold down the Option key, for instance, and note where the ¢ sign is located.

- Once you discover that the ¢ is found under the 4 (which is also the $ sign), then you can go back to your document and press Option 4—the ¢ will appear. *It's exactly the same idea as pressing Shift 4 to get the dollar sign or Shift 8 to get an asterisk!*

You can "type" the characters on the Key Caps keyboard, copy them (select the characters first, then choose Copy from the Edit menu), and then Paste the characters into your document (they will paste in wherever the insertion point is flashing). This works fine as long as the font you are using in your document is the same font you chose from Key Caps, or at least that they share the same character. Otherwise when you paste the character it will take on the *format* (font, size, style) *of the character to the left of the insertion point,* which may not be what you want at all. So if that happens, do it this way:

- At the Key Caps keyboard, find the character you want to use.
- Remember which font and what keys to press to get that character.
- Go back to your document, click the insertion point at the spot where you want the character to appear, *select the font you need,* and then press the appropriate keys to type the character.
- Can you find the apple?

Also see pages 140–141 for more information about special characters and Key Caps, including how to type accent marks over letters. There is a very tricky method for discovering the keyboard combination for many of the accent marks that take two steps to create, such as Ê, for which you type Option i, let go, and then type Shift e. For now, you can use the chart of special characters at the end of the book as a quick reference for typing.

If you find you need special characters regularly, I suggest you go to www.shareware.com and download PopChar Lite. It's free. Read the directions. It makes finding and using special characters so easy.

Which Fonts are Loaded on your System?

Using Key Caps is a great way for discovering which fonts are installed at the moment in any Macintosh! Just choose Key Caps from the Apple menu, then press on the "Fonts" menu item that appears—you will see the fonts that are currently installed and available, as shown on the opposite page.

Note Pad

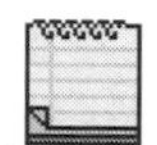

In Mac OS 9.1, find the Note Pad in the Apple Extras folder, which is in the Utilities folder.

The **Note Pad** is no longer added to the Apple menu, but you can find it in the Apple Extras folder. It's a great little accessory that allows you to write up to eight pages of notes. This is a great place to leave prearranged messages, notes about particular formatting used in a document, reminders, or more love notes. Any messages in the Note Pad are automatically saved.

When you open the Note Pad, the insertion point is flashing; type into it just as you type anywhere else in the Mac. You can backspace/ delete, cut, copy, paste, etc. Turn the pages by clicking on the little turned corner on the bottom-left; click on the *very* bottom corner to turn the pages backwards.

The Note Pad has a scroll bar running along the right side. This is a **visual clue** that you can type more text than will fit on the page you see, then you can scroll through it.

To make a "clipping file," select text, then press-and-drag that text to the Desktop or into a window. You can open this clipping file in other applications or just drag it directly onto open pages. Keep a list of web addresses in the Note Pad: drag an address from the Note page and drop it onto a browser page to open that address—drag it *onto the page itself* and drop it (not into the Location box where you usually type addresses!).

Add more pages: *Go to the File menu and choose "New Note."*

Search for words: *From the Edit menu, choose "Find," then type the word you want to find.*

Change the font and size: *From the Edit menu, choose "Preferences...."*

Print a note: *Use the options in the File menu.*

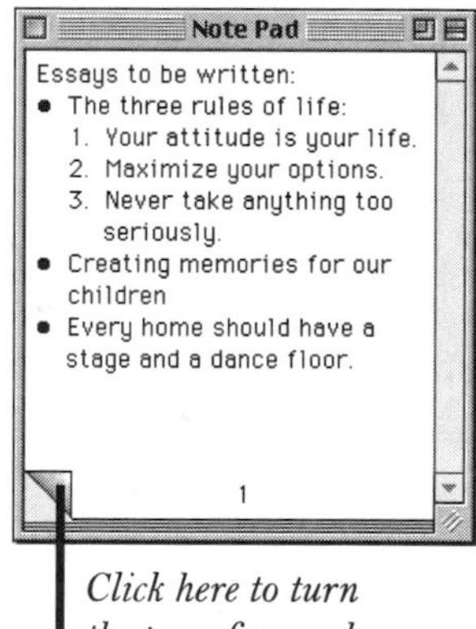

Click here to turn the page forward.

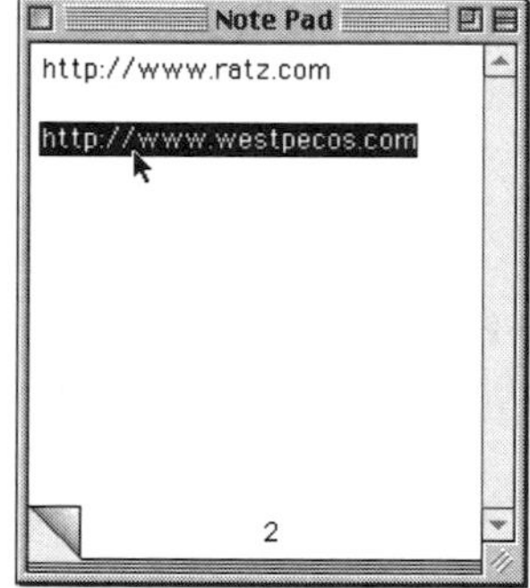

If you select the text in the Note Pad, you can then press on it and drag it somewhere. When you let go, the text appears in that spot.

If you drag the text to the Desktop, it makes a clipping file (shown to the left). Double-click to open a clipping file, or open it in another application.

You can drag text from the Note Pad into almost any application, like your word processor, page layout program, or web authoring application.

Rename text clippings so you know what they are! Click once on the name—after you see the outline around the name, just type the new name in.

text clipping

Note to Jimmy

Jigsaw Puzzle

The **Jigsaw Puzzle** is not included with Mac OS 9, but you might have it leftover from an earlier operating system. It acts just like a regular jigsaw puzzle, but you can customize it.

- Choose "Jigsaw Puzzle" from the Apple menu. You'll get a new menu item called "Options" along with the completed puzzle.
- From the Options menu, choose "Start new puzzle...." You can choose to have large, small, or medium pieces. Click OK.
- So now solve it.
- Play around with that Options menu—everything is self-explanatory.

  Want a challenge? Use the Fun Tip to create a puzzle out of one of your Desktop Patterns! Ha!

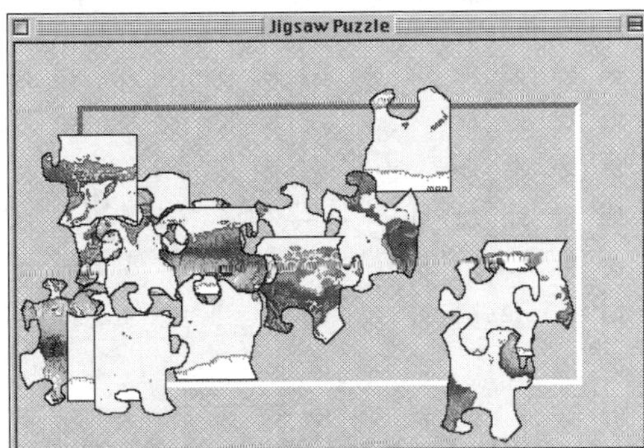

This is the original jigsaw puzzle.

This is a custom puzzle. Copy or create any art and paste it in here.

If you have clip art, you can copy the clip art, open the puzzle, and paste. That clip art image will then be the new puzzle. Put the face of someone you love in here.

Fun Tip!
Open the Scrapbook or the Desktop Patterns control panel, ***and*** *open the Jigsaw Puzzle. Drag any image from the Scrapbook or the Desktop Patterns over to the puzzle and let go—that image is the new puzzle!*

Another Great Tip!
View many graphic files by dragging an icon onto the open Jigsaw Puzzle! If it displays as puzzle pieces, just choose "Solve Puzzle" or "Show Picture" from the Options menu.

Scrapbook

The **Scrapbook** is a place where you can permanently store text, graphics, movies, and sounds from virtually any program; then in any other program you can take a copy of any of those items back out from the Scrapbook and paste it into your document. Once you put something in the Scrapbook it is saved to your hard disk automatically. The Scrapbook holds the entire object or text, even though you can't always see all of it in the window.

▼ **To paste something into the Scrapbook:**

1. From your document, *select* and *copy* the item you want to place (this puts a copy on the Clipboard, as shown on the next page).
2. Open the Scrapbook from the Apple menu.
3. Paste the item into the Scrapbook: from the Edit menu choose "Paste." The Scrapbook will make a new page for the new item, and everything else *will move over one; nothing is replaced.*
4. Close the Scrapbook to get back to your document, or just click on any visible part of your document.

▼ **To copy an item out of the Scrapbook:**

1. Open the Scrapbook.
2. Scroll through until the item you want *is visible.*
3. Copy it: from the Edit menu choose "Copy."
4. Close the Scrapbook.
5. Go to your document and paste it in. Usually text, and sometimes graphics, will insert itself wherever the insertion point is flashing; in some applications the item will be pasted into the middle of the page.

▼ **To delete an item from the Scrapbook:**

1. Scroll through until the item you want is *visible.*
2. From the Edit menu choose "Clear" (Clear *removes* the item *without* putting it on the Clipboard). Notice you can use the keyboard shortcut Command B to clear an item.

Limitations and troubleshooting

Not every item you see can be pasted into any document of any kind. For instance, you usually can't paste a movie into a spreadsheet cell. If nothing happens when you try to paste from the Scrapbook, one of two things is happening: either it can't be done, or you have inadvertently pasted the item somewhere other than where you expect. For instance, your insertion point might be flashing on page 7, but you are looking at page 15. Remember, when you paste, the item will paste onto the page *where the insertion point is flashing!* In a spreadsheet, it will paste into the selected cell or cells. In a database, it will paste into the selected field. Be conscious!

Clipping and dragging

As in the Note Pad, you can drag a file out of the Scrapbook directly onto the Desktop or into a window, where it becomes a "clipping file." You can open this clipping file in other applications. You can drag files out of the Scrapbook directly into some applications without having to copy and paste. You can drag items from the Scrapbook to the Desktop Patterns or the Jigsaw Puzzle.

The Scrapbook and the Clipboard

The information right here is not critical to know because the Mac takes care of putting items into the Scrapbook automatically. But if you are teaching Mac classes or if you like to know why things happen, here is the simple and brief explanation: When you paste items to or from the Scrapbook, they automatically go through the Clipboard (the Mac's temporary holding place) on their way in or out. That's why the Clear command is important—if you have something temporarily stored in your Clipboard and you don't want the Scrapbook item to replace it, use Clear instead of Cut. Or if the file in the Scrapbook is large, Clear it instead of cutting it so the large file does not sit in memory (the Clipboard) while you work.

See pages 138–139 if you want more information on the Clipboard.

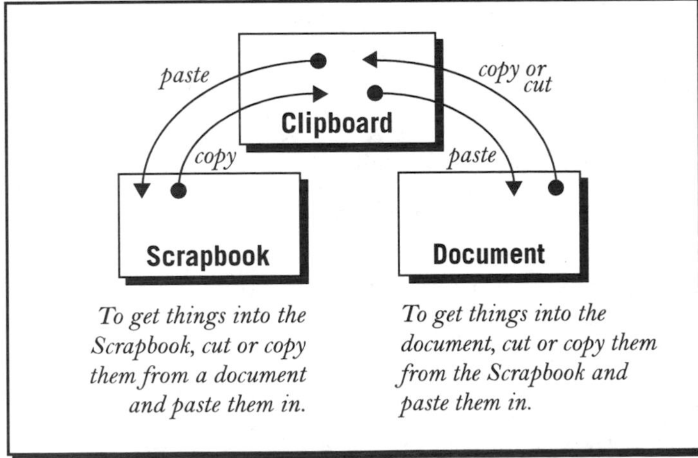

To get things into the Scrapbook, cut or copy them from a document and paste them in.

To get things into the document, cut or copy them from the Scrapbook and paste them in.

Stickies

Stickies are electronic Post-It® notes. Some people like them, some people don't bother with them. Use Stickies for a bit and see what you think. (They don't really turn at angles, as shown to the left.)

Scarlett, I put the report in your folder! Mom

Jimmy, Get your homework done before you play pool! Love, Mom

Ryan, I missed you! It's good to have you home again!

From the Apple menu, choose "Stickies." The first time you choose this, you'll see these messages:

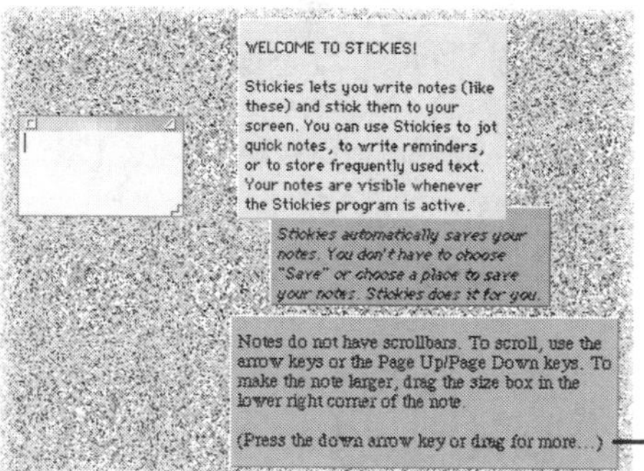

Ooops—they left out a step here: first you must click at the end of this sentence before you press the down arrow key.

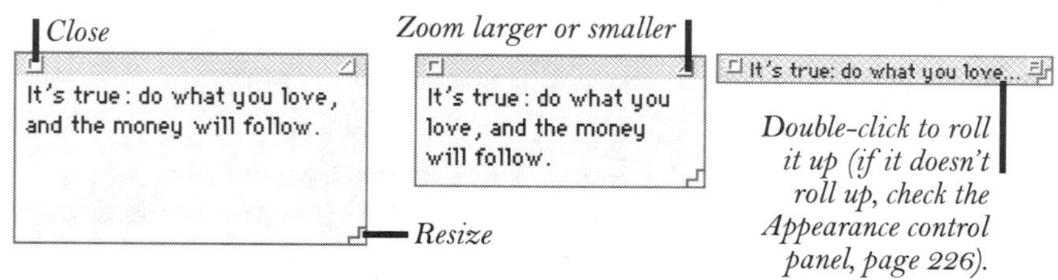

Double-click to roll it up (if it doesn't roll up, check the Appearance control panel, page 226).

Stickies Preferences

- [ ] Confirm window-closing
- [ ] Save All on deactivate
- [x] Zoom-box collapses window
- [x] Launch at system startup
  - [x] ...in the background

Cancel | OK

If you choose "Launch at system startup," all your Stickies will automatically open when you turn on the Mac. Choose "...in the background" if you want your Desktop windows to be in front when you startup, rather than Stickie windows.

These little stickies act like windows: you can move them around by dragging their title bars, resize them, zoom them smaller or larger, double-click their title bars to roll them up, and click the close box or press Command W to make them go away. You can change the color, typeface, and typeface size for each note from the Color and Note menus that appear when a stickie is an active window. You can "import" text (bring in text from a document you created) and "export" text (which saves it as a SimpleText document) from the File menu, and you can choose to print all the notes in one collection.

From the Edit menu, choose "Preferences..." to customize some of the Stickie features to your own liking (shown to the left).

If you want all your Stickies to be a certain format, make one exactly the way you want it (typeface, size, and color) and position it on the screen where you would want a new one to show up. Then from the Edit menu choose "Use as Default."

You'll get this message every time you close a Stickie unless you uncheck "Confirm window-closing" in the Preferences.

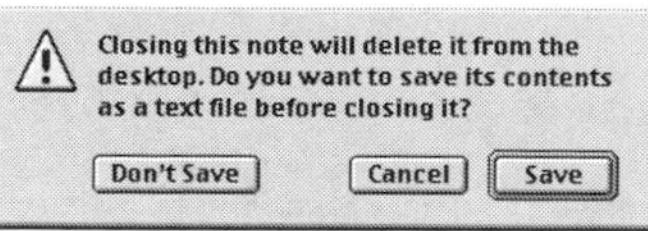

Remember, *not all of the items in your Apple menu are desk accessories.* You won't often need to know which ones are or aren't except when you are **installing** them and want to know where to put them.

If you need to know whether a file is a desk accessory, click once on its icon, then choose "Get Info" from the File menu and check the "Kind." If the file is *really* a desk accessory, meaning the Mac knows it is a desk accessory and not just something you want to put in your Apple Menu Items folder, then to install it you can just drag the icon and drop it onto the top of the *closed* System Folder. You'll see this polite message:

Installing Desk Accessories

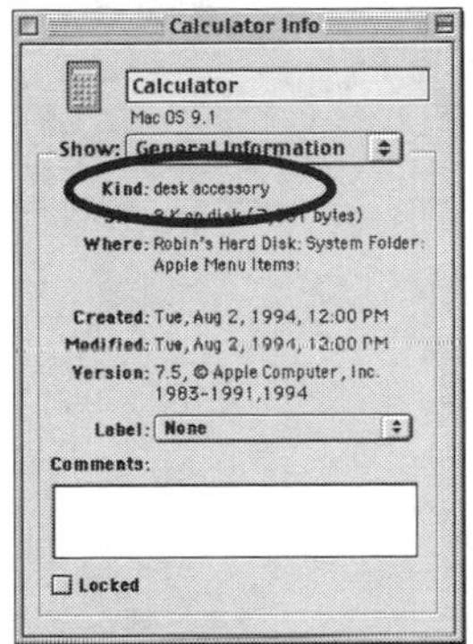

The Get Info box will tell you if the file is actually a desk accessory.

You can also place the desk accessory icon directly into the Apple Menu Items folder, found inside the System Folder. As soon as you drop it in, it appears in the Apple Menu and you can use it.

If you use a particular desk accessory so much that you would like to have it available for instant clicking, just move it to the Desktop—it will work just fine from there. You might want to keep an alias (see Chapter 25) on the Desktop and the original file in the Apple Menu, or vice versa.

Closing Desk Accessories

To close any desk accessory, click in its little close box in the upper left of its window, *or* press Command W, *or* press Command Q, *or* go up to the File menu and choose "Quit."

Match the task with the appropriate desk accessory you could use to accomplish the task. One DA might apply to more than one task.

Scrapbook — **Scrapbook**

Calculator — **Calculator**

Key Caps — **Key Caps**

Chooser — **Chooser**

Note Pad — **Note Pad**

Jigsaw Puzzle — **Jigsaw Puzzle**

AppleCD Audio Player — **CD Player**

Stickies — **Stickies**

Graphing Calculator — **Graphing Calculator**

1. Play a music CD . . . .
2. Find out how to type this character: © . . . .
3. Save a graphic image to put into your letterhead next week . . . .
4. Leave little notes all over the Desktop . . . .
5. Tell the computer to print to a different printer . . . .
6. Add up the itemized list for an invoice total and copy it into the invoice . . . .
7. Discover which fonts are installed . . . .
8. Keep a to-do list and notes about your garden . . . .
9. Graph an equation . . . .
10. Hang out and enjoy yourself for a few minutes . . . .

Answers on page 425.

23 Apple Menu

The **Apple menu** is under the tiny picture of the apple in the upper-left corner of your menu bar. No matter which program you are in, you always have access to anything in the Apple menu.

You can customize your Apple menu by adding files to it that you use frequently. Documents, folders, programs, desk accessories—stick 'em in the Apple menu. This chapter fills you in on all the juicy tidbits of how to customize your Apple menu and how to take advantage of it.

Apple Menu

The **Apple menu** is *meant* for you to customize—it is designed to help make your work easier and more efficient. Take advantage of it! But keep this is mind:

> Except for desk accessories (as you read about in the previous chapter, right?), you should put an *alias* of any item into the Apple menu—don't install the original file!

Aliases

An alias looks just like the original item, but its name is always in italic.

An **alias** is a *substitute* for the real thing. When you choose an alias, *the alias goes and gets the real thing.* You can have lots of aliases for the same item, since all any of them do is find the real object you want—they're "go-fers." You know, kind of like your kids: "Jimmy, go fer this and go fer that." Even though I'll explain how to create aliases in this chapter, you might want to read Chapter 25 for details. Aliases are great. And they are a very important part of managing your work.

> If you install an alias of a **folder** in the Apple menu, the name of the folder in the menu will have an arrow pointing to the side and the contents of the folder will be listed in a separate submenu so you can choose any item in the folder right from the menu.
>
> If you install an alias of an **application** in the Apple menu, selecting it will open the application for you.
>
> If you install an alias of a **document** in the Apple menu, selecting it will open the application it was created within, plus put the document on your screen.

What Are All These Things?

I explain each of the items in the Apple menu somewhere in this book, if not right here in this chapter. Below is a brief list of what each item is and where you can find more information about it.

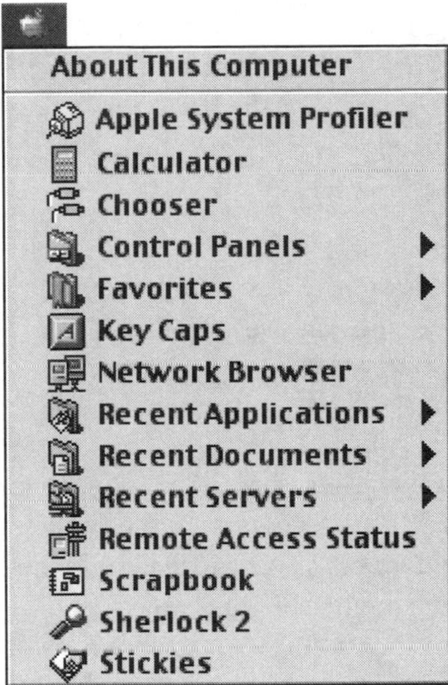

This is the Apple menu as it looked after I installed brand new Mac OS 9.

About This Computer
see pages 323–406, Chapter 29

Apple System Profiler
see page 235, Chapter 36

Calculator
see page 214, Chapter 22

Chooser
see page 152, Chapter 16

Control Panels
see Chapter 24

Favorites
see page 228 (next page)

Key Caps
see pages 216–217, Chapter 22

Network Browser
see page 301, Chapter 27

Recent Applications
see page 228 (next page)

Recent Documents
see page 228 (next page)

Recent Servers
see page 228 (next page)

Remote Access Status
see page 369, Chapter 33

Scrapbook
see pages 220–221, Chapter 22

Sherlock 2
see Chapter 26

Stickies
see page 222, Chapter 22

Favorites

www.apple.com

This icon is already in the Favorites folder in Mac OS 9. If you choose this favorite from the menu, your Mac will log on to the Internet, open a browser, and go to the Apple web site.

Favorites is a link to a folder that contains items you have designated as Favorites: You might assign a document as a Favorite, and then it would appear in the Apple menu under Favorites and you could open it from there. You might assign an entire folder as a Favorite, and then you could access the entire contents of the folder from the Apple menu. If you are connected to a network, you can put other network locations in your Favorites menu and connect to them with a click. If you have applications that use the new Open and Save As dialog boxes, your Favorites will be accessible there also.

To save a file as a Favorite, either:

- Click once on the file to select it. From the File menu, choose "Add To Favorites." In Mac OS 9.1, you can press Command T.
- **Or** hold down the Control key and click on the file; from the little menu that pops up, choose "Add To Favorites."

You can save your own **web addresses** as favorites, then when you choose an address from the Apple menu, your Mac will connect to the Internet and go to that address. Save an email address as a Favorite, and when you choose that address from the Apple menu, the Mac will open your email program and create a new email form addressed to that person. For details about working with these "Internet locations" and using them as Favorites, see Chapter 32, page 355.

Automated Tasks

About Automated Tasks
Add Alias to Apple Menu
Share a Folder
Share a Folder (no Guest)
Start File Sharing
Stop File Sharing

Automated Tasks is no longer in the Apple menu with OS 9, but you might still see it if your computer was updated from Mac OS 8.6. The items listed under Automated Tasks are just easy ways to accomplish things that you can also accomplish through control panels and dialog boxes. There are "scripts" you can install for more automated tasks—check the "Apple Extras" folder on your hard disk, look in the "AppleScript" folder. Drag any of the scripts you want to use into the Automated Tasks folder in the Apple Menu Items folder (found in the System Folder), and they will appear in this menu item.

Recent Applications
Recent Documents
Recent Servers

These "recent" menu items list the applications, documents, or servers (other computers that you send or retrieve files to or from) you have used recently; having them listed in the Apple menu makes the files or applications easier to return to. You can control how many items each of these recent options lists, and you can choose to turn each one on or off completely if you like (see page 235). If you are not on a network, turn "Recent Servers" off completely so it doesn't clutter up your Apple menu. See page 235 for a few more details.

Installing Apple Menu Items

If you still have the "Automated Tasks" item in your Apple menu, this is the quick, easy, and automatic way to put an alias in the Apple Menu Items folder. I'll also explain the manual method because Mac OS 9 no longer includes this Automated Tasks list.

Automatically

- If you plan to make an alias and put the alias in the Apple Menu Items folder, here's the easiest way:
  - Select the file by clicking once on it.
  - From the Apple menu, slide down to "Automated Tasks" and choose "Add Alias to Apple Menu."
  - It's done! Check the Apple menu. You can skip to the next page.

Manually

Follow these manual steps to install any file in the Apple menu.

- Unless the file is a desk accessory,* first make an alias of it (it probably isn't a desk accessory). To make an alias:
  - Click once on the folder, application, document, etc., that you want in the Apple menu. If you're viewing your files as buttons, click once on the *name* (not the button) to select it.
  - From the File menu, choose "Make Alias," or press Command M. The Mac will make an alias of the item.

    How do you know it's an alias? The most important **visual clue** is that the name of the alias file is in *italic.* Alias file names *are always italic.*

**If you don't know whether the file is an actual "desk accessory" or not, click once on the file icon, then press Command I to check the Get Info window, (shown below). Or check the window: when you view a window as some sort of list, the column "Kind" is usually showing. It will state "desk accessory" if the selected file is one.*

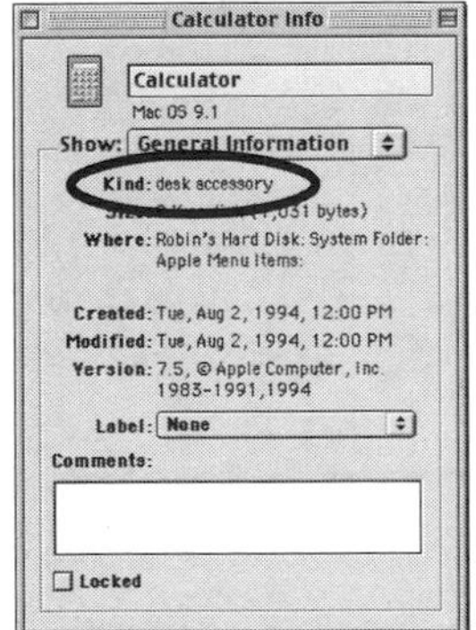

Icon view

List view

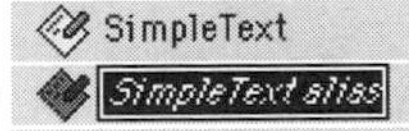

This is what you will see when you make an alias. Oh, look—the name is highlighted and has a border around it. That must be a ***visual clue!*** *What does it mean?!? ***

*** The highlight and border are clues that the file is ready for you to rename—just type if you want to rename it.*

—continued

Put the alias in the Apple Menu

- Now to put the alias in the Apple menu, open the System Folder.
- There is a folder in the System Folder called **Apple Menu Items.** You can type **appl** to select it, even if you don't see it.

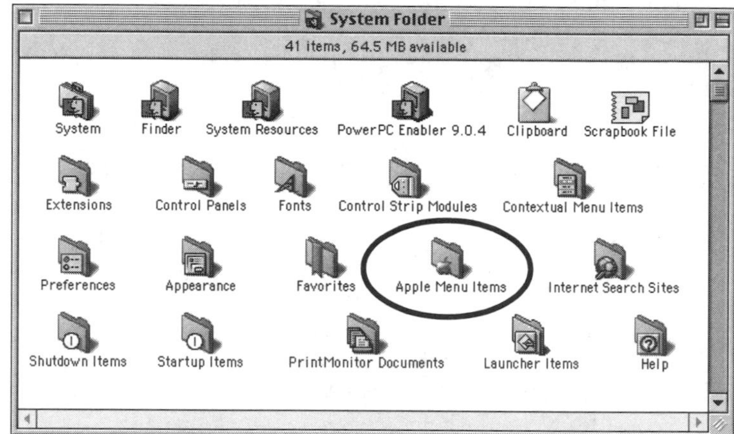

Here is the Apple Menu Items folder, inside the System Folder.

- The trick to putting the alias into the Apple folder is that you need to be able to see both the alias of your file *and* the Apple Menu Items folder at the same time; you may need to rearrange windows and the alias file to do so.
- Drag the alias and drop it onto the "Apple Menu Items" folder.
- The item will appear in the menu instantly; you don't need to restart the computer for it to take effect.

  Note: You can also use the spring-loaded folder feature to open all these folders, then have them close up behind you automatically (see page 84).

Alphabetizing, or "sorting"

The Apple menu displays items alphabetically, as I'm sure you've noticed. When the Mac alphabetizes, blank spaces and certain punctuation are "sorted" (alphabetized or otherwise organized) in front of any other character. So if you add a blank space, a hyphen, or a bullet (•, press Option 8 to type a bullet) as the first character in a name, that file will be first in the Apple menu list. The more blank spaces or hyphens, the higher on the list the file will be located. (Don't start a file name with a period—it can corrupt the file.)

Suggestions for Customizing

I keep an alias of the Apple Menu Items folder right on my Desktop so when I want to add something to the menu, I just open this folder and drop the alias directly into one of my organized folders.

Here are **suggestions for customizing your own Apple menu.**

- The Mac automatically places an alias of the Control Panels folder in the Apple menu. But if there are control panels you use regularly, you can make things even easier on yourself by installing aliases of the individual control panels right into the menu directly. For instance, if you use the Extensions Manager all the time, then put an alias of it into the Apple menu.
- Rather than dig into all those folders to get an application that you use regularly, put aliases of your favorite applications directly into the Apple menu.
- If you have a folder of important items that is filed within other folders, install an alias of the important folder into the Apple menu. When you choose it, the folder will open and you'll have easy access to all those related files.
- If you have documents or templates that you use regularly, such as a fax form or letterhead stationery, put their aliases in your Apple menu.
- If you have a floppy disk or cartridge hard disk or CD that you use regularly, or you can even do this to your hard disk, put an alias of it in the Apple menu and you'll get a submenu of all the items on the disk without having to open the windows. Any folders on the disk will have their own submenus. It's really amazing. If you change stuff on the disk, such as add files or change document names, it will be reflected in the Apple menu.

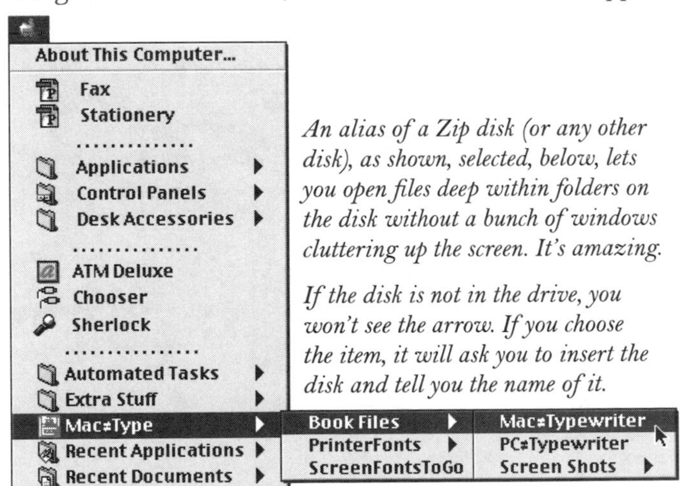

An alias of a Zip disk (or any other disk), as shown, selected, below, lets you open files deep within folders on the disk without a bunch of windows cluttering up the screen. It's amazing.

If the disk is not in the drive, you won't see the arrow. If you choose the item, it will ask you to insert the disk and tell you the name of it.

Hey—Let's Get Obsessive!

If you really want to create a nice, neat, customized Apple menu, you can group the files into clusters and even create separators between the clusters. Below is an example of an organized Apple menu.

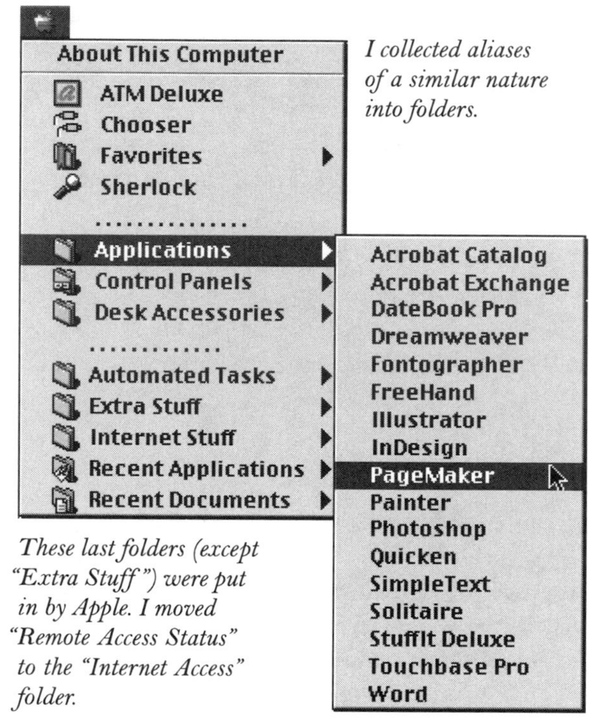

I collected aliases of a similar nature into folders.

These last folders (except "Extra Stuff") were put in by Apple. I moved "Remote Access Status" to the "Internet Access" folder.

Why would you put aliases of your applications in the Apple menu when you could put aliases on your Desktop and open them without having to go to a menu? For the simple reason that you can get to aliases in the Apple menu at times when you can't see your Desktop.

How to Organize your Apple Menu

I made a folder inside the Apple Menu Items folders for all my applications, one for all the desk accessories, and one for the extra stuff that I don't know what to do with yet, and look how short and neat the menu is! And still just as convenient. I also organized the files that were not in folders, as you can see. Directly below is an illustration of how things are organized in the Apple Menu Items folder to make the Apple menu (shown on the right) appear the way it does.

I typed two blank spaces in front of each of these file names so they are grouped together.

I typed one blank space in front of each of these file names.

I didn't add any blank spaces to these files.

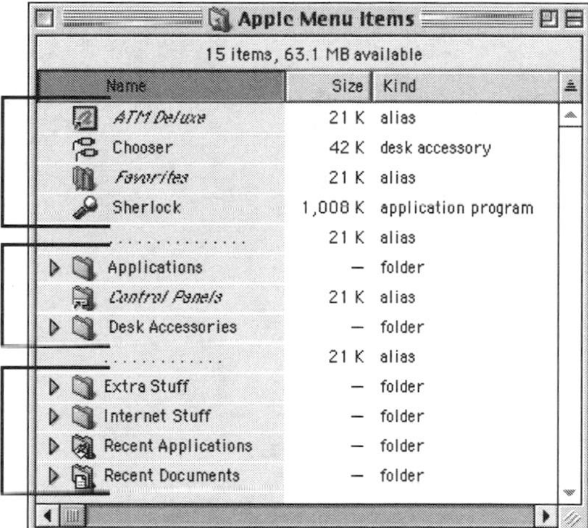

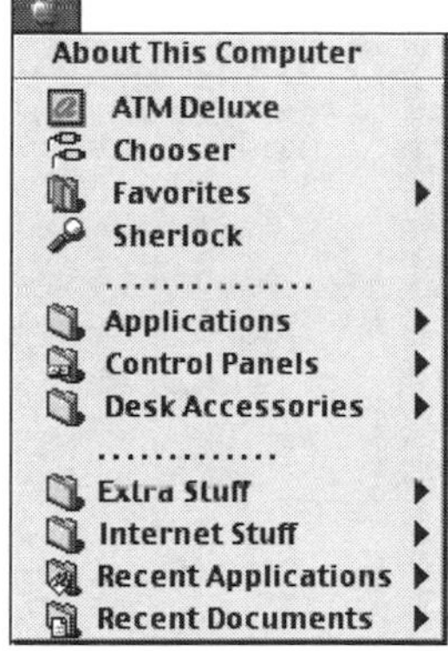

This is what the folder to the left looks like in the Apple menu.

I created ***the separators*** *by making two aliases of a blank page. I renamed the aliases by typing spaces and periods. I typed none or one blank space in front of each name. They each "alphabetized" at the top of the different groups of files because a period precedes an alphanumeric character.*

You could, of course, type several bullets or hyphens and then a name to indicate the cluster. For instance, instead of • • • • • • •, the divider might be • • Desk Accessories • • .

You don't see an icon for the blank document because I turned the file's icon into a white box, which essentially makes it invisible. *See page 98 for details on changing icons.*

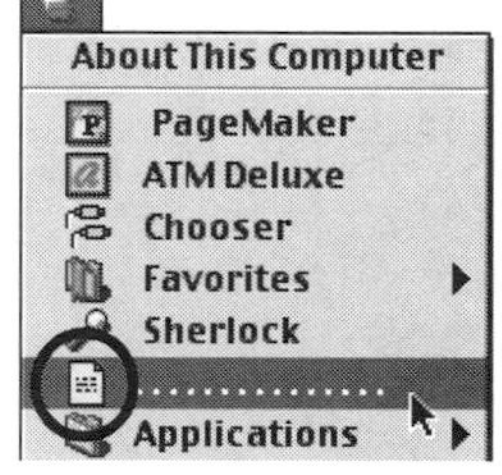

I removed the icon from the file so it doesn't show up in the Apple menu.

Apple Menu Options

You'll notice there are several folders in the Apple menu that Apple has placed there for you. Through the control panel **Apple Menu Options** you decide whether or not these folders show up, how many files each folder will keep track of, and if you want the little side menus (hierarchical menus). This is what each option does, and you can decide whether they are useful enough to keep or not.

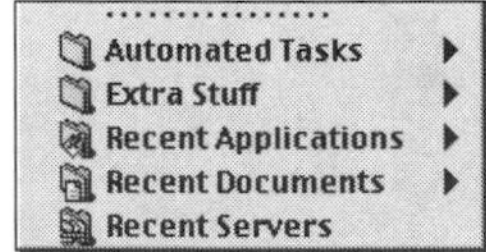

These folders are automatically placed in the Apple menu (except "Extra Stuff"— I put that in myself).

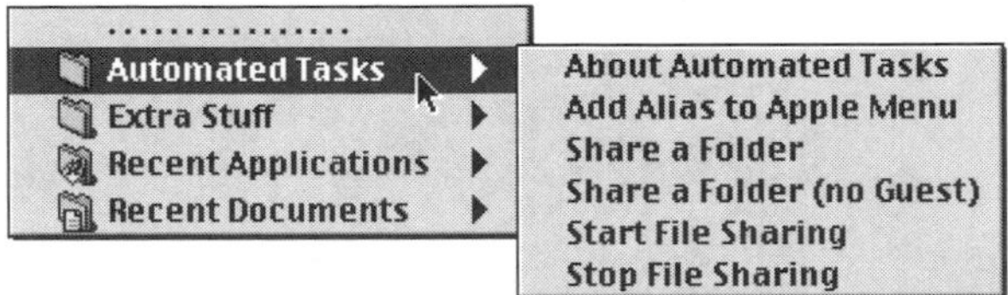

"Automated Tasks" is not included in Mac OS 9, but if you have it leftover from OS 8.6, it's great. I often use the task "Add Alias to Apple Menu." These items are all pretty self-explanatory.

Once you start file sharing, you will appreciate the automated task of turning file sharing on and off.

I don't use the "Recent Applications" menu item much since I have aliases of all my applications in my Apple menu anyway. If you don't find it very useful either, go to the Apple Menu Options control panel (shown on the next page) and set the number in "Remember recently used items" to 0 (zero). The folder will disappear from the Apple menu.

I love the "Recent Documents" menu item. The Mac keeps track of the documents you've opened and lists them here. Rather than having to dig back through folders to re-open something, you can just select it from this menu. You control how many recent documents you want the Mac to keep track of.

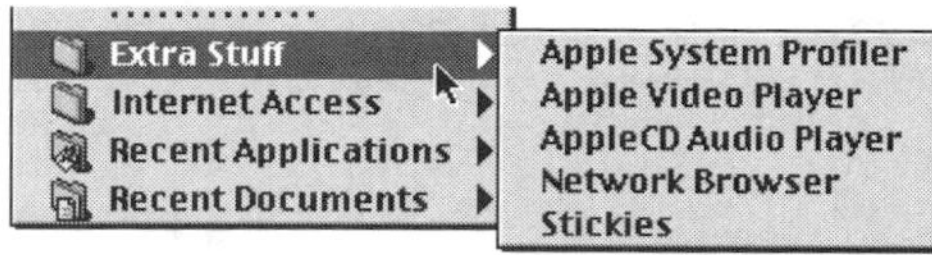

This folder "Extra Stuff" is not in your menu—I added it to mine. I put things in here that I don't need very often so I don't want them to clutter my menu. You can also hide something in there if you don't know what it is yet but are afraid to throw it away.

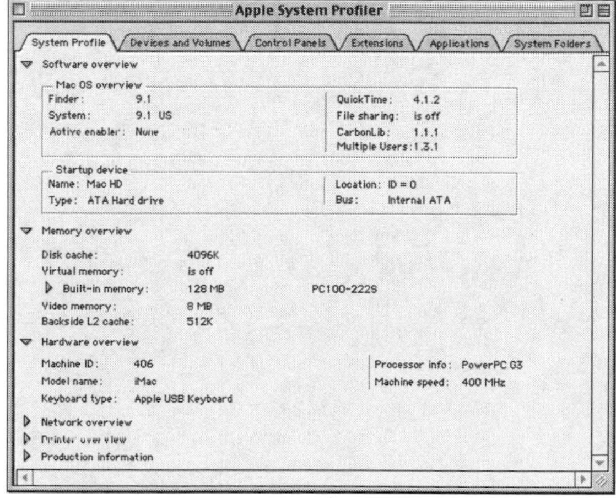

This is what you see if you choose "Apple System Profiler" from your Apple menu. Keep this in your menu and remember to look at it if you ever have to call tech support. See Chapter 36 for more information.

Apple Menu Options Control Panel

Use the **Apple Menu Options** control panel to customize those "Recent" folders and to turn on or off the hierarchical menus (the submenus, the ones the arrows in the menus point to). To get this control panel, slide down the Apple menu to "Control Panels," then out to the side to choose "Apple Menu Options."

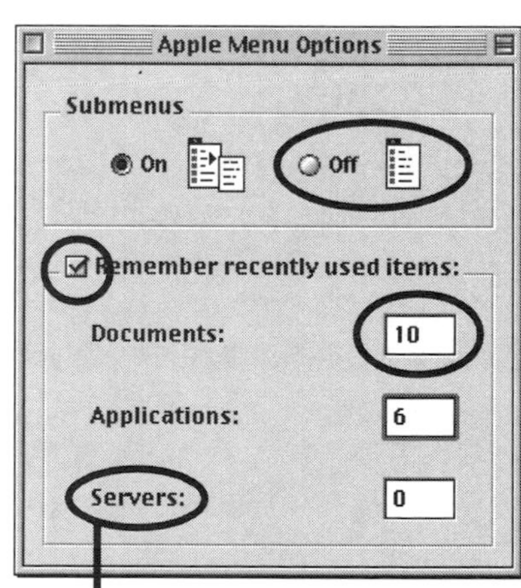

If you don't want the hierarchical menus at all, check the "Off" button.

If you uncheck the box "Remember recently used items," then those three extra folders for Recent Documents, Applications, and Servers will not appear at all in your Apple menu.

You can change the number of items you want the Mac to remember. If you type in "0" (zero), then that folder will disappear from the Apple menu altogether. Anytime you want it back, come back to this control panel and type in another number.

If you are file sharing, you can choose to see the servers you last used. If you are not file sharing, set this to zero to remove the folder from the menu.

1. When you start to customize your Apple menu, are you going to install original files or aliases in the Apple Menu Items folder?

2. What is an alias anyway?

3. Where do you put desk accessories or aliases when you want them to show up in the Apple menu?

4. Which of the following items can be stored in the Apple menu as aliases: folders, applications, documents, floppy disks, CDs, hard disks

5. How can you force a set of items to be grouped together in the Apple menu?

6. What is the fastest and easiest way to get an item into the Apple menu?

7. How can you get rid of the folder in the Apple menu called "Recent Servers"?

8. If you know that a file is technically a "desk accessory," do you need to make an alias of it before you put it in the menu?

9. What is the visual clue that tells you a file is an alias?

10. Can you name three items that you, personally, would find useful having in the Apple menu?

Answers on page 425.

Control Panels

24

The **control panels** concept is a very important feature of the Macintosh that lets you customize the look and feel of your computer, plus gives you added features. Each control panel controls a certain aspect of the Mac, such as what you see in your windows and how the items are displayed, what sound you hear and how loud it is, whether or not you want to share folders and files with other people on other computers, and many other features. A certain number of control panels are provided by Apple, and you will run into others provided by other vendors.

Control panels are stored in the Control Panels folder found in the System Folder. *Many control panels will not work unless they are stored in this folder!* You can open the Control Panels folder and double-click on any file to open the panel itself. Most of the features are self-explanatory, and different sorts of computers have different sorts of control panels. In this chapter I'll go through the most common ones so you can quickly get an idea of what they do and how you can control your Mac.

If you need more help with any control panel, go to the **Help** menu (in your Desktop menu bar, next to "Special") and choose "Show Balloons." Then position the pointer over parts of the control panel: a balloon with information in it will pop up, and if you're lucky you'll learn something. Or click the Help icon (the question mark) that is visible on most control panels. This will bring up the Apple Guide, which is usually more helpful than the Balloons.

Get either Balloons or the Help guide from here.

Wherever you see one of these icons, click on it to get Help. Sometimes it's useful, sometimes it isn't.

Control Panels

The actual Control Panel files are stored in this folder, found in the System Folder.

Control panels are accessible through your Apple menu (an alias of the Control Panels folder was automatically installed in the Apple Menu Items folder for you).

There is a little arrow pointing to the side next to the Control Panels item, indicating another menu (an *h-menu,* remember?). You can slide out to the side and select the control panel you want without having to open the entire folder.

If you *do* want to open the actual folder that contains all of the control panels, just let go when "Control Panels" is highlighted in the menu, *without* sliding over to the side.

If you find you are using certain control panels regularly, you may want to put an alias of the panel itself directly into the Apple menu (see the previous chapter) or directly on the Desktop (see Chapter 25).

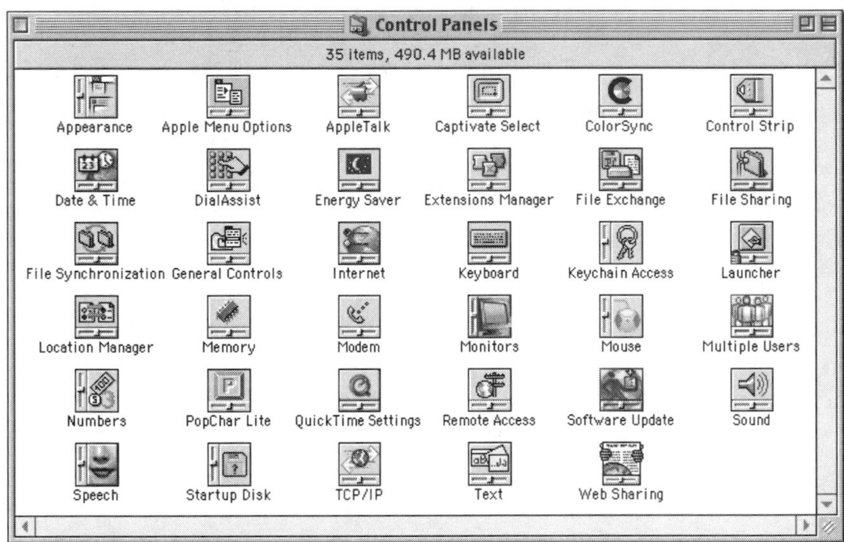

These are some of the Control Panels you might find in your folder. You might not have some of these, and you probably have lots of others that aren't shown here.

Apple Menu Options

The **Apple Menu Options** control panel determines whether your Apple menu has *hierarchical menus* or not. Hierarchical menus are the little submenus that come off to the side, indicated by a little arrow. In this control panel you can turn them off altogether if they annoy you.

If you check the box to "Remember recently used items," then you will have three new folders in your Apple menu. One will create a submenu that holds aliases of the last several documents you opened, one holds applications, and one holds servers (which is only useful if you work in a heavily networked environment where you have access to several other computers through your own). The number you type in is how many items the Mac will remember. If you type in "0" (zero), the folder will disappear from the menu.

If you have any number typed in the "Documents" box, the Mac will monitor *all* the files that are opened, including all the filters of some programs that use them. If it seems that your applications are taking an unusually long time to launch, open this control panel and type in a zero in the Documents edit box.

ColorSync

The **ColorSync** control panel is useful for graphics professionals who want to make sure the color on the monitor is as close to the color that will be printed as possible, to see how web graphics might appear on other monitors or on Windows machines, or just to make the color on your own monitor look pleasing regardless of whether anything you create will be printed or posted on the web. This control panel works in conjunction with the Color section of the Monitors control panel—any new profiles you create will appear in the "System Profile" list in the ColorSync control panel.

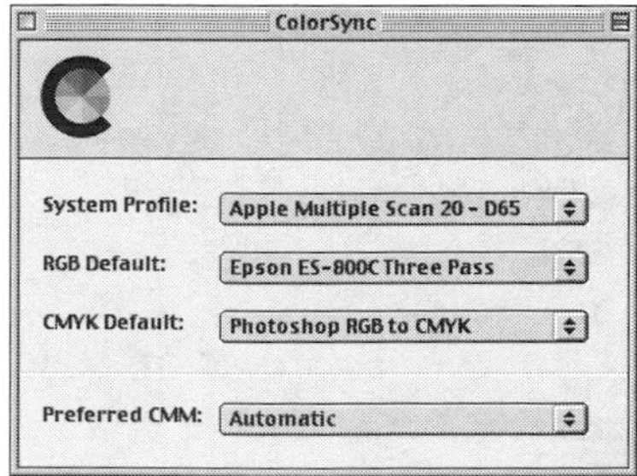

If you know what you're doing with monitor and printer color, you can adjust these choices to suit you. If none of this makes sense to you, don't worry—the default settings will be just fine.

Appearance

The **Appearance** control panel lets you adjust a number of items that affect the way things appear on your monitor, such as colors, patterns, fonts, sounds, scroll bars, etc. The big deal is that you can make sets of preferred choices and save these sets as "themes." These themes are particularly great if more than one person uses the computer: each person can set up their preferences and apply the whole set with a click; the next person can apply their own set of preferences with a click. For instance, perhaps your teenage son likes the Roswell flying saucers as a background, lots of sounds, an ugly typeface, and bright orange highlights. He can save these options as his own theme. You might have another theme with large type for the icons, a flat background of a soothing color, and no sounds. You can save these options as a theme. Either one of you can open this Appearance control panel, choose the theme you created, and it will be applied instantly.

Themes

To create a theme, as described above, open the Appearance control panel. Then:

1. Click on each of the individual tabs (Appearance, Fonts, Desktop, etc., are all explained on the following pages), and make your choices.
2. When you've made all of your choices, click again on the "Themes" tab. You'll see a theme highlighted, and it will be called "Custom Theme."
3. Click the button "Save Theme…" and give this one a name. Now your customized set of options is saved in this scrolling list of themes, and you can choose it whenever you like.

If you ever want to ***change the name of your theme,*** *select its picture in the scrolling examples, as shown to the right. Then from the Edit menu, choose "Theme Name…." Type to rename it, then click* OK.

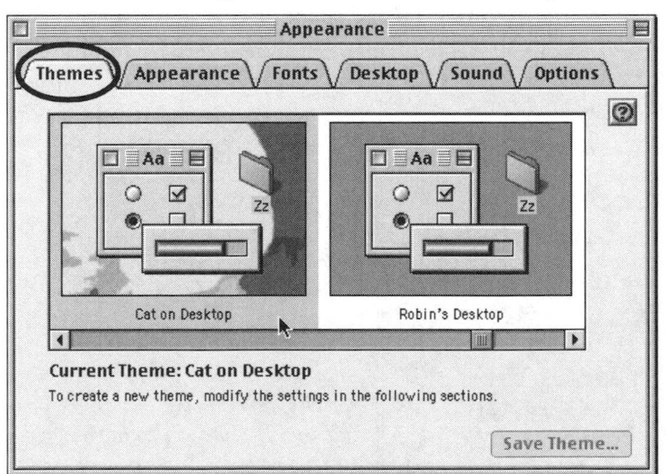

Appearance

These are all pretty self-explanatory. The "platinum look" might make some of your menus and dialog boxes look funny in certain applications (white squares or blotches), but it doesn't hurt anything. "Highlight" color is the color of the highlight when you drag over text, and "Variation" is the highlighted color in menus. Choose a variation color and then pull down a menu to see its effect instantly.

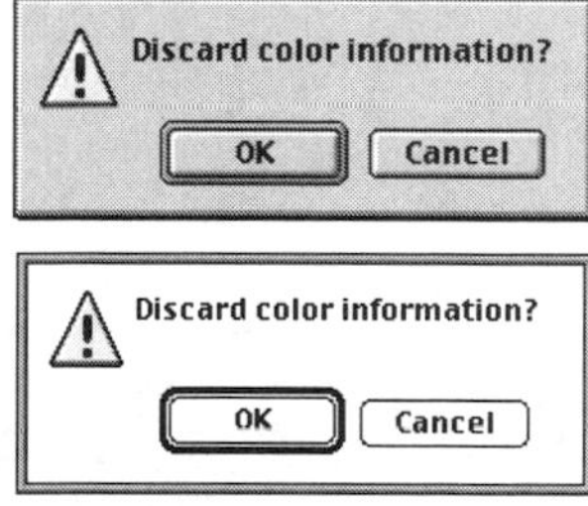

This is the difference between the platinum appearance (top) and the normal appearance (bottom).

Fonts

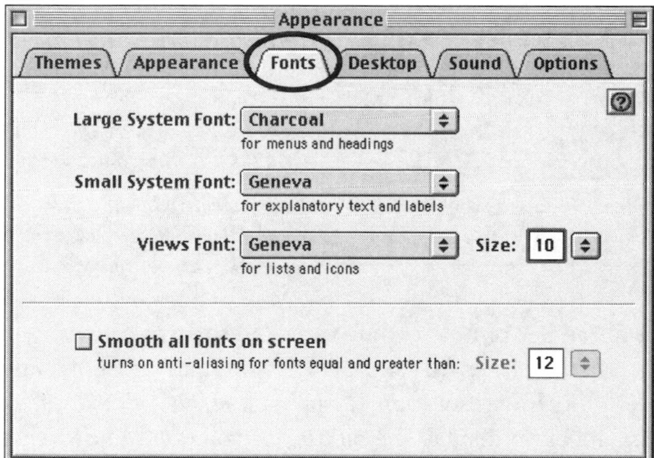

Each option explains where that particular font will appear.

The choice to "Smooth all fonts on screen" makes the edges of most typefaces smoother and prettier on the screen, as shown in the example to the right. ("Aliasing" is the stair-step jaggies on type or certain graphics; anti-aliasing blends the letterforms with the background color. It's best for on-screen.)

For what?

Aliased type, above; anti-aliased, below.

For what?

Desktop

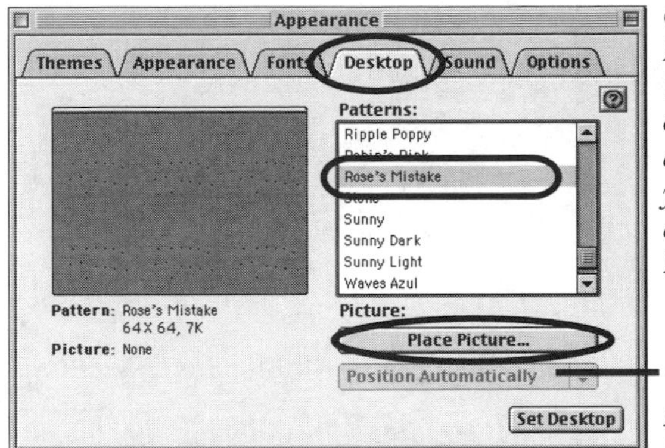

Click a pattern for your Desktop background. You'll see it in the preview on the left side of the control panel. To see it on your Desktop before you close this box, click "Set Desktop."

Once you've placed a picture (see below), use this menu to position it.

Make your own patterns

To make your own patterns, *select and copy a piece of any graphic you have in any of your graphic programs, including AppleWorks (or you can even select text). Then click on the preview, and paste. The image will "tile," or repeat itself on the screen. Your new pattern is called "Untitled Pattern." Change its name: select it in the list, then from the Edit menu, choose "Pattern Name..." and give it a name. Click* OK.

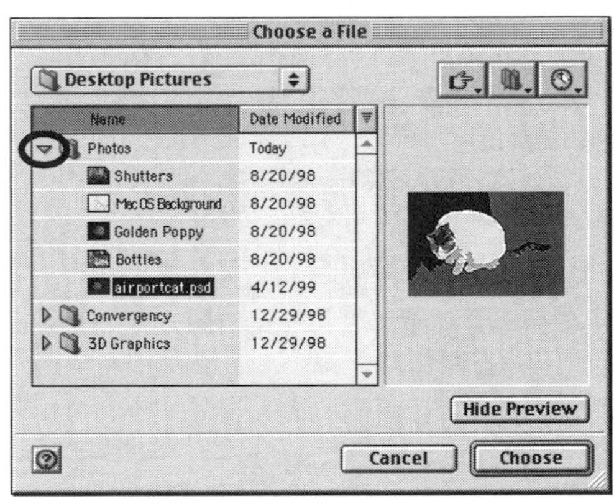

To place an image on your Desktop, click the "Place Picture..." button (circled above.) In the Open dialog box (left), you are automatically taken to the folder called "Desktop Pictures." Click the tiny triangle to see what is inside each folder. Click the "Show Preview" button to see what the image looks like. Double-click the file name you want to use.

Experiment with the "Position" menu (above). The picture sits on top of the pattern you chose.

Use your own photos or images

Apple supplies a number of images, but you can use any of your own. The file format must be either GIF, JPEG, PICT, or a "native" Photoshop file, and it's best if it's low resolution (72 ppi is fine) so it doesn't take much of your memory to display the picture. If you don't know what all this graphic stuff means, ask a graphic friend. Or check your software—if you can open a photograph or image in any of your applications, then you can probably save in a variety of file formats.

Tip: *Drag an entire folder of images into the preview box, and each time you turn on your Mac, a different picture from that folder will appear on your Desktop!*

Once you have images in the proper format, put them in the Desktop Pictures folder (which is inside the Appearance folder, which is inside the System Folder) and open them through the dialog box, as explained above. Or **you can simply drag an image and drop it into the picture box right here in the control panel.**

Sound

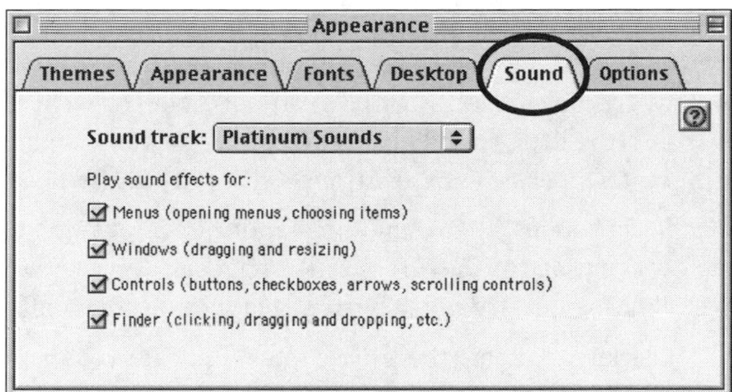

You can choose from different sound tracks for sound effects. If you like to hear your menus opening, your windows dragging, and your mouse clicking and dropping, choose a sound track and check the boxes. If you like a silent Mac, choose the sound track "None." This does not affect the volume level nor the alert sounds.

Options

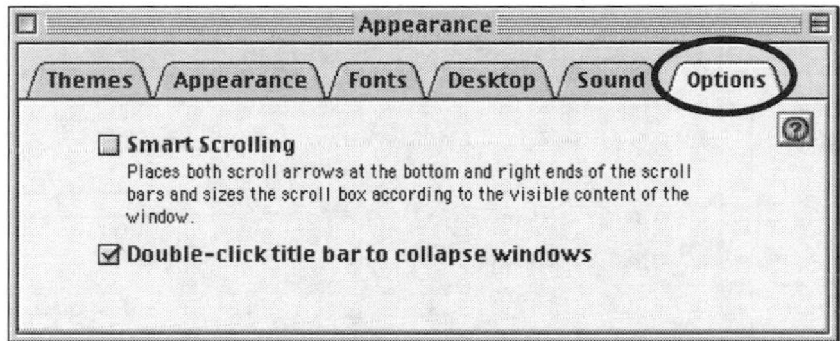

Choose "Smart Scrolling" to put both of the scroll arrows at the same end of the scroll bar, as shown in Chapter 7. This also makes the scroll box change size to indicate how much of the window is out of your sight. If you've been using a Mac for a while, Smart Scrolling takes some time to get used to. If you're a new user, you might want to start off with Smart Scrolling now.

As explained in Chapter 7, you can click the Collapse box in the upper left of windows to collapse a window to just its title bar. If you check the box to "Double-click title bar to collapse windows," then you can double-click ***anywhere*** *in the title bar. I really like this option because I don't like to have to find that tiny little box to collapse the window. Also, with this button checked you can collapse windows or palettes that don't have Collapse buttons. For instance, in many applications you can double-click to collapse the floating tool palettes if you check this box.*

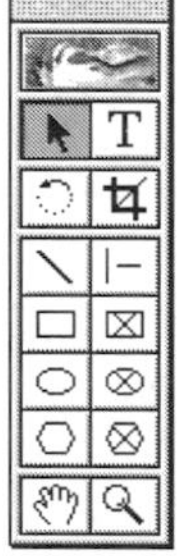

The tool palette, left, doesn't have a collapse box. But if I check the box in the Appearance control panel, I can double-click to collapse the tool box so all that's left on the screen is the title bar, as shown above.

General Controls

The **General Controls** panel has some interesting features. Below is a screen shot of the entire control panel, and I'll go through each item separately. This panel is a good example of the difference between radio buttons (the little round ones) and checkboxes (the square ones). Their different shapes are not arbitrary—they are **visual clues.**

Radio buttons (the round ones) indicate you can choose *one and only one* of the options, like on a car radio. When you choose one, any other button that was on turns off.

Checkbox buttons (the square ones) indicate you can choose *any number* of the options, including *none of them or all of them.* If you click in an empty box, you get a checkmark (✔); if you click on the checkmark, the ✔ is removed. (This is a toggle switch—it toggles back and forth between on and off as you click on it.)

The control panels looks slightly different in Mac OS 9.1 (below-left) and Mac OS 9 (below-right), but they act just the same.

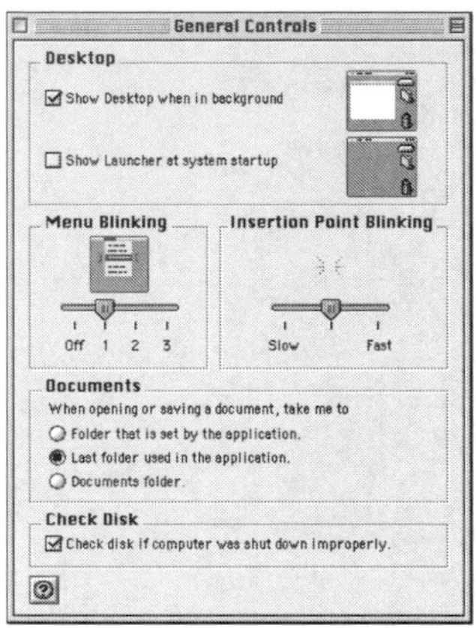

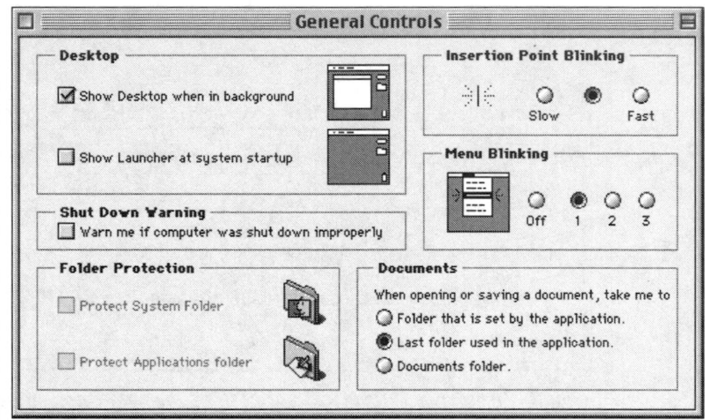

Desktop

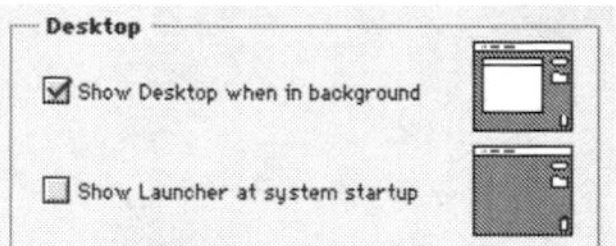

If you choose **Show Desktop when in background,** then no matter which application you are in you will be able to see the Desktop and all the icons on it while you are working on your documents. This is confusing to beginners because if you accidentally click on that Desktop, you will pop out of your application and over to the Desktop without knowing what happened. More advanced users like to have that option turned on, though, because it allows you to bounce back and forth between your application and your Desktop (the Finder).

If you **un**check that option (click in the checkbox), then the only way to get back to the Desktop (Finder) is to choose "Finder" from the Application menu (the icon on the far right end of the menu bar)—you cannot accidentally "lose" your application. If you uncheck this box, use the tear-off Application menu to get to the other applications (see pages 325 and 326).

Show Launcher at system startup

If you choose **Show Launcher at system startup,** then guess what—the Launcher will show up when you start your computer. The Launcher is this interesting little panel upon which you can place your favorite applications and documents. Then when you want to use one of them, you just click once on its icon on the Launcher panel. It's similar to viewing your windows "as Buttons," but you can just put the files you use regularly in the Launcher so you don't have to see everything else.

All the details about the Launcher are on pages 248–249. If you like it and use it, you can choose in this control panel whether or not you want it to automatically appear when you turn on (startup) your Mac.

Shut Down Warning

Sometimes the computer crashes, freezes, bombs, or otherwise stops functioning properly. Usually when this happens you have to either restart the computer (see page 411) or turn it off. Remember, the Mac doesn't like to be turned off unexpectedly. It likes to go inside itself and tidy up important things before shutting down. So if you had to follow undesirable procedures because of some problem, when you next turn on the computer you get a message telling you the Macintosh was shut down improperly. Well, if you **un**check the box to **Warn me if computer was shut down improperly,** then you won't see that message anymore.

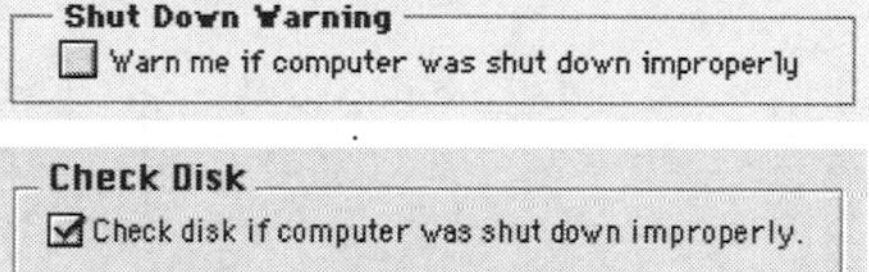

Mac OS 9 uses the first warning above, top; OS 9.1 uses the second warning shown.

Insertion Point Blinking

The **insertion point** is that little flashing bar that appears whenever you can type. You can choose how fast it blinks. If you choose "Slow" it can get lost on the page because it is gone for so long. Fast is rather annoying to many people.

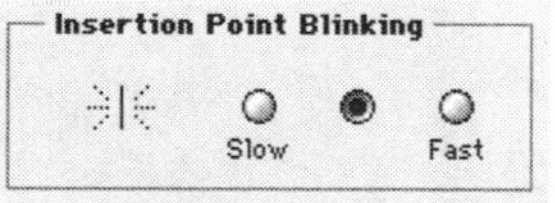

Menu Blinking

When you choose a menu item, the **menu blinks** either one, two, or three times. You can choose the number, or choose to have no blink at all. I like to have at least one blink as my **visual clue** that I really did get the right menu item.

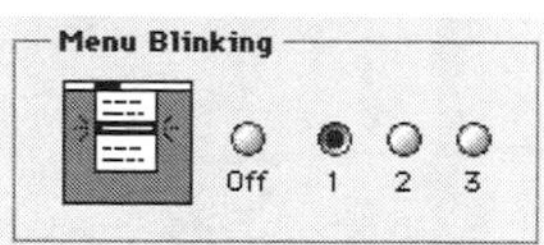

Folder Protection

(This is in Mac OS 9 only.) If you check either of these boxes, **Protect System Folder** or **Protect Applications folder,** no one can throw away anything from those two folders, nor can they move items out of them, nor can they rearrange files. You can still save documents into either folder, though. Some Macs have folder protection on as a default.

If you try to change things in the System Folder or Applications folder while they are being protected, you'll get a thoughtful message that tells you how to fix the problem:

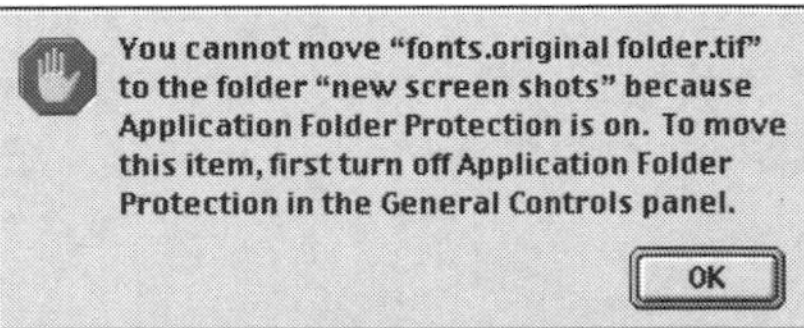

Documents

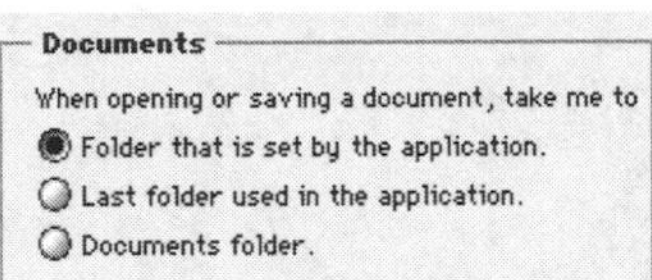

In the **Documents** setting you can choose where your "Open" and "Save As" dialog boxes automatically open to. For instance, let's say you are at the Desktop and you double-click a word processing document stored in a folder called "Letters" that you created yesterday in AppleWorks. So when you double-click the document, it opens AppleWorks and puts the letter in front of you. You want to Save As so you can edit this letter and send the edited version to your mother.

If you chose **Folder that is set by the application** in the General Controls control panel, then when you Save As, the dialog box will open right to the same folder that the letter came out of (usually, depending on the application). This is perfect. This is what we want. This is good.

If you chose **Last folder used in the application,** when you Save or Open you will get a dialog box displaying the last folder you used in this particular application. Depending on how you work and what you do, you might like this option. Generally, most people find it annoying because the last folder you used in that application often has nothing to do with what you are working on now.

The Mac will create this Documents folder for you. On some Macs, the Documents folder option is checked by default.

If you chose **Documents folder,** when you Save As or Open you will get a dialog box that automatically chooses to Save your file *into* a folder called Documents, or Open a file *from* the Documents folder. Don't worry if you didn't see any folder called Documents—the Mac will automatically create one for you on the Desktop. This might be okay for a while, but as soon as you figure out how to organize your files with folders and how to save them into their own folders, you will never want this Documents folder again. It's like putting every piece of paper in your office into one file folder in your filing cabinet.

Date & Time

Date & Time

Use the **Date & Time** control panel to (duh) change the date and time. Just click on the day or time and press the arrows or type the numbers. To accept the new information, click anywhere, close the control panel, *or* press the Return key.

- Click on any of the numbers and you will get little arrows. Click the up or down arrows to move the selected number higher or lower. Or you can just type some numbers in to replace the selected ones. Click anywhere to set it.
- Any button you see with an ellipsis (three dots ...) takes you to another dialog box where you can set the specifications for all those things.

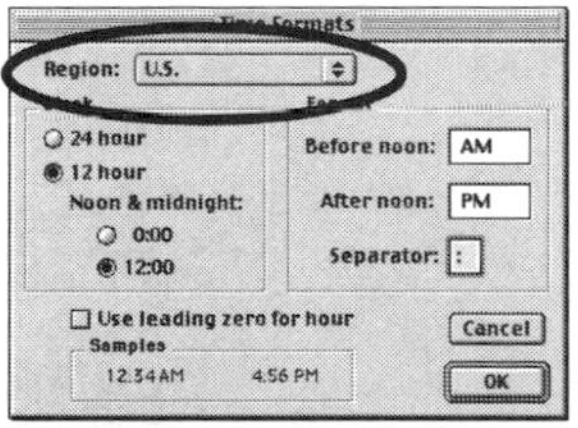

Click on the time in the menu bar and you'll see the date.

This control panel also lets you change the *formats* for the date and time. Click the button "Date Formats..." or "Time Formats..." to get a list of options. As you change options, a sample of the new format appears in the bottom portion of the box. If you have any other language versions installed in your System, you can choose to display date and time in that language's standard format: choose the language from the "Region" menu by pressing on the arrows (it probably says "U.S." at the moment). As soon as you make any changes to these boxes, the Region menu will display "Custom."

When you use an application that automatically inserts the date or time, the numbers will appear in the format you have determined here.

Poke around in all the dialog boxes—they're very self-explanatory. You can change the typeface for the clock that shows up in the menu bar, or change the time zone you're in (which is especially handy if you take your computer traveling), or even set up the correct Daylight Savings time, then click "Set Daylight-Saving Time Automatically" and your Mac will change the time on those two days. Have fun!

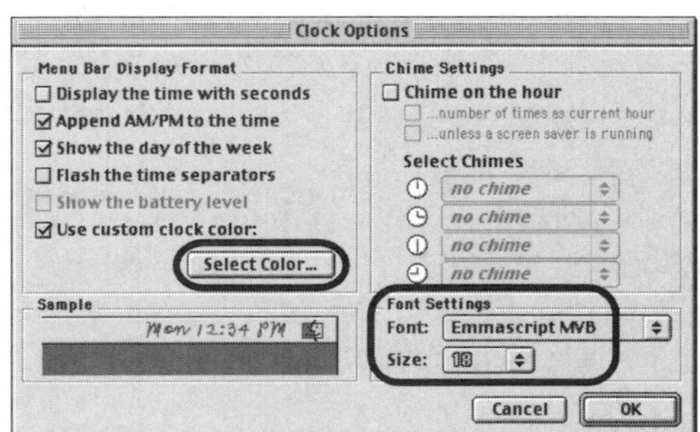

Change the color, typeface, and size of the time in your menu bar!

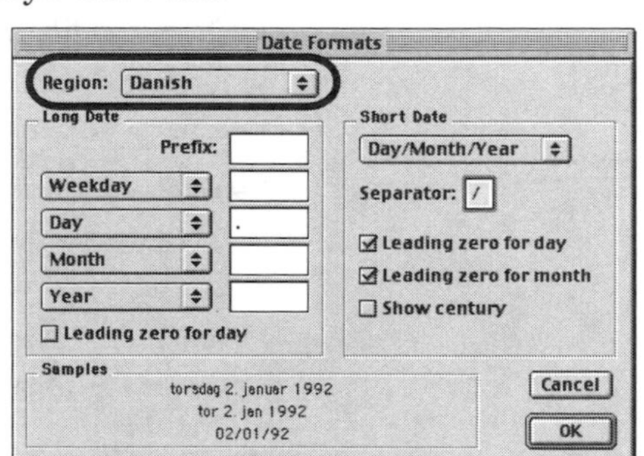

The settings for "Long Date" will appear under the "Date Modified" heading in your windows.

Launcher

The **Launcher** control panel opens a special "window" with buttons. You click these buttons *once* to open, or "launch," applications and documents. This can be a very wonderful feature for beginners—all you see are the buttons that do what you want to do, and you can ignore the rest of your Mac for a while. If you're not comfortable with your Mac yet, have someone set this up for you. This is what the Launcher looks like once it's been customized with all your files:

Across the top are ***category*** *buttons. You can add or delete categories.*

If you prefer, ***resize*** *the Launcher so it's vertical.*

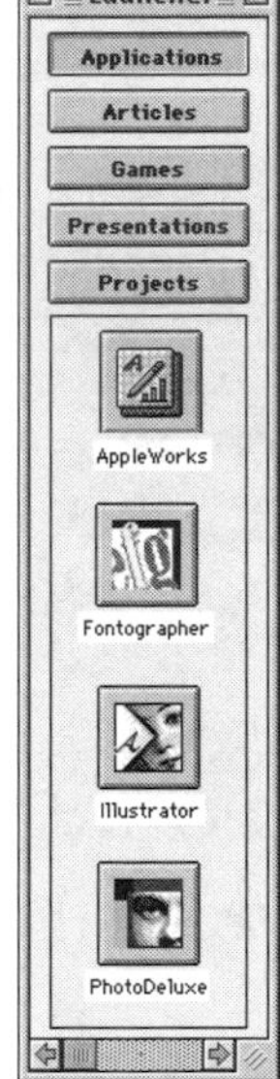

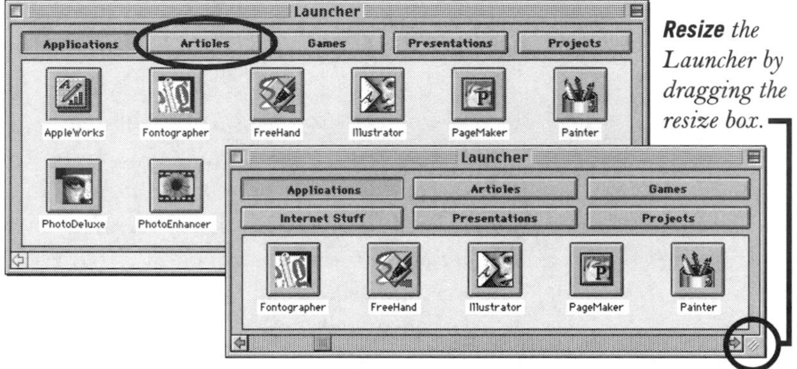

Resize *the Launcher by dragging the resize box.*

Customize your Launcher. Everything on the Launcher is an alias (page 266); when you add items to it, the Mac automatically creates the alias for you. When you throw items away, you are throwing away an *alias*, not the *original*.

To add an item to the Launcher:

- Open the Launcher if it isn't open already (in the Apple menu, slide down to "Control Panels," then choose "Launcher").
- On the Desktop, find the file you want to add. It can be a document, folder, application, sound, etc.
- Drag the file onto the category *button* where you want the file to be placed. If that category is already open (its button is depressed), just drag the file right onto the Launcher *window.*

To remove an item from the Launcher:

- Hold down the Option key and drag the icon from the Launcher to the trash, or drag the icon to a folder if you want to keep it.

  Remember, everything in the Launcher is an alias so it's completely safe to throw anything away! Your original files stay right where you left them.

To move an item to a new category:

- Hold down the Option key and drag the item to one of the other category *buttons.* Let go.

To put a file into a folder on the Launcher:

- First, do you *have* a folder on the Launcher? You can put one into any category: Make a folder anywhere, then drag it to the Launcher and drop it. The Mac makes the alias for you.
- Drag a file from your hard disk and drop it on top of the folder button on the Launcher. *Anything you put in the Launcher folder will really go into the real folder on the hard disk.*

To resize the Launcher buttons:

- Hold down the Command key and press the mouse pointer inside the Launcher window. This makes a little menu pop up. Keep holding the mouse button down and choose another size.

Command-press to get this little menu to change the size of the icons.

To open category button folders:

- Hold down the Option key and click on a category *button.* Its original folder will appear.

To make new category buttons, and to remove others:

- From the System Folder, open the Launcher Items folder.
- **To make a new category,** make a new folder with the name of the category you want. At the beginning of the name, type a bullet (press Option 8 to type a bullet). That folder will now appear in the Launcher as a category.
- **To remove a category** from the Launcher, take the bullet off of the name in the Launcher Items folder.

Any folder name starting with a bullet (•) will appear as a category. The "Applications" category is already made for you—although there is no visible folder for Applications, any file you drop directly into this Launcher Items folder will automatically be placed in the Applications category.

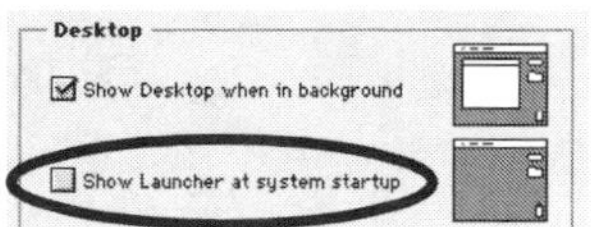

You can put an alias of the Launcher right on your Desktop so you don't have to go to the Apple menu to get it. Or go to the General Controls control panel and click the box to "Show Launcher at system startup," and then every time you turn on your Mac the Launcher will be up and ready to go.

Launcher Items

If you find you use the Launcher Items folder often, make an alias of it and leave it on your Desktop. Or drag the Launcher Items folder onto your Launcher so you have a button of the folder!

Memory

Memory

*This control panel assumes you know what **memory** is in the first place. Read Chapter 29 called* Very Important Information *for a better understanding of the difference between hard disk space, memory, and virtual memory.*

Use the **Memory** control panel to set a *disk cache* (pronounced "cash") for your Mac, turn *virtual memory* on or off, or create a *RAM disk.*

The **disk cache** is a part of the memory your Mac uses to hold information about the most recent things it's done on your disk, like getting files and saving them. Getting this data from the disk cache is much quicker than going back to the disk to retrieve it. The Mac will set a default (an automatic choice) for the cache size, depending on how much memory is available. You can override this default by changing the Cache Size yourself. It might seem like setting a larger cache size would be better, but it actually isn't because then that much memory is unavailable to any applications you open. In OS 8.5 and up, the Mac grabs much too much of your RAM for cache, based on how much RAM is installed. It's safe to click "Custom setting" and set a smaller amount.

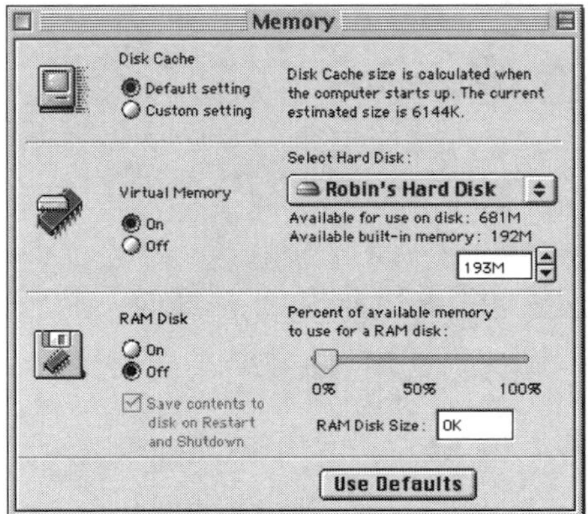

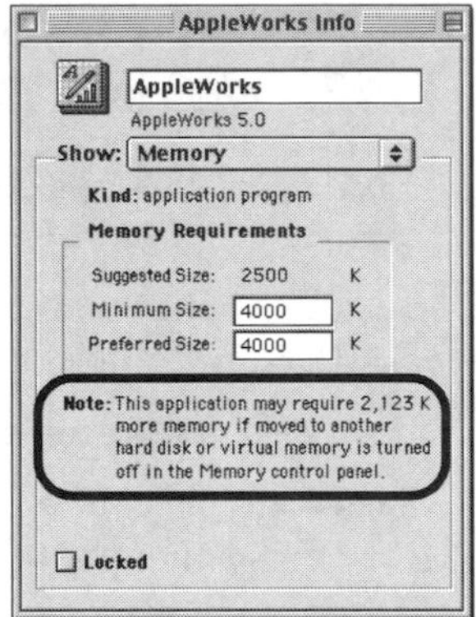

Most applications on newer Macs like to have virtual memory on.

Virtual memory

Virtual memory is when the Mac *pretends* some of the hard disk space is memory. Since you're probably using Mac OS 8 or higher, you're probably using a Power Mac, G3, or G4. These machines utilize memory differently from older machines, and applications written for these machines actually function better with virtual memory turned on, even if you allocate just a megabyte (older Macs generally function better with virtual memory turned off). So go ahead and turn it on, if it isn't already.

You determine how much of your hard disk space to let the Mac have. Don't ever give it more virtual memory than you actually have installed. That is, if you have 32 megabytes of real RAM installed, don't allocate any more than 32 megabytes of virtual memory. In fact, allocating just 1 megabyte will satisfy your Mac and your applications that want virtual memory turned on.

RAM disk

After you restart, you'll see the RAM disk on your Desktop. It will appear in your Save As dialog boxes, also.

A **RAM disk** is a pretend hard disk made out of memory. (Virtual memory is a *hard disk* pretending to be memory; a RAM disk is *memory* pretending to be a hard disk.)

When you create a RAM disk, you are telling the computer to take some of your real memory and set it aside. The Mac will create an icon of a floppy disk on your Desktop, and then you can copy things to this disk, or save things onto it. Why? For speed. RAM disks are blazingly fast. If you copy your favorite application to a RAM disk, you will notice a decided difference.

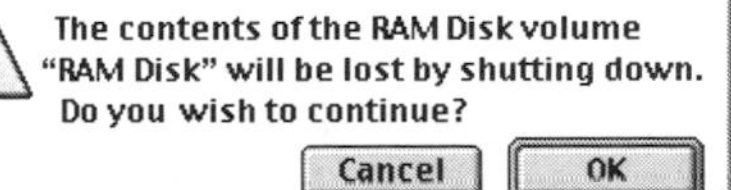

But RAM is temporary, remember? Anything stored in RAM or on a RAM disk will disappear when you shut down or when you crash or when the lights flicker. (It will stay during a restart, though.) So you don't ever want your only copy of an important document saved to a RAM disk. ***Unless*** you are running Mac OS 9 or 9.1—then you have an extra button in the Memory control panel, as shown to the right, so the Mac will automatically save the contents on Shutdown and, on OS 9.1, on Restart.

If the button is gray when you want to turn the RAM disk off, first turn off file sharing.

To create a RAM disk, click the button On. Move the slider to the amount of RAM you are willing to give away, and restart. The RAM disk icon will appear on your hard disk. (If you're not using a version of OS 9, remember to copy anything out of the RAM disk and onto your hard disk before you shut down!)

Mouse

Use the **Mouse** control panel to determine how "fast" the mouse moves. The terms "Slow" and "Fast" are a little misleading. The "slower" the "Mouse Tracking," the farther you have to move the mouse across the desk to get the pointer to move across the screen. Try it—click different speeds, especially the fastest and slowest, and notice how far you have to move the mouse to get the pointer across the screen.

Slower speeds are good for drawing or for editing images in a program like Photoshop. Set the mouse tracking to "Fast" to move the cursor all the way across the screen while moving the mouse a much smaller distance. It's great for small work spaces. It may drive you nuts to work on someone's computer who has the mouse tracking set to one of the slower speeds. Now you know what to do about it.

The "Double-Click Speed" lets you set the speed at which the mouse will interpret two clicks as a double-click (as opposed to two single clicks). If you're kind of slow with your finger, set it to the slow speed. If you set it to the fastest speed (the far-right button), you may find that the mouse sometimes thinks a single-click is a double-click.

Monitors

The **Monitors** control panel provides several options for your monitor. Your control panel will probably not look exactly like what you see here—you might have more or fewer options. (If you're using an older operating system, you might have a control panel called "Monitors & Sound" that combines both this control panel and Sound in the same panel; see Sound on page 254.)

Color Depth

The **Color Depth** lets you choose how many shades of gray or colors your screen will display. The number of grays and colors to choose from depends on your particular monitor, plus how much RAM and video RAM you have, and what kind of video card (if any) is in your computer. If you're short on RAM, choose to display fewer colors.

Resolution

If you have a "multi-sync" monitor, you can change the **resolution** of your screen. It doesn't really change the "resolution" like you think of in a printer—on a monitor, more pixels make things appear smaller and farther away ("bird's-eye view," which might make you think it is in higher resolution); fewer pixels make things bigger and closer ("close-up view," which might make you think it is in lower resolution).

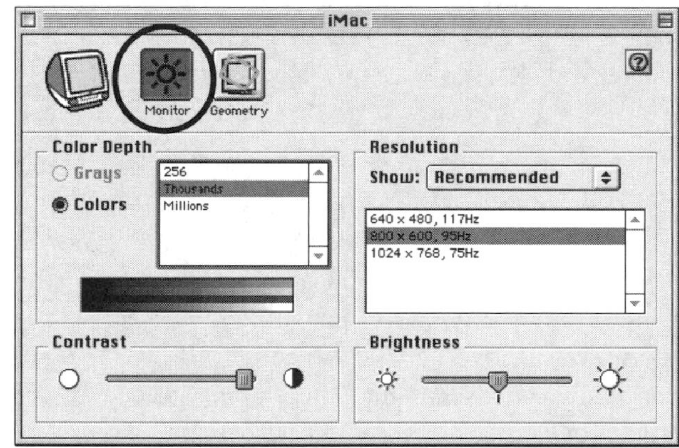

The "Color Depth" number refers to how many actual colors your monitor is capable of displaying at the moment. The more colors you choose, the more memory it takes to display them.

The "Resolution" numbers represent pixels; "640 x 480" means your monitor will display 640 pixels across and 480 pixels down. If you choose a higher number of pixels, each pixel will be smaller so more can fit on your screen. The more pixels you have, the more memory it takes to put color into every one, so with a higher resolution you may have to be content with fewer colors, like thousands instead of millions.

The "Hz" number is the refresh rate (in hertz), which is how many times per second the computer re-energizes the phosphors on the screen. Less than 65 Hz will display a flickering on your monitor.

More than one monitor

If you have **more than one monitor** attached to your computer, your Monitor control panel will have an extra button called something like "Arrange." This lets you determine which monitor should function as your main one, and which side of the main monitor your pointer will float across to the second monitor. Follow the directions in the control panel to arrange things how you need them; for instance, drag the picture of the second monitor around and put it on the same side of your main screen as your second monitor is positioned on your desk. The cursor will move off the main screen in that direction. (Now, don't ever go into your boss's or your sweetheart's Monitors control panel and switch the second monitor picture to the opposite side of their main monitor—that would be naughty.) To change which screen is the startup, first check the box, "Identify the startup screen." Then you'll see the happy face and you can drag it to the other monitor.

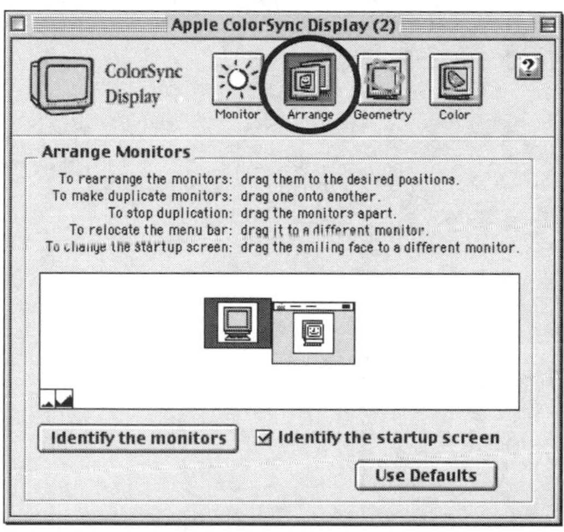

If you want the menu bar to appear on the other monitor, drag its tiny picture (right here in this preview) to the other monitor picture.

Extra features

Your monitor might provide you with extra features in the control panel, as this one below does. Experiment!

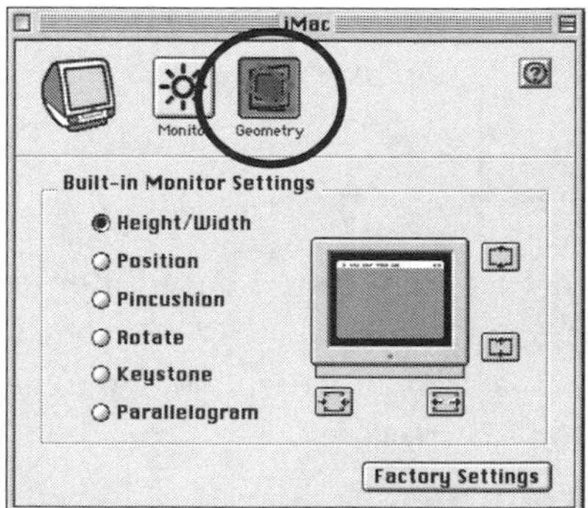

If you see that the little red, green, and blue colors are not lined up exactly, click "Convergence..." (if you have it in your control panel) and it will help you put all the colors right where they belong. If you don't have this button, you probably have buttons directly on your monitor that will adjust the color alignments. Check your monitor manual.

Sound

Use the **Sound** control to determine the volume of all the sounds that come out of your Mac, change the alert sound, make new sounds, and determine which input device will input sounds for you (microphone, CD, etc.). The options you see here and whether they actually work or not depend on what kind of computer you're using, what kind of monitor you have, and what kind of speakers or earphones you've got plugged in.

You have different volume sliders for the main volume, the Alerts (the beeps you hear when the Mac wants your attention), and for your external speakers, monitor, or earphones. Just move the slider bars left or right. If you set the volume slider all the way to the left or click the "Mute" button, you will see the menu bar flash silently instead of hear the computer beep at you.

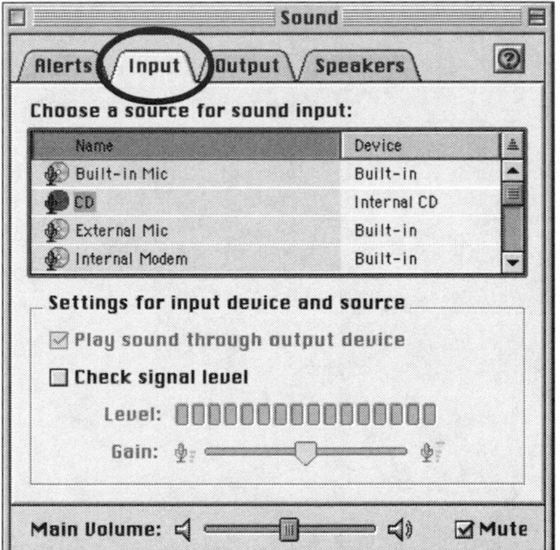

This is the Sound control panel for Mac OS 9.1.

To listen to audio CDs on your built-in CD player, change the "Sound Monitoring Source" to "CD." *See page 215.*

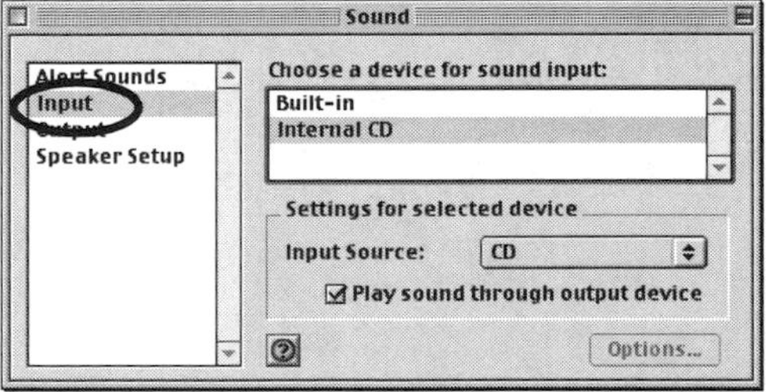

This is the Sound control panel for Mac OS 9. It's almost exactly the same, except you choose the panel from the list on the left instead of from tabs, as shown above.

The "Output" option lets you choose a different sound output device that you might have attached to your computer, something you added. "Speakers" or "Speaker Setup" adjusts the balance of earphones and the speakers on a monitor (if your monitor has speakers).

Alerts

Also see the Speech control panel.

Click the **Alerts** tab or button to choose which sound you want to hear when alerted to something. Click on the name of a sound to hear it. The last one you choose before you close the control panel is the sound the Mac will use when you need to be beeped.

If you *don't* have one of the Macs that came with a microphone, your control panel might not have the "New Sound" or "Add…" button. If you *do* have a microphone, then you can have lots of fun. Plug the mike into the little port on the machine (there's only one spot the plug will fit into). (If you have a phono jack adapter, you can directly record sounds from other sources, such as music CDs and tapes.) Click the "New Sound" or "Add…" button, then record sounds using the buttons as you would on a tape recorder. When you save the sound, it will automatically appear in the list and you can select it. Even if you don't have a microphone, if the button is there, try making a sound anyway. Your built-in speakers just might be enough to pick up a recordable sound.

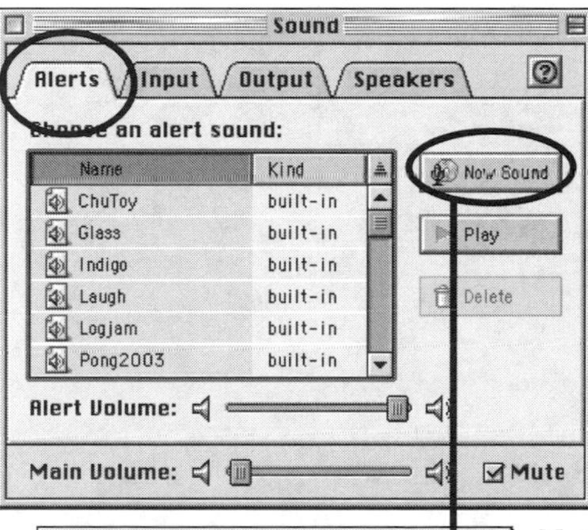

If your Mac came with a microphone, you'll have the "New Sound" or "Add" button and the dialog box shown below.

Notice it will record a sound from the input device you chose from the Input tab (opposite page). If you want to record your own voice, first click the Input tab and choose the type of microphone you have attached.

These sound files are actually kept in the System file (the Mac puts them there for you). My Uncle Floyd recorded himself hollering, "Woman—get back in the kitchen!" and moved the sound from the System file to the Startup Items folder so when my Aunt Jeannie turned on the machine she got yelled at. (Don't worry —she didn't get mad, she got even.)

File Exchange

File Exchange has several parts. It combines the previous control panels called PC Exchange and MacLinkPlus into one.

PC Exchange

The **PC Exchange** section controls which applications on your Mac will *open* which PC documents ("PC" meaning any computer that's not a Mac, such as any machine running Windows 95/98/ 2000). For instance, in the example shown below the Mac will open any document with a PC *extension* (the two or three letters at the end of a file name) of ".bat" in SimpleText. Click the "Add…" button to tell the Mac which applications should open which extensions.

If you send or receive files to or from a PC, you might want to read Windows for Mac Users *by Cyndi Baron and me. It goes into great length about creating and reading cross-platform files.*

This control panel is what automatically mounts PC disks on your Mac.

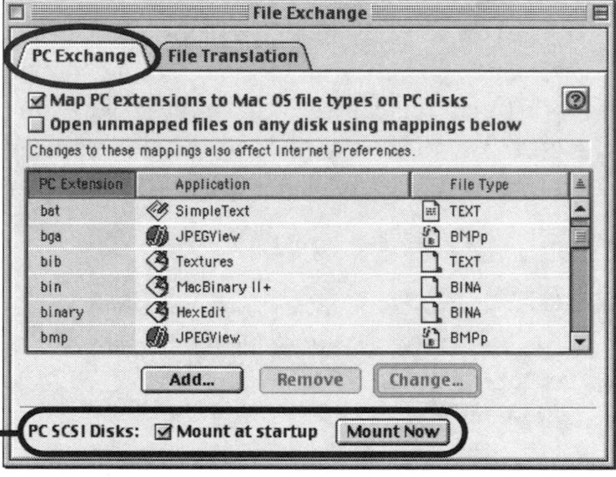

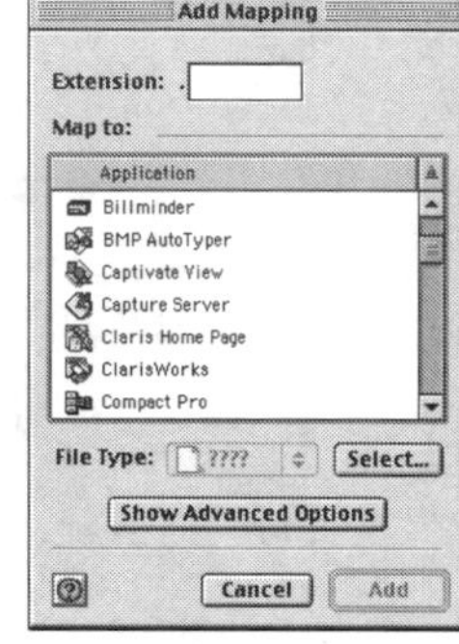

If you know which extensions should be "mapped" to certain applications, do it here.

File Translation

The **File Translation** section lets you make some decisions about how things should be *converted* when you bring a PC file to your Mac (as opposed to PC Exchange, which tells the Mac which program to use to *open* a PC file).

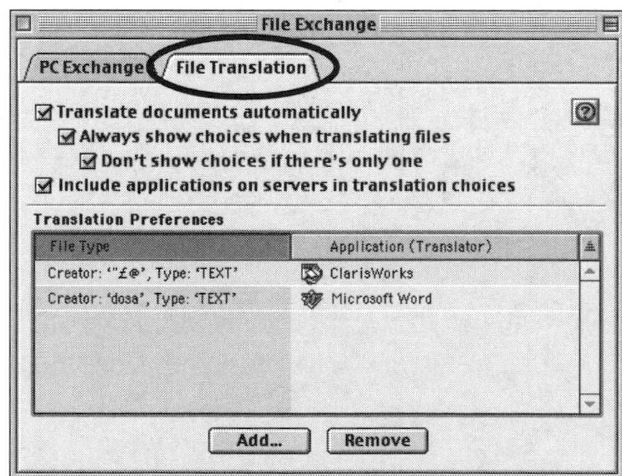

If you get PC files regularly that you need to read on your Mac, click the "Add…" button and create more preferences for more file types.

Use the **Numbers** control panel to determine how numbers and currency will display. This can be important in international work, where numbers in the thousands may be separated with a period instead of a comma. The format you choose here will affect the numbers in spreadsheet cells, database fields, and headers that use a currency or number format automatically.

Numbers

The **Text** control panel is only useful if you use more than one language on your Macintosh. Different languages will be listed in the menu in the control panel and you can choose the one you need to work with.

Text

The **Keyboard** control panel gives you several extra controls.

Keyboard

- The "Key Repeat" is handy. Every key on the Macintosh keyboard will repeat, meaning if you hold the key down it will continue typing that character across the page. "Key Repeat Rate" lets you control just how fast that key repeats across the page.
- The "Delay Until Repeat" options, from "Short" to "Long," give you control over how long you can hold your finger on a key before it starts to repeat. This is wonderful if you're heavy on the keys—set it for a long delay so even if your fingers plod along on the keys you won't end up with extra characters all over the place. If you choose "Off," the keys will not repeat at all.

If you notice you seem to type double spaces between words often, or perhaps double letters as in "tthe" or "yyou," you might want to lengthen the delay.

- You have files in your System Folder that provide other keyboard layouts; choose to have them available here. If you select more than one language, you'll see a new menu item in the upper right of your menu bar—a flag. The flag (a **visual clue**) represents the country whose language you have chosen as your current keyboard layout. It's also a menu, as shown to the right, so you can switch between the chosen languages.

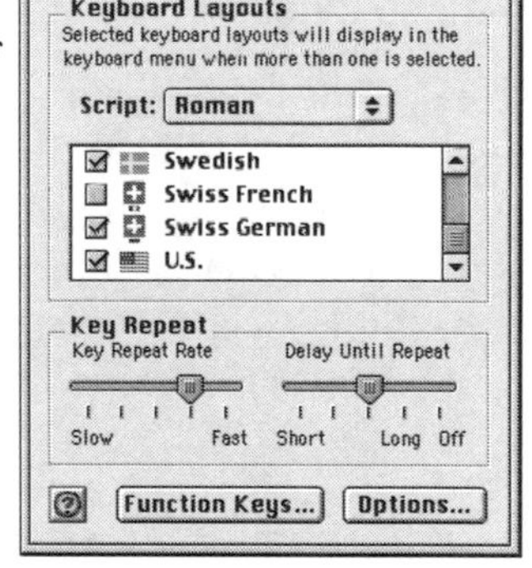

If you choose any keyboard layouts at all, you'll have this new menu item. The choice "Customize Menu…" opens the control panel.

- **"Function Keys…"** opens a dialog box so you can choose to make an Fkey (above the main keyboard) open an application or document or connect to a server: just click the Fkey button in the dialog box, then choose the file you want to open when you press that Fkey. If you want the Fkeys to maintain their original functions (see page 65 for details about Fkeys) in addition to yours, check the box under "Function Key Settings"; then when you want to activate *your* choice, hold the Option key down before you press the Fkey.

Extensions Manager

The **Extensions Manager** control panel is an extremely important tool, but it's not something you should fool around with if you don't know what you're doing.

Extensions are tiny little programs that work behind the scenes (usually) to do all kinds of little tasks for you. Because there is such a wide variety of extensions and because they go directly into the system, they have a long history of causing minor to major trouble when certain ones conflict with others. The Extensions Manager helps you control conflicts by allowing you to turn extensions—or other control panels—on or off, depending on what you are doing.

Sets of extensions and control panels

While the Extensions Manager is open, use the ***File menu*** *to create new sets, or to rename, delete, or duplicate sets.*

You can create **sets** of extensions and control panels so when you restart the Mac, customized groups of extensions will load, depending on what you are doing and what you have determined is conflicting with what you are doing. How do you determine what is conflicting? By turning certain ones off through this Extensions Manager and restarting to see if the problem persists. For instance, I was crashing regularly while cruising around the Internet. So I made a set of extensions and control panels that are the minimum necessary for me to use the Internet. I do have to restart between being online and being offline, but it's better to restart the computer than to crash.

If you think you have an extension conflict, find your local power user or ask at your local user group for someone to help guide you through to the solution.

If you have a clue about what you're doing and you want to control extensions, hold down the Spacebar as you boot or restart. Hold it down until you get the Extensions Manager. Select your extensions and control panels, or choose the set, "Mac OS 9.1 Base" to get rid of everything except what's absolutely necessary. Then either close the Extensions Manager window to resume startup, or click the "Continue" button.

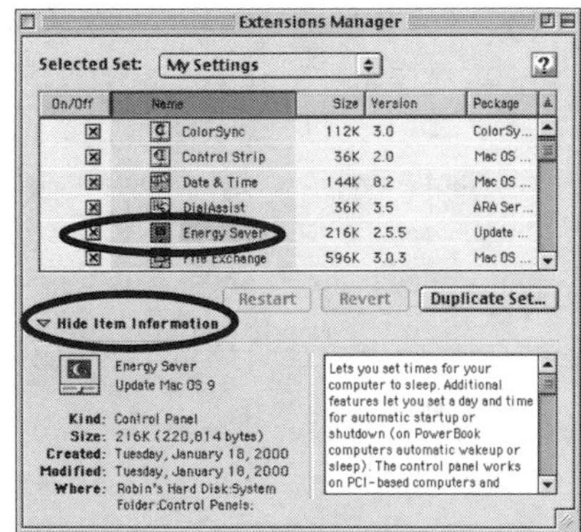

This is the Extensions Manager. To find out what some of these items are, you can click on one to select it, then click the arrow that says "Show Item Information." The bottom section of the control panel appears with information which may or may not be very helpful. (When the information is showing, as in this example, the arrow changes to "Hide Item Information.")

The Extensions Manager looks very scary. You can ignore it for a long time, as long as everything is working fine. If you want to poke around and get used to this thing (which is a good idea because it's guaranteed that one day you will need to deal with it), experiment with the various ways you can view the items: check out the View menu while the Extensions Manager is active.

Different views of the Extensions Manager

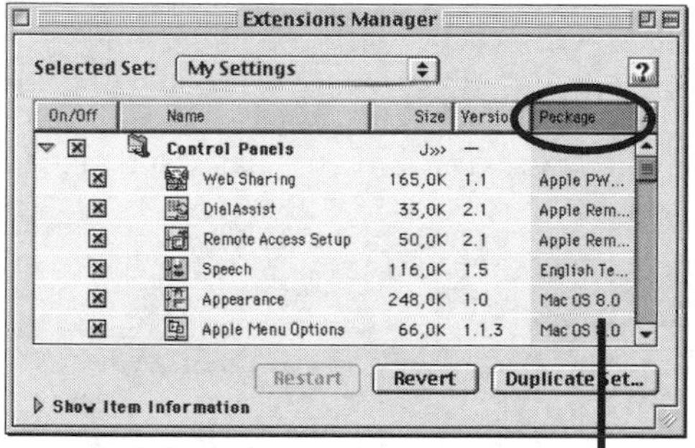

Click the **Package** column heading to collect items into related groups, groups that work with each other to accomplish various parts of a similar task.

When you **View as Folders,** *the items are grouped into Control Panels and Extensions, just like they are in the System Folder. This helps when you know you want to find one or the other.*

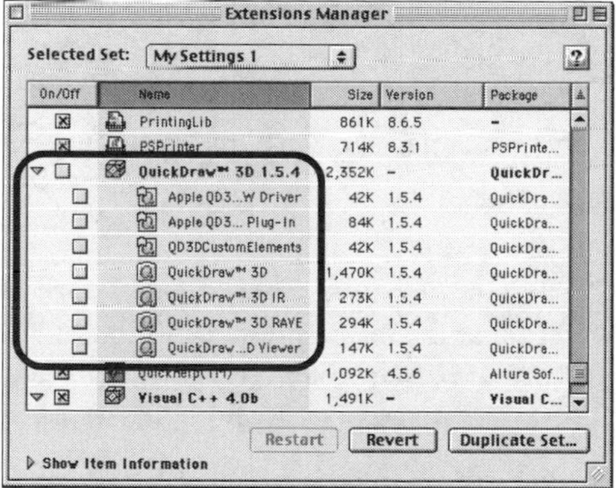

View as Packages *to collect the items into related groups. This makes it easy to turn off related items. If, for instance, you have no need for the QuickDraw 3D files, group them as a package and then you can turn them all off with one click on the package.*

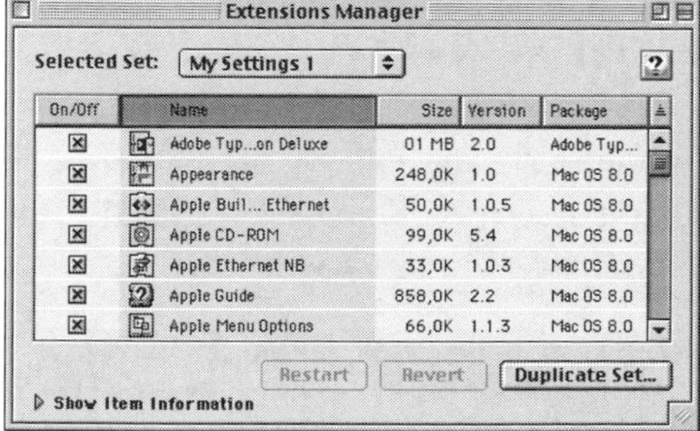

View as Items *just lists all of the items in a long, alphabetical list.*

Speech

Speech

For Speech to work, you also have to have the following items in your Extensions folder, which is inside your System Folder:

MacinTalk 3

Speech Manager

Voices

This is such an incredible hoot. If you have the items shown in the column to the left, your Mac can talk to you. If you haven't consciously removed those items, they're probably still there. Open the **Speech** control panel and first make sure "Options" is set to "Voice." Choose any voice from the menu in the control panel. Click on the speaker icon and hear that voice speak a phrase, such as, "We do not communicate with these carbon units," or "I sure like being inside this fancy computer." You can change the speed with the slider bar.

Then from the Options menu, choose "Talking Alerts." Check "Speak the phrase," and the voice will speak the phrase that's shown. The one you choose from this menu will be the phrase you'll hear instead of a beep the next time the Mac tries to warn you about something. Make your own phrases: choose "Edit phrase list" from that same menu. Check "Speak the alert text" and the voice will also read the alert message that appears on your screen, such as "Are you sure you want to shut down your computer now?"

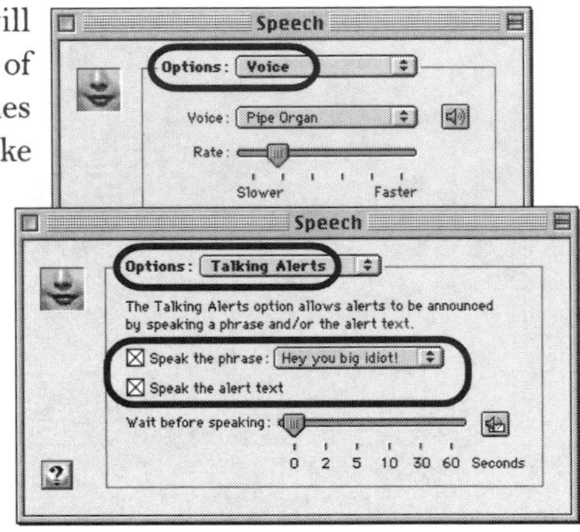

If you hear the lady read the alerts to you and it makes you nuts, open the Speech control panel and uncheck "Speak the alert text."

Control Strip

Control Strip

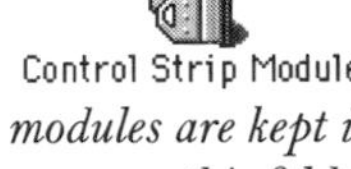

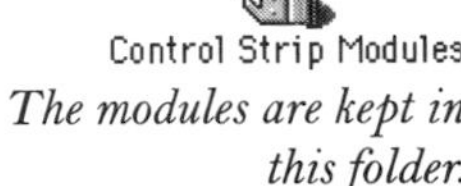

Control Strip Modules

The modules are kept in this folder.

Monitor Resolution

File Sharing

These are examples of control strip modules. Their icons appear in the strip.

The **Control Strip** is a retractable bar of icons. These icons represent other control panels or shortcuts, and you can click on icons in the strip to access them. Try it. For instance, if you have the Monitors & Sound Control Strip Module, you can change the volume from the Control Strip. Some modules are installed when you install certain software, others you have to go get from somewhere, like a web site. Once you find a module, put it in the Control Strip Modules folder in the System Folder and it will appear in the Control Strip.

You can move the Control Strip to anywhere else on your screen. Just hold down the Option key, press on the very end of the control Strip (whether it's open or closed), and drag it up, down, or over to the other side of the screen. Wherever you let go, there it will stay.

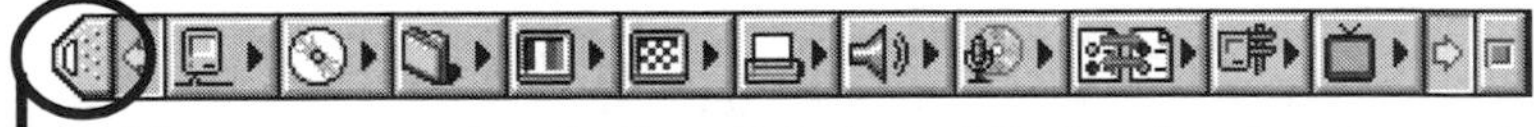

Click here to open or close the Control Strip, and Option-drag here to move it.

Networking Control Panels

The Mac has several built-in **networking** features, and there are two control panels that let you change those settings. These are explained in Chapter 27 on Sharing Files.

File Sharing lets you set your user name, choose a password for yourself, and turn on your Mac's ability to share files over the network. The network might be as simple as two computers that share the same printer, like in your home office. The control panel includes a **Users & Groups** feature that lets you restrict access to your computer to specific people, or lets everybody see what you've been working on.

Startup Disk

If you have more than one hard disk attached to your Mac that has a System Folder on it, or perhaps more than one *partition* to your hard disk, you can use the **Startup Disk** control panel to determine which hard disk to use to start your computer. Each attached or mounted hard disk will appear as an icon in the control panel; any disk without a System Folder will appear as gray. Depending on whether you are running Mac OS 9 or 9.1, you will see one of the control panels below.

You need to restart the computer for the new disk to become the startup disk. You can always tell which hard disk is booting the computer—its icon is always first in the upper-right corner.

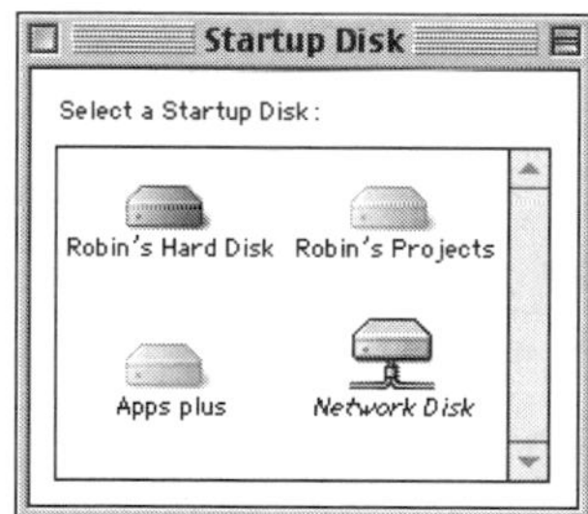

You can see the **visual clue** *that tells you which disks are capable of starting the computer.*

Internet Control Panels

There are several control panels that are specifically for connecting to the Internet and the World Wide Web. I go into those in detail in *Part Three, The Internet.*

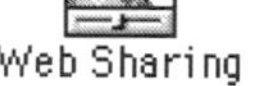

Energy Saver

Energy Saver

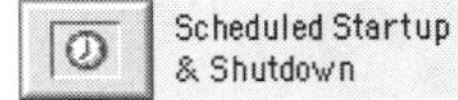

Even if you have buttons instead of tabs, your control panel will do basically the same things as the one shown. Get the "Notification" settings from the Preferences menu that appears when you open the control panel.

This is a wonderfully useful control panel. You can schedule your computer to "sleep" when you're not using it (tap any key on your keyboard to wake it up), or click the "Scheduled shut down instead of scheduled sleep" button to make your Mac turn itself off if no one's using it for a while. Click "Show Details" to get more options (shown below). You can choose to have just the display go to sleep (which makes your screen turn black), or just the hard disk go to sleep (which leaves your monitor bright). No matter what goes to sleep, when you wake it up, have patience for about fifteen seconds while everything spins up.

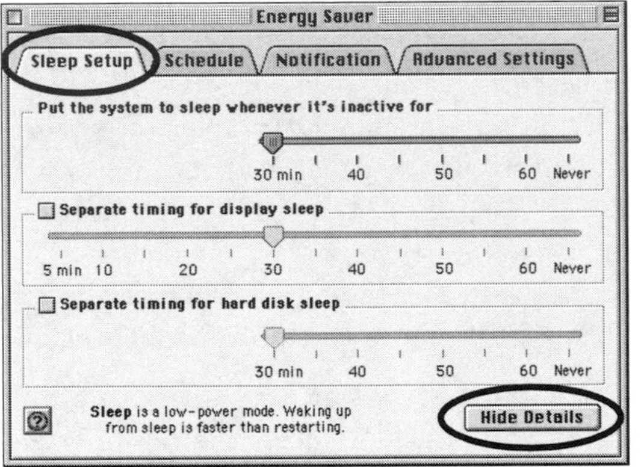

If you don't see these details, click the "Show Details" button (in this example it says "Hide Details" because they're already showing).

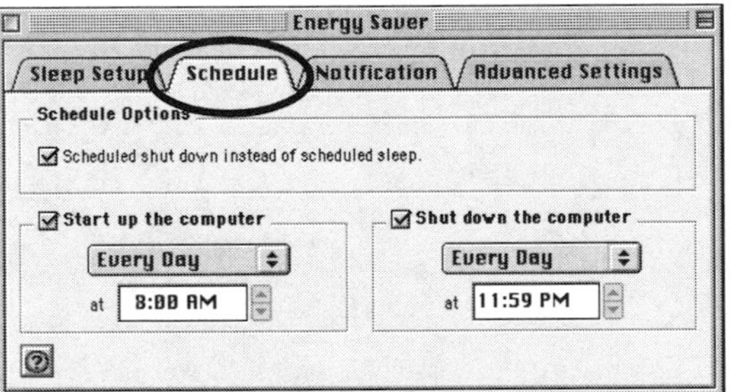

This is my favorite part— I like my Mac to turn itself on in the morning.

Some Macs let you turn the Power button (or ***one*** *of the Power buttons, if you have one on your monitor as well as on your keyboard, like iMacs) into a Sleep button so when you press it, instead of turning the computer off, it puts it to sleep.*

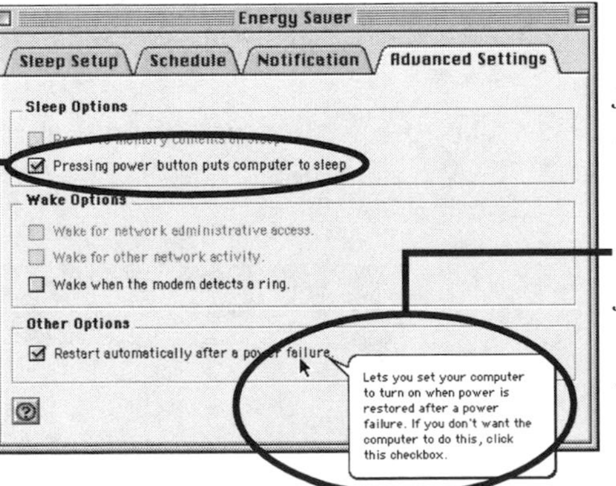

If you don't see "Restart automatically after a power failure" as shown to the left, go to the Preferences menu and choose "Server Settings."

To get specific details about every feature, go to the Help menu and choose "Show Balloons." Then position the pointer over the item about which you want more information.

Location Manager

Location Manager

If you are new to your Mac, you probably won't need the **Location Manager** for a while. If you share your Mac with anyone else, or if you carry a PowerBook from home to work and back again, then the Location Manager can be incredibly useful. It allows you to set up all sorts of custom parameters in sets (locations) and then you can change them with the click of a button. For instance, perhaps your teenager uses your computer and she likes to use the Launcher, the color inkjet printer, America Online, and listen to loud music while she works. You ignore the Launcher, use a black-and-white laser printer, have a direct Internet connection with an ISP, and like to mute the sound. Set up a location with all of the specifics for yourself and another location for your teenager. Maybe you take your PowerBook to work and use an Ethernet connection to log on to the intranet and have your work user name and password, then you come home to a modem connection to the Internet and use a different user name and password: set up two different locations for yourself.

Before you set up locations, you do have to make sure none of the current specifications are the "defaults" set by the Mac. You have to go to each setting, make your own choices (even if they're the same as the defaults), and name the new settings; then you can add those new settings to the location.

Depending on which settings you choose, you may or may not have to restart when you change locations. Use the Preferences (from the Edit menu) to make the Location Manager ask you which location you prefer when you startup (see below, right).

When the Location Manager is open, poke around the menus and see the other options available. As this shows, you can export your settings, take that exported file to another Mac, and import them into the Location Manager on the other computer.

Robin's Computer

This is an exported file.

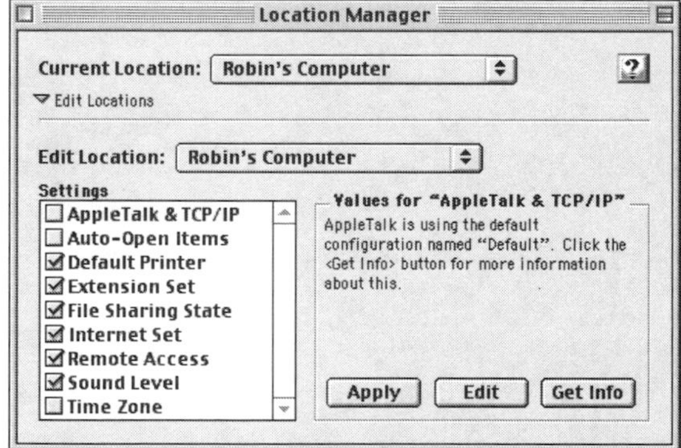

Click in the little boxes to choose settings that you want the Location Manager to keep track of for you. Click the "Apply" button to apply the current values in the selected settings, or select a setting and click the "Edit" button to edit the values.

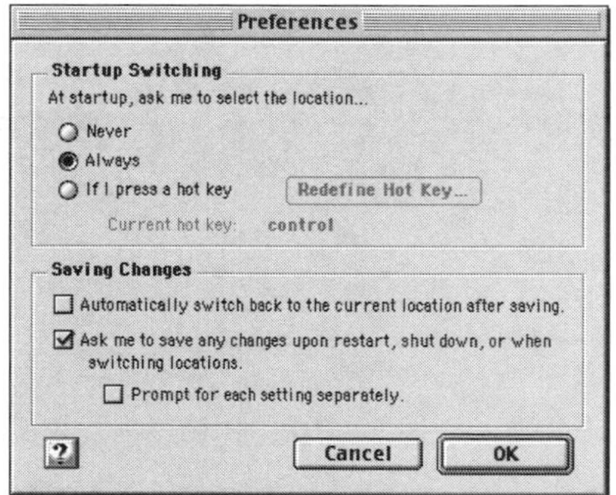

A "hot key" is a key that does something special when you press it. In this case, you can choose your own hot key to press when you turn the computer on to make the Location Manager ask you to select a location. Otherwise, you can choose to have it never ask you on startup, or to always ask you.

Which control panel would you use to accomplish the following, and which settings would you set?

1. Make the mouse move quickly across the screen without your hand having to move much at all.

2. Change the pattern of your Desktop.

3. Start file sharing between several computers.

4. Change the rate of how fast a keyboard character will repeat across the page when you hold the key down.

5. Enlarge or reduce everything you see on the screen.

6. Change the time that shows up in your menu bar.

7. Set it so you *don't* see the icons on the Desktop when you are working in an application and so when you accidentally click on the pattern in the background, you *don't* pop to the Desktop.

8. Use fewer colors on your monitor to save memory.

9. Record your own sounds to surprise and startle your coworkers.

10. Get rid of the "Recent Servers" option in the Apple menu.

Answers on page 425.

25 Aliases

Aliases are one of the greatest features of the Mac. An alias is a fake icon that *represents* the real thing. Aliases only take up about 2 or 3K of disk space, so you can make lots and store them all over the place, wherever they come in handy.

You see, many applications must stay in the folder they were installed into because when the application opens, it calls upon resources within its folder. If you store the application itself in a different folder or on your Desktop, you run the risk of it not being able to function properly. That's where the alias comes in. You make an alias, which *represents* the application, and you can put that alias anywhere. In fact, you can make a dozen aliases of the same application and store them in all sorts of handy places. When you double-click an alias, it goes into the application's folder and tells the application to open.

You might make an alias of a folder or of the trash can. When you put items into the *alias* of the folder or the trash can, the item actually gets put into the *real* folder or trash can.

Say you have an application you use frequently—your word processing program, for instance. You can make an alias of AppleWorks or Quicken or whatever you use and put it just about anywhere. You might want to put it right on your Desktop. Or in your Apple menu. Or in your Startup Items folder so AppleWorks opens automatically whenever you turn on your machine. Since you can have many aliases of the same file, you can put aliases to the same item in several places! Learn to use and take advantage of this seriously cool feature.

Aliases

You can make **aliases** of programs, documents, desk accessories, disks, folders, control panels, the trash can, etc. Aliases are wonderful tools for organizing your work—anything you want to use is only one click away from wherever you are. Remember, an alias is just a picture that goes and gets the real file. It's a go-fer.

Using Aliases

Before I tell you *how* to make them, here are ideas for **using aliases** so you will *want* to make them (how to make an alias is on page 269).

- Put an alias of an often-used Control Panel out on your Desktop or in your Apple menu.
- Use aliases to store documents in two or three places at once, including right on your Desktop. For instance, you may want to keep budget reports in folders organized by months, as well as in folders organized by projects. When you update the real document, all the aliases will open the updated document.
- If you have a document you use frequently, put an alias of it in the Apple menu: just open your System Folder and drag the alias into the "Apple Menu Items" folder.

  You can use the "Automated Task" to do this for you: select the file you want an alias of, then from the Apple menu slide down to "Automated Tasks," then slide out to "Add Alias to Apple Menu." The Mac will make an alias, take the word "alias" off the end of the name, and put it in the Apple Menu Items folder. (See Chapter 23 for more info on the Apple menu.)
- In fact, if you find you use your Apple Menu Items folder regularly, make an alias of the folder and leave it on your Desktop. Dropping a file in the alias folder automatically puts it into the real folder, which puts it in the Apple menu.
- If you have an application, a document, or a folder that you want to open automatically whenever you turn on your Mac, put an alias of it in your "Startup Items" folder, which is in the System Folder.
- Leave aliases of applications neatly organized directly on your Desktop or in your hard disk window. This way you don't have to dig into folders to open the applications. This also makes all your applications available to you for the **drag-and-drop trick of opening files,** including files from other programs.

Remember: you can drag any document onto the icon of the application to open the document. Many applications can open files created in other programs this way, so if you come across a file from a program you don't have, or perhaps you don't know where it came from, you can drag it over the top of all these aliases that are sitting on your Desktop. Any icon that changes color when you drag the document on top of it will open that document.

The Eudora and Netscape aliases sit on my Desktop to make it easy to pop in quickly and check my mail or the web.

- Some of the more advanced uses for aliases aren't apparent unless you're on a network. For example, you can make an alias of your file server so you can connect to it quickly. And you can make an alias of your hard disk, copy it onto a floppy (since the alias is only about 2K), and take it to somebody else's computer on the network. Then you can quickly connect back to your own computer just by clicking on the alias on the other computer (provided you have set up the sharing privileges first; see Chapter 27 on simple networking and sharing). This concept is sometimes called the "office-on-a-disk."

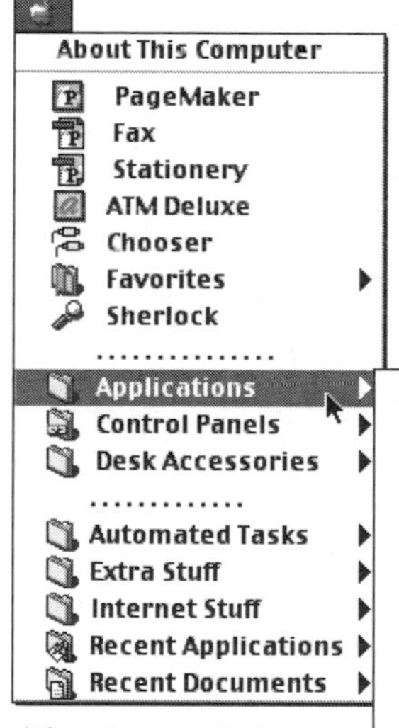

This Apple menu has aliases of the PageMaker documents I use for faxes and stationery; their originals are nested deep within folders. I also keep an alias of PageMaker right here at the top because I use it every day.

In the Apple Menu Items folder, I made another folder and named it "Applications." Inside that folder I put aliases of all the applications I use regularly so I can open them without having to go all the way back to the Finder. Notice I also have PageMaker in this menu, just in case I want to grab it from here.

(When aliases are in the Apple menu, their names are not italic anymore.)

(If you're wondering why this Apple menu looks so organized, see Chapter 23.)

Finding Files with Aliases

▼ **Use aliases to find files that you keep stored on floppy disks or cartridge hard disks.**

- Make an alias of an original file on the disk; *the original file must be on the removable cartridge disk already.* Be sure this disk has an identifiable name, and be sure you put a label on the disk with this name so you can find it again.
- Drag the alias from the cartridge to your hard disk. Now you can eject the disk and store it safely.
- When you double-click on the alias you have on your hard disk, you will get a dialog box asking for the disk that contains the original file (that's why you named the disk memorably and actually labeled it, right?).

▼ Since aliases only take up about 2K, you can keep a folder of many of the files you use only occasionally but that you do want to keep track of. This folder of aliases is your "secretary" who knows just where everything is filed. (Also see "Finding the Original File," page 271.)

▼ You can put an alias of an entire floppy disk, cartridge, or CD in your Apple menu and get hierarchical menus (those little submenus with the arrows) of all the files on the disk. Then you don't have to open all the windows to get to things—just follow the hierarchical menu, as shown below.

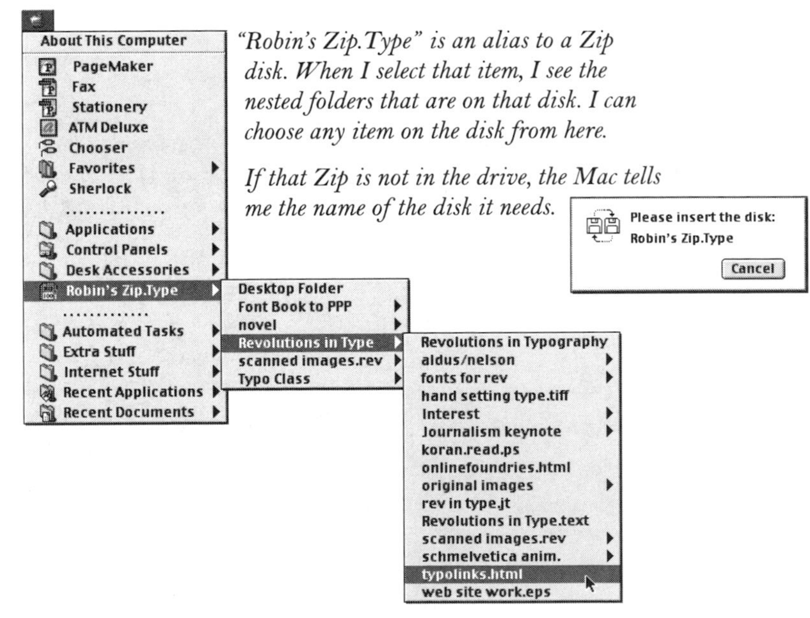

"Robin's Zip.Type" is an alias to a Zip disk. When I select that item, I see the nested folders that are on that disk. I can choose any item on the disk from here.

If that Zip is not in the drive, the Mac tells me the name of the disk it needs.

Making an alias is so easy.

1. Select the item you want to make an alias of (click once on it).
2. Choose one of these four easy ways to make an alias:
   - **a.** From the File menu, choose "Make Alias."
   - **b. Or** press Command M instead of going to the File menu.
   - **c. Or** hold down the Control key and click on the item you want to make an alias of. A menu will pop up; select "Make Alias."
   - **d. Or** hold down Command Option and drag the file—if you drag it to a *different* folder or to the Desktop, when you let go you have an alias with the word "alias" removed from its name; if you drag to somewhere else in the *same* folder, you have an alias with the word "alias" at the end of it.

You now have an alias.

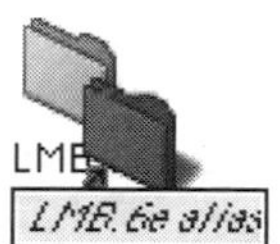

This is what it looks like when you make an alias using the Control-click method. After you click on the "Make Alias" command, the new alias will be sitting right next to the original file.

- The new alias icon will look the same and will be named the same, with the word *alias* added (unless you used the Command Option–drag trick). An alias name is in italic so you can always recognize the file as an alias.

  (I like to remove the word "alias" from my files because it makes the name too long. Move the alias out of the folder the original is in before you change the name because you can't have two files with the same name in one folder.)
- Drag the icon to wherever you want to keep it. Rename it if you like. The new file does not have to have the word "alias" in its name. *And it doesn't matter if you move the original file*—the alias can always find it.
- To put the alias in your Apple menu, drag the alias icon to the "Apple Menu Items" folder in your System Folder and drop it in. (You'll notice that when the alias appears in the Apple menu, its name is no longer in italic.)

Making Aliases

An alias looks just like the original, but the name is italic and there's a tiny arrow (your visual clues).

I like to remove the word "alias" so the name is shorter.

Even when you view your windows as a list, an alias looks like an alias.

Details of Aliases

Making aliases is easy, but there are a couple of **details** you should understand.

- An alias isn't really a *duplicate* of anything but the icon; it's just a **representation** of the real thing. If you double-click on an *alias* of Quicken, you'll start your *original* Quicken program running, even if the original Quicken is stored in a completely different folder.
- If you **delete** an alias of something, you don't delete the original—the original is still stored on your hard disk. So you can keep revising your filing system as your needs change. Don't want that alias of Budget Charts cluttering up your Project Plans folder any more? Fine; throw it away. The original Budget Charts is still where you stored it.
- If you put an item into an *alias* of a **folder,** the item actually gets put into the *original* folder.
- If you put an item into an *alias* of the **trash can,** the item actually gets put into the *original* trash can. Only the original trash can will bulge.
- You can **move** an alias and even **rename** an alias. The Mac will still be able to find the original and open it whenever you double-click on the alias.
- Even if you move or rename the **original** file, the alias can still find it.
- If you **eliminate** the *original* file, the Mac does *not* automatically eliminate any of the aliases you created for that file. When you double-click on an alias whose original has been trashed, you will get a message telling you the original could not be located. See your choices below.

If you click the "Fix Alias..." button, you'll get a dialog box where you can navigate to the original item. If you don't know how to navigate yet (see Chapter 28 to learn how), just click "Delete Alias" and then make a new alias from the original item.

Finding the Original File

To find the original file belonging to an alias, follow these steps:

1. Click once on the alias.
2. Use any of these easy techniques to find the original file:
   - **a.** From the File menu, choose "Show Original."
   - **b. Or** press Command R.
   - **c. Or** hold down the Control key and click on the alias. From the menu that pops up, choose "Show Original."

The original file will appear in front of you, selected.

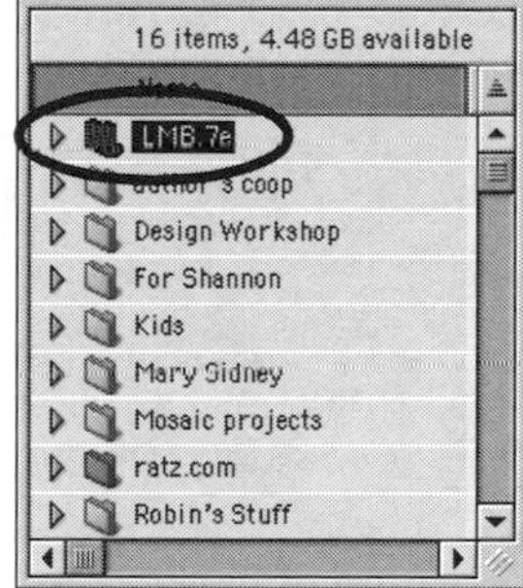

As soon as you use any technique to show the original file, it will appear in front of you, as shown.

- If you choose "Show Original" *or* if you double-click on an alias that has its original stored on a removable disk of any sort, you will get a message telling you which disk to insert.

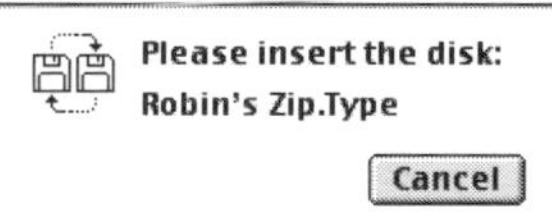

If the original file is on another disk and the disk is not in the computer, you will get a message telling you which disk to insert.

Linking an Alias to a New Original

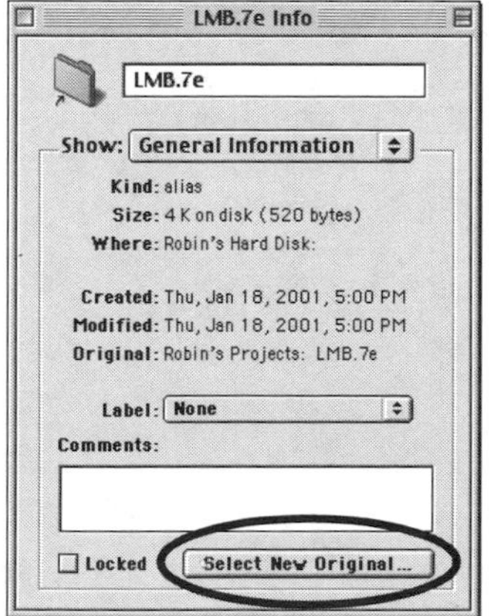

If necessary, you can link an alias to a different original.

1. Click once on the alias to select it.
2. Press Command I to get the Get Info box.
3. Click the button at the bottom, "Select New Original…."
4. Find the original file you want to link to this alias, and click OK. Close the Get Info box.

1. What is an alias, anyway?

2. How large, in file size, is a typical alias?

3. Name at least four ways to create an alias.

4. What is the quickest way to put an alias into the Apple menu?

5. If you throw away an alias, what happens to the real item?

6. If you throw away the real item, what happens to all of its aliases?

7. What is the easiest way to find the original of an alias?

8. If you use the Monitors & Sound control panel several times a day, where would be a good place to keep an alias of the control panel?

9. If you want the document for a particular project to automatically open on your screen every day this week, where would you put its alias?

10. If you put a file into an alias of a folder, what happens to that file?

11. What happens if you make an alias, then rename the original?

Answers on page 425–426.

Sherlock (find things)

26

Sherlock is a wonderful time-saving and frustration-reducing feature that helps you search for any file on your disk or attached disks, and it can even search the *contents* of any file. If you are connected to the Internet, Sherlock can also find shopping bargains on the web, old friends and lover, the latest news, research items, products and support from Apple, and more.

In your Apple menu, Sherlock is called Sherlock 2, which is to distinguish it from a less robust version in previous operating systems. I'm just going to refer to it as Sherlock in this chapter.

The Many Faces of Sherlock

Sherlock has expanded, along with the Mac, to the Internet; that is, it helps you find items not only on your own hard disk, but out in the global world. It's not a complete replacement for the search tools you find on the web itself, but it can provide a quick and easy way to locate many things. Let's look at a general overview of Sherlock.

Note: If America Online is your only email/Internet service, you must first open and log on to AOL before you can use Sherlock to search the Internet!

The buttons across the top of Sherlock represent what Apple calls "channels," or customizable sources of information. Position your mouse over any of the buttons and pause a few seconds—a tag appears that tells you what that channel can help you find (shown to the left). Try it.

Across the row, the channels are Files, Internet, People, Shopping, News, Apple, References, an empty channel called My Channel that you can customize, and in Mac OS 9.1 only, there is also a channel called Entertainment. (All of the channels except Files search for information on the Internet.)

Click on a channel to select it; the window will change with each channel. Try it.

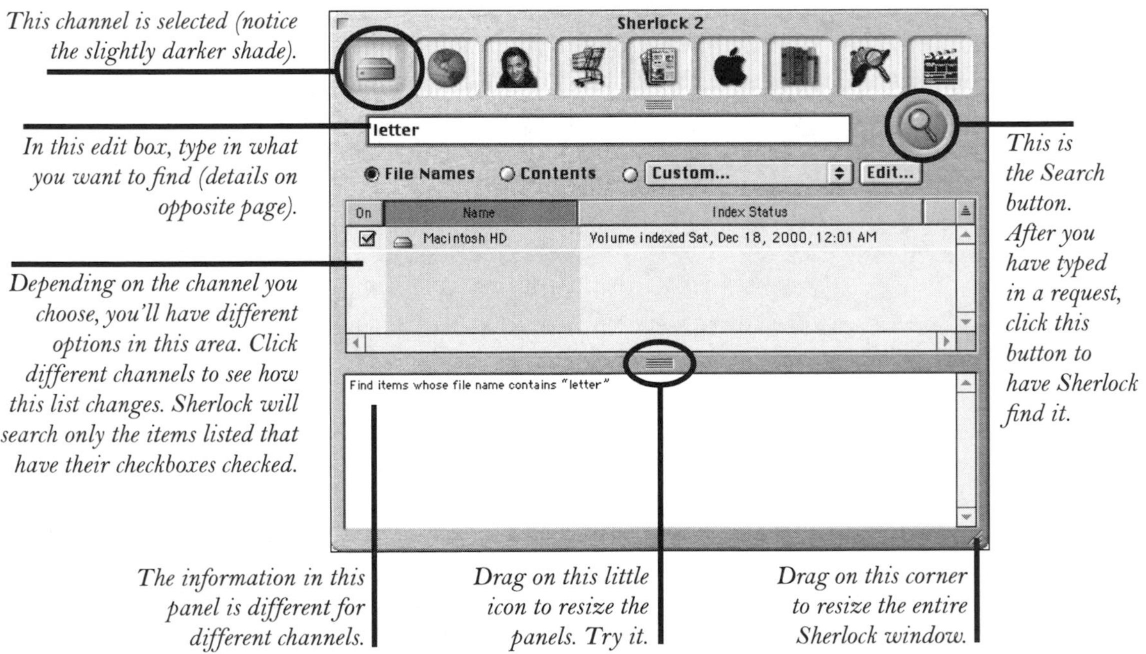

This channel is selected (notice the slightly darker shade).

In this edit box, type in what you want to find (details on opposite page).

Depending on the channel you choose, you'll have different options in this area. Click different channels to see how this list changes. Sherlock will search only the items listed that have their checkboxes checked.

This is the Search button. After you have typed in a request, click this button to have Sherlock find it.

The information in this panel is different for different channels.

Drag on this little icon to resize the panels. Try it.

Drag on this corner to resize the entire Sherlock window.

How to Quit Sherlock

When you want to put Sherlock away, either press Command Q to quit, or click in the little close box in the upper-left corner of the window.

Find a File on Your Hard Disk

First of all, a *file* is anything on your hard disk. Documents, folders, applications, fonts—everything is considered a file. And every file on your Mac is represented by an icon. So search for something on your hard disk.

Search for a file on your hard disk

1. If you are at the Desktop, go to the File menu and choose "Find…," or press Command F.

   If you are in any application (or even if you're at the Desktop), from the Apple menu, choose "Sherlock 2."
2. Click the first channel button, the one with the picture of a hard disk (circled, below; it's probably already selected).
3. In the upper portion of the window you'll see the name of your hard disk (as shown below). Depending on how your computer is set up, you might see other items in that area. Make sure there is a checkbox in any item you want to search.
4. In the edit box (see below), type a word that you think is in some of the files on your computer. For instance, type "letter" or "setup."
5. Make sure the round radio button for "File Names" is checked (shown below).
6. You'll notice in the lower area that Sherlock reiterates what you are looking for.
7. Click the Search button (the round one with the magnifying glass; circled, below). Then turn the page and continue.

Note: *It doesn't matter whether you type capital or lowercase letters. If you don't know the exact name of the file, just type any part of it that you think is in the file name.*

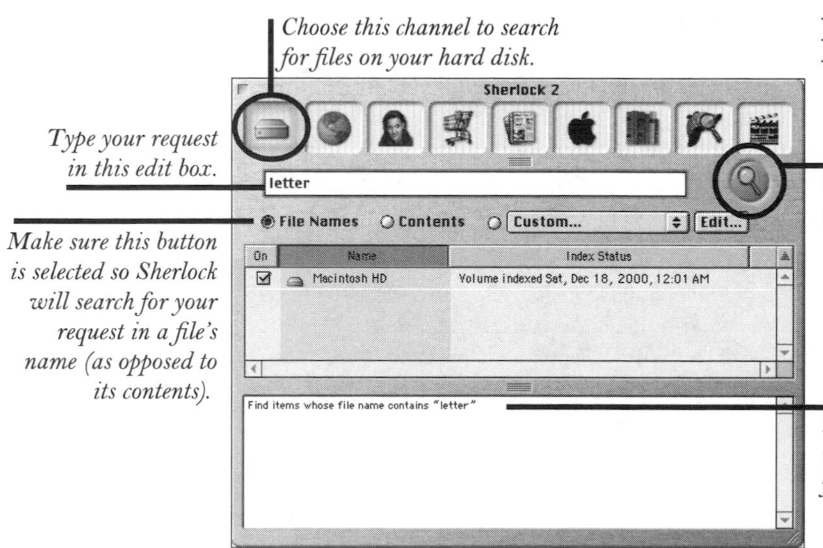

Choose this channel to search for files on your hard disk.

Type your request in this edit box.

Make sure this button is selected so Sherlock will search for your request in a file's name (as opposed to its contents).

Click this button to search.

Right now this panel reminds you of what you are looking for.

Opening a found file

Sherlock will take several seconds to search your entire hard disk. The results will look something like those shown below. In the upper portion of the window is a list of all the files that have your request in the file name; click once on any one of those files and in the lower portion, Sherlock will tell you where that file is stored.

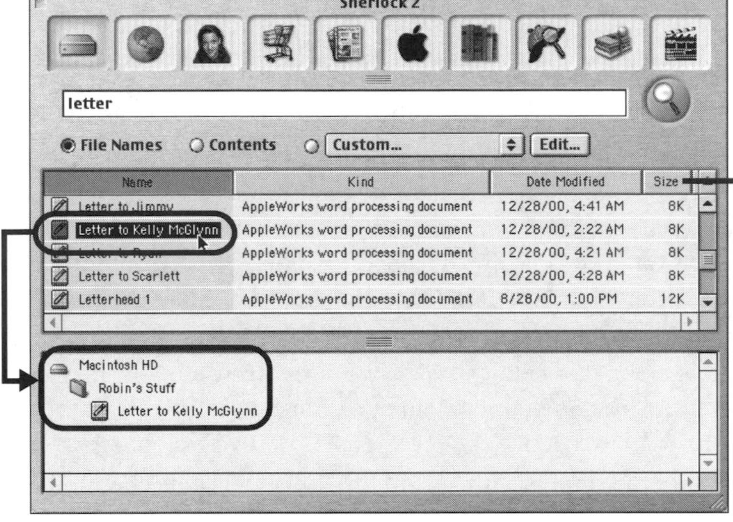

Click once on the file you were looking for, and in the lower portion of this window you'll see exactly where that file is stored. This example shows that the selected letter is in a folder called "Robin's Stuff," and that folder is on the Macintosh HD (the hard disk window).

Click on any of these column headings to organize the content by that heading.

Once you have located the file you want, there are several things you can do. First, click once on the file name in either the upper or the lower portion of Sherlock to select that file. Then do one of the following:

- **To open the file,** double-click the file name, or press Command O (for Open).
- **To open the enclosing folder** in which the file is stored, press Command E.
- **To print the item** (if it's a document), press Command P.
- **To delete the file,** drag the file from the window to the trash can, or select the file and press Command Delete.
- **To make an alias of the file,** hold down the Command and Option keys and drag the file to the Desktop or into a folder; let go and an alias will appear (see Chapter 25 for information about aliases).

Tip: *Click on a file name to select it, then go to the File menu to see what your options are for that particular type of file.*

Narrow Your Search

If the quick and easy search gave you too many results, you can **narrow the search** to more specific attributes.

To narrow a search

1. Open Sherlock and click the "Files" channel button (the hard disk icon).
2. Click the "Edit..." button; you'll see the dialog box shown below.
3. Take a few moments to see what your options are here. Once you click a checkbox, the gray options will become available to you. For instance, you can see below that the "date modified" choice is checked, so the menu next to it is now available. Check the boxes, then click on the menus to see what you can do. Be sure to uncheck any options you don't want to apply before you click the OK button!
4. Once your parameters are set up, click the OK button. You'll go back to the main search window and Sherlock will summarize your search options in the bottom portion of the window. Then click the Search button.

Tip: *If you're looking for a file you created or worked on today or yesterday, try the "Custom..." menu.*

Click in the checkbox, then click on the menu to see what your choices are.

See page 288 about saving your search criteria.

Search a Specific Disk or Folder

Sometimes you want to **search a specific disk,** such as a Zip or CD you inserted, or perhaps you want to search only in one particular folder. That's easy to do.

To search a particular disk or folder

1. Find the icon for that disk or folder on your Desktop.
2. Drag the disk or folder icon and drop it in the top portion of the Sherlock window. Sherlock calls all folders or disks "volumes."
3. Make sure there is a check in the box next to each volume you want to search.
4. Continue with the search as you did on the previous pages.

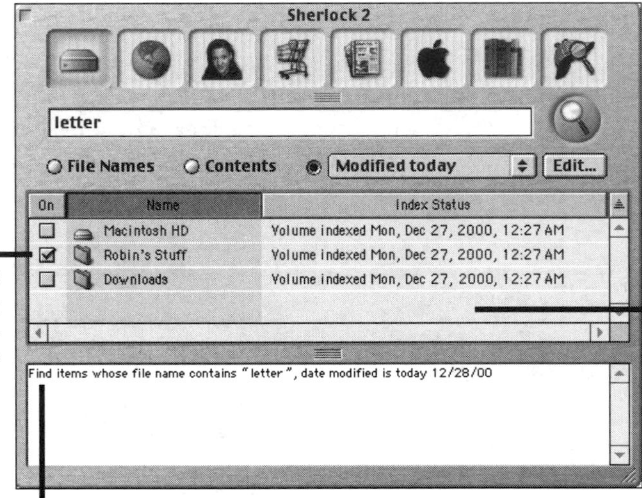

Drag the icon of the disk or folder you want to search and drop it in this space.

This shows that of the three "volumes," Sherlock will search only the folder called "Robin's Stuff."

Here Sherlock displays the options I chose when I clicked the "Edit..." button (explained on the previous page).

The "Contents" Button

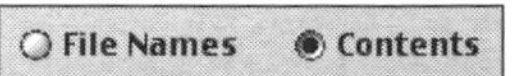

Sherlock will **search through the contents** of any file. For instance, maybe you're working on a research project and you've created dozens of files on the topic of chess. You want to find all the papers in your collection that mention "en passant." That's when you click the "Contents" button; instead of searching for just the *name* of a file, Sherlock will actually read the *contents* of files. For instance, you might have written an article that you named "Special Moves in Chess," and in the article itself you wrote about the en passant move, but you also mention en passant in three other articles with different names—Sherlock will find every file that includes the phrase "en passant" in the text.

BUT Sherlock cannot search the contents of your files *until* it has first indexed every file. That is, Sherlock has to read every file on your computer and then organize every word into a database that it can search when you request it. Logically, if you write more articles after Sherlock has indexed the files on your hard disk, Sherlock has to index things again to update and add those new files to its database.

Apple has set Sherlock to automatically index your hard disk at a certain time every day. You should check to see what the schedule is because it can take an hour or so for Sherlock to index (depending on how many files you have on your hard disk); you might want to change the schedule so it indexes when you are not working on your iMac.

Depending on how many files you have, indexing can take a while.

Check the indexing schedule and change it if necessary

1. Open Sherlock (at the Desktop, press Command F; or go to the Apple menu and choose "Sherlock 2").
2. From the Find menu, choose "Index Volumes…."
3. There is probably a checkmark in the little box in the "Use Schedule" column. If not, you can click the little box so Sherlock will automatically index the hard drive (it will use the schedule you are about to set).
4. Click the "Schedule…" button in the bottom left. *—continued*

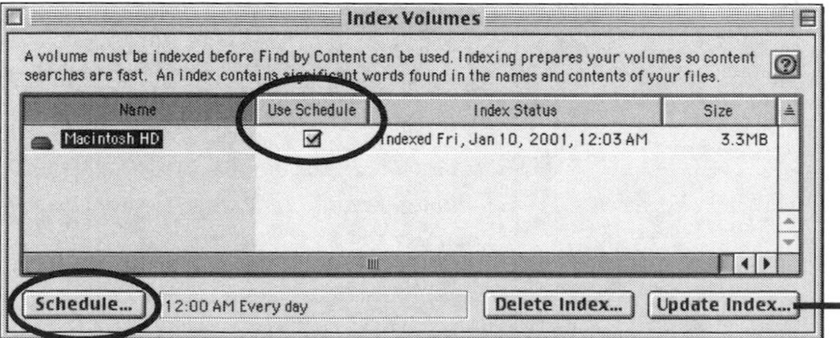

Note: *If you don't want the index to be updated automatically on a regular schedule, uncheck the "Use Schedule" box. Then when you* ***want*** *to index it, you can open this dialog box, select the disk you want to update (click on its name), and click the "Update Index…" button. (If you have never indexed the disk, this button says, "Create Index….")*

5. The "Schedule" dialog box opens, as shown below. Do you see the time it's scheduled for? The hour in that time slot is selected (it's highlighted).

   To change the hour, either type in a new time or click the tiny arrows to the right.

   To change the minutes, either tap the Tab key on your keyboard to select the minutes or click on the minutes; then type or use the tiny arrows.

   To change the AM or PM, either tap the Tab key on your keyboard to select the AM or PM or click on the letters; then type or use the tiny arrows.

   To change the days, click in the checkboxes to check or uncheck each day—a check tells Sherlock to index on that day each week.

6. Click the OK button when you're finished, then close the "Index Volumes" dialog box by clicking in its little close box in the upper-left corner.

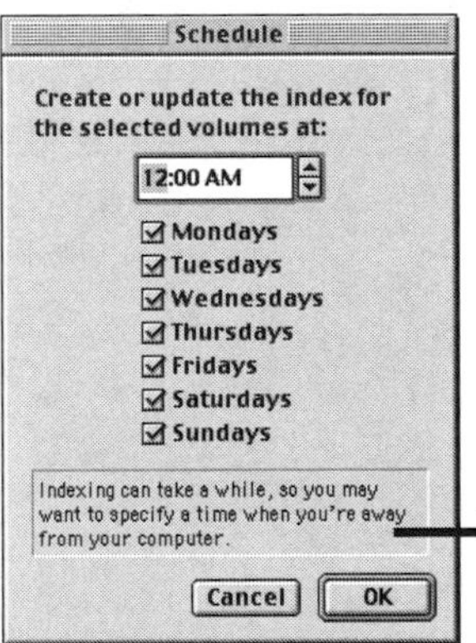

This is good advice—just remember that your Mac must be turned on for Sherlock to do its business.

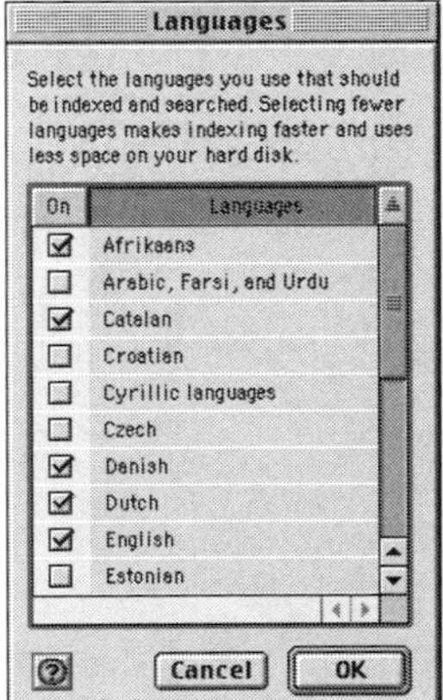

Tip: *While Sherlock is open, go to the Edit menu and choose "Preferences...." Click the "Languages..." button. You might see many languages in this list that have a checkmark next to them. If you don't have files on your disk in those languages, uncheck each one you don't need. Then click OK in both this dialog box and the "Preferences" box.*

As the note in the box says, "Selecting fewer languages makes indexing faster and uses less space on your hard disk."

Delete the Index

In the "Index Volumes" dialog box (shown below), you'll notice a column labeled "Size." This is the size of the database that Sherlock has made. As you create and install more and more files, this database can become huge, which means it uses a large chunk of your hard disk to store the index. You can't throw this file away because it's invisible (which means you can't even find it), but you can use Sherlock to delete it.

1. When Sherlock is open, go to the Find menu and choose "Index Volumes...."
2. Click once on the name of the disk to select it, then click the "Delete Index..." button.

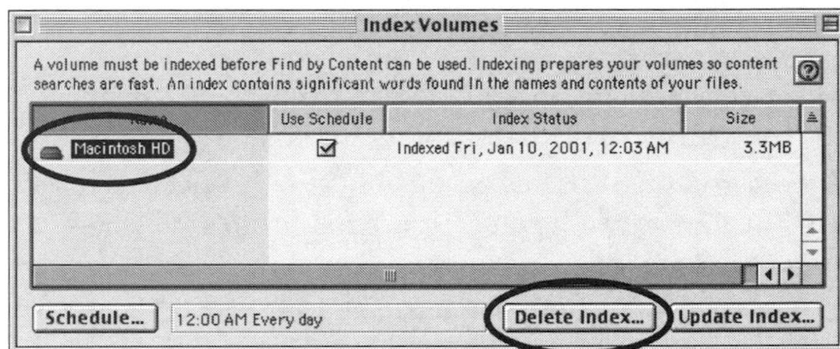

Find Something on the Internet

Besides searching your disk, Sherlock will also search the Internet and the web. Each of the buttons across the top of Sherlock is called a "channel." Each channel is set up to search specific areas of the web (except the very first channel, which finds files on your hard disk). When you click on a channel to select it, you'll see the bottom portion of Sherlock change to fit the channel's specifications. Try it.

To search the Internet, Sherlock has to *go* to the Internet, which means you must have your Internet connection already set up and working before you use this feature of Sherlock. **If America Online is your only email/Internet/web service, you must first open and log on to AOL before you can use Sherlock to search the Internet!**

To search the Internet

Internet

People

Shopping

News

Apple

Reference

My Channel

Entertainment
After you use this one, its icon changes!

1. Open Sherlock (choose "Sherlock 2" from the Apple menu; or if you are at the Desktop, press Command H).
2. Make sure the "Internet" channel button is selected (it should already be selected if you pressed Command H); click once on it to make sure.

   If you are looking for a person, click the "People" channel button instead of the "Internet" channel. If you're looking for news, reference material, or Apple support information, click the appropriate channel. If you want to go shopping, take a look at page 258.
3. Type in the item you wish to look for. If it is a phrase, put quotation marks around the phrase; for instance, if you are looking for a recipe for chocolate pecan pie, type in "chocolate pecan pie" in quotes.

   If you don't use the quotes, Sherlock will find every web page with the word "chocolate" on it, plus every page with the word "pecan" on it, plus every page with the word "pie" on it. But with the phrase enclosed with quotes, you should only get pages that contain the entire phrase "chocolate pecan pie."
4. Click the Search button (the big one with the magnifying glass). Sherlock will log on to the Internet through your ISP (Internet Service Provider). Remember, if you use AOL you must first open and log on to AOL before you click the Search button.
5. You will get a list of "results," as shown on the opposite page. Click once on a result and details of that web page will be displayed in the middle panel (also shown). To go to that web page, either double-click the title in the top portion of Sherlock, or single-click the underlined link in the details portion. Read the captions on the illustration on the opposite page.

1. *Click the appropriate channel to search.*

2. *Type in what you're looking for.*

3. *Click the Search button.*

4. *Using the scroll bar, scroll through this list of results.*

5. *Click once on a result to see details below, or double-click to go directly to that web page.*

Tips: *To resize the results and the details boxes, drag this little symbol.*

To resize the entire window *so you can see the names of pages and the addresses better, drag this corner.*

To resize the columns, *press on the dividing line between the column headings at the top (Name, Relevance, Site) and drag left or right.*

6. *If you want to see this web page, click once on this link.*

Tip: *If you see a link that says "Find similar pages," click it to get a list of more results that match the selected web page.*

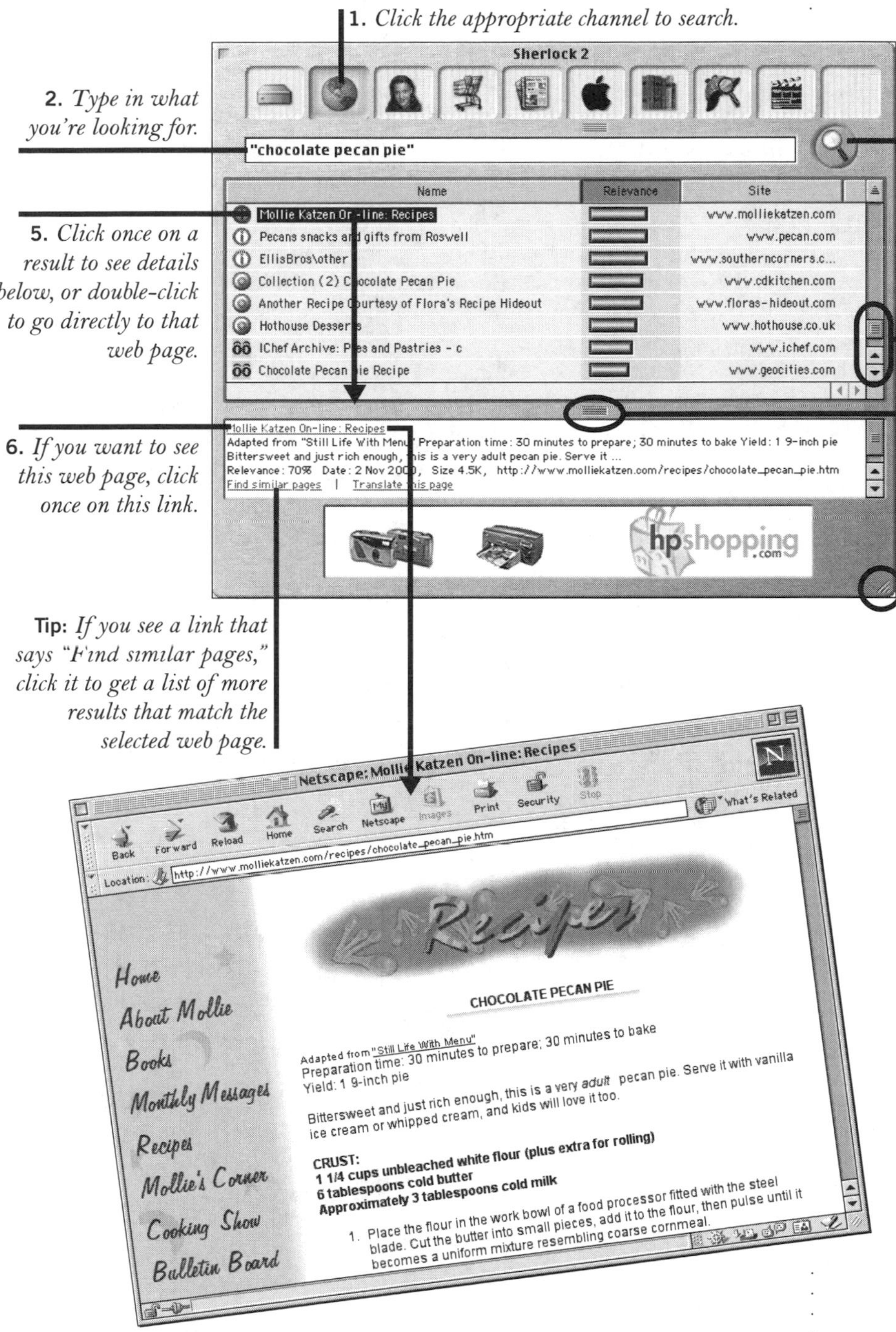

Shop on the Internet

Sherlock doesn't just *find* the items you want that are for sale on the Internet—it actually provides you with their prices and availability. Amazing.

Keep in mind that what Sherlock finds is dependent on what is being offered for sale through the selected search sites; in the case of the shopping channel, you can see below that Sherlock is only looking through selected sources. That is, if you're looking to compare prices of a down jacket from Lands End, L.L. Bean, and Orvis, Sherlock is not the right tool to use. But considering there are literally millions of items for sale in the search sites listed in Sherlock, it's not a bad place to look for many things.

Search using the shopping channel just as explained on the previous two pages: **1)** Click the Shopping channel button, **2)** type in your request (use quotation marks for phrases), **3)** click the Search button, then **4)** double-click the result of your choice, *or* **5)** single-click your choice to see if there are more details, then if you still want to go there, click the link in the details box.

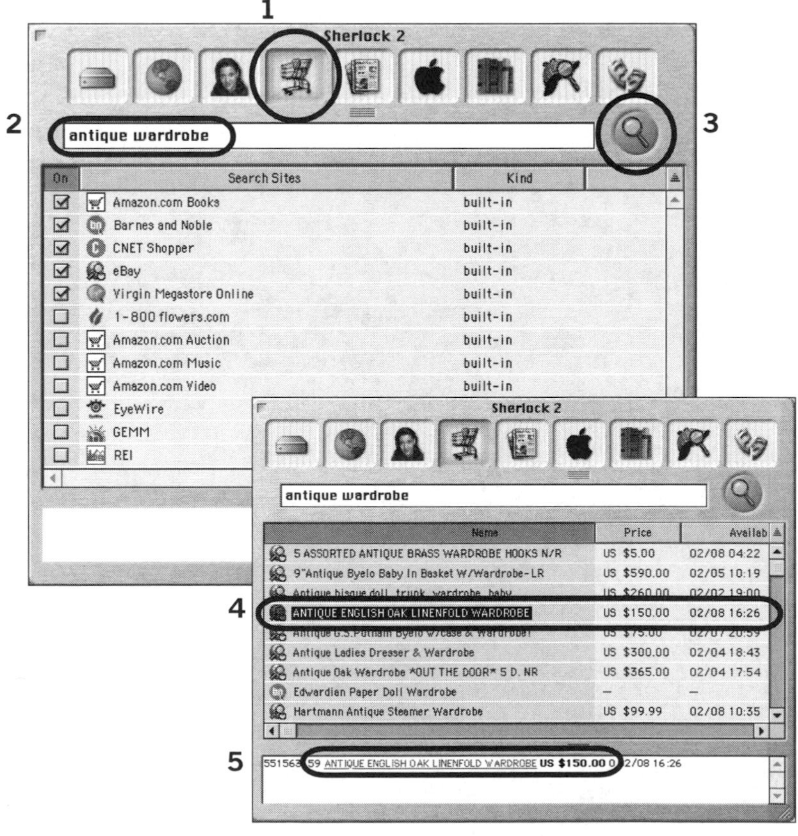

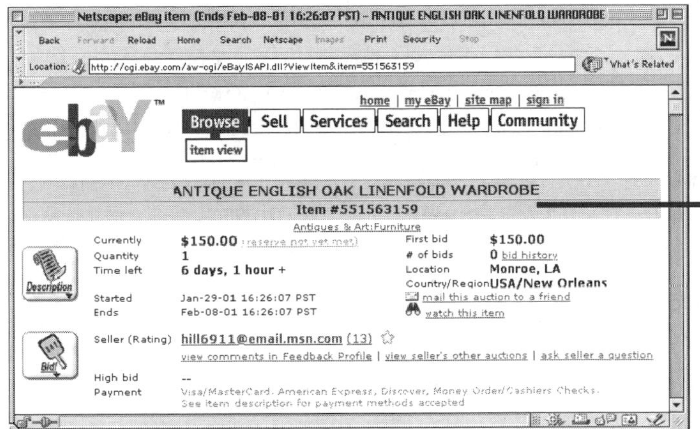

Depending on which web site you go to, you can choose to buy the selected item.

The intimidating term "Boolean operators" simply refers to using words like AND, NOT, and OR in your search. For instance, in the example below, I was able to limit my search to sites that had the words "Mary Sidney" *plus* the word "Countess" on the page.

Boolean Operators

Most of the search engines on the web use Boolean operators. For more information, go to just about any search engine site and click the "Help" button or the "Advanced Search" button.

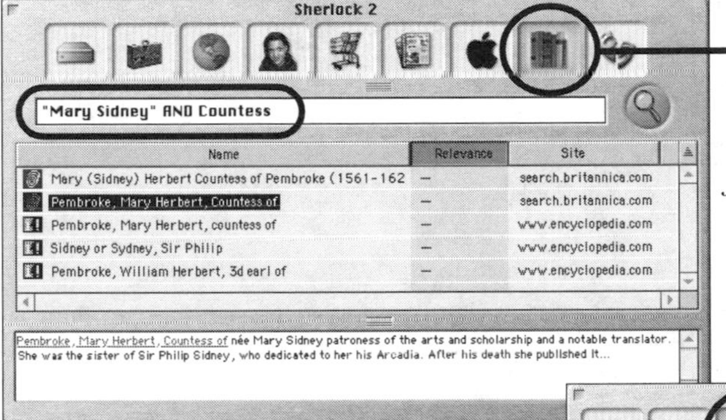

I clicked the "Reference" channel to search for encyclopedia and reference articles.

After the search above, I clicked the "Internet" channel to search for web sites about the same topic. The Boolean operator prevented me from getting a lot of results from Sidney family or genealogy web sites.

Sherlock will search a large number of search engines at once, bringing you the best of each.

Internet Search Sites

Sherlock does what it does by using special "plug-ins" for the various search sites. In your System Folder is a folder called "Internet Search Sites." This folder contains all the plug-ins for all the search sites that Sherlock looks through. If the plug-in for your favorite search tool is not in this folder, Sherlock can't search it.

To get the latest plug-ins, go to Apple's web site at www.apple.com/sherlock/plugins.html. Click on the plug-in you want and it will download to your Desktop as an **.src** file. Drop that .src file onto your System Folder; the Mac will put it into the "My Channel" folder in the Internet Search Sites folder for you, and then Sherlock can search with it. Sherlock can also update certain files itself, as explained below.

When you drop an .src file on the System Folder, the Mac puts it into this channel, called My Channel. You can always open the Internet Search Sites folder and put the .src file directly into the folder of your choice. Also see the following information.

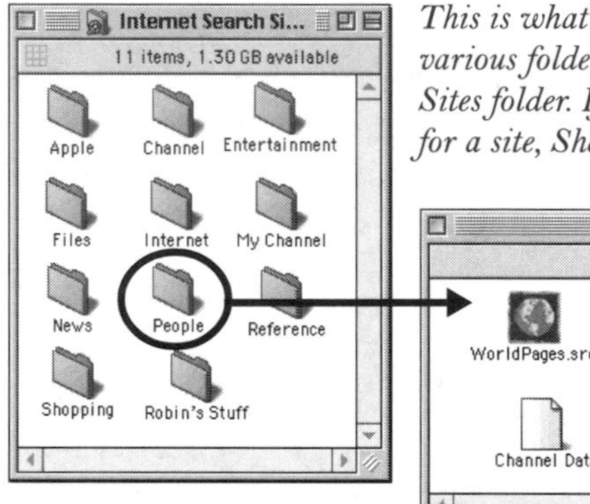

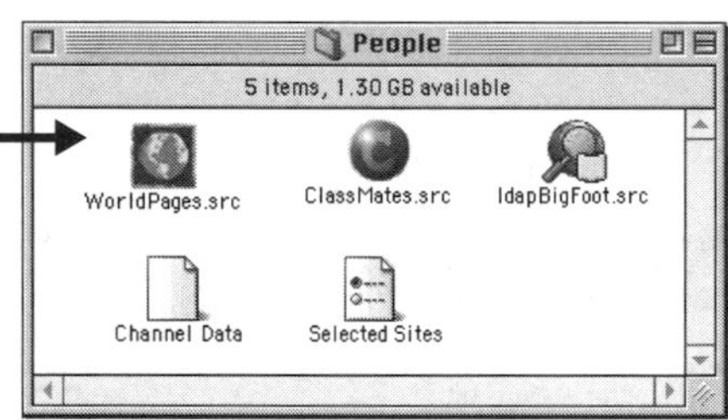

This is what the .src files look like in the various folders in the Internet Search Sites folder. If you don't have an .src file for a site, Sherlock can't search it.

Make New Channels and Customize Existing Channels

You can make your own new channels and you can customize existing channels by adding search sites to them.

To make a new channel

1. Open Sherlock.
2. From the Channels menu, choose "New Channel...."
3. In the "New Channel" dialog box (shown below), type the name and, if you like, a description of this new channel.
4. Press on the menu for "Channel type" and choose the sort of channel you want this to be.
5. On the top-right, click the scroll arrows to cycle through a selection of icons to represent your channel. Or drag any graphic file from your hard drive and drop it into that little window, as shown to the right.
6. Click OK. Now in the Sherlock window you will see your new channel.

To move a channel, *drag and drop it into a new slot.*

If you drag one channel directly on top of another, it will ***replace*** *the existing one. You can't* ***replace*** *any of the default channels—you'll have to move them out of the way first, then move your own into position.*

Drag this little marker to make more or fewer channels visible. If you can't display all the channels and slots, first enlarge the entire Sherlock window by dragging the size box in the very bottom-right corner.

To find and add new search sites

1. Connect to the Internet and open your browser.
2. **To update any of the default Apple search sites,** go to www.apple.com/sherlock/plugins.html. Click any of the plug-in links and it will be downloaded to your hard disk. Skip to Step 4.
3. **To get new search sites,** go to www.apple-donuts.com. Click any of the plug-in links and the plug-in will be downloaded to your hard disk. You will actually find three new files on your hard disk, as shown below.

LawCrawler.sit.hqx

This is the encoded file. It will automatically unencode and create the compressed file. Throw this away.

LawCrawler.sit

This is the compressed file. It will automatically uncompress and create the actual file. Throw this away.

LawCrawler Folder

This is the actual file, a folder that contains the plug-in. Open this folder and find the .src file, which is the plug-in.

LawCrawler.src

This is the plug-in. Go to Step 4.

4. Open Sherlock. Click on the channel that you want to add this plug-in to. Drag the plug-in and drop it into the window, as shown below.

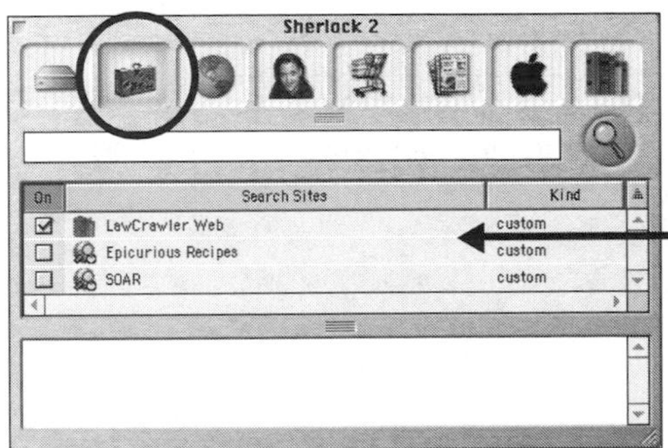

Drop the plug-in into the window. New plug-ins you add will appear as "custom" instead of "built-in."

This will automatically put the plug-in into the correct channel folder in the Internet Search Sites folder.

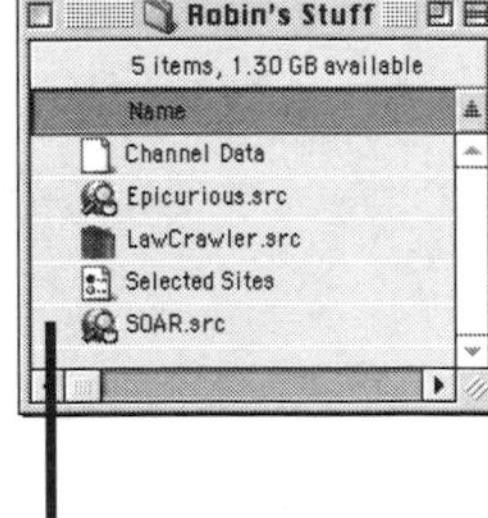

Saving a Search for Files on Disks

You can choose to **save the search criteria.** Sometimes you create a great, narrow search that takes you to exactly the files you're looking for on a disk. If you save this criteria, Sherlock will make an icon for the saved criteria file, and when you want to find that same information, simply double-click the icon. Sherlock will open, run the search, and display the results.

This is what the icon looks like for saved search criteria.

To save the criteria:

1. Open Sherlock and set up the criteria you like.
2. From the File menu, choose "Save Search Criteria...," or click the "Save..." button at the bottom of the "More Search Options" window (shown on page 277).
   You'll get the Save As dialog box.
3. Name and save your criteria, and choose where to store it on your hard disk, just like you save any file.

To use the criteria, either:

- Double-click on the icon representing the saved criteria. Sherlock will run the search and display the results.
- **Or** Open Sherlock and choose "Open Search Criteria..." from the File menu. Choose the file you want and Sherlock will run it.

Saving a Location for Information on the Internet

You can choose to **save the location of a web page.** When you get a list of results, often there are many pages you want to go to but you can't at the moment. You can save any web page location as a tiny file and later, double-click that file to go to that exact web page. It's this easy:

womenwriters.about.com

This is an Internet location file. Put it anywhere on your Mac, then double-click it to go to that page.

To put this in your Favorites menu, hold down the Control key, click once on this file, and choose "Add to Favorites."

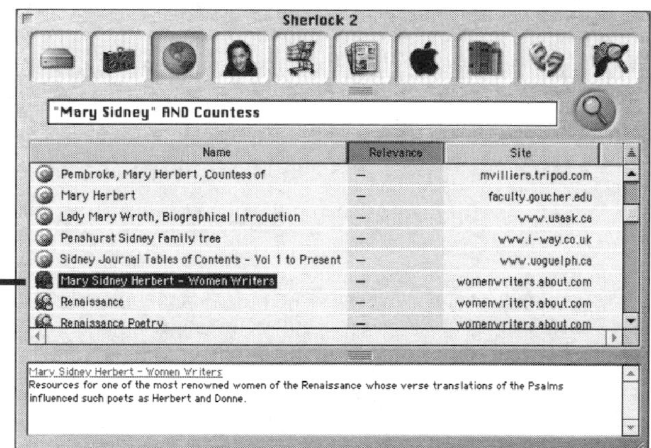

Just drag any of these results to your Desktop. The Mac will make an Internet location file for you, as shown to the left.

Chances are that when Sherlock finds some good sites for you, you'll want to bounce back and forth between Sherlock and your browser—clicking on the Sherlock links, checking them out in the browser, going back to Sherlock to click another link, and so on. To make this process easier, drag down the Application menu palette (directions below). Then you can just click the palette button icons to pop back and forth between Sherlock and your browser.

Extra Little Tip

To make the Application palette

1. Position your pointer directly on the Application menu, which is the one in the far, upper-right corner of your menu bar. It names the current application you are in.
2. Press on that menu and drag your mouse down through the menu and off the bottom, still holding the mouse button down. The menu will "tear off."
3. Resize the floating Application palette: hold down the Command key and click in the tiny little zoom box (circled, below).
4. Let the palette float around on your screen. When you want to go to Sherlock, click the Sherlock icon. When you want to go to Netscape, click the Netscape icon.
5. To put the palette away, just click in its tiny close box in the upper-left.

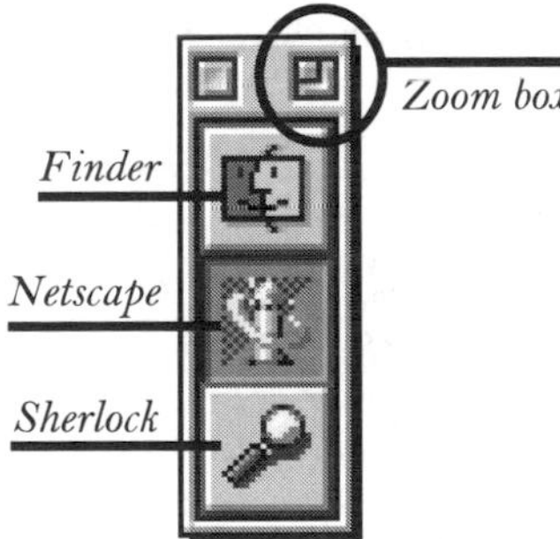

This is the floating Application palette.

1. Do you have to type in the exact and entire name of the file you're looking for?

2. Do you have to type caps and lowercase exactly as in the file name?

3. Do you have to type spaces in exactly the right place?

4. How do you tell Sherlock whether to search **a)** by file name, **b)** by content, or **c)** the Internet?

5. How would you find a file you wrote sometime in January '01 that you know had the word "budget" in the file name? You have hundreds of reports with the word "budget" in the names.

6. If you are not at the Desktop, how can you open Sherlock?

7. Once Sherlock has found a web site you want, what is the easiest way to display that site?

8. What keyboard shortcut can you press to open the ***folder*** that contains a file found on your Mac?

9. How can you trash a file on your Mac that's displayed in the results list?

10. Sherlock found lots of files for you on your hard disk (not web sites). How can you organize them in the results window so they're grouped according to what sort of file they are?

Answers on page 426.

27 Sharing Files

This chapter is only for you if you have more than one Mac in the same house or small office. If you do have more than one Mac, it is incredibly easy—in fact, it's so easy it's spooky—to **share files** between Macs. You can just drop a file into a shared folder and it instantly appears on the other computer. Or you can set it up so each person can get to the other person's entire hard disk. This works even if the other Macs are not using a version of Mac OS 8.

You must be **networked** together (your Macs must have some sort of cable connecting them to each other or both to the same printer), but networking a couple of Macs is a simple procedure. There are entire books written on networking, and the procedure *can* get very complex, so complex that people make a living being network specialists and in a large office there is usually a *network administrator*. I am only going to explain the simplest method to get a couple of Macs talking to each other. I do this in my office with one other person and it is the coolest, most efficient way for us to get work done.

If you have a number of machines in your home office or small office, you can get something called a *router* that can connect all of your machines together, including your printers. Have your local connectivity person get it set up and wired, then follow the directions in this chapter, starting with Step 2.

File Sharing Software

You need to have installed and turned on the **file sharing software** that came with your Mac. It's probably already there—open the Extensions Manager (find it in the Apple menu, under Control Panels) and look for the control panels *Apple Talk*, *File Sharing*, (if you're using software earlier than Mac OS 9, you'll also need the control panel *Users & Groups*) plus the extensions *AppleShare*, *File Sharing Extension*, and *File Sharing Library*. Make sure they each have a checkmark in their little boxes. If they are in the list but don't have checkmarks, check them and restart.

If some of those items aren't in the Extensions Manager list at all, they're apparently not installed. You can run the Installer again from your original CD that came with your Mac (have that power user friend of yours help you). In the Installer, click "Customize," and choose those items that are missing.

AppleTalk, LocalTalk, and Ethernet

The Mac has the **AppleTalk** networking software built into it that allows you to connect with other kinds of networks, and it's free.

LocalTalk is the networking protocol proprietary to the Mac. To use LocalTalk, you will plug in a LocalTalk-compliant cable to your printer port or modem port and connect two computers either directly, or more commonly, connect two computers to the same printer. Then whether the printer is on or not, the two computers can send files back and forth to each other.

The AAUI port has this symbol above it: <••>. This is the same symbol as on an Ethernet port. For more information on ports, see Chapter 34.

Ethernet is a much faster connection than LocalTalk. Most newer Macs have Ethernet ports. Look at the back of yours—if you see what looks like an extra-large phone jack, you have Ethernet. If one of the machines you want to connect has an Ethernet port and the other one has an AAUI port (see sidebar), you can get an adapter (called a transceiver) for that AAUI port so you can plug the Ethernet cable in. In fact, you can attach transceivers to two machines, neither of which have a built-in Ethernet connectors, but which do have AAUI ports.

An Ethernet connection might be what's called 10BASE-T or 100BASE-T, both of which refer to how fast the information travels through the wires. 100BASE-T, of course, is faster than 10BASE-T. The newest Macs have 10/100BASE-T Ethernet ports, which means they are really 100BASE-T but you can connect them to other Macs that "only" have 10BASE-T connections.

You have a network!

Once you have connected two or more computers, you have created what is called a **LAN,** or local area network.

Networking Options

Even on a Mac, networking has gotten more complicated. See which of the following situations applies to your arrangement of computers and printers, then turn the page to find your solution.

What kind of printer do you have?

A common way to share files between two computers is to hook both computers up to the same printer, because we often want to do that anyway. But not all printers can be networked.

You don't ***have to*** *network through a printer; you can connect two Macs directly to each other.*

PostScript printer: If your printer cost at least $1000, prints only black toner, and is fairly large, it's probably PostScript. If it cost around $4,000 or more and prints color, it's very possibly PostScript or at least PostScript-compatible. With this printer you have a great solution and can network your computers easily because these computers use LocalTalk.

Non-PostScript printer: If you have a relatively inexpensive color printer (one that cost less than about $500), or a black-and-white printer that cost even less, your printer is not PostScript and probably doesn't use LocalTalk.

Many **non-PostScript printers** are meant to be hooked up to one computer only, which means you cannot network them. If only one computer can be hooked up to your printer, then you can't use it as a solution to share files. You still can, however, connect the two *computers* together directly with a LocalTalk cable (see the next pages).

If you already have an investment in a printer that isn't networkable, check InfoWave's web site at www.infowave.com or Farallon's site at www.farallon.com to see if they have a printer/networking solution that is right for you.

Some **non-PostScript printers,** such as several of the Epsons, have Ethernet interfaces. This is a great solution and you can network easily.

If you haven't bought a printer yet or plan to buy a new one, make sure you get one that has a networking solution if you want to print from both computers to one printer, which automatically allows you to share files. The printer needs to be a "LocalTalk" printer, or use an individual network solution that might include software, special adapters, and special cables.

What kind of "ports" do you have?

Check the back of your computer and see if you have Ethernet ports, (plugs) the ones that look like large phone jacks. All G3s and iMacs and many PowerBooks have Ethernet ports. See the opposite page for information about Ethernet.

Even if you don't have Ethernet, you can directly connect two Macs through your serial ports with LocalTalk cables, or add transceivers to the AAUI ports. See Chapter 34 for illustrations of the ports.

The AAUI port doesn't have pins; it has a little horizontal slot. It has the same symbol above it as an Ethernet port: **<••>**

STEP 1: Connect the Computers

Note: *iMacs do not have built in serial ports, nor do the translucent G3s or G4s. But they do have 10/100BASE-T Ethernet connections.*

For almost any connectivity solution, check out Farallon at www.farallon.com. They are constantly coming up with new products to make connections and networking easier and faster no matter what arrangement of computers and printers you have.

The first thing you must do before you can actually share files is connect the two computers together with a cable. Read the previous page and decide which of the solutions below you will create. Match the solution with the information on the opposite page.

A. Connect two computers to a PostScript printer (either through Ethernet ports, if the printer and the computers have them, with Ethernet cables; or through the regular serial port with LocalTalk cables).

B. Connect two computers to a networkable non-PostScript printer with Ethernet cables or a solution provided by the vendor.

C. Connect two computers directly to each other using a LocalTalk cable and the serial ports (the little round ones with eight tiny holes; they have icons of a printer or a telephone handset above the ports). This would be an option if you have a printer that is not capable of networking.

D. Connect two computers directly to each other using an Ethernet cable for the fastest connection (for instance, iMac to iMac or iMac to G3). The computers might also be connected to one or more printers through serial or USB ports.

E. Connect two computers directly to each other with Ethernet cables using an Ethernet port on one machine and a transceiver (adapter) on the other machine (G3 or iMac to Mac 8100, for instance). The computers might also be connected to one or more printers through their serial ports.

Depending on your particular solution, you will most likely have to buy cables. In buying Ethernet cables, the most common type is "twisted pair, cat 3 or cat 5" (cat 5 is more protected and is usually used in professional networking situations). In buying a transceiver, the most common is a "10BASE-T transceiver," although 100BASE-T is rapidly becoming very common. Make sure you buy a transceiver that is compliant with your computer.

If you're connecting computers through your serial ports, you can use LocalTalk-compatible cables that you get at your computer store or through mail order. The PhoneNET kit from Farallon is very inexpensive, and with PhoneNET you can use plain ol' telephone cables from the hardware or grocery store when you need to rearrange things. You can get extra long telephone cables and connect computers in different rooms to each other and to the same printer. Just follow the directions in the Farallon PhoneNET kit you buy.

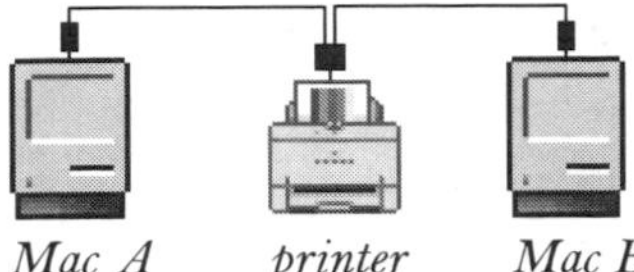

A. *This is one possible arrangement. If all three devices have Ethernet ports,* use Ethernet cables to connect them in this arrangement (you won't need the little boxes shown on the computer ends). If all three devices have serial ports, get the Farallon PhoneNET kit (you will need the little boxes on the cables, as shown; they come in the kit).*

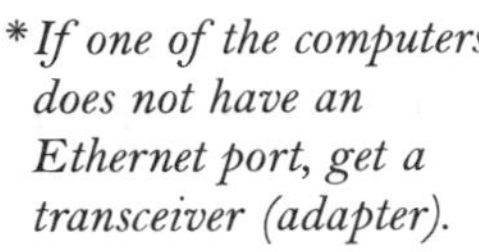

**If one of the computers does not have an Ethernet port, get a transceiver (adapter).*

***IMPORTANT:* Always shut down the computer before you connect or disconnect any cables! The only exception is a USB cable, found only on the newer Macs!**

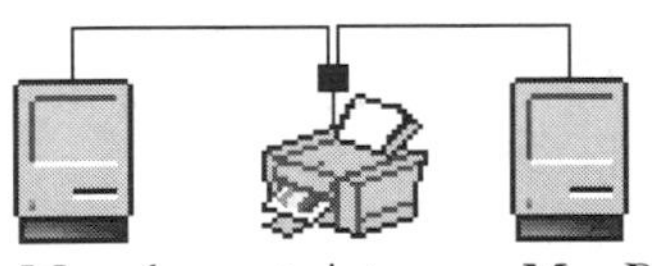

B. *Use Ethernet cables if all three devices have Ethernet ports,* or use the solution provided by the printer vendor, which might be cables and connectors as shown in A, above. You probably need an attachment so you can plug two cables into the printer.*

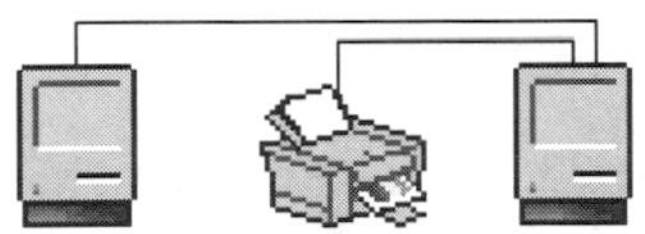

C. *Use LocalTalk cables plugged directly into serial ports. Now, you only have (at the most) two serial ports—one labeled for the printer and one for the modem. If you have both a printer and a modem attached, you will have to unplug one of them to attach the LocalTalk cable so you can share files. Then to print or use your modem you'll have to disconnect that cable and reconnect the modem or printer cable.*

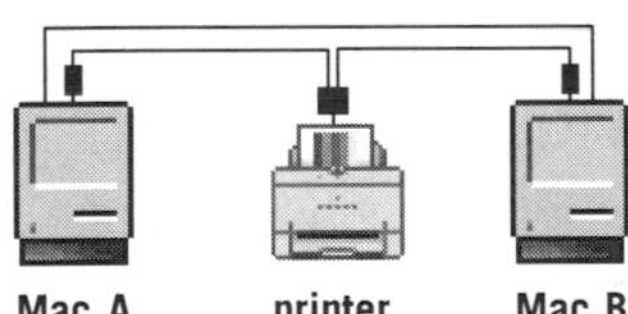

D. *This is the fastest method of file sharing. Get Ethernet cables and plug them right into the ports. In this example, two Macs are sharing a printer through the serial or USB ports, and the Macs are directly connected to each other with an Ethernet cable.*

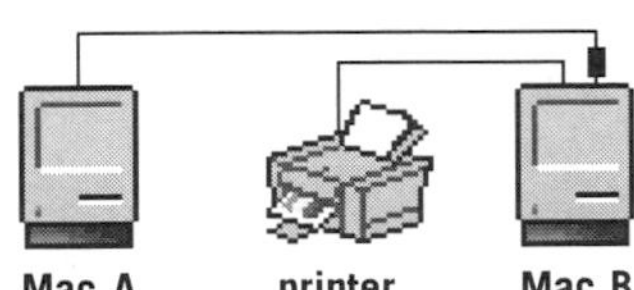

E. *Use Ethernet cables, and buy a transceiver for the Mac that doesn't have a regular Ethernet port. The transceiver will plug into the AAUI port, the one with this symbol over it:* <••>.

STEP 2: Turn AppleTalk On

Before you begin to connect, make sure **AppleTalk is turned on** or nothing will work anyway. Turn it on on both computers.

- From the Apple menu, slide down to Control Panels, then choose "AppleTalk."
- If you don't see an "Options…" button, go to the Edit menu, choose "User Mode…," click the "Advanced" button. Click OK.
- Click the "Options…" button.
- If it isn't already on, click the "Active" button. (If it's off, it probably means you have a non-PostScript printer. If so, you'll have to switch AppleTalk back and forth for printing and sharing.)
- Don't close the AppleTalk control panel yet . . .

Apple recommends that you use this control panel to turn off AppleTalk, ***not*** *the Chooser or the Control Strip.*

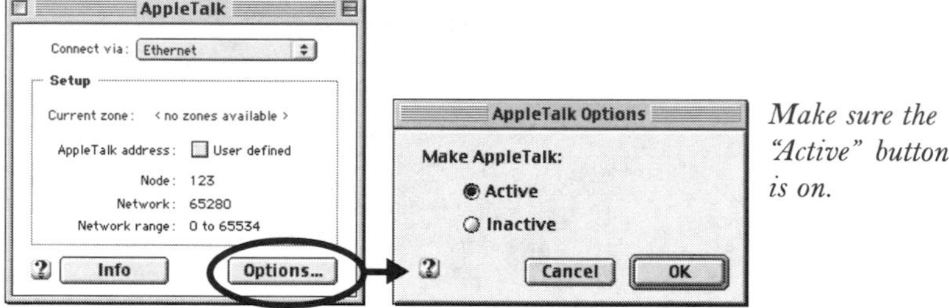

Make sure the "Active" button is on.

STEP 3: Choose Your Connection Method

Check the AppleTalk control panel and make sure it's set to the correct choice, depending on whether you are using Ethernet cables (plugged into the Ethernet ports) or serial cables (plugged into the printer or modem ports, the little round ones). Do this on both computers.

- If it's not already open, open the control panel "AppleTalk."
- Choose "Ethernet," "Printer Port," or "Modem Port," depending on which port you have the cables connected to.
- To close this control panel, click in the little close box. It will ask if you want to save these changes; click "Save."

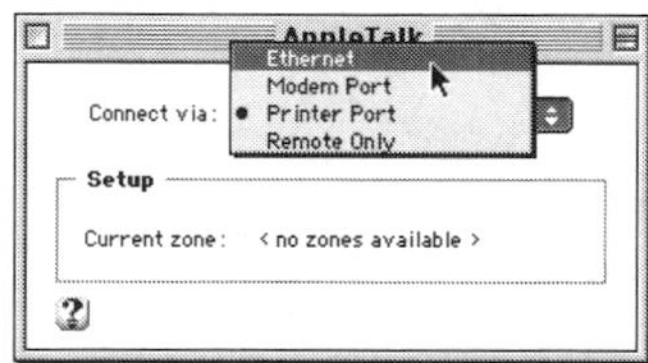

If you use a router and your entire office is connected through it, you don't ever have to switch AppleTalk to anything else.

Note: You have to come back to this dialog box when you need to use another connection. For instance, on my G3 I choose Ethernet when I want to share files with my iMac, but when I want to print directly to my laser printer (which uses LocalTalk), I have to open this AppleTalk control panel again and switch to "Printer."

STEP 4: Name the Mac

Now you must **name the Macintosh** and the owner. Generally the biggest computer will be your *file server,* or the one to which the other computers will connect. In large offices or school labs, there are one or more computers that do nothing except act as file servers. In your home or small office, one of the Macs will be considered the file server, but to you it will still be your working Mac.

File Sharing control panel

Name the Macintosh (I'm going to refer to this serving Mac as **Mac A**) through the File Sharing control panel:

a. From your Apple menu, slide down to Control Panels, then choose "File Sharing." The control panel is shown below.

b. Type your name in the edit box "Owner Name."

c. Make up a password, up to eight characters, which will give you control over whether other people have access to your files.

After you type your password, the letters turn into bullets, like so: (••••). Remember this password!

If you ever do forget your password, follow Step 6 to set up a Guest user; a Guest doesn't need a password.

d. Type a name for your Mac (this is still **Mac A**). This is the name that the person on the other computer (Mac B) needs to know to connect to you. This name will appear in their Chooser when they try to connect to your computer. If you are connecting several Macs together, create memorable and distinct names. Notice I named this one "Robin's Hard Disk." Very creative.

Turn on file sharing

e. Click the "Start" button to turn File Sharing on. (If the button says "Stop," then file sharing is already on—don't click it!)

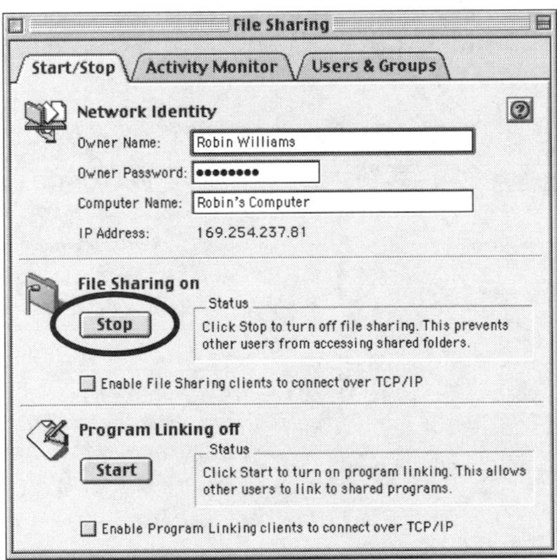

After you click the "Start" button, that button turns into "Stop." Notice the message above the Stop button now says "File Sharing on." Notice also that the folder has wires coming out the side, a ***visual clue*** *that information is flowing in and out of the folder.*

"Program Linking" allows other users on your network to link to applications that are sharable. Not all applications are sharable, and most applications that can be shared must be first set up for sharing, which often includes paying a higher fee for the application if more than one computer is going to use it.

f. Click the close box to put this control panel away.

STEP 5: Make a Folder to Share

Make a new folder on **Mac A** *or* select an existing folder and give this folder sharing privileges (instructions below). Mac B users will be able to see this folder on their hard disk, they can see anything inside of it, and they can put items into this folder on their own computer; the files they put in this folder will show up on your **Mac A.**

a. Click on a folder to select it. You can select more than one folder at a time.

If you're not on Mac OS 8.5 or higher, *you can't use the Get Info box to apply sharing privileges; instead, go to the File menu and choose "Sharing…."*

b. From the File menu, slide down to "Get Info, then choose "Sharing…" (shown below) to get the Sharing dialog box.

Or hold down the Control key and press on the folder. From the menu that pops up, choose "Get Info," then "Sharing…" (shown below) to get the Sharing dialog box.

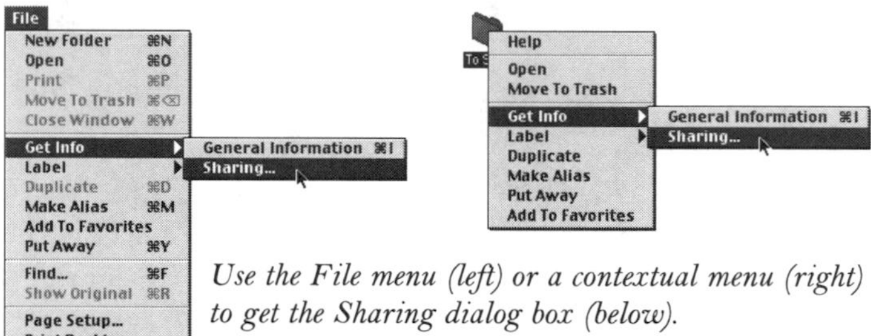

Use the File menu (left) or a contextual menu (right) to get the Sharing dialog box (below).

c. Click to put a ✓ in the box, "Share this item and its contents." You can change the privileges: the person at the other computer can "read only" (glasses icon; they can't make changes), "write only" (pencil icon; to make a folder so people can give you files), or they can have "read-write privileges" (glasses and pencil icon) where they can do anything.

Click the close box *or* press Command W to close the dialog box.

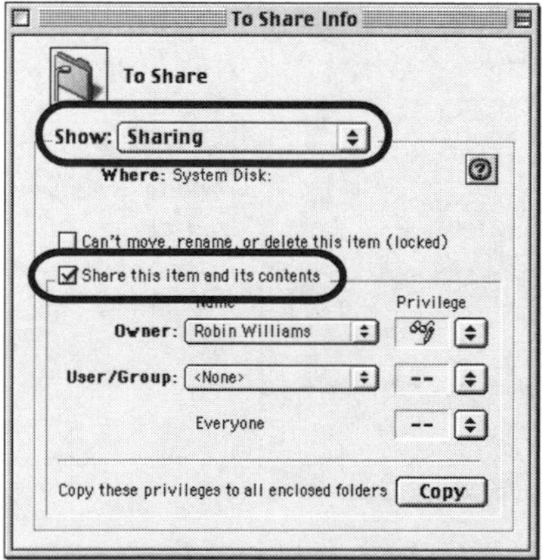

If this "Show" menu says "General Information," click on it to choose "Sharing." If it doesn't have the option "Sharing," the selected item cannot be shared. Maybe it's an alias?

If you want the other person to be able to read these files and/or perhaps to make changes to the file, you can grant permission right here. Just check the boxes of your choice.

d. Now the folder will show wires coming out the side, as shown below. The wires are a good **visual clue** that this folder is willing to share. Anything you drop into this folder will be available to the person on the other Mac.

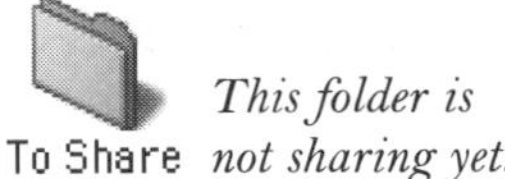

This folder is not sharing yet.

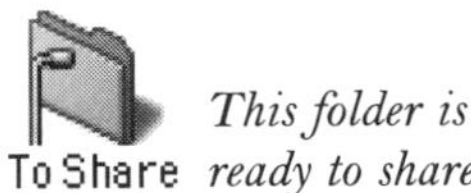

This folder is ready to share.

Share your entire hard disk

You can, if you choose, **share your entire Macintosh.** Instead of choosing individual folders to share, choose your hard disk icon and share it (Steps 5a–5c). You must first make sure there are no existing shared folders on the hard disk (see below). You won't see wires coming out of your hard disk icon once it's sharable.

To find folders that are being shared, use Sherlock:

a. From the Apple menu, choose "Sherlock 2."

b. Click the "Edit..." button.

c. Put a checkmark in the last box, called "folder," as shown below. To its right, from the menu choose "shared."

d. Click OK. Any folders that have been set up to share, whether they are actually being shared right now or not, will appear in the list. Right in this list, you can select the folder, get its Get Info window, and turn off the sharing.

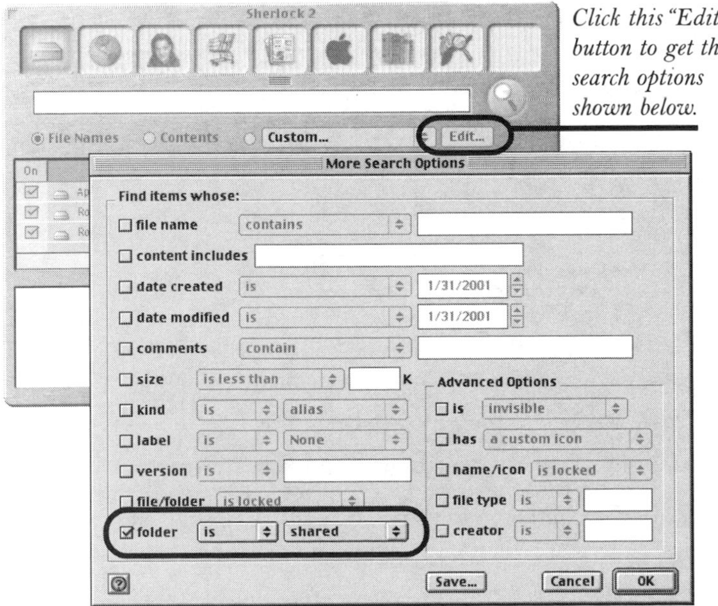

Click this "Edit..." button to get the search options shown below.

You might be surprised at the folders you find that you forgot you shared!

STEP 6: Set up Guest Access

You don't have to do this step—you can skip it altogether. If you *don't* do this step, then to share your computer a person has to know the correct name and password to connect to your machine, and they will be able to see and have access to your entire hard disk.

If you *do* follow this step, you can arrange it so a person does not need a password—they can log in as a "guest," and they will only have access to the specific folders you gave them privileges to.

To provide access as a guest:

a. On **Mac A,** from the Apple menu, get the control panel "File Sharing," then click the tab "Users & Groups." It looks like this:

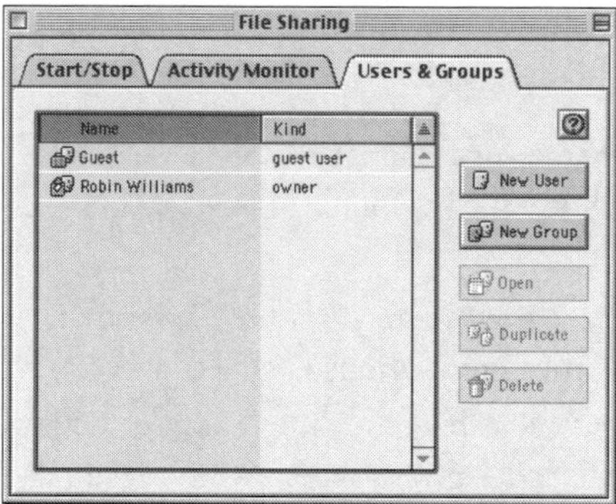

b. Double-click the name "Guest." You'll get this dialog box:

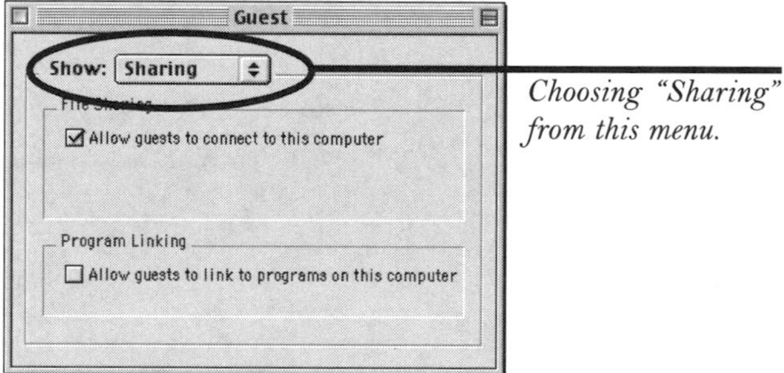

Choosing "Sharing" from this menu.

c. The "Show" menu in this dialog box probably says, "Identity." Click on it and choose "Sharing," as shown above.

d. Check the box "Allow guests to connect to this computer."

e. Click the close box, then close the File sharing control panel.

Continue on to the next step. You can always come back here and add new users, give entire groups certain access, and more. If you know that much about networking, you'll know what to do with these other options here.

STEP 7: Connect the Other Mac to Yours

Now the *other* Macintosh, **Mac B,** needs to connect to *your* Macintosh, Mac A. Once you do this, you won't need to do it again unless the file-serving Mac (Mac A) turns off the sharing. After you set this up the first time, make an alias of your server icon so you can just double-click to connect to the server (see page 306).

To actually connect to the other computer, you can use either the Network Browser or the Chooser; both are in the Apple menu.

Using the Network Browser (instead of the Chooser)

To connect using the Network Browser:

Note: The file-serving Mac (Mac A) must be turned on and have file sharing on.

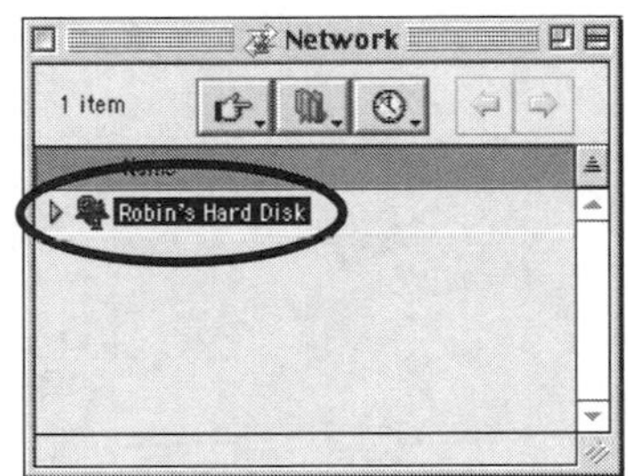

- **a.** On **Mac B,** from the Apple menu, open the Network Browser.
- **b.** You should see the name of the file-serving Mac (Mac A, here named "Robin's Hard Disk"). Click on the little triangle.
- **c.** You'll get the dialog box below. If you followed Step 6 to set up a Guest, that option is available. If Mac B logs on as a Guest, the Network Browser displays the folder you set to share (shown below, left). If Mac B logs on as a Registered User, the Network Browser displays the entire hard disk (below, right).

A Guest does not need a password, but access is limited to the individual items that were set up to share on Mac A.

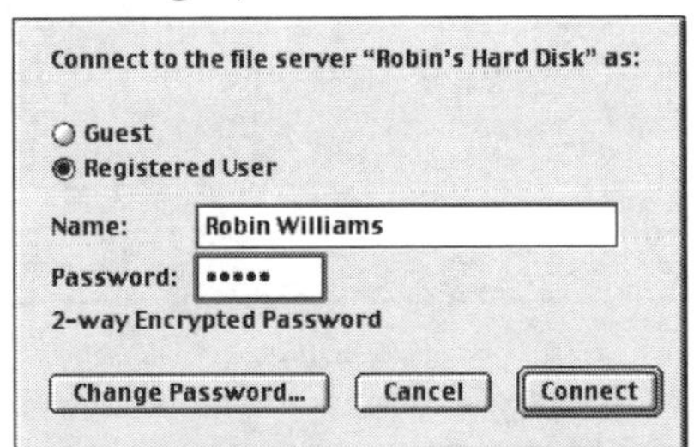

- **d.** Double-click the shared item you want access to. An icon will appear on the Desktop of Mac B, and its window will open automatically. It can be confusing—watch the folder names! Go to Step 8.

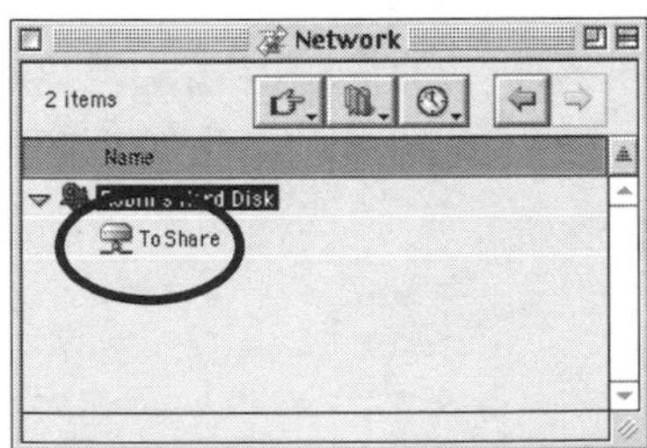

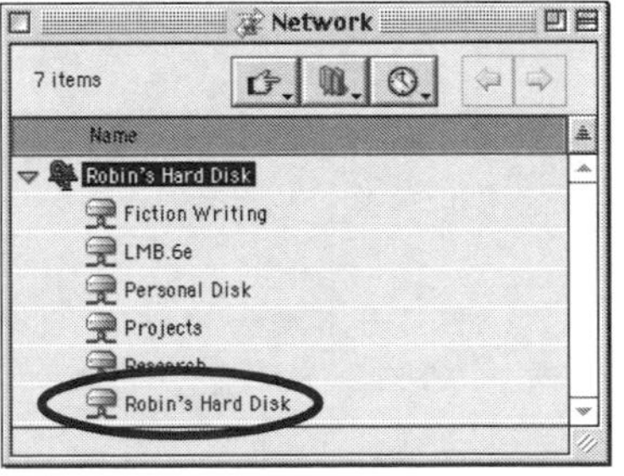

The icons for a shared folder or a shared disk look the same.

Using the Chooser (instead of the Network Browser)

To connect using the Chooser:

Note: The file-serving Mac (Mac A) must be turned on and have file sharing on.

a. On **Mac B,** from the Apple menu, open the Chooser (shown below).

b. Click the AppleShare icon. (If you were on a big network with "zones," you would see all the zones listed here also.)

c. You should see the name of the file-serving Mac (Mac A, here named "Robin's Hard Disk") on the right. Click on that name.

d. If you followed Step 1, the AppleTalk button is already on. You cannot share files without it.

AppleShare

This is the AppleShare icon that must be in your Extensions folder.

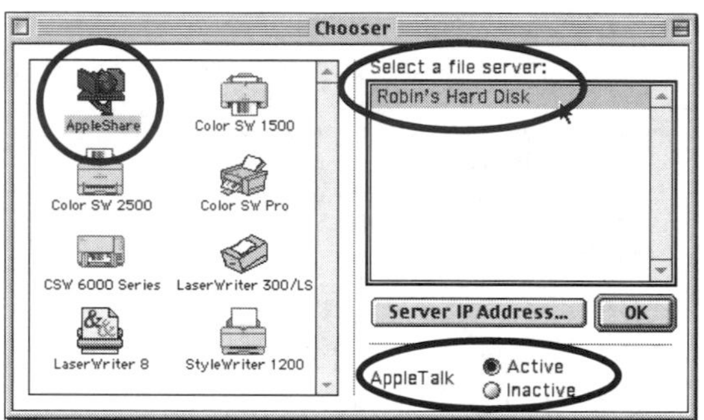

The AppleShare icon is critical. You must have the AppleShare file in the Extensions folder in your System Folder.

e. Click OK. This will give you one of the dialog boxes shown below:

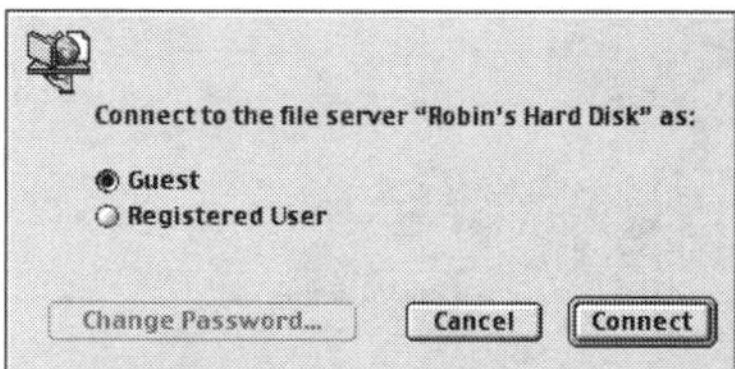

If you followed Step 6 to set up a **Guest** *user, the Guest button will be available and the user does not need to know a password.*

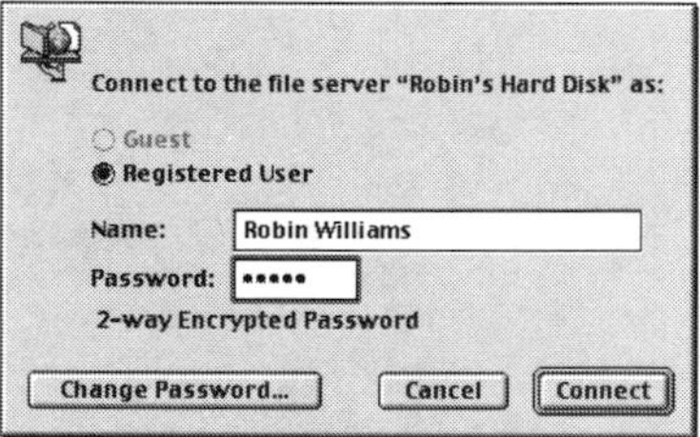

If you did not follow Step 6 to set up a Guest user, the Guest button will not be available. The **Registered User** *must know the correct name and password, including capitalization and spaces.*

You can change the password here, but you need to know the original password to do so.

f. Click "Connect." This will give you one of the dialog boxes shown below. Click the names to select the folders or disks you want to share.

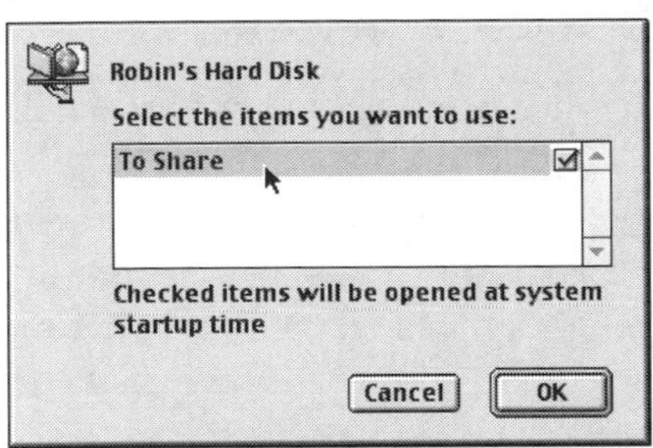

If you logged on as a ***Guest,*** *you will see only the specific folders that were set up to share in Step 5.*

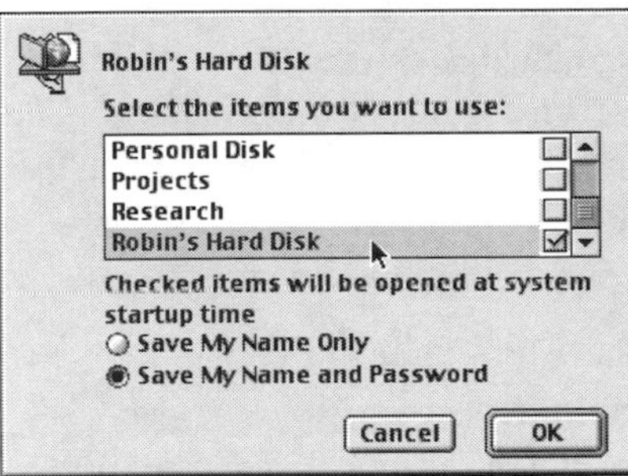

If you check "Save My Name and Password," you won't have to enter those next time you log on.

If you logged on as a ***Registered User,*** *you will have access to the entire hard disk. In this example, each of the individual partitions of my hard disk are available.*

Be sure to ***highlight*** *the name of the disk you want access to—the checkmark does something else!! The* ***highlighted*** *disk is the one that will be shared for you—the* ***checkmarked*** *disk will be opened next time you turn on* ***Mac B.***

g. The checked items, as the note in the dialog box says, will be opened and shared every time you turn on Mac B. They will only open and share at startup on Mac B ***if*** Mac A was turned on first and ***if*** file sharing is activated on both computers!

h. Click OK in this sharing dialog box, and the Chooser will again appear in front of you. *Don't click OK on the Chooser or it will think you want to connect to the server again!* Instead, click in the close box in the upper left of the dialog box.

i. On the Desktop of **Mac B** you should see an icon like this for each folder or disk you have chosen to share:

The icons for a shared folder or a shared disk look the same.

STEP 8:
***Now* You Can Share Files!**

On **Mac B,** you can double-click on this "file serving icon," which represents the folder on the file-sharing Mac A, and it opens to a window just like any other folder. Anything you put in this "folder" will be **copied** to Mac A.

On **Mac A,** the shared folder icon changes when Mac B has successfully connected (a **visual clue**). Can you believe how cute this is—happy little people sharing files? Any file you drag from Mac A to this folder will **move** into that folder, and then the person on Mac B can drag that file out of their "To Share" folder, and it will be **copied** onto their Desktop on Mac B.

If Mac B has access to the entire hard disk of Mac A, the hard disk window from Mac A will appear on the Desktop of Mac B. You can drag any files from any Mac A folder onto the hard disk of Mac B, and you can drag any files from Mac B into the hard disk window for Mac A and the files will copy over. It's really amazing.

Twitching while file-sharing?

While the computers are file-sharing, you'll notice they go through little spasms and twitches and your typing stops for a second or two, menu commands take longer to happen, and other little annoyances will irritate you because the computers are trying to do two things at once—the work you want, plus send a file.

Where are those shared files?

Important—please read this!

Let's say I'm working on **Mac A** and I put a file into the shared folder so You on Mac B can use it. When I put the file into the folder on **Mac A** (the server), I am actually just *moving the original file* into the folder because I am on the file-server Mac **(Mac A).**

You, on **Mac B,** want to use that file. You double-click on your shared folder on **Mac B** and see the file. **Don't double-click on that file that's inside the folder!!** What *You* see in that shared folder is the original file that is still on *My* hard disk, Mac A, and if You open that file, *You will be using My computer!*

Instead: Copy the file to your hard disk on **Mac B** and then open it! To copy the file, just drag it from the shared folder onto your hard disk window.

You, on **Mac B,** when you put files from your hard disk into the shared folder, you'll see that the computer **copies** the files from your hard disk on **Mac B** onto my hard disk on **Mac A.** This means that when I open my shared folder on **Mac A,** all of the files in it are already copied onto my machine. Thank you.

Disconnecting

When either computer shuts down, file sharing is automatically **disconnected.** You can also disconnect yourself from the "network" in several other ways:

- Drag the icon of the *file server* on **Mac B** to the trash. You will not see any icon of the file server in the trash can window, so you can't go get it to reconnect.
- **Or:** select the file server icon on **Mac B,** then press Command Y (the keyboard shortcut for "Put Away" from the File menu).
- **Or:** on the file-serving **Mac A,** go back to the File Sharing control panel and click the "Stop" button. **Or** choose "Stop File Sharing" from the Automated Tasks item in the Apple menu.
- You can selectively disconnect users on **Mac A** through the File Sharing control panel, the same one you used to start the connection process: Open the control panel, then click on the tab labeled "Activity Monitor" (shown below).

  Click once on the name of the connected user you want to disconnect, then click the "Disconnect" button. Notice you can also change the privileges of any shared items from here.

This is the icon of the file server on Mac B.

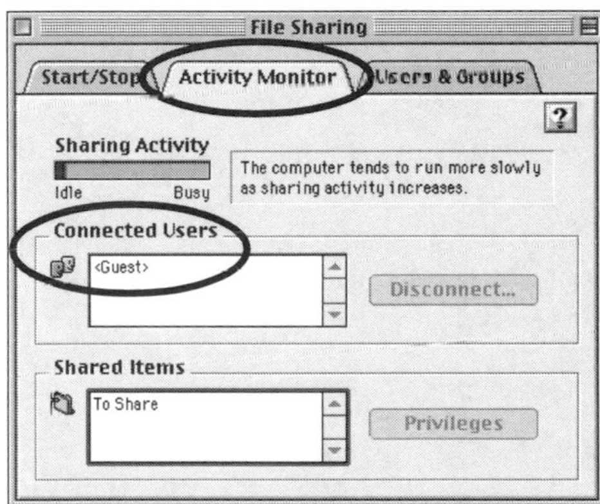

You will get a dialog box that says users will be disconnected in, for instance, 10 minutes. You can change that number to 0 (zero) and they will be disconnected immediately. They'll get a message on their screen telling them they have been disconnected.

Also use this control panel to change privileges or disconnect users.

Turn Off File Sharing

If you need to turn off file sharing, do one of the following:

- In the Control Strip, click the file sharing button and choose "Turn File Sharing Off."
- From the Apple menu, slide down to Control Panels, choose "File Sharing," and click the "Stop" button.

You can, of course, use any of these techniques to turn file sharing back on.

Reconnecting

Double-click the alias to automatically start file sharing without having to go through the Network Browser or the Chooser.

To reconnect Mac B to the file-sharing **Mac A,** you *can* go through the process of getting the Network Browser or the Chooser and logging on again, just like you did the first time. Or you can do this great trick:

> In the Network Browser, select the icon of any of the folders or disks you want to connect to—drag the icon out of the Network Browser and drop it on the Desktop or into any folder. It will automatically make an alias for you (without the word "alias").
>
> If you used the Chooser, then when you *are* connected, make an alias of the file server icon on **Mac B** that represents the shared folder. To make the alias, click once on the icon, then press Command M.

Store this alias wherever you like. **When you need to connect to Mac A, just double-click the alias.** This trick will also work if you make an alias of some file in the shared folder.

28 Navigating and Saving

Whenever you save a document, the Mac creates an icon to represent your file. This file/icon has to go somewhere on the disk. Have you ever saved a document and wondered where it went? Have you ever lost things? Have you ever opened a document only to discover it does not contain the last several hours of your work, and you know you saved the document beyond that point?

The problem is that you aren't quite clear yet on how to **navigate** through the dialog boxes with all the different levels and folders on the Mac to get where you want to be, either to open the correct document or to save it where you will find it again. Navigating is one of the most important skills you can master. It seems so befuddling at first, and then one day it will just click and make perfect sense. Once you learn how to navigate you will never misplace documents when you save them, you will always be able to find the clip art you're looking for or the extra report you wanted to open along with the one currently on the screen, and you will amaze your friends and coworkers as you whip through those lists knowing exactly where you are going.

Visual Reference

It helps to have a **visual reference** to see how things are organized on the Mac. Let's follow the document **"My Friends"** through the navigation process.

*The **Hard Disk** is on the **Desktop**.*

***Personal** is a folder in the **Hard Disk** window.*

***My Kids** is inside the folder **Personal**.*

*The **Scarlett** folder is inside the folder **My Kids**.*

***My Friends** is inside the **Scarlett** folder.*

Take a look at these folders inside of folders where the file **My Friends** is stored. Imagine the Desktop to be your office. In your office is a filing cabinet, called the Hard Disk. In the filing cabinet are lots of folders. Each of these folders can have folders inside. Think of each of these things—the Desktop, the Hard Disk, each folder—as a separate *level* where you can choose to place a document. For instance, you sometimes want to file a document in a very specific compartment, nested into a number of folders with each folder getting more specific than the last, as in the case here for Scarlett's story about her friends.

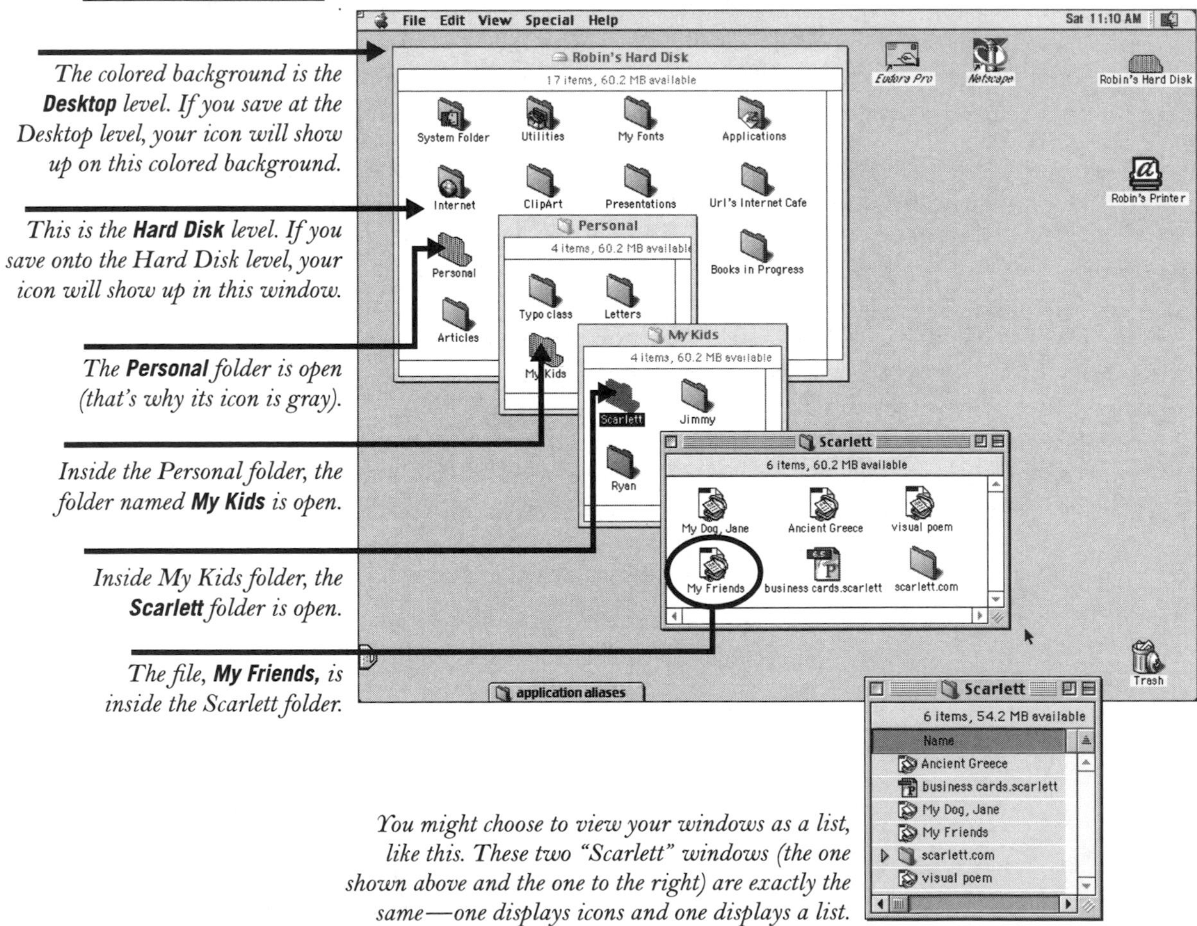

*The colored background is the **Desktop** level. If you save at the Desktop level, your icon will show up on this colored background.*

*This is the **Hard Disk** level. If you save onto the Hard Disk level, your icon will show up in this window.*

*The **Personal** folder is open (that's why its icon is gray).*

*Inside the Personal folder, the folder named **My Kids** is open.*

*Inside My Kids folder, the **Scarlett** folder is open.*

*The file, **My Friends**, is inside the Scarlett folder.*

You might choose to view your windows as a list, like this. These two "Scarlett" windows (the one shown above and the one to the right) are exactly the same—one displays icons and one displays a list.

Since you have been working on your Mac for a while, you have created your own folders for organizing your own information. (Well, you *should* be creating them—just press Command N to make a new folder in the *active* window; read Chapter 10 on *Folders*). Making a folder on the computer called "Personal" is the equivalent of marking "Personal" on a manila folder and sticking it in a drawer in the filing cabinet (Hard Disk) in your office (the Desktop/Finder). When you open that folder in your real office, what do you see? You see all the documents you've stored in that folder, right? When you double-click on a folder on your Hard Disk, that's what you see—all the documents stored in that folder.

- The trick to navigating through dialog boxes is to understand that **the dialog box is just a different way of looking at the contents of the folder.** When you choose to see that folder in a dialog box, the list (sometimes called the directory) displays all those files.

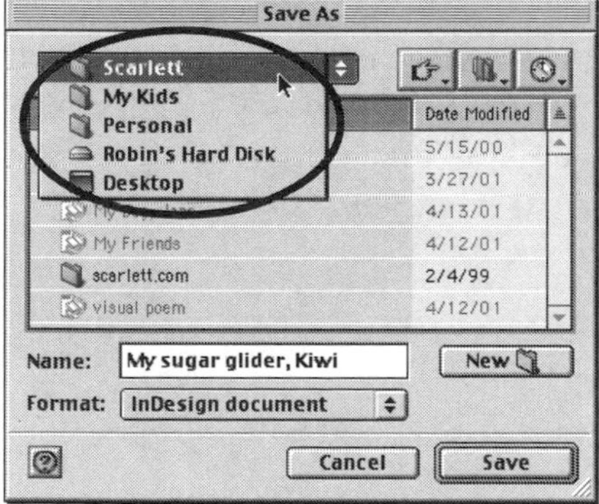

Take a minute to look carefully at the menu in the Save As dialog box and notice the order is exactly like the order you see in the picture on the opposite page—this is a list of the folders that "My Friends" is nested into. This list just looks upside down compared to the one opposite—but it leads back to the "root level," which is the Desktop.

Your Save As and Open dialog boxes might look like this if the application you're using is new enough. It's basically the exact same dialog box.

You could view the same thing another way: At the Desktop, hold down the Command key and press on the name of the open folder. You see the same hierarchical list (called the "path") telling you where this particular folder is nested.

Different Ways of Looking at the Same Thing

***My Friends** is inside the Scarlett folder.*

*The **Scarlett** folder is inside the folder **My Kids.***

My Kids** is inside the folder **Personal.

***Personal** is a folder in the **Hard Disk** window.*

*The **Hard Disk** is on the **Desktop.***

The list above is exactly the same hierarchy as the list on the opposite page—it's just listed in the reverse order.

Where Does the Document Go?

This is how to save a document into exactly the spot you want so when you quit you know where the document went. Ready?

So here you are in your word processor with a new document open. You choose "Save As..." from the File menu.

If you were to name your document and press the Save button right now, your document icon would appear in the folder or disk whose name is in the label above the list, as shown below.

The document you just named, "Sources of plays," will be saved into the folder "Article" (see the folder icon in the label), which is on the disk "Research," whose name is at the bottom of the label menu, above "Desktop" (see the disk icon).

This is the "Article" folder that is on the "Research" disk that is on the Desktop.

This is the list of other files that are in the "Article" folder.

This is the document you are saving.

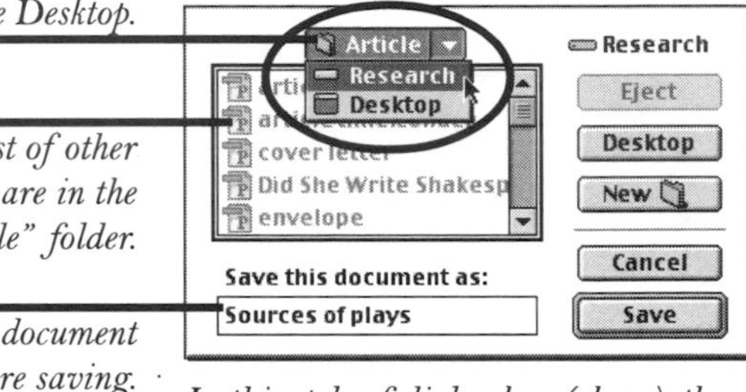

In this style of dialog box (above), the name of the disk you are saving onto is also shown at the top-right.

You can save on any one of several different "levels" on a disk: on the Desktop (on a hard disk), on the disk itself (hard or floppy), or into any folder (folders can be on any level, or they can be "nested" inside of other folders). The following pages explain the steps to save into various places on your computer.

Save onto the Desktop

If you want to save onto the Desktop of your Hard Disk, in the Save As dialog box click the button "Desktop" or choose "Desktop" from the Shortcuts menu (shown below-right), depending on which style of Save As dialog box you have (both are shown below). No matter what is showing in the dialog box or how confused you are, choose "Desktop" to take you to *the Desktop level of your Hard Disk.*

If you save onto the Desktop level, your document icon will be displayed on the far right of the screen (circled, below).

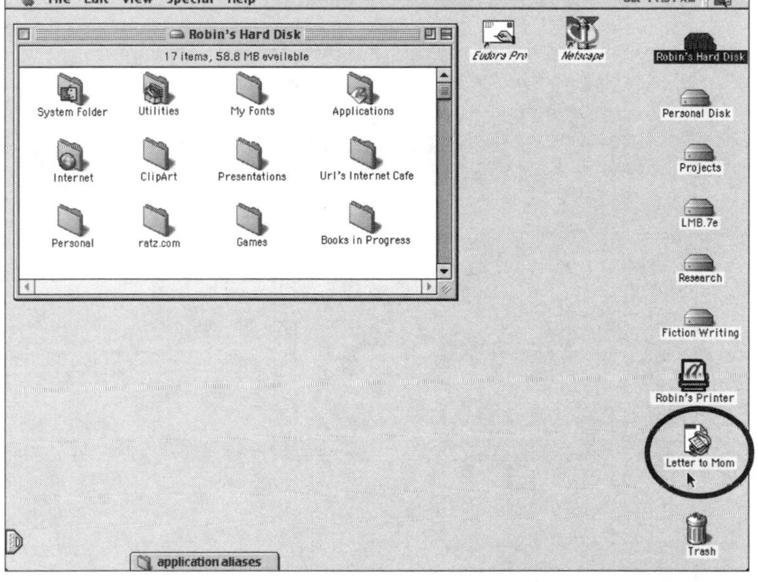

(All of these other hard disk icons are actually "partitions" of my main hard disk. Each one acts like a separate hard disk. They appear in dialog boxes as individual hard disks, as you can see below.)

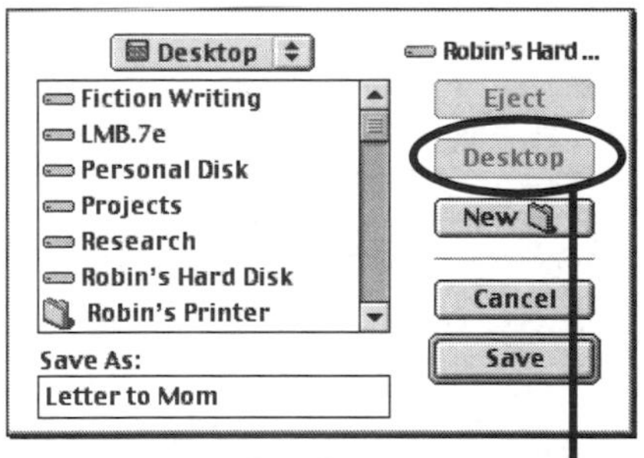

Click the Desktop button (or press Command D) to go directly to the Desktop. This button is gray at the moment because I already clicked it—notice the label above the directory now says "Desktop."

This is the "Shortcuts" menu.

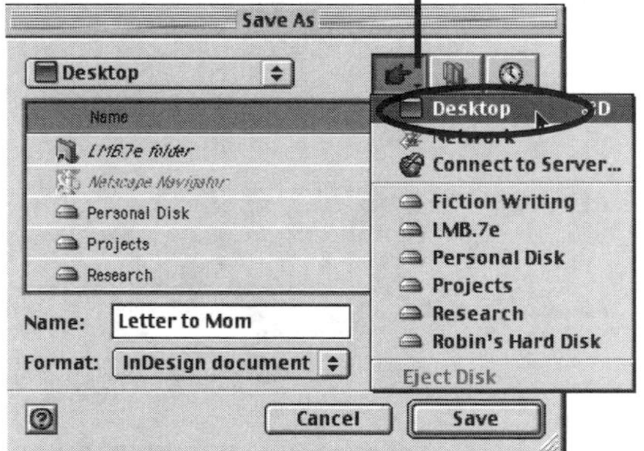

In this kind of Save As dialog box, choose "Desktop" from the Shortcuts menu, as shown (or press Command D).

Save into your Hard Disk window

If you want to save into the Hard Disk window (meaning you want your file to be visible in the *window* of the Hard Disk, but not in any folder), you have to choose your Hard Disk. Depending on which style of Save As dialog box you have (both are shown below), follow these steps:

Older dialog box: Click the button "Desktop" to make sure you are viewing your hard disk. Then in the list, double-click the name of your Hard Disk.

Newer dialog box: From the Shortcuts menu (shown below), choose the name of your Hard Disk.

If you save onto the Hard Disk, the icon for your document will be displayed in the window for the Hard Disk.

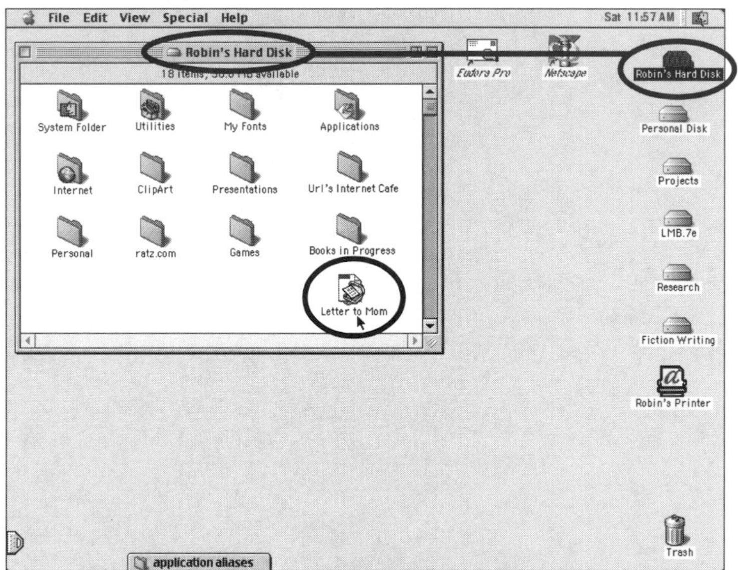

This is the Shortcuts menu.

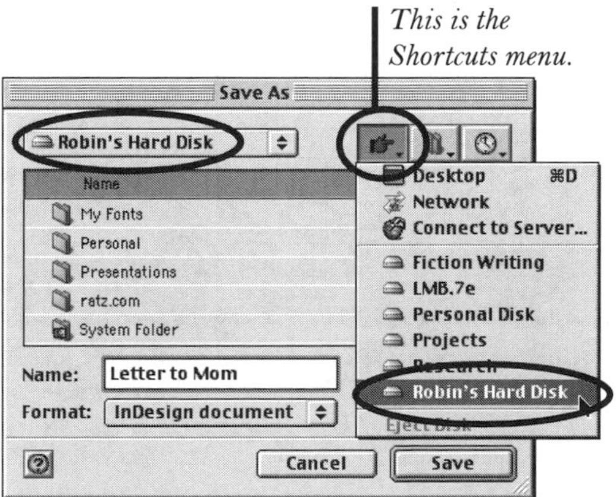

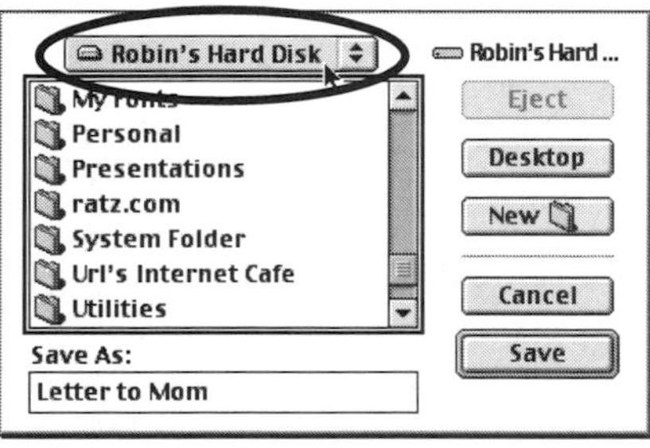

Before you click the Save button, you should see the name of your hard disk in the label at the top of the list. This will make sure your file is saved into the window for your hard disk.

If you want to save onto a floppy disk or a cartridge disk, make sure that floppy disk is inserted or the cartridge is mounted. When you get to the "Save As" dialog box, you probably have to navigate over to the disk:

Older dialog box: Click the button "Desktop." The name of any other disk will appear in the list. Double-click its name.

Newer dialog box: From the Shortcuts menu (shown below), choose the name of the disk.

If you save onto the other disk, the icon for your document is displayed in that disk's window.

Save onto a floppy, cartridge, Zip disk, or other disk

Tip: *Go to the Save As dialog box* ***before*** *you put the removable disk in. Then, while the Save As dialog box is open, insert the disk. In a couple of seconds the inserted disk will display itself in the Save As dialog box.*

You can't use the Save As dialog box to save anything onto CDs from your Mac yet, even on recordable CDs.

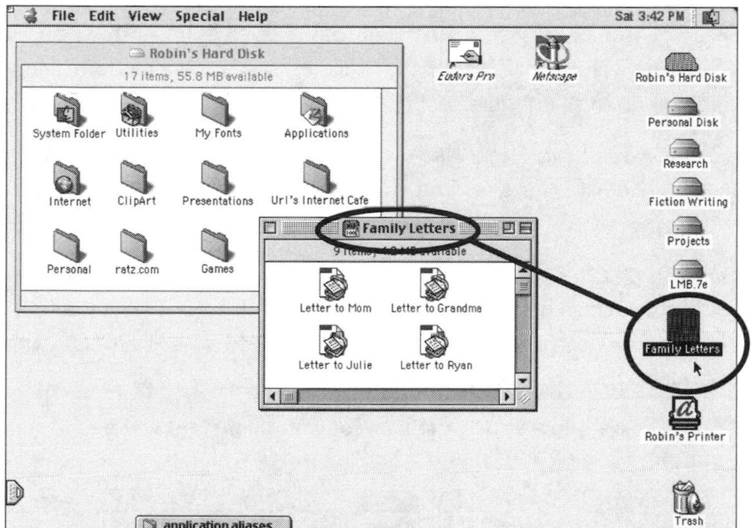

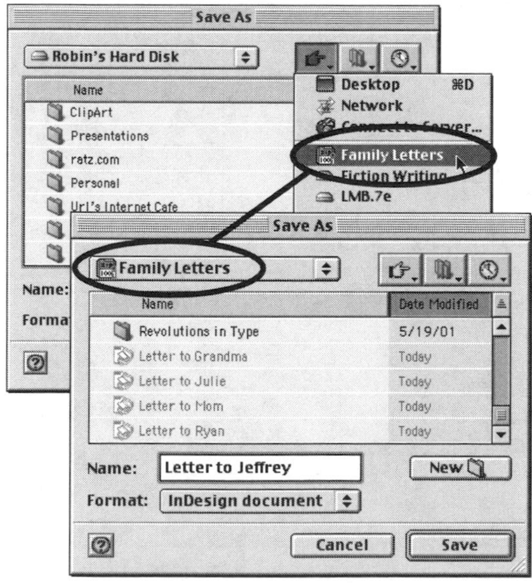

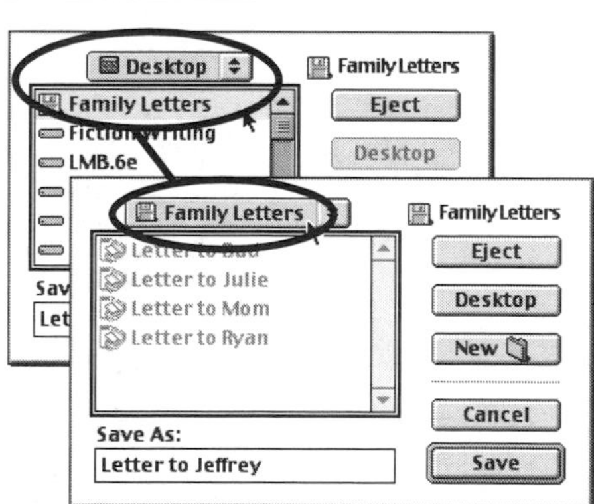

Before you click the Save button, make sure you see the name of the disk in the label above the list box. Notice the icon indicates that "Family Letters" is a disk, not a folder.

Save into a particular folder on any disk

If you want to save into a particular folder, first navigate to the folder.

- If the folder is on the Hard Disk, then first make sure you are viewing the Hard Disk: Click the button "Desktop," then double-click the name of your Hard Disk. In newer dialog boxes, choose your hard disk from the Shortcuts menu (as shown on page 312).
- If the folder is on another disk, then first make sure you are viewing the other disk: follow the steps on the previous page.

Now you must find the folder. Do you see the folder listed on the disk? Yes? Then just double-click the name of that folder. Its name will appear in the label with a tiny icon of an open folder. **That open folder icon is your visual clue that if you were to save right now, the document would end up in that folder.**

Is the folder you want inside another folder that you see in the list? Double-click the other folder first and then the one you want will be available for opening.

Did you forget to create a folder before you tried to save the document? Most applications have a "New" folder button in the Save As dialog box. Keep in mind that any new folder you create *will drop right into the folder or disk whose name is showing in the label!*

If you save into a folder, the icon for your document will be displayed when you open the folder's window.

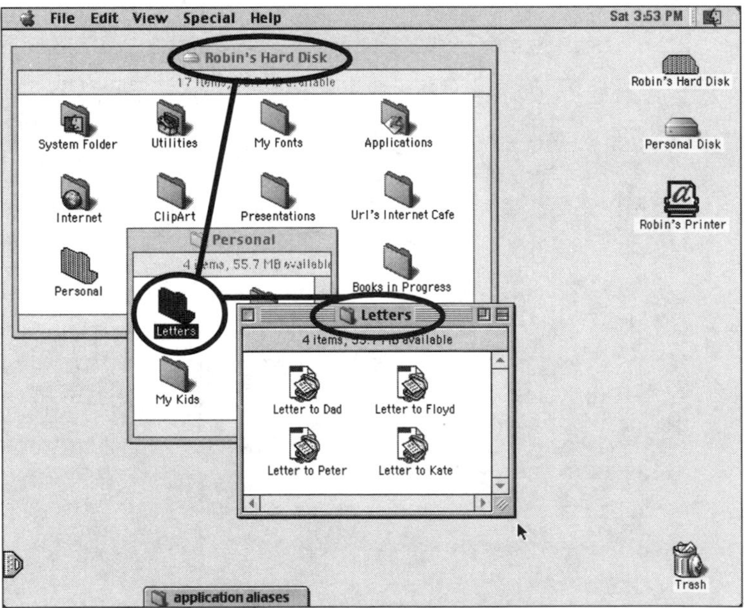

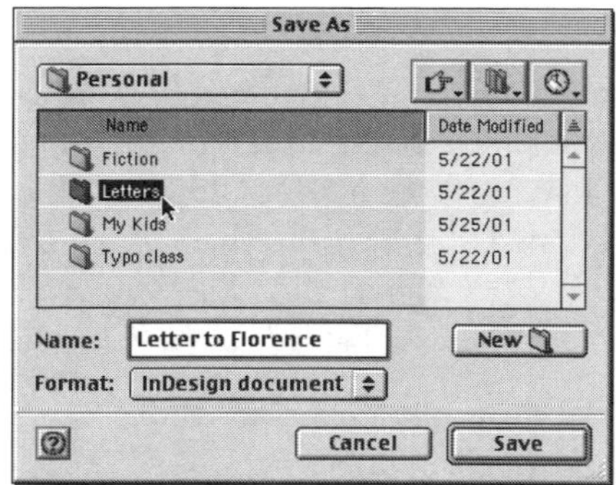

As you can see on the opposite page, the folder "Letters" is inside of the folder "Personal." Here you can see the folder "Personal" is open (its name is in the label), and "Letters" is inside of it. To open "Letters" so you can save into it, double-click "Letters."

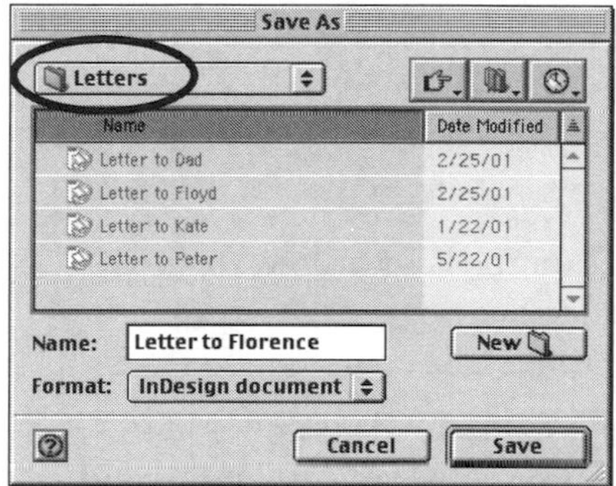

After you double-click that folder's name, you will see its name in the label.

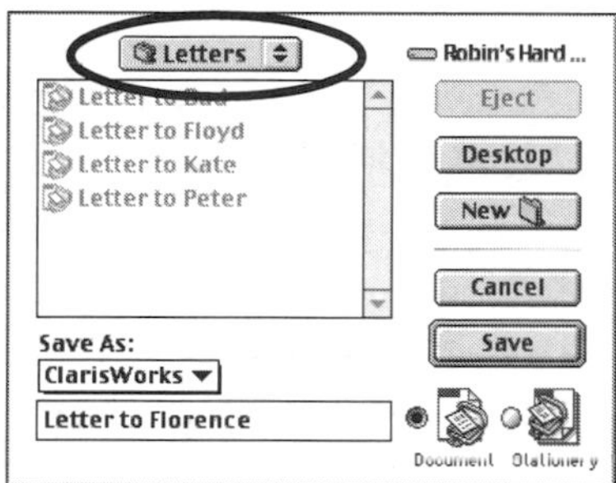

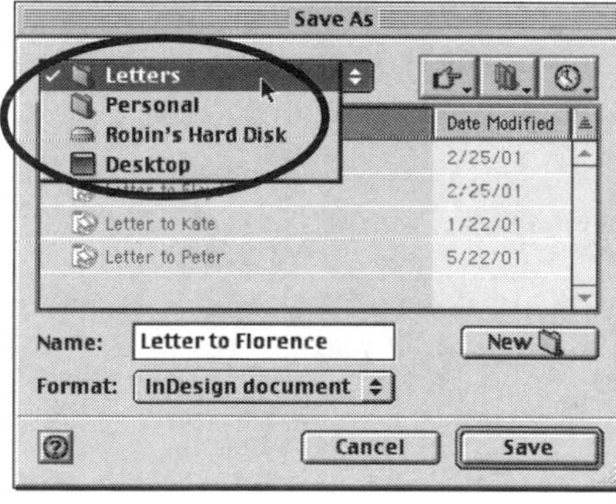

If you click (or press) on the label, you can see the folders inside of folders on the hard disk, just like they are on the Desktop (shown on the opposite page). Once you understand how this works, you can always save documents into specific places and always find anything you need to open.

If you click the "New" button to create a new folder, the new folder is placed in the folder whose name is showing in the label above the list box. For instance, if you were to click the "New" button in the dialog box above, you'd have a new folder inside the folder "Letters." Try it.

If the application you are using doesn't have a "New" folder button, then you have to make the folder you want to store things in *before* you Save As! If necessary, go back to the Finder by choosing "Finder" from the Application menu (far-right of the menu bar) and create a new folder where you need it (see page 106). Then go back to your document and Save As.

For Instance

a
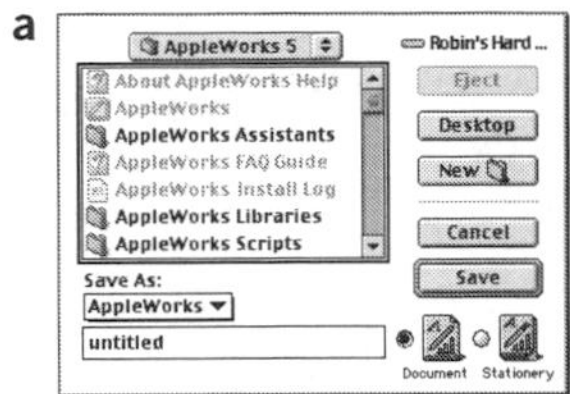

b
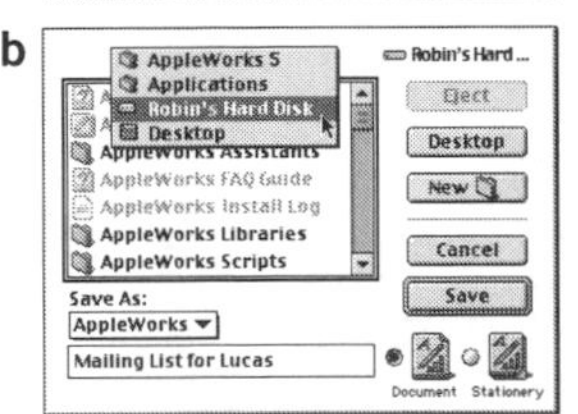

c
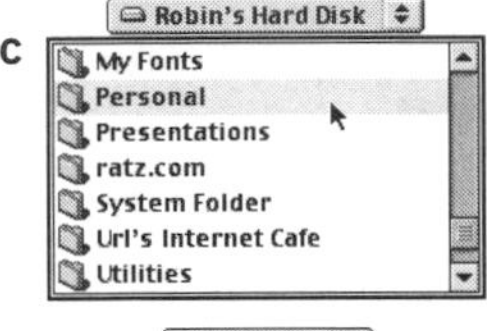

d
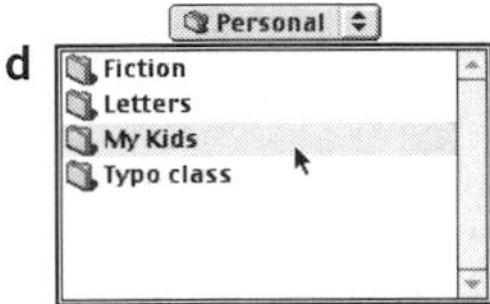

e
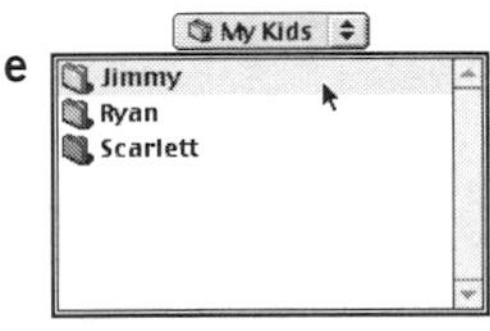

f

g
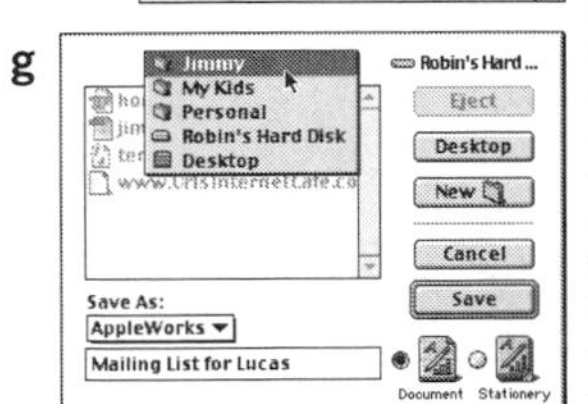

This menu displays the same folders-inside-of-folders as on the Desktop.

If your Save As dialog box looks like the one shown to the left:

Okay. You want to save a new document into a particular folder. Let's say you are working with your teenage son, Jimmy, on a mailing list for his rock band, Lucas. You're making the mailing list with the database in AppleWorks, so you opened this new database page by double-clicking on the program AppleWorks (also called ClarisWorks). You want to save it in the folder named "Jimmy" that he's already made.

a When you choose to save the Mailing List for Lucas, the "Save As" dialog box usually automatically opens to the folder in which AppleWorks is located, or to the Documents folder.* Well, you don't want to store this database file in that folder—you want to store it into **Jimmy**'s folder. Remember where Jimmy's folder is? Right—it's in **My Kids,** which is in the **Personal** folder on the **Hard Disk.** So you need to navigate to that folder.

b You know the **Personal** folder is on the **Hard Disk** so you press on the menu bar in the label and slide down to the **Hard Disk** (of course *your* hard disk might be called something different!).

c Now in the list you see all the files on the **Hard Disk.** Find the folder called **Personal** (you might have to scroll to find it) and double-click its name to open it.

d Now **Personal** is in the label at the top of the list and all the files in *that* folder are listed. You want the folder called **My Kids**, so double-click **My Kids** to open it.

e Now in the list for **My Kids** you see **Jimmy**'s folder. Double-click **Jimmy** to open it.

f Now the label at the top of the list has **Jimmy**'s name in it, and you know if you click the Save button this file will be stored into **Jimmy**'s folder.

g This is just the same as digging through folders on the Desktop! It just looks a little bit different.

* *You have a little bit of control over what the Save As and Open dialog boxes display by using the General Controls Panel. If you haven't already, you might want to read the "Documents" section, page 246.*

* *On some Macs, the default (the automatic choice) is to open the dialog box to the "Documents" folder. If you find this annoying, see page 246.*

If your Save As dialog box looks like the one shown to the right:

Okay. You want to save a new document into a particular folder. Let's say you are working with your teenage son, Jimmy, on a CD cover for his rock band, Lucas. You're making the CD cover in a page layout application called InDesign, so you opened this new document by double-clicking on the program Adobe InDesign. You want to save it in the folder named "Jimmy" that he's already made.

- **a** When you choose to save the CD cover for Lucas, the "Save As" dialog box might open to the last folder you used in this application, or to the Documents folder.* Well, you don't want to store this CD cover in that folder—you want to store it into **Jimmy**'s folder. Remember where Jimmy's folder is? Right—it's in the folder called **My Kids,** which is in the **Personal** folder which is on the **Hard Disk.** So you need to navigate to Jimmy's folder.
- **b** You know the **Personal** folder is on the **Hard Disk** so you press on the menu bar in the label and slide down to the **Hard Disk** (of course *your* hard disk might be called something different!).
- **c** Now in the list you see all the files on the **Hard Disk.** Find the folder called **Personal** and double-click its name to open it.
- **d** Now **Personal** is in the label at the top of the list and all the files in *that* folder are listed. You want the folder called **My Kids**, so double-click **My Kids** to open it.
- **e** Now in the list for **My Kids** you see **Jimmy**'s folder. Double-click **Jimmy** to open it.
- **f** Now the label at the top of the list has **Jimmy**'s name in it, and *now* if you click the Save button this CD cover file will be stored into **Jimmy**'s folder.
- **g** This is just the same as digging through folders on the Desktop! It just looks different.

* *You have a little bit of control over what the Save As and Open dialog boxes display by using the General Controls Panel. If you haven't already, you might want to read the "Documents" section, page 246.*

* *On some Macs, the default (the automatic choice) is to open the dialog box to the "Documents" folder. If you find this annoying, see page 246.*

For Instance

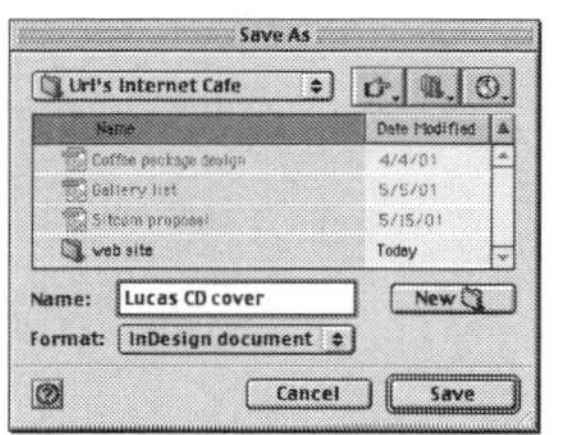

a

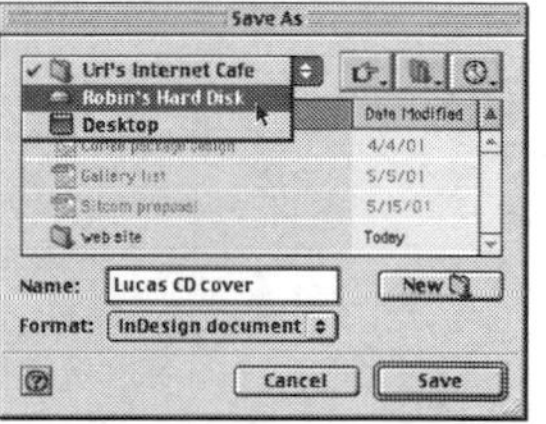

b

c

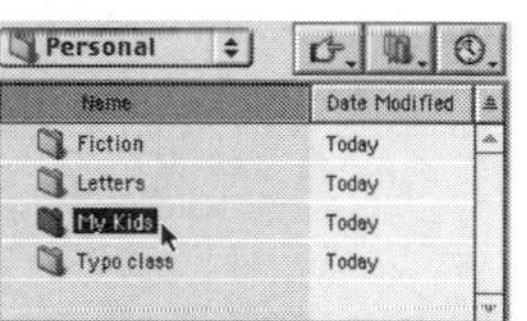

d

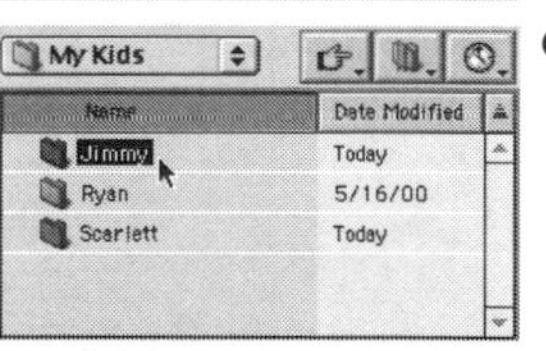

e

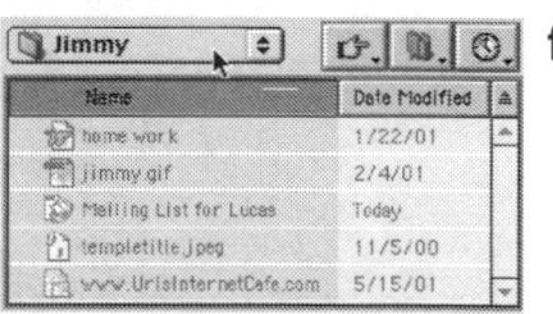

f

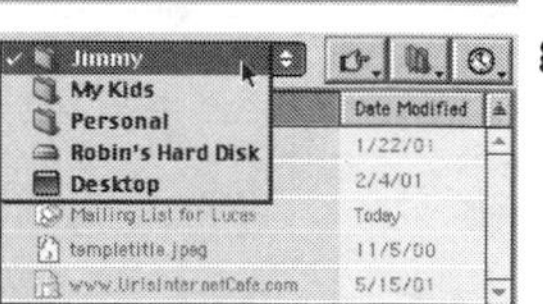

g

Keyboard Shortcuts for Navigating

You can use **keyboard shortcuts to navigate** the folders at the Desktop and in the dialog boxes.

- **In any active window on the DESKTOP:** If you press Command UpArrow, the window in which the current active folder is *stored* will pop up in front of your face. For instance, if you are at the Desktop looking at Scarlett's open folder, you can press Command UpArrow to bring the folder My Kids forward. You can keep pressing Command UpArrow all the way to the Desktop level.

  Press Command Shift UpArrow to go straight to the Desktop.
- **In any DIALOG BOX:** If you press Command UpArrow, the dialog box will display the folder in which *this* folder or document is stored (meaning you will go up one level in the hierarchy). It will display the next folder and list the files in it. You can keep pressing Command UpArrow all the way to the Desktop level.
  - If a folder in the list is selected, press Return or Enter to open it (which moves you one level deeper in the hierarchy).
  - Press the DownArrow or UpArrow to select files in the list.
  - Type the first letter or several letters to select specific files in the list.
  - Press Command D to select the Desktop level where you can find any attached hard disks or inserted disks.
  - Press Command RightArrow or LeftArrow to cycle through the disks or volumes you have connected or inserted.
  - Press Command Period to Cancel.
  - Press Command E to eject a selected disk.
  - Press Return or Enter to Open, OK, or Save—whichever option is currently available.

▼ **In a "SAVE AS" DIALOG BOX:** When you choose "Save As...," the dialog box opens and the edit box where you type the name of the file is automatically selected (it's *highlighted*). *If you type while the current name (which may be "Untitled") is highlighted, or while there is an insertion point flashing in the edit box*, then what you type will appear in the edit box.

The edit box (where you give the file a name) is highlighted. Whatever you type will replace whatever is already here. That means you don't have to hit Delete first—just go ahead and type! Try it.

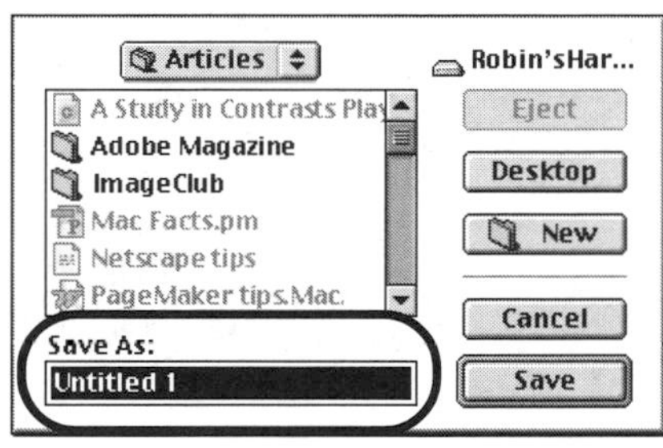

But if you move the pointer and **click in the directory** (the list box), the *directory* becomes highlighted—notice the double border around it. *If you type while the directory is highlighted*, the letters you press will select any file with those letters, or the next file in the alphabet.

*The directory, or list, is selected, indicated by the double border around it. Notice the difference between the border around **this** list box and the border around the list box in the illustration above.*

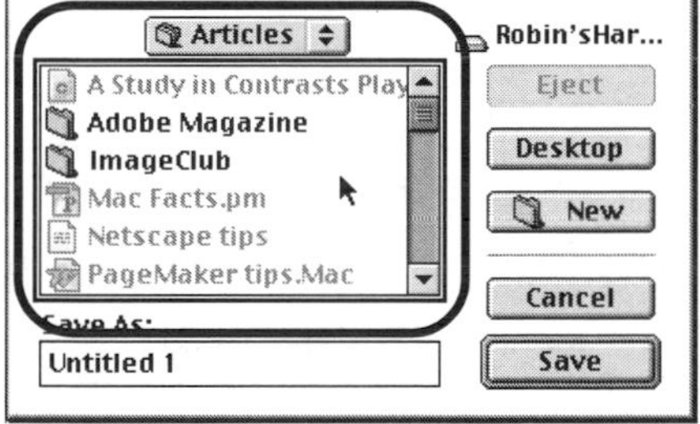

Very useful tip: To bounce back and forth between selecting the list (to choose other files or folders) and selecting the edit box (to type a name), press the **Tab key.**

For instance, if the **edit box** is highlighted or has an insertion point in it, *but you want to select a folder in the* **directory** by typing its first letter, then press the Tab key. When you have selected the folder and *want to name your new file*, press the Tab key. Try it—press the Tab key several times and watch the selection change. *This selection thing will drive you nuts for a while. Eventually, in about a year, you'll get used to it and you'll start remembering to hit the Tab key to switch to the mode you need—either for selecting files or for typing a name.*

1. What does "navigating" mean, anyway?

2. If the Desktop is analogous to your office, what is the Hard Disk analogous to?

3. Finish this sentence: The "Open" and "Save As" dialog boxes are just another way of looking at . . .

4. How do you know which disk you are saving onto or trying to open a file from?

5. How do you know which folder you are saving into or trying to open a file from?

6. If you choose to save onto the Desktop, where would you find its icon later?

7. If you save into a folder, how do you find the file?

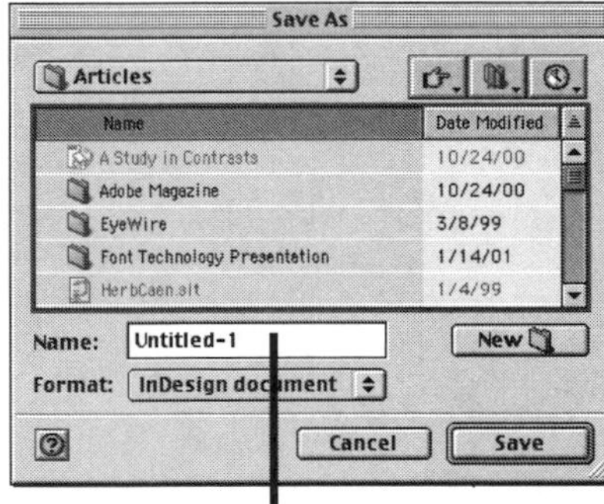

This is the edit box.

8. In the dialog box to the left, which button is the Shortcuts menu?

9. In the dialog box to the left, if you start to type the name "August Vacation," what will happen?

10. In the same dialog box, if you want to change the file name, which key can you press to select the edit box?

Answers on page 426.

Very Important Information

29

It used to be so easy. And you used to not have to worry about what wasn't easy. But now you have no choice. Now you have to be conscious. Now you have to take responsibility for certain things on your Mac. Sigh.

This chapter covers several aspects of the Macintosh "operating system" that are all inextricably interrelated: hard disk space, memory, and virtual memory. I know, you don't wanna know this stuff. But believe me, if you don't understand this particular information you will constantly find yourself frustrated and confused. Spend a few minutes here to empower yourself and gain control over your Mac. It's not hard to understand.

Hard Disk vs. Memory

There are 1024 megabytes in each gigabyte (sort of like ounces in a pound).

I have worked with thousands of new and not-so-new Mac users and have heard so many people wail in confusion, "My Mac keeps telling me I'm out of memory, but I have 2.5 gigabytes left on my hard disk!" Well, I myself have a hard time figuring out all this technical stuff so I create analogies. What follows is my personal analogy for answering the heart-breaking cry, "What the heck is the difference between **hard disk** and **memory** anyway?"

Think of the hard disk in your computer as a filing cabinet in your office. Picture each megabyte of space as one drawer, so if you have a 200MB **hard disk,** your filing cabinet has 200 large drawers. Well, if you are working in your office and you need something out of the filing cabinet, you don't climb into your filing cabinet to work on it—you take the information out of the file drawer and put it on your desk, right? Well, the computer does the same thing. The computer cannot climb into the hard disk to work any more than you can climb into your filing cabinet. It does the same thing you do—it takes things out of the hard disk and puts them on its desk, but its desk is called **memory** (**random access memory,** or **RAM,** to be precise). When you turn the computer on, it goes to the hard disk, just like you go to your filing cabinet, and gets the System out of the hard disk and puts a copy of it into the memory, RAM (onto its desk), to run the machine. When you open an application, such as your word processor, the computer gets a copy of that word processing application and puts the copy into memory (kind of like taking a typewriter out of the filing cabinet and plopping it on the desk).

Well, you can see that the bigger the desk, the more things you can work on at once, or the bigger the project you can work on. When you turn on your computer, the System that runs the machine, plus the typefaces and extensions you are using, and a few other items are all automatically placed (loaded) into RAM (onto the "desk"). All these things take up a certain amount of space. When you open an application, that application goes into RAM. When you work on a document, everything you haven't yet saved onto a disk floats around in RAM. When you work on large graphic files, such as scans of color photos or a large poster, there is an extraordinary amount of information that has to be held in RAM for the computer to be able to work on the image.

This is the hard disk.

This is memory (RAM).

Why do you crash?

If RAM gets full, **you will crash** (well, that's *one* reason for crashing). Sometimes you will get a warning, but often the System just goes belly up, "unexpectedly quits," or gives you some sort of "system error" message. It's like you put one thing too many on your desk and the desk just collapsed. Type 1 errors are usually out-of-memory problems.

How much RAM do you have?

It's very easy to tell how much memory you have in your Mac. At the Desktop, go to the Apple menu and choose "About this Computer." You will get the dialog box shown below (although yours will look a little different).

- Do you see where it says "Built-in Memory"? That's how much RAM you have installed in your Mac.
- The term "Virtual Memory" refers to how much of your hard disk space your Mac is *pretending* is memory. We'll talk about that on page 329.
- The amount of "Largest Unused Block" is how much RAM is still available for the computer to work in (how much free space is left on the desk).

This is how much RAM is installed in your Macintosh.

Thirty-two megabytes of RAM is about the minimum you can run your Mac with, especially if you want to get on the Internet with the current browser software. With some versions of the System you can function with less than that, but you will bump into "out of memory" problems often. Increasing the amount of RAM in your computer is the single most effective way to increase the potential of your Mac. On many Macs it's just a matter of ordering RAM chips from your favorite catalog, opening the case, and popping them in. Well, you should read the directions, though, before you actually do it, of course. Ask your power user friend.

SUGGESTIONS **If you don't have a lot of memory** in your computer, here are a couple of suggestions to avoid running out of it:

Quit, Don't just Close

1. QUIT the application when you are finished using it (press Command Q). Don't just ***close*** the document you were working on by clicking in the little close box or by choosing "Close" from the File menu. Closing makes you *think* the application is put away because you don't see it anymore. But you must actually *quit* the application (choose "Quit" from the File menu) so the computer can remove it from RAM.

It's like this: When you open a word processing application, it's as if you pulled a typewriter out of the filing cabinet and put it on the desk. When you *close* the document you were typing, you have essentially *put the piece of paper back into the filing cabinet (the hard disk), but the typewriter itself is still sitting on your desk (in RAM).* If you then open a spreadsheet application, you have essentially pulled a large calculator out of the filing cabinet and put it on the desk. When you close the worksheet for the day, you have *put the paper documents back into the filing cabinet, but you have left the calculator itself still sitting on the desk.* Well, eventually this desk is going to get so full of applications (appliances) that it will collapse. For instance, if you still have the typewriter *and* the calculator *and* the System sitting on the desk, and then you put an easel on the desk to paint a picture (like a paint program), the desk will collapse, and you will get a message that "the application has unexpectedly quit," or the entire System may crash. SO—the point is, *quit* the application itself (which puts the appliance back into the filing cabinet); *don't just close* the current document (which just puts the piece of paper back into the filing cabinet).

Clicking in the close box (circled) or choosing "Close" from the File menu **does not** *put away an application! It just puts away that page, or document.*

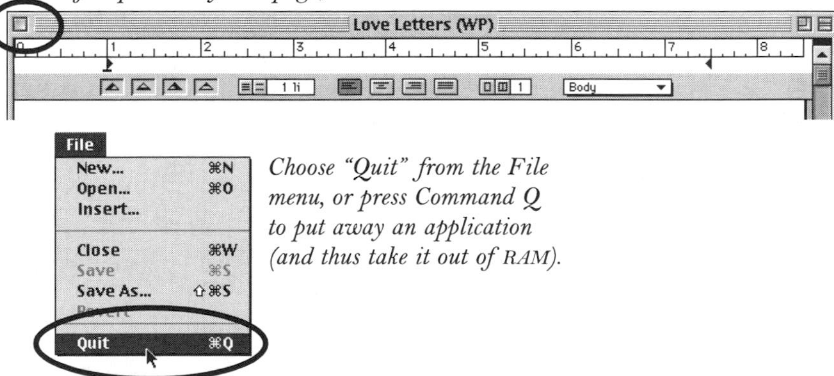

Choose "Quit" from the File menu, or press Command Q to put away an application (and thus take it out of RAM).

Which applications are still open?

So let's say you haven't been quitting—you've just been closing documents—and now you're getting messages or clues that you are running out of memory. You need to know how to check to see which applications are still open, and then quit each one. In the upper-right corner of the menu bar is the **Application menu.** Press on it to see a list of all the applications *that are still open on your Macintosh.* If you see any application name besides "Finder" on the bottom half of that menu, *that program is still open.*

This is the Application menu. This icon will change to indicate which program is currently active (open in front of you).

There will be a checkmark next to the name of the application that is active right now, the one that is open in front of your face. Even if you don't see it anywhere, trust it. Look at the menu bar.

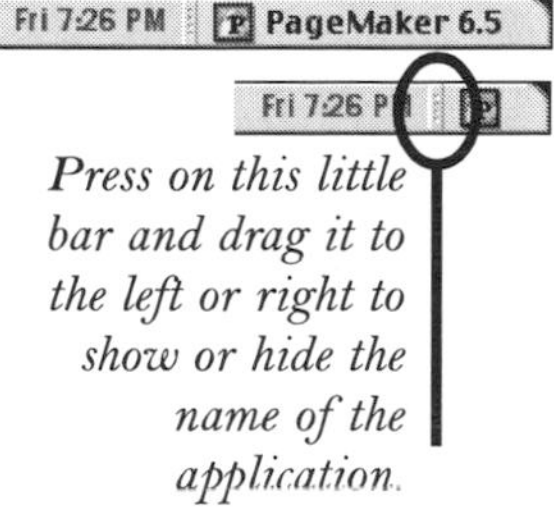

Press on this little bar and drag it to the left or right to show or hide the name of the application.

To make it really easy to see what is still open, "tear off" the Application palette, like this: Press on the tiny icon of the Application menu. Drag your mouse down the menu, keep holding the mouse button down, and drag right off the end—an outline of the menu will "tear off" and follow your mouse. When you let go of the mouse, you will see the Application menu in a little window, or palette, called the Application Switcher. Try it. It looks like this:

If you keep this Application Switcher floating around on your screen, you will always know exactly what is open and taking up memory on your Mac. Click any name to switch to that program. The "depressed," or darker button, indicates which program is active at the moment.

Like any window, drag the title bar of the Application Switcher to move it around the screen. Click its little close box to put it away, and the collapse box to roll it up. Click the zoom box to narrow the palette down to just the icons, like this:

Every item listed in this menu is some sort of application, control panel, game, or program that is open right now and taking up RAM.

Choose one of the open applications, besides Finder, either from the menu or from the Application Switcher, **and notice the menu bar change.** Even if you see no other change, you will see the menu bar change. You might still see the Desktop and the trash can, but *you are now in that program whose name you chose from the Application menu.* Really. You no longer see "View Special Help" in the menu, right? Check the Apple menu and you'll notice that it says "About [the name of your program]." So now, **to put this application away,** either choose "Quit" from the File menu or press Command Q. Even if you still don't see the program, trust me. Press Command Q and watch your menu bar change.

Have you accidentally switched programs?

Do you ever find you are working in a program and suddenly it disappears? Or the menu bar changes? Or you closed a document and now you're back at the Desktop when you didn't want to be? *It happens inadvertently all the time!* That's because the Macintosh lets you have several things going on at once, such as having those several applications open at the same time. The important thing to know is that all it takes is a click of the mouse on a window to pop you back and forth into the various applications. You may be happily working away on a letter when you accidentally click on the patterned background of your Desktop (you didn't even know it). The Mac thinks that since you clicked there, you want to go there. So suddenly all your Desktop windows flash in front of your face. To help control this:

Use the Application Switcher!

I suggest you tear off the Application menu as described on the previous page, and let it float on your screen all the time. You will always know exactly where you are, and you can pop into any open program by clicking on its name in the palette. Here are a few other tricks with the Application Switcher.

- Hold down the Option key and click on a button; you will switch to the other program or Finder and the windows of the current program will hide.
- Press Command Tab to switch to the next program in the list; press Shift Command Tab to switch to the previous program.

Option-click here to enlarge the buttons.

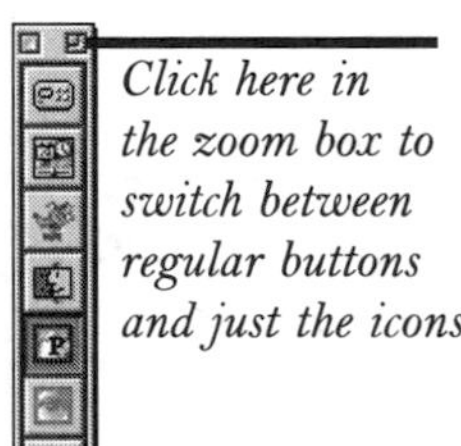

Click here in the zoom box to switch between regular buttons and just the icons.

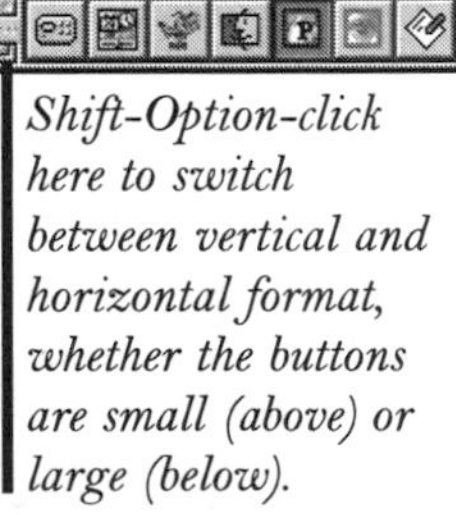

Shift-Option-click here to switch between vertical and horizontal format, whether the buttons are small (above) or large (below).

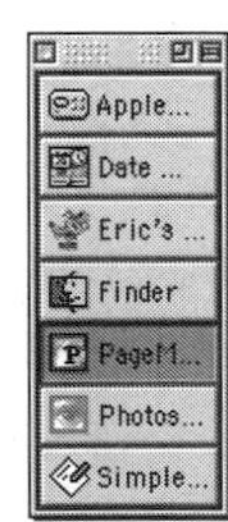

Change the width by dragging the right edge of any button.

Click the zoom box once to display just large icons, still horizontal, instead of these full buttons.

Save Regularly
SOS

2. **Save regularly.** The entire time you work on a document, anything you do not *save* is stored in RAM (and you know that anything in RAM will disappear when the computer crashes, right?). When you *save* the document, the current information gets "written" to the hard disk and just the parts the computer needs still sit in RAM. If you work on a document for several hours without saving, the RAM fills up and so your computer crashes. If you work on large graphic files for even half an hour without saving you run the risk of filling RAM and crashing. Oooh. Don't do that to yourself. SOS—Save Often Sweetie. Just hit Command S every couple of minutes.

Check the Memory Allocation of your Applications

3. **Check the application memory allocation.** If you find that you crash regularly in a particular application, you may need to change the memory allocation for that program (details below), or check the allocation of other applications you have open at the same time. The application memory is the amount of RAM the computer sets aside just for that program. If you allocate too little or just the bare minimum, the program information gets poured into that amount and takes its chances on finding any more when it needs it, like when it needs to perform a complex maneuver such as checking spelling or flipping a graphic. You don't want to set the amount too high or you may not have enough memory for the other things the computer needs to do or for other applications that are open at the same time. Experiment to discover the amount that keeps you from crashing or "unexpectedly quitting."

1. Make sure the application is not open. (If its icon is gray, the application is open. Check the Application menu, choose the application, and Quit.)
2. Click once on the original application icon to select it. You can't change the memory allocation of an alias to that program, nor of any document that belongs to that program. You have to find the application icon itself. If you can find the alias, click once on it to select it, then press Command R to get the true application icon. Use Sherlock if necessary (Chapter 26).
3. Press Command I to see the Get Info window.
4. In the "Show" menu, right there in the Get Info box where it probably says "General Information," choose "Memory."
5. In the middle of the Get Info window, the "Memory Requirements" tell you a **Suggested Size,** which is what the vendor suggests is the optimum amount of memory necessary to run the program efficiently. It's rarely enough.

—continued

Minimum Size is the minimum amount necessary to open and run the application.

Preferred Size is what the program likes to have to run at its best, but it always wants more than the vendor has set in this box. Add about 20 to 40 percent more than the existing "Preferred Size," or even more if you are working with large documents, lots of windows in one application, and if you have enough RAM to allocate. Any amount you allocate in this window will be hogged by the application and nothing else can use it, so don't set so much that other applications won't be able to get enough.

6. Change the "Minimum Size" amount to match "Preferred Size" so your application doesn't try to stuff itself into the minimum necessary, then crash while you are working in an important file.
7. Close the Get Info window and continue with your work.

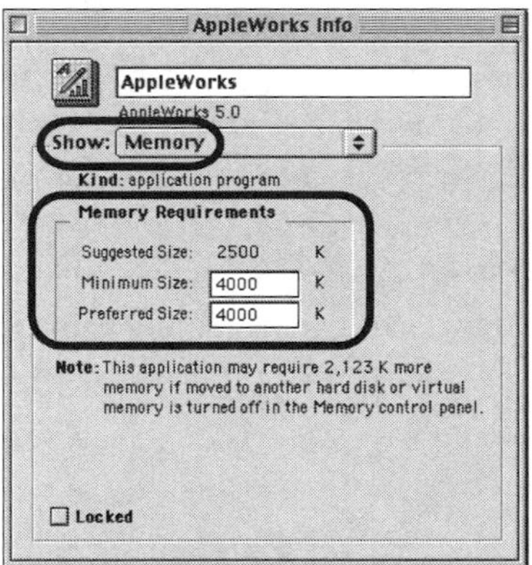

Enlarge these numbers by selecting them and typing new amounts.

If you don't see "Memory Requirements" in the Get Info box, then the selected file is not an application. Really.

AppleWorks Robin's Address Book

These two icons look very similar, but only one is the actual application icon. How can you tell? ***Documents*** *almost always have the upper-right corner turned down. Also, the Get Info box will tell you whether a file is a document or an application.*

Virtual Memory

Virtual memory is pretend memory—your Mac pretends part of your hard disk is memory. You determine how much of your hard disk you are willing to give up. Anything you give to virtual memory you cannot use for hard disk space. Power Macintoshes use virtual memory differently from older Macs, so on a Power Mac (which includes G3s, G4s, iMacs, and many PowerBooks, especially if they're less than five years old) you should turn virtual memory on, but on older Macs, only turn it on temporarily when you need more memory for a certain project. On a Power Mac, turning virtual memory on and allocating even just one megabyte will make your Mac happy.

You control virtual memory on your Mac through the **Memory control panel,** which is explained on pages 250–251.

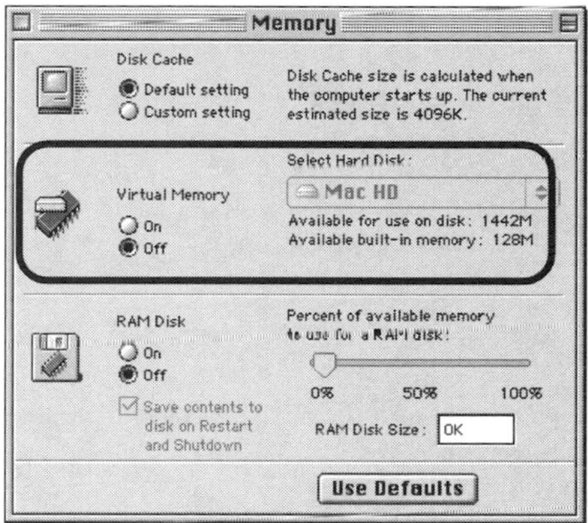

If your Mac allows virtual memory, you can turn it on in the Memory control panel.

The Upshot

So the **upshot of all this memory stuff** is this:

- Your **hard disk** is like a filing cabinet where you store your work and your "appliances" (your applications).
- **Memory** is like your desk where you actually do your work—you put your applications and projects on the desk.
- **Virtual memory** is like taking a couple of drawers out of your filing cabinet, setting a board across them, and using them as extra desk space.

Circle the choice that most pertains to the phrase.

1.	Filing cabinet	**RAM**	**hard disk**	**neither**	**both**
2.	Temporary storage	**RAM**	**hard disk**	**neither**	**both**
3.	System running	**RAM**	**hard disk**	**neither**	**both**
4.	System stored	**RAM**	**hard disk**	**neither**	**both**
5.	"unexpectedly quit"	**RAM**	**hard disk**	**neither**	**both**
6.	"disk is full"	**RAM**	**hard disk**	**neither**	**both**
7.	Permanent storage	**RAM**	**hard disk**	**neither**	**both**
8.	Document you have saved	**RAM**	**hard disk**	**neither**	**both**
9.	Document you are working on	**RAM**	**hard disk**	**neither**	**both**
10.	Desk	**RAM**	**hard disk**	**neither**	**both**
11.	Application menu	**RAM**	**hard disk**	**neither**	**both**
12.	Application memory	**RAM**	**hard disk**	**neither**	**both**
13.	Application size	**RAM**	**hard disk**	**neither**	**both**
14.	Virtual memory	**RAM**	**hard disk**	**neither**	**both**

Answers on page 426.

30 Visual Clues

The Mac, with its famed graphical user interface, provides many **visual clues** to tell us what's going on. Most of these clues, though, aren't documented anywhere and we have to just kinda figure them out as we go along. Some of the clues are loud and clear, like the picture of the bomb that we used to see a lot—you might not know exactly why you bombed, but you knew something was bad. The trash can is another easy visual clue, as are the icons of a hard disk or floppy disk.

But many of the visual clues are much more subtle. And to beginners especially, there is so much information going in through the eyes that it takes a while to absorb everything. I want to point out some of the clues the Mac is constantly providing, which should help you work more efficiently.

Ellipsis in the Menu

The ellipses indicate that the command will show you a dialog box.

Whenever you see a menu item followed by an **ellipsis** (three dots ...), it indicates that if you choose that menu item you will get some sort of dialog box. Dialog boxes always have a Cancel button in them, so it's a great way to explore a new program—choose any menu item with an ellipsis, check out its dialog box, then click Cancel and you'll never wreck anything. Any menu item that is *not* followed by an ellipsis will just execute when you choose it, which has the potential to create unexpected results if you don't know what you're doing.

Occasionally you will find applications where the programmers did not follow the rules, and it's frustrating to try to predict what will happen when you choose the item. If you find menu items that are unpredictable because they don't have an ellipsis when they should, write to that company and ask them to please be more considerate.

Default Button

Any button with a thick double border around it is the **default button** ("default" means it is the automatic choice). This means if you hit the Return or the Enter key, the button with the dark border around it is the one that will take effect.

Typically (not always) the default button is the safest option, as in these examples.

Almost anywhere on the Mac you can press Command Period to Cancel (there's no visual clue for this shortcut!).

Highlighted Text

When **text is highlighted** (text on a black or colored background), it's a visual clue to you that you are in typing mode and whatever you type is going to replace the highlighted text. *You don't need to hit the Delete key first—just type.* This is true in every dialog box, in every program that uses type, in every Save As box, etc.

Simply type to replace any highlighted text anywhere on the Mac.

Save As Dialog Boxes

In the **Save As dialog boxes,** have you noticed that sometimes the name of the file is highlighted, and sometimes it isn't? Have you sometimes tried to type a name for your document and nothing happened? That's because you're missing a valuable visual clue.

When the text is selected (highlighted), it is ready for you to type a new name. **If the text is not highlighted, then the list box, or directory, above the name is selected.** The visual clue is the border around the list box (look carefully at the illustrations below). When the list box is selected, you can type a letter or two to select files within the list box. In a Save As dialog box, the only files that will be black (which indicates you can select and open them) are folders or other disks. All the other files you see are in gray just to show you what is stored in that folder.

Press the Tab key to toggle the selection between the name edit box and the directory list! Try it!

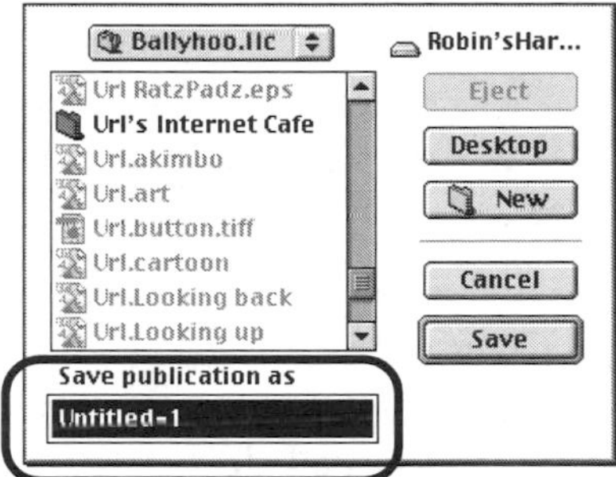

The edit box is selected/highlighted, ready for you to type a file name.

The list, or directory, has a double border around it, indicating it is selected. You can type a letter to select a file.

Radio Buttons vs. Checkboxes

The very buttons themselves are visual clues. **Radio buttons** (the little round ones) are called radio buttons because they act like your car radio in that you can only choose one option at a time. Clicking on any radio button deselects any previously selected button in the same list. And you have to select at least one—it's not possible to have no radio button selected.

When a button is a **checkbox,** it's a clue that you can choose more than one. In fact, you can choose from none to all of them.

You can actually click anywhere in the word, not just within the tiny checkbox or circular button, to turn the buttons on or off.

- ◉ Arabic numeral
- ○ Upper Roman
- ○ Lower Roman
- ○ Upper alphabetic
- ○ Lower alphabetic

You can select only one radio button.

☐ Normal ☑ Italic ☐ Outline ☑ Reverse
☑ Bold ☐ Underline ☐ Shadow ☐ Strikethru

You can select any number of checkbox buttons.

Mini-Menus

In dialog boxes, whenever you see a shadow behind a little box it means if you press on the name in the box you'll get a **mini-menu,** or **submenu** (sometimes called a **pop-up menu** because it pops up into your face). These are kind of subtle, so you have to know to look for them. Some pop-up menus are indicated by little arrows (a stronger visual clue), in which case you can press on the arrow itself.

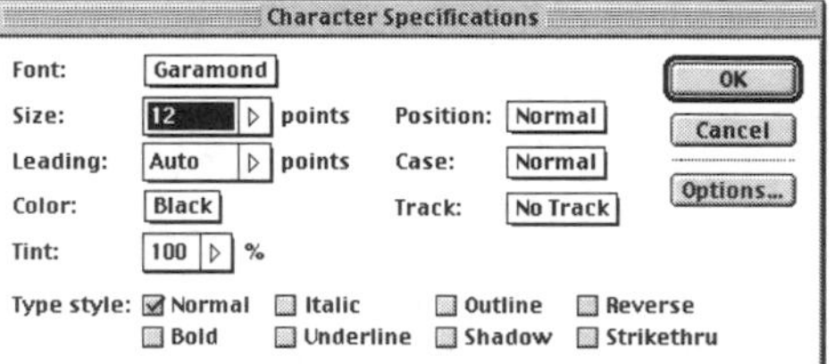

Press on any box with a slight shadow behind it to see the mini-menu. There are eight menus in this dialog box.

Mini-Menus above a List

Along the same lines as the previous clue, the **label above the list** in any dialog box (such as when you Save As, Open, Export, etc.) has that little shadow behind it, indicating a **menu** lurks beneath. The visual clue is strengthened by the little double arrow.

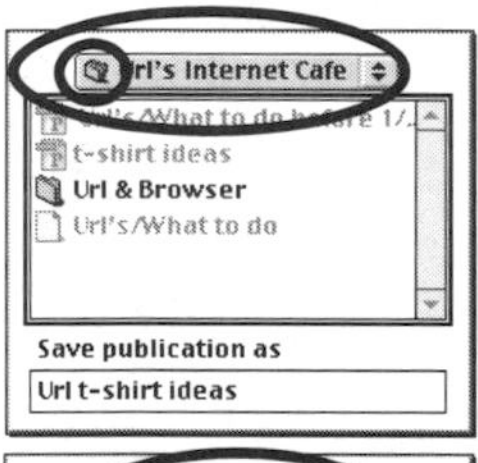

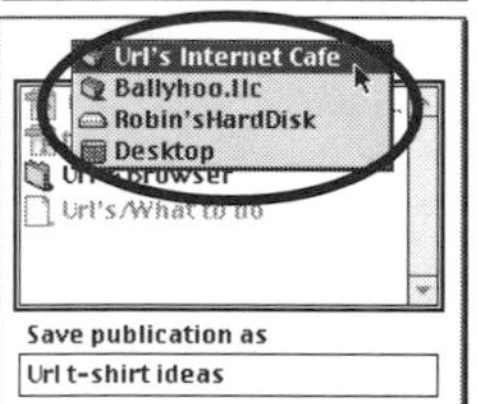

The label above a list box tells you where the items visible in the list are located.

In the label there is always a tiny icon, either a Desktop icon, a disk icon (either hard or floppy), or an open folder icon. This tells you where the items visible in the list are located. For instance, if the icon is an open folder, the items in the list are found within that folder. And if you **click on that label** with the open folder icon, you will see the menu showing the hierarchy—that is, where that folder is located, perhaps within another folder which is within another folder which is located on the hard disk. You can, of course, select any other folder or disk in the menu to open it and display its contents.

By the way, you can also see the **hierarchical menu of any window on your Desktop** (also known as the Finder). This feature is completely clueless: hold down the Command key and press on the name in the title bar of any active window at your Desktop. Slide down to choose any of the folder names in the list and that folder will instantly open.

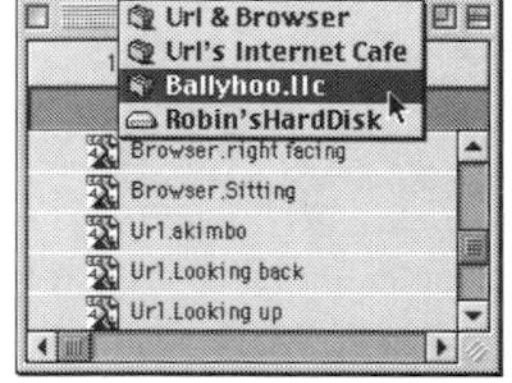

Command-press the title bar to see the hierarchy of any window on the Desktop.

Matching Icons

Icons, of course, are major clues. You've probably noticed that Desktop icons can generally be grouped into several categories: disk, folder, document, application, and system icons. Document icons (usually shaped like pieces of paper with the top-right corner turned down) often match the application they were created in, which is a very thoughtful and helpful visual clue. See Chapter 9 on Icons and Files.

Document icons usually match the application icon.

If a document icon is **blank,** it is often a clue that the application in which the document was created cannot be found on the disk (see page 80 for elaboration).

A blank document is also a clue.

You can **customize** any of your icons, thus potentially weakening this system of recognition. Is the icon to the right a folder, a document, an application, an extension, a graphic file? Be careful. (See page 98 for details on how to change your icons if you really want to.)

Changing File Names

The Mac lets you know when you are about to **change the name** of a file on the Desktop/Finder. When you single click on the *name* of the icon (*not* on the picture) *or* select an icon and press the Return key, a border appears around the name, which is the visual clue that what you now type will replace the current name. If you wait long enough before you type, you'll notice that the pointer turns into an I-beam when you position it over the name.

The border around the name indicates you can now change it. If you make a mistake, press Command Z right away.

Gray Icons

A **gray icon** is a visual clue that the disk, folder, or application is already open. If you don't see its window anywhere, double-click on the gray icon to bring the window or application to the front. (You don't see any sign of your application? The visual clue that your application is active is in the menu bar; see page 96.)

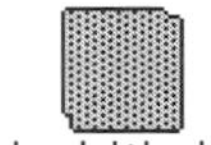

A gray icon indicates the file is already open.

View Clue

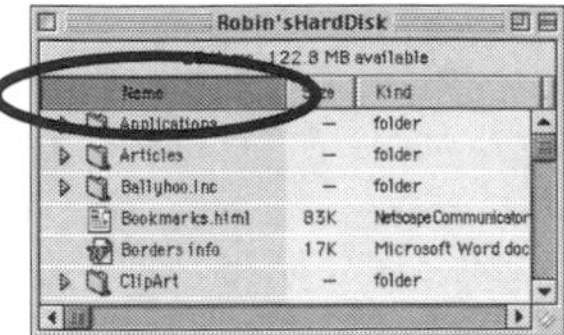

When you view the items in a window in some sort of list, such as By Name, By Size, By Kind, etc., notice that the particular **view** you have chosen is **dark gray.** You can simply click on one of the other categories in the information bar to switch to that view. See Chapter 8 on *Desktop Windows* for details.

Number of Items

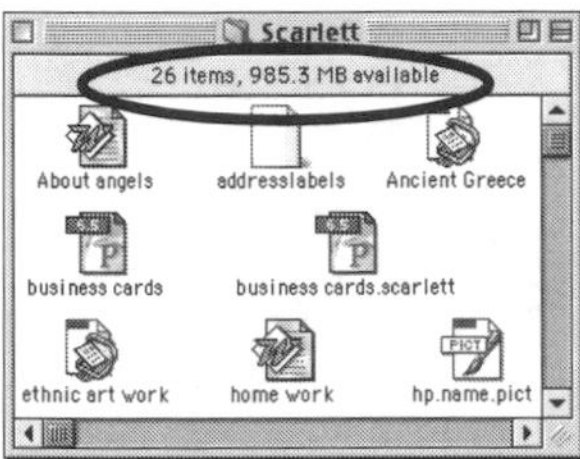

The information bar under the title bar tells you the total **number of items in the window.** I have seen countless people complain that their document is missing while the info bar says "5 items" and the window only displays 4 icons. If the number in the information bar is higher than the number of items you can see, then there is more stuff in that folder. The scroll bars, of course, are another big clue; see below.

Scroll Bars

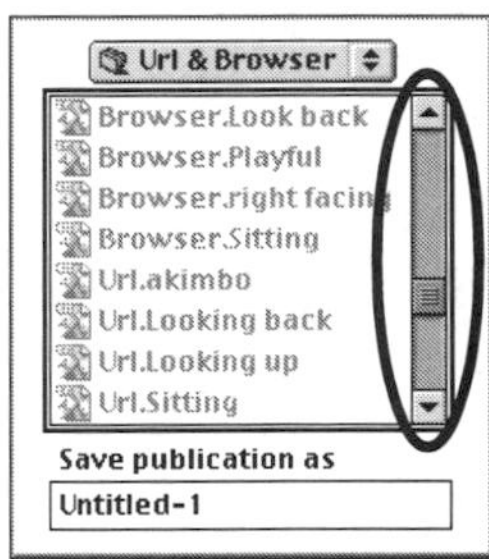

Scroll bars, whether in a window or in a dialog box, may be white or gray. When the scroll bar is white, it's a visual clue that you are seeing all the items in that list, or viewing all the icons in that window—nothing is hidden from sight. If a scroll bar is **gray,** it indicates there are other items that are not currently visible, and you need to press the scroll arrow to display them.

Often the difference between white and gray scroll bars is minimal. If a scroll bar is gray, there is a scroll box in it. So **if you don't see the scroll box,** there is nowhere to scroll to.

Scroll Box

Check the position of the scroll box on the scroll bar —it indicates where you are in relation to the outer edges of the entire window. ***If you turn on Smart Scrolling*** *(see page 73), the scroll boxes themselves are a visual clue as to where you are in the window (smart scroll boxes don't appear in every application).*

The **scroll box** shows you where you are in that list or in that window, not only at your Desktop or in dialog boxes, but within applications

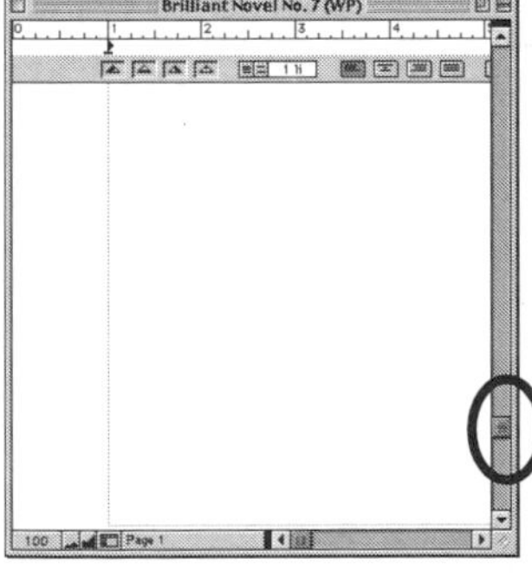

also. If you're typing in your word processor and your text suddenly disappears, check the scroll box—is it at the bottom of the bar? Drag it back to the top to find your text. Did you place something on the pasteboard in PageMaker and then turn the page and can't find that item on the pasteboard? Go back and check the horizontal scroll box on the other page.

Menu Checkmark or Lack of Checkmark

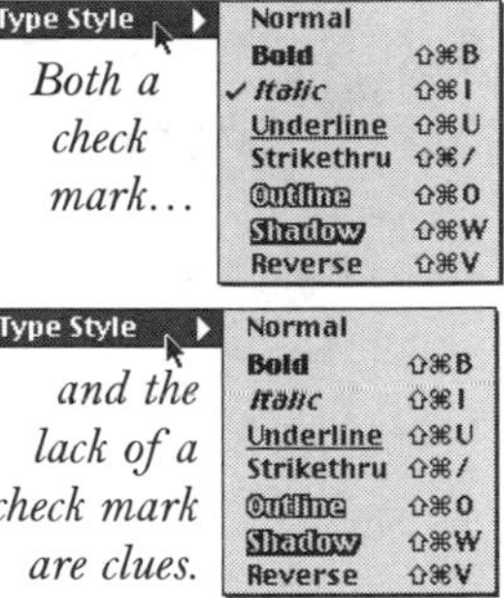

Both a check mark… and the lack of a check mark are clues.

You've surely already noticed that when you look at a menu, a little **checkmark** often appears to tell you what is currently selected or what is considered "on." The lack of a checkmark is also a clue—if you pull down a font menu or a size menu and you notice there is **no checkmark** at all, it means there is more than one font or more than one size of type in the text you selected. Sometimes the Mac can't tell you more than one thing at a time so it tells you nothing instead—*but that nothing is actually a valuable clue.*

To find out what the actual font or size is, select a smaller portion of text, or just click the insertion point within the text. Maybe *you* can't see any other font or size, but the Mac sees blank spaces and blank lines as characters. If even one of those selected blank spaces or blank lines is formatted in a different font or size or style than the rest of the text, you won't see a checkmark in the menu. To make everything the same, select everything and apply new formatting.

Boot Disk

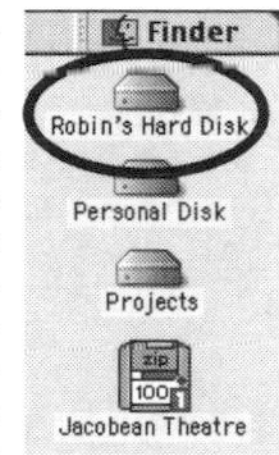

Sometimes you may have more than one disk in the computer, you may be connected to more than one hard disk, or you may have a large hard disk "partitioned" into separate pieces. You can always tell **which disk is booting,** or running, the computer: its icon is the one at the top in the upper right of the screen. (You may be surprised one day when you discover you actually need to know that bit of information. Then again, you may live a long time and never have a use for it.)

Diamond in the Application Menu

If you see a little **diamond shape** next to an item in the Application menu (the menu at the far right), it is an indication that the progam wants to tell you something. It's usually not good news. Choose that item from the menu—typically you will get a message from the troubled program with a suggestion of what to do about it.

Look for Clues!

Once you become aware of these visual clues, you'll start noticing more and more of them. Cursors change to tell you what will happen if you press now; each program has a way to indicate that an item is selected; buttons sometimes give you a clue as to what will happen if you click; etc. Take advantage of what they are showing you!

Use the dialog box below to answer the following questions.

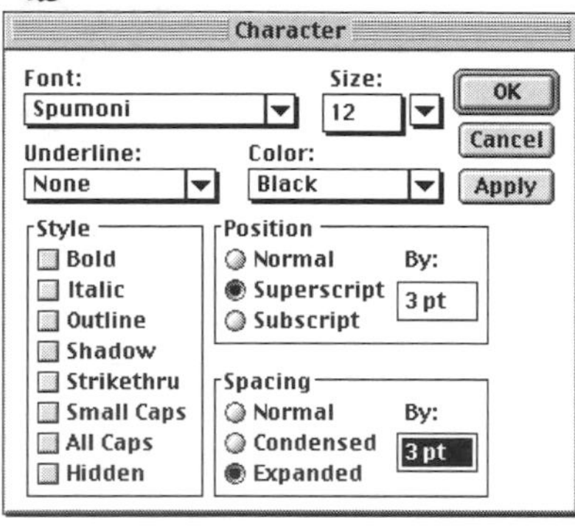

1. How many menus are in this dialog box?

. . . .

2. If you were to type, where would the text go?

. . . .

3. How many edit boxes (places where you can type) are in this dialog box?

. . . .

4. How many Styles can you choose?

. . . .

5. How many Positions can you choose?

. . . .

6. How many regular buttons (not checkboxes or radio buttons) are in this dialog box?

. . . .

7. If you hit the Return key, what would happen?

. . . .

8. Can you move this dialog box around? How do you know that?

. . . .

9. Extra Credit: In almost all dialog boxes, what will happen when you press Command Period? (This is clueless—but it's in this chapter and it's good to know.)

. . . .

10. Of the three icons to the left, which will change its name when you type?

. . . .

Answers on page 426.

PART Three

The Internet

Whether you have ever used the Internet and the World Wide Web before or not, you are probably aware of its impact on our world. This impact is only going to get greater, so you might as well join the crowd now and see what it's all about. This section explains what the Internet and the Web are, the difference between the Internet and America Online, how to get around on the Web, and how to use the Mac's features for getting online.

See you there!

31 What is the Internet?

This chapter explains what the Internet is and how the World Wide Web is part of the Internet. It explains the difference between America Online and the World Wide Web and how they are related. This chapter also clears up a lot of the jargon you probably hear all the time, such as modem, browser, newsgroup, etc.

One of the first things you might want to do on the Internet is check out the sites that are devoted to helping you use your Macintosh. Every vendor has a site, and their sites usually include tips and tricks for using their products. Apple, of course, has a great and huge site with many things that are useful to beginners. On page 305 I explain how to decipher web site addresses, and I'll give you some important addresses.

The Internet

The **Internet** is a system of computers all over the world that are linked together using phone lines or other sorts of cables. This linking together of computers is called a "network." It was created by the United States government in the early '60s as a means of communication that couldn't be controlled by outside forces. Now the government can't even control it and I'm sure they regret that. Anyway, this connectivity lets people send messages all over the world. The messages bounce from one computer to another along the network until they reach their destination. If one of the computers along the route is down or has been blown up by enemy forces, the message just finds another route.

Modems

Many computers, especially home computers, send these messages out from the computer to the phone line and onto the Internet network using **modems.** A modem is a piece of hardware that might be a little box attached to your Mac, or it might be built inside your Mac. You connect the modem to your computer with a special cable (unless it's an internal modem), plus you connect it to your phone jack or telephone with a phone cable, just like the cable you plug into your telephone.

You see, your computer is *digital*, meaning it can only work with countable, finite information, like ice cubes. The phone lines are *analog*, meaning they only work with information that is flowing and infinite, like water. So the modem takes the digital info (ice cubes) from your computer and translates it into analog info (water) so it can be sent over the phone lines. The modem on the other end takes the analog info (water) and turns it back into digital info (ice cubes) so the other computer can understand it.

These other connections also use modems, but different kinds.

There are other ways of connecting to the Internet besides phone lines, such as ISDN lines, DSL, fiber optics, cable, and more. They are all faster than phone lines, but more expensive also. This will change, of course.

You might hear the speed called the "baud rate" or "bps" (bits per second).

Modems come in a variety of *speeds*, which indicate how much information can be sent at a time. The faster the speed, the more "ice cubes" can be translated into "water" and sent through the lines. Below is a chart of the most common speeds at the moment. This will also change, of course.

To get on the Internet, you must have a modem of at least 14.4.

speed	say it	write it		how is it
2400	twenty-four hundred	2400	(2.4)	s l o - o - o - o - o - w
9600	ninety-six hundred	9600	(9.6)	not much better
14,400	fourteen-four		14.4	frustratingly slow for the Internet
28,800	twenty-eight eight		28.8	faster; the Internet isn't too bad at this speed
33,600	thirty-three six		33.6	pretty good for home or business
56,000	fifty-six k		56K	very common now for home

Email

For over thirty years people have been using the Internet to send **email,** which is a message typed on a computer and sent over the wires to another computer. The "e" in email stands for "electronic." One of the first things you'll use the Internet for is to send and receive email. With all the things we can do on computers, it seems to have evolved that our favorite thing to do is to communicate with other humans. Far from being an isolating medium, the computer and the Internet have helped develop millions of relationships between people.

Newsgroups

Another original feature of the Internet is **newsgroups,** which are sort of like online clubs. Each newsgroup is a collection of people with a common interest, such as golf, the Shakespearean authorship question, llama breeding, Zoroastrianism, Esperanto, and about 25,000 other topics. Members of newsgroups "post" ongoing discussions on a public "bulletin board," which is similar in concept to tacking notes on a cork bulletin board in the lounge. Whenever you like, you can pop in to the newsgroup, read the messages, and post your own response, question, or opinion. This is a wonderful resource for information about your favorite topic. These groups often form strong communities, since they are people bonded together with a common interest.

Mailing lists, or listservs

Mailing lists, or **listservs** (yes, "listserv" is spelled correctly) are another popular feature of the Internet. A listserv is similar to a newsgroup in that it is a collection of people who want to discuss a common interest, but instead of posting messages on a bulletin board, they send email. Piles of email. When anyone sends an email message to the mailing list, it goes to every single person on the list. There are about 30,000 different mailing lists.

Why didn't you hear about the Internet before?

So with all this going on for over thirty years, why is it that you've only recently begun to hear about it? Because all these years the "interface" for the Internet, the way it looks and how you use it, has been pretty ugly and geeky. Only nerds were attracted to it. (Now, don't be offended; "nerd" is not a pejorative term—I'm a nerdette myself.) Getting on the Internet was very DOS-like, with command lines and backslashes and codes, and a typical computer monitor displayed yellow text on a black background, monospaced and ugly. Then a miraculous event occurred.

The Macintosh was invented.

—continued

The World Wide Web

Now, it's not part of official Internet history, but I do personally believe the World Wide Web would not have happened if the Macintosh computer had not been invented. It was the Mac that changed computing. For the first time, we had a monitor capable of displaying professional type, and it was black type on a white background, so much easier to read. We became accustomed to color, graphics, sound, animation, beautiful text, etc. Microsoft, of course, "borrowed" this technology and soon other computers were able to act (albeit clumsily) like Macintoshes.

This new expectation of computers—graphical and colorful—paved the way for the invention of new software several years ago that allowed full pages to be sent over the Internet and displayed on a computer screen. These pages could have color, graphics, sound, animation, beautiful text, etc. Finally the Internet started to look like something regular people would be interested in. These pages are called **web pages,** and this is the **World Wide Web.** The World Wide Web is a collection of millions of individual pages displaying text, graphics, sound, and more.

So the Web, then, is one more facet of the Internet. The Internet is used to send the web pages of information and graphics from the computer they are stored on, over the lines, to your computer.

Web Sites and Home Pages

As I mentioned, these pages are called web pages. A collection of related web pages about one topic—say, for instance, about your worm farm—is a **web site.** A web site is like a book in that there may be several parts to it, like chapters, and there is a "table of contents" that shows you the organization of the book. On a web site, this table of contents page is called the **home page.** You'll return over and over again to the home page; it's sort of like home base.

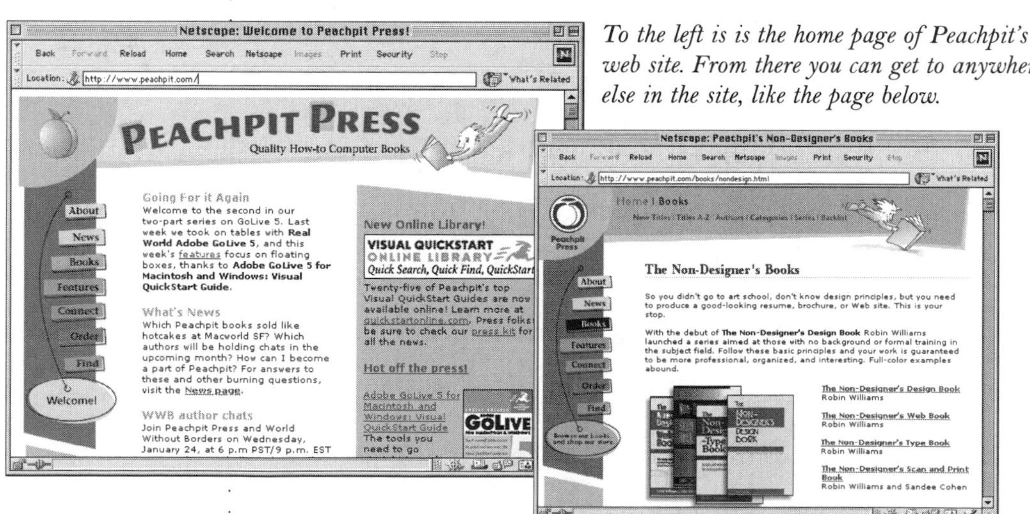

To the left is is the home page of Peachpit's web site. From there you can get to anywhere else in the site, like the page below.

To see web pages, you need special software that can display them. It's just like anything else on your Mac—if you want to crunch a bunch of numbers, you need spreadsheet software; if you want to write a letter, you need a word processor; if you want to view web pages, you need a **browser.** A browser is simply the software that displays web pages.

Along with your Mac operating system software you got browsers—Netscape Communicator and Microsoft Internet Explorer. You really only need one, and the browser by Netscape is preferred by most people (judging from what the people in my seminars are using).

There are other browsers. For instance, when you use America Online (which I explain on the next page), you can view web pages through America Online's special browser. There are quite a few browsers, each with loyal fans. You can keep as many browsers as you like on your hard disk. You can switch between them as often as you like. They each display web pages a little differently, and they each have their own special features. As I mentioned in the last paragraph, though, a Netscape browser is what most of the world uses, and it's the best. I recommend you start with Netscape and experiment with the others after you feel comfortable with Netscape.

Browsers

Below are the icons for several browsers.

Netscape Communicator

Internet Explorer

If you don't have a Netscape browser on your Mac already, use whatever browser you have, go to the Netscape site (home.netscape.com), and "download" it (copy it to your computer). Have a friend help you, if necessary.

Internet Service Providers

So how do you get to the Internet and the World Wide Web? You need a computer, a modem, a browser, and an **Internet Service Provider.** You see, there are thousands of special computers around the world hooked into the Internet 24 hours a day, and they provide Internet connections to people like us who only want to be connected several hours (or minutes) a day. From your home or business, you need to pay a provider to give you a connection to the Internet. You pay them; they give you the necessary software, instructions for connecting, and a local phone number; your modem dials the phone number; that puts your computer in touch with their computer and its Internet connection; and you can go anywhere in the world from there, on a local phone call. It's truly amazing.

There are probably several Internet Service Providers (also called ISPs) in your area. There are also a number of national providers that can set you up with a connection. Ask around your town and at your local Mac user group for the names of the favored providers.

There is an alternative to getting a connection through an Internet Service Provider, as described below.

America Online is not the Internet

These buttons change as AOL redesigns the service. They might not look exactly like this on your machine, but they will still take you to the World Wide Web.

Another way to get to the Internet and the World Wide Web is through **America Online.** But America Online is not the Internet! This is how it works: America Online (AOL) is an online service that you join for a monthly fee. You dial a local number and "log on" (connect) to the service. **You are not on the Internet**—you are safely contained in the AOL "village," where there are clubs and organizations, conferences, chat rooms, a "post office" for sending and receiving email, online magazines, news sources, kids' places, teen hangouts, parent support groups, research resources, and much more. There are live guides to help you figure things out; there are "police officers" who make their rounds and kick out people who act inappropriately; there are classes and interviews; there are friends to make and parties to crash. Everything is nicely organized and easy to find. Wherever you go on America Online, you are still within the village—**until you click the button that says "Go to the Web,"** type in a web address, or click a link that takes you to the web. When you head for the web, you're going out the back door of the village, onto the Internet, straight to the Web itself. It opens AOL's own special browser and you can surf the world. There are no guides, no police officers, no maps. You're on your own. You have actually left America Online, even though the AOL menu bar is still there. AOL has integrated the web into their own system so well that it is often difficult to tell when you have left—but don't worry, it's not that important to know when you have left.

America Online and Netscape

Using America Online is actually a great way to get to the Internet and the World Wide Web. The AOL service acts as your Internet Service Provider. You pay a monthly fee, something like $20 a month, which is fairly comparable to what you might pay an Internet Service Provider for a direct connection to the Internet.

If you don't like AOL's browser, you can actually **surf the Web using Netscape while connected to AOL.** You have to be using America Online version 3.0 at least. This is how you do it:

1. If you don't already have an alias of Netscape sitting on your Desktop, make an alias (page 269) and put it within easy reach.
2. Log on to America Online as usual.
3. Then double-click the Netscape alias on your Desktop.

   Et violà! You're on the Internet using Netscape to browse the World Wide Web through your AOL account. After you quit Netscape, be sure to log off from America Online.

Should You Choose America Online or a Service Provider?

America Online is a wonderful service. There are complaints about it, of course, but when you're trying to make twenty million ardent users happy, there are bound to be problems here and there. In general, AOL is the easiest, most fun, and least painful introduction to the online world. If you've never been online before, it's not a bad idea to start with AOL. You can explore the Internet and the World Wide Web very easily from America Online. You can have seven separate email addresses, each with its own password, so your whole family can use it. There are parent-controlled features to help keep your kids out of trouble.

If America Online is not already installed on your Macintosh, you can install it from any of the hundreds of disks you've probably received in the mail, inside magazines, or on airplanes. Just put in the disk and double-click the file called "Install." After it's installed, double-click the AOL icon and it will walk you through the registration process. You're on. **You do not need to establish a connection with an Internet Service Provider to use America Online, not even if you want to use a different browser from the one that AOL supplies.**

If, however, you have no need for America Online and its services, then you might want to get a "direct" Internet connection from a local **Internet Service Provider.** This connection, along with a browser, will get you to the Internet and the World Wide Web, newsgroups, mailing lists, and email. The Internet is the wild outside world, whereas America Online is the nice little village. And it's certainly possible to do both, but you will have to pay both the service provider and America Online.

1. What are the four major ways people use the Internet?

2. Which is a faster modem speed, 28.8 or 2400?

3. If you wanted to get a lot of email, would you join a newsgroup or a listserv?

4. What is a collection of web pages called?

5. What is the "home page" of a web site?

6. Why do you need a browser on the World Wide Web?

7. Explain the connection between America Online and the Internet.

8. If you use America Online exclusively, do you need to get an Internet connection through an Internet Service Provider?

9. Explain how to use Netscape to surf the Web if your connection is through America Online.

10. What great invention was a critical factor in the development of the World Wide Web?

Answers on page 426.

32 Using the World Wide Web

The World Wide Web is addictively fun to use. That's one of the amazing things about this incredible technology—it's so easy. You just need to know a few things about getting around. This chapter contains only a brief introduction, but it's probably more than many people know who are surfing the Web already.

What are Web Pages?

***Hypertext** is a term coined in the 1960s by Theodor Nelson. He explained, "By hypertext, I mean nonsequential writing—text that branches and allows choices to the reader, best read at an interactive screen. As popularly conceived, this is a series of text chunks connected by links which offer the reader different pathways [through the information]."*

In the last chapter, I explained that the World Wide Web is comprised of millions of individual web pages. These pages are literally the same as the pages you create in your word processor—in fact, many of them *are* created in word processors, and the code for any web page can be viewed in a word processor. The big deal about web pages is that they have "hypertext links"—text you click on to make another page appear in front of you. It's like this: Imagine that you could open a book to its table of contents and touch, say, "Chapter 3," and the book instantly flips to Chapter 3. In Chapter 3, there is a reference to Greek mythology. You touch the word "Greek mythology," and a book about Greek mythology instantly appears in front of you, open to the page you want. That's what web pages do, that's what hypertext is. That is incredible.

Links

Every web page has **links** on it. You click on a link with your mouse and a new web page appears. A link might be text, or it might be a graphic. If it's text, it has an underline; if it's a graphic, it sometimes has a border around it. Even if the **visual clues** of the underline or the border are missing, you can always tell when something is a link because the pointer turns into some sort of hand with a pointing finger, as shown below.

These are the "pointing hands" you'll see in your browser.

America Online

Netscape, Internet Explorer

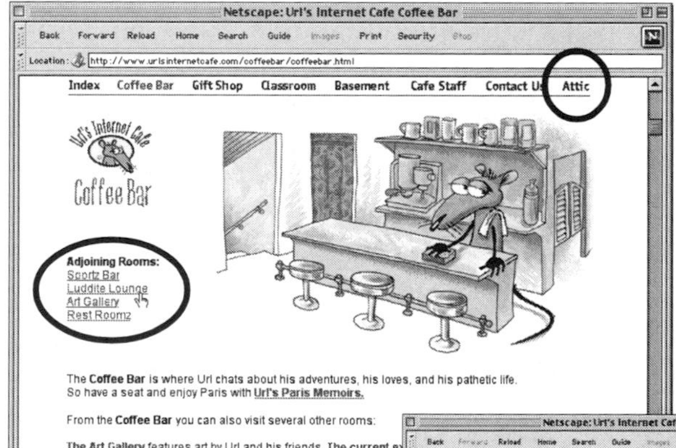

To the left is a typical web page. You can see the pointing hand positioned over underlined text, about to click the link. You also see a row of buttons across the top that look like you should probably click on them.

When you click on the link above, "Luddite Lounge," the browser jumps to another page, the page shown to the right. You can see there are more links on this new page. You can click links for the rest of your life and still not have time to read everything. That's the World Wide Web.

Web Addresses, also known as URLs

Something you will become intimately familiar with is a **web address.** Just as every home in the country has an address so you can find it, every web page on the World Wide Web has its own address. The address is also called a **URL** (pronounced *"you are ell"*), which stands for Uniform Resource Locator (who cares). A typical web address looks like this:

http://www.ratz.com/robin/hats.html

Knowing what a web address represents helps you find your way around on the web. This is what the different parts mean:

http:// These letters stand for hypertext transfer protocol, but who cares. The important thing to know is that the **http** means this address leads to a web page. You might also see addresses that start with news:// or ftp://. Those are different from web pages.

www This stands for World Wide Web, of course, but this is not the definitive clue that tells you (and the browser software) that the address goes to a web page! The www is just a convention; many addresses don't include it. (The "http" means it's a web page.)

The period is pronounced "dot." So "ratz.com" is pronounced "ratz dot com."

ratz.com This is the **domain name.** Typically it is the name of the business or vendor. The **com** stands for **commercial.** You can buy your own domain name; it costs $70 for two years, renewable every year after that for $35. I bought ratz.com. Ask your service provider to help you buy a domain name.

Domain names
The domain name gives you a clue as to the general nature of the site:

.com	*commercial*
.edu	*educational*
.gov	*government*
.mil	*military*
.org	*organization, usually non-profit*
.net	*network business*

/robin The slash tells the browser to go down one more level, to look into the next folder. So in this address, the slash tells the browser to go to the domain name "ratz.com" and look inside the folder named "robin."

/hats.html So here's a slash again, which tells the browser to look inside that folder and find the page that has been saved with the name "hats.html." The "html" is a clue that this is a web page because all basic web pages (just about) end with ".htm" or ".html."

You will often see web addresses such as "www.adobe.com." If there is no file or folder name *after* the domain name, the browser finds the web page that has been named (usually) "index.html" and displays it automatically. This is usually the home page. So if you are at a page with a long address, you can always delete the part of the address after the domain name, hit Return, and you will go to the home page that belongs to that domain.

Using a Browser

The browser, as you learned, is the software that displays web pages on your screen. You enter the address of a web page in the browser, you use search tools through your browser, you watch movies and hear music through your browser, you can print from your browser, and on and on. So it's important to know how to use it. The Help files are usually very good—while you're in your browser, go to the Help menu and choose the command for your software. Right here I'm just going to give you some basic tips that will get you started right away.

Entering a web address

To enter a web address, type it into the "Location," "Address," or "Go To" box (or it might be called something else) at the top of the window, in the toolbar. After you type it in, hit Return or Enter to tell the browser to go find that page.

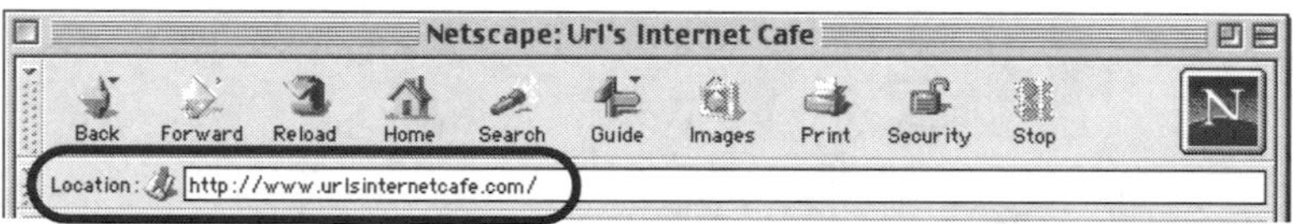

Type the address in here. Make sure it is spelled absolutely correctly, that caps and lowercase letters are in the right places, and that there are no empty spaces in the address. ***Hit Return or Enter after you type it.***

Going back and forth from page to page

You see buttons in your toolbar. The ones you will use most often are "Back" and "Forward." The "Back" button, of course, takes you back through pages you have visited. If you've gone back, then the "Forward" button appears so you can go forward again. You can also use the Go menu to go through pages you have visited. But keep this in mind: the browser can only keep track of one path. You'll notice, as you wander around the web, that often you can't get back to a page you visited. If you backtrack over pages and then go off in a *different* direction, the browser keeps track of that *new* direction. It's as if, as you backtrack, the browser picks up the breadcrumbs that marked your trail. Don't worry too much about it—just keep in mind that the page you loved a few minutes ago might not be accessible through the "Back" button or through the Go or History menus. If you really like a page, make a Bookmark or Favorite of it (see page 355). Then that web page will always be available to you with the click of a button.

Press anywhere and you'll get Back/ Forward menu options.

Shortcut: You can go Back or Forward by pressing on any *blank* spot on the web page. As you press *and hold the mouse button down,* a tiny menu pops up with the options "Back" and "Forward." Try it.

Open a new browser window

You can have lots and lots of browser windows open. This comes in handy when you really like a page, or maybe this page has lots of links you want to follow so when you go to another page you don't want this one to disappear. So instead of *clicking* on the link to get another page, *press* on it (hold the mouse button down). You will get a menu right there in the middle of the page, and one of the options is something like "New Window with this Link." Choose that, a new window with the new page will open, and the previous window will still be open on your screen as well.

Press—don't click—on a link to get this menu.

Shortcut to enter address

And here's an extra-special shortcut you will love. If you are using Netscape or Internet Explorer (on a Mac), you don't have to type in the entire ugly web address with the http:// and all. For one thing, unless you are using very old browser software, you never need to type "http://." So skip that part altogether. If the rest of the address is in this format, "www.**something**.com," all you need to type is "**something**." Really. For instance, to get to http://www.**apple**.com, all you need to type is **apple**, then hit Return or Enter.

So try this: In Netscape, type Command L (in Internet Explorer, type Command O) to get the Location or Open box. Type "apple." Hit Return.

If the address uses another top-level domain, such as .org or .net instead of .com, you'll have to type .org or .net, etc. And if the address has other slashes and stuff, you'll have to type everything after the domain name.

Customize your toolbar

You can customize your toolbar. One of the first things you might want to do is get rid of the big buttons so you have more room for the web pages. Find your browser's preferences settings—they're usually in the File or Edit menu, called "Preferences" or maybe "Options." Find the section that controls the toolbar. Experiment.

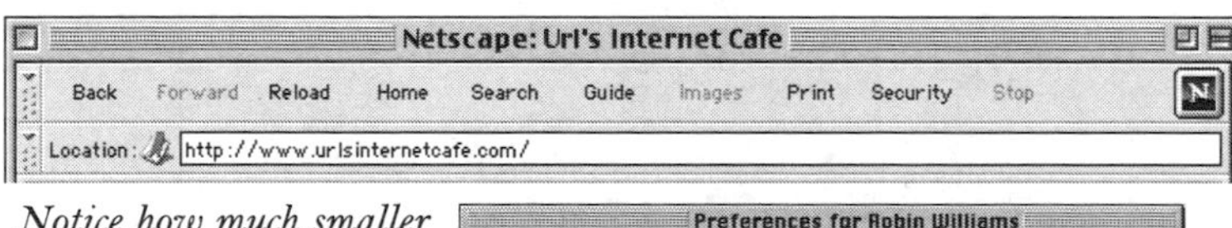

In the Preferences dialog box, choose "Show ToolTips" to display these little clues when you pause the pointer over a button. Or turn them off if they bore you.

Notice how much smaller this toolbar (above) is than the one on the facing page. Find the Preferences for the toolbar and experiment with the options.

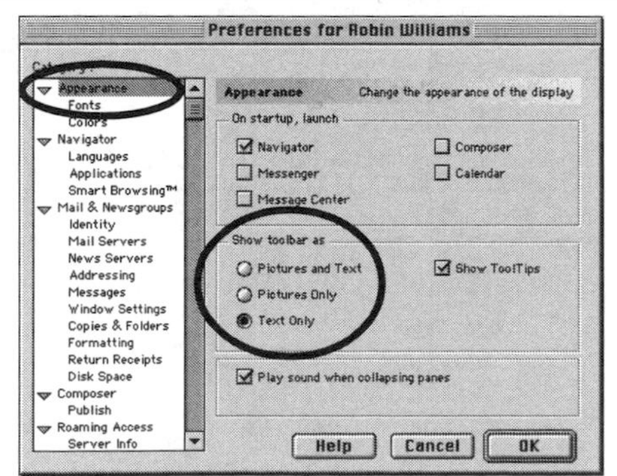

This is the Preferences dialog box for Netscape Communicator.

Customize your typeface

The other most important feature to customize is the typeface. The default that has been set for you is usually Times, 12 point. On a Macintosh screen, Times is very difficult to read. New York, however, has been designed specifically for the resolution of a monitor. Change your font to New York 10 or 12 point and see what an incredible difference it makes. Or use Geneva instead of Helvetica, or try Verdana, which looks lovely on the screen.

On the left is New York 12 point. On the right is Times 12 point. Which is easier to read, especially on a screen?

THE ENEMY CAMP
Dr. Richard Hallmark examines the Apple/Microsoft deal in his editorial "An alliance reborn?" It's a thought-provoking piece that really makes you wonder if Rick's been hanging around with Puff Daddy.

THE INTERFACE POLICE
Lunetta and Howe, fresh from their stint as Honda's ad agency, say--"Here's an idea, Simplify." And we agree! See any old copies of Windows 95 cluttering up your office? Simplify--toss 'em in the incinerator.

THE ENEMY CAMP
Dr. Richard Hallmark examines the Apple/Microsoft deal in his editorial 'An alliance reborn?' It's a thought-provoking piece that really makes you wonder if Rick's been hanging around with Puff Daddy.

THE INTERFACE POLICE
Lunetta and Howe, fresh from their stint as Honda's ad agency, say-'Here's an idea, Simplify.' And we agree! See any old copies of Windows 95 cluttering up your office? Simplify-toss 'em in the incinerator.

PAINTER TIPS AND TRICKS
David Roberts, (who once posed for a famous statue in Rome), says 'Make mine Monet.' David, I hate to tell you this, but any art historian can tell you Monet did not use Painter. He used Photoshop. (kidding, just a joke!)

Change the font in the Preferences or Options dialog box in your browser. The option might be called "Text," "Typeface," "Variable Width Font," "Proportional Font," or a variation thereof.

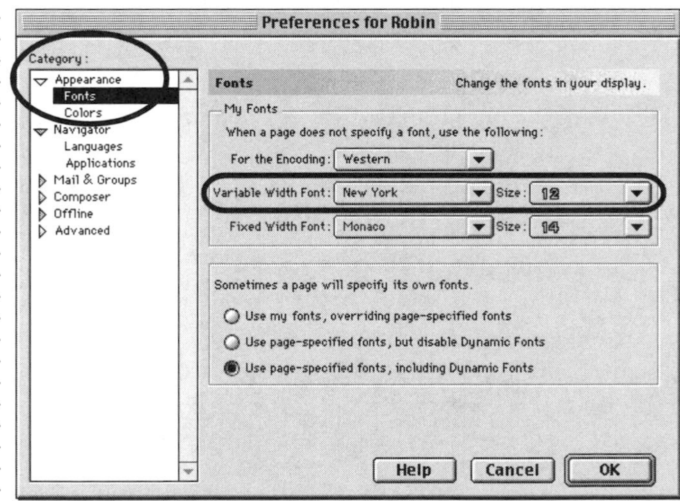

Bookmarks or Favorites

As you wander around the Web, you'll run across web sites you really like and want to come back to. For these sites, make a Bookmark (Netscape) or a Favorite (Internet Explorer). Once you have a bookmark, the title of the page shows up in your bookmark list and you can just choose it from the menu, as shown below.

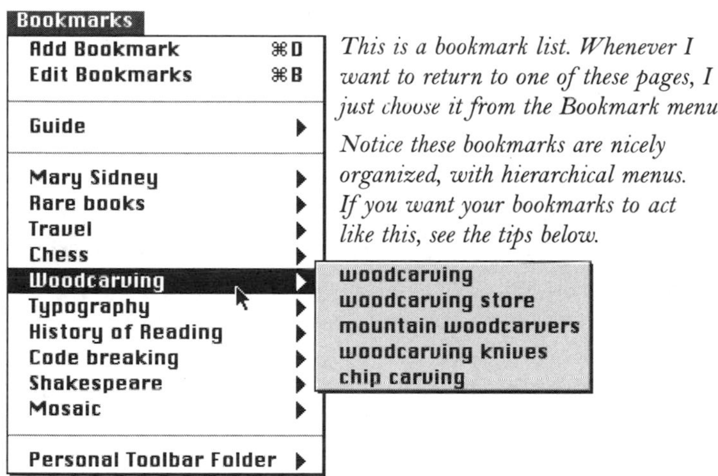

This is a bookmark list. Whenever I want to return to one of these pages, I just choose it from the Bookmark menu.

Notice these bookmarks are nicely organized, with hierarchical menus. If you want your bookmarks to act like this, see the tips below.

To make a bookmark or favorite: Simply view the page you want to make a bookmark for. Press Command D. The title of the page is now in your Bookmark or Favorites menu.

To organize your bookmarks or favorites: In Internet Explorer, you have a few self-explanatory options in the menu for making new folders and putting favorites into those folders. In Netscape, there are lots more things you can do with bookmarks. You can read all about them in the Help menu, but here is a quick tip that will help you keep them organized.

Press Command B to get the Bookmarks window, as shown to the right. When this window is active, your menu bar and the commands in it change—look through the menus for items like "New Folder," "Set as New Bookmarks folder," "Alphabetize Bookmarks," and others. Experiment.

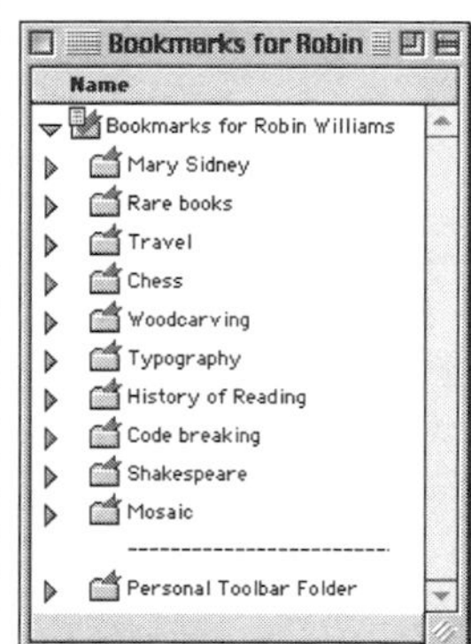

Also in that Bookmarks window, you can drag bookmarks into and out of folders, Option–double-click to change the names of folders or bookmarks, delete bookmarks, drag bookmarks into new positions in the list, and more.

You can even save your bookmark list as a web page and then open it in your browser (from the File menu, choose "Save As"). Each folder will appear as a heading, and each bookmark will be a link!

Search Tools

URLs for several popular search tools:

google.com
yahoo.com
altavista.com
infoseek.com
excite.com
about.com
hotbot.com
search.com
goto.com

Once you know how to use your browser and start surfing, you'll quickly run up against this problem: There are literally many millions of web pages out there. How do you find the one you want? You find it with a **search tool,** often referred to as a search engine. You don't have to buy or install search tools—they are just on the web, like any of the other web pages. But they are different from other web pages in that you can type in subjects you want to find, and the search tool will look for it.

Oh, there is so much to tell you about search tools, but that's not the purpose of this book. I can only tell you a couple of important points, and you will have to move on from there.

Important Point Number One

When you enter a query in a search tool, it does not go running all over the world looking for pages that match your query. **It looks only in its own database** that it has compiled according to its own special criteria. There are many search tools, and they each have their own criteria and their own way of adding sites to their database. So you might ask three different search tools to find "Briards" and come up with three very different lists of web pages about Briards (a dog breed).

Important Point Number Two

Every search tool has different rules for finding information. **Read the Tips or Help section.** It will tell you critical details about how to enter a query so results can be found. As search tools are improved, their rules change a little, so when you see a new look on your favorite search page, check the Tips or Help section again.

This is for the web address, also known as the URL.

Enter (type) your query in here. Put quotation marks around words that you want to find as a whole phrase (for instance, "shakespeare authorship question". Then press Return or click the "Google Search" button. See the results on the opposite page.

These are the results of the simple search shown on the previous page. If you want to narrow the search, read the Help or Tips page of the web site! Every search tool gives you tips on how to find specifically the item you want.

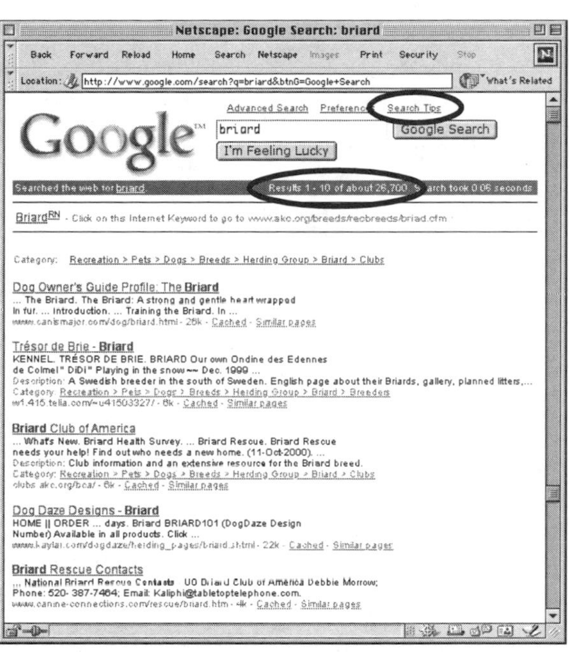

There is a good, hearty chapter on search tools in another book of mine, written with John Tollett, called ***The Non-Designer's Web Book,*** *which is about creating and posting your own web site.*

There is a great book from Peachpit Press called ***Search Engines for the World Wide Web, Visual QuickStart Guide,*** *by Alfred and Emily Glossbrenner.*

Other sorts of tools

Some search tools work best by entering words or phrases within quotation marks. Others work best by "drilling" down through their selection of web sites. You will probably find yourself using the directory called Yahoo, or a similar one called Google Web Directory, shown below. Instead of typing in a word for the directory to find, try clicking your way down through the list. Click on a category and keep clicking down to narrow your choices.

How do you know which is the best way to search for something? Read the Help or Tips section in each search tool you find. For lots of information, drill down through the Computer category in Google until you find the articles on "Searching the Web." The Internet itself is the best source of information about how to do things on the Internet. You just have to find the stuff.

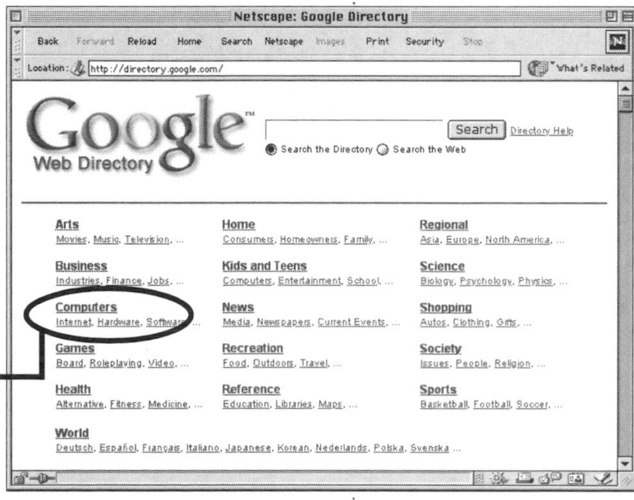

Click Internet, then on the page that comes up click WWW, then click Searching the Web, then click Help and Tutorials, then choose any of the many articles about searching the web.

1. The World Wide Web is made up of millions of:
   a. spiders
   b. individual pages, similar to word processing pages
   c. individual corporations
   d. government troops

2. You can tell an item on a Web page is a link because:
   a. it is underlined
   b. it has a border around it
   c. the cursor turns into a hand
   d. any of the above

3. Hypertext refers to:
   a. text that branches out non-sequentially, and the reader can choose which path to follow
   b. text on drugs
   c. text you can read really fast
   d. any text on a web page

4. A URL is a:
   a. rat
   b. search tool
   c. web page address
   d. domain name

5. The letters "htm" or "html" at the end of a file name indicate:
   a. any web page
   b. a domain name
   c. a server
   d. only home pages

6. To view web pages, you need a:
   a. search tool
   b. domain name
   c. bookmark or favorite
   d. browser

7. To find the information you need, use a:
   a. search tool
   b. domain name
   c. bookmark or favorite
   d. browser

8. If you want the URL of your web site to be the name of your business, you need to buy a:
   a. search tool
   b. domain name
   c. bookmark or favorite
   d. browser

9. To save the location of a page that you want to find again, use a:
   a. search tool
   b. domain name
   c. bookmark or favorite
   d. browser

10. In the browsers Internet Explorer or Netscape, to get to a web page with the address **http://www.peachpit.com** what is the minimum you have to type:
   a. http://www.peachpit.com
   b. www.peachpit.com
   c. peachpit.com
   d. peachpit

11. In the browsers Internet Explorer or Netscape, to get to a web page with the address **http://www.newmexico.org** what is the minimum you have to type:
   a. http://www.newmexico.org
   b. www.newmexico.org
   c. newmexico.org
   d. newmexico

12. Which of these fonts will be the easiest to read on the screen?
   a. Times
   b. New York
   c. Helvetica
   d. Palatino

Answers on page 426.

33 The Internet Features on your Mac

The Mac has a number of features designed specifically for getting on the Internet quickly and easily, and for customizing various parts of the connective process. What you will need to do to connect yourself depends on many variables. I suggest using this chapter, when and if you ever need it, along with your manual and the Help files. If you're connected to the Internet and the World Wide and everything is already working fine, don't even look in here. Go back to the web and enjoy yourself!

Where to Begin

If you are not connected to the Internet at all yet, first be sure to read the previous two chapters. Then read through this chapter up through page 368 (where it begins to talk about control panels and other features specifically) so you have an overall view of the process.

Mac OS 8.5 and above have something called the **Internet Setup Assistant** that walks you through getting yourself connected to the Internet. You must first have made a decision whether you are going to use America Online, or get an individual connection through an Internet Service Provider (an ISP), or use the network connection at work, as explained on the opposite page.

After the section about getting your connection established, the rest of this chapter explains the individual control panels and special dialog boxes on your Mac where you can customize settings. If you get your connection working and everything is fine, don't mess with anything else unless you see the need. You might want to read through the information just so you have a better understanding of what all these things are.

You Need a Modem

Of course, before you can get connected in the first place, you must have some sort of modem for connecting to the Internet. If there is a phone jack on the side or back of your Mac, along with the other ports, you have an internal modem. Don't get the modem port mixed up with the Ethernet port! The modem port is exactly the size of a regular phone cable; the Ethernet port looks very similar, but it's larger—a phone cable won't snap into it neatly. If you have a modem port, just plug one end of a phone cord directly into it, and the other end into the wall or into another phone.

If you don't have an internal modem, you'll have to buy one and plug it in before you set up your Internet connection (a modem plugs into the serial port, which is one of the little round ones just like your printer port). Follow the directions with the modem manual; typically you connect a modem cable from the Mac to the modem, then a phone cable from the modem to the wall. Or you might connect your phone between the computer and the modem, or use a slightly different combination. Read the directions.

If you have a special line for a fast connection, such as DSL, ISDN, cable, T1, or anything else, you have a special modem that uses an Ethernet connection and you are usually considered to be on a network. Have the person who helped you configure the network also help you get connected to the Internet through your Mac.

Using the Internet Setup Assistant

The **Internet Setup Assistant** facilitates connecting you to an Internet Service Provider. There are two important things to know before you jump into this Setup Assistant:

1. **If you are using America Online as your Internet connection, you do not need to use this Internet Setup Assistant at all.** Ignore it. See pages 346–347 about AOL and the Internet.
2. If you are not using America Online, or you are using it but you want a direct Internet connection *in addition* to AOL, **you must first establish a relationship with an Internet Service Provider.** A "relationship" means you either **a)** call up a local or national ISP (Internet Service Provider), tell them you want to connect to the Internet through their service, register yourself with them, and pay them money. They will give you all the strange information you need to enter into this Internet Setup Assistant.

   Or **b)** if you don't want to use a *local* ISP, the Internet Setup Assistant will give you a national provider option (EarthLink). Have your credit card handy, and you can register during the setup process. All of the strange information will be entered for you automatically and you can just log on right away.

   Or **c)** if you are in an office and use a LAN (local area network, meaning your computers are all in the same office complex or building), talk to your network supervisor instead of an ISP.

To use the Internet Setup Assistant:

1. If the Assistant is already open and in front of you, go to Step **3.**

   If the alias to the Internet Setup Assistant (shown to the right) is sitting on your Desktop, double-click it.

   If you don't see the Internet Setup Assistant icon (it's usually in a folder called "Assistants"), use Sherlock (Chapter 26) to find it for you. Double-click it.

This is the icon you want to double-click to start the process.

2. The first window that appears is this one you see to the right. Since you have gotten this far, you most likely want to click "Yes."

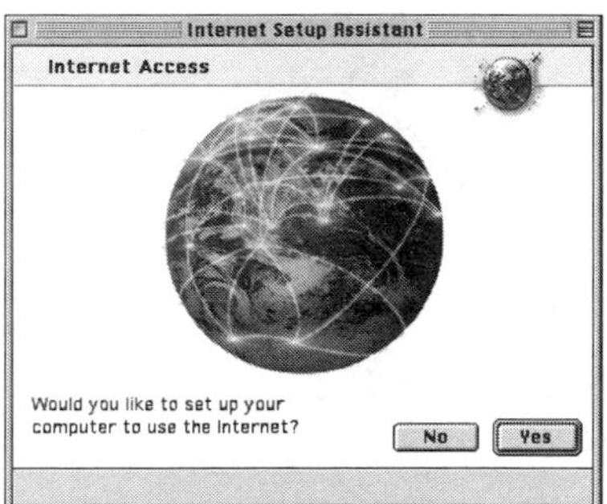

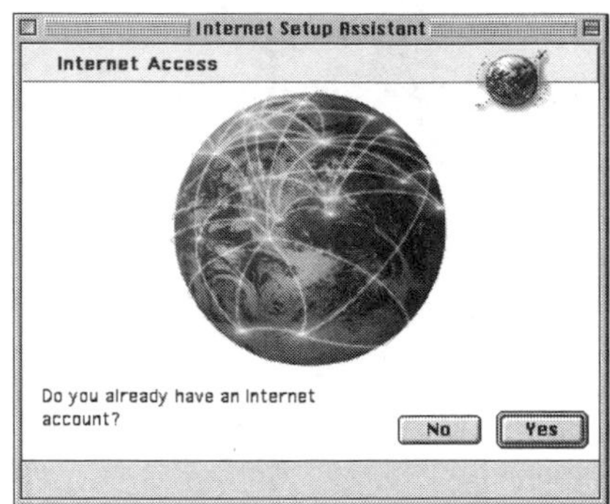

3. This is an important question.

Answer **No** if you have never had your own connection to the Internet on any computer, **or** if you want to make *another* one. For instance, you might have America Online but you also want a direct connection to the Internet. Or two people use the same computer and each pay for their own Internet connection separately. *Continue to **Step 4A,** below.*

Answer **Yes** if: You have/had an individual connection on another computer, either at home or work, and you want to establish that same connection on this computer. **Or** you contacted a local or national ISP and set up a relationship with them and you have the appropriate information to enter. **Or** you are on a local network (LAN), as is typical in a large office environment, and want to connect this computer to that network. *Skip to **Step 4B** (page 365).*

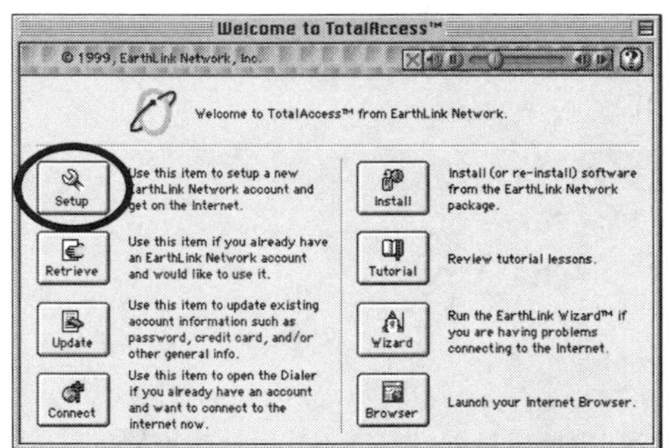

4A. If you have no Internet connection at all yet and you click the "No" button, you'll get this TotalAccess assistant to help you establish an account with EarthLink. EarthLink will be your ISP and your email address will be something like "robinwilliams@earthlink.net."

EarthLink can be a great solution if you are in a city in which EarthLink offers a local phone number and you are in the contiguous United States. At the moment the basic service is $19.95 a month, but if you live in Hawaii or Alaska, expect to pay an extra $9 PER HOUR on top of that. If EarthLink doesn't have a local phone number in your area (which is very likely if you live outside the major towns in places like New Mexico or Arkansas), you can ask for an 800 number which costs about $5 PER HOUR extra.

You can follow this process through to the point of checking for local phone numbers in EarthLink (Step 7A), and if they don't have one for you, you can cancel the process with no harm done. If you decide EarthLink isn't the best solution for you, call a connected friend or computer consultant and ask about local providers.

EarthLink does have great tech support 24 hours a day, and the service is pretty good and very convenient.

- Click the "Setup" button to start a new account and a new email address.
- Click the "Retrieve" button to set up an existing EarthLink account, if you already have one, on your new computer.

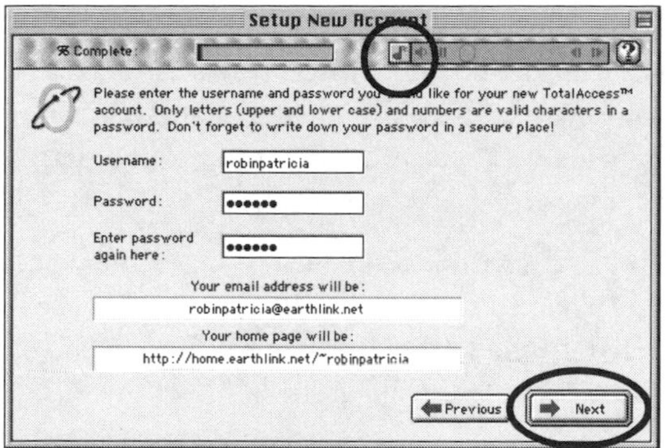

5A. Continue to fill in the dialog boxes and click the button in the bottom-right to go to the next one. It's all pretty self-explanatory. You'll be asked to fill in your name and address, phone number, billing information, including credit card, etc.

Anytime you need more details about a dialog box or process, click the little musical symbol in the upper-right; the lady will tell you all about it.

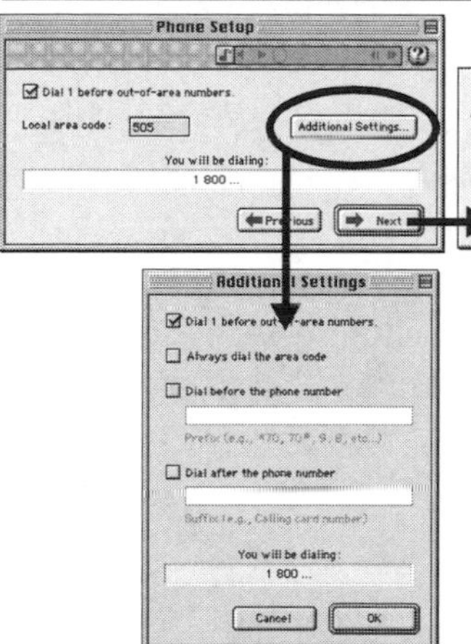

6A. If you are in an office where you need to dial 9 or some other number to get out, or *70 to turn off call waiting, or you are in a location where you must always dial the area code before the phone number, etc., click "Additional Settings..." here and make your choices. Click OK and move on.

7A. EarthLink (TotalAccess) will connect to the Internet through your phone connection and show you a list of local phone numbers for your account. Choose one and click the Next button.

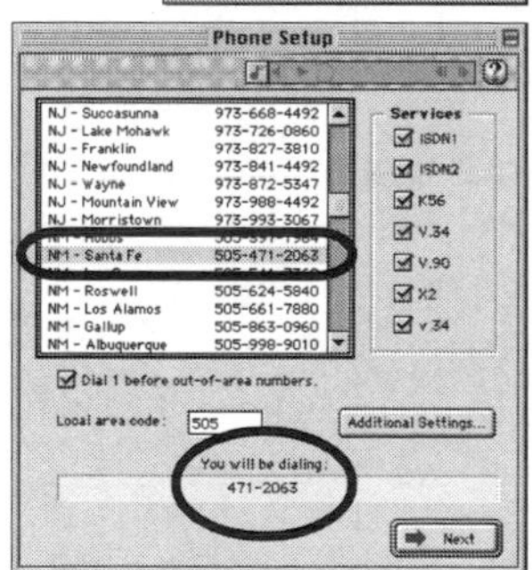

Click a number in the list to choose your access number. The number you have chosen will be displayed below.

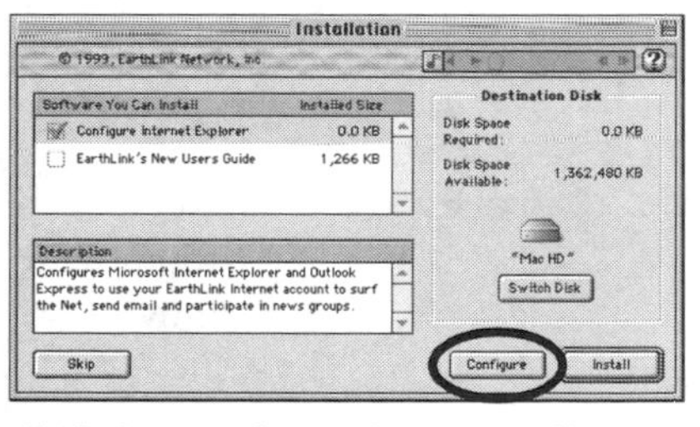

Click the "Configure" button to tell the browser Internet Explorer how to check to see if you have mail. This way every time you open your browser (as long as you use Internet Explorer), you will know if you have mail waiting for you. If you want to check your mail right there on the web page, as opposed to using your email program (like Outlook Express), you can do so; see the next page. Even if you configure the browser to check your email, you can still use your email program as well.

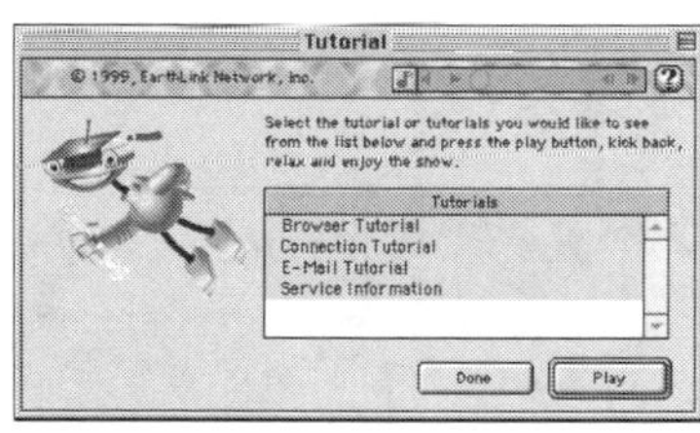

You'll see this dialog box at some point. Double-click any of the tutorials in the list to see them play. You'll learn a lot.

If EarthLink doesn't log you on to the Internet at the end of this process, see page 369 to log on. Then read page 364.

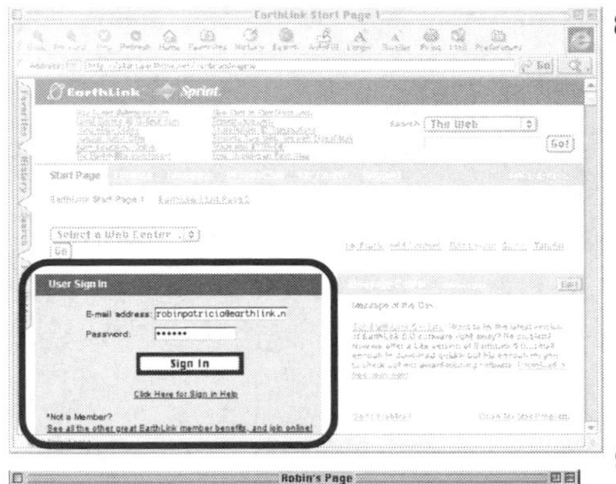

8A. Log on, if you aren't already (see page 369), then open the browser Microsoft Internet Explorer. You'll see a very messy and confusing web page, which is your "Start Page" at Earthlink. Yikes.

Web pages change, but if yours look somewhat like the one to the left, you'll see a sign-in area (circled, to the left). Enter your information, then click the "Sign In" button.

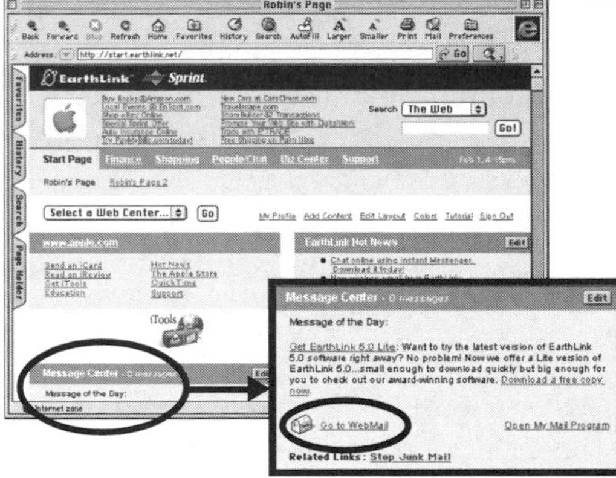

9A. Once you sign in, try to find the "Message Center," as circled to the left. You might have to scroll down to see it (which is bad design).

In the Message Center area, you can click the button to "Go to Web Mail," which will take you to a web page where you can access your email. You can open mail, send new mail, etc., as shown below. The advantage of having a web page for mail is that you can check it at any computer anywhere in the world, as long as they have a browser.

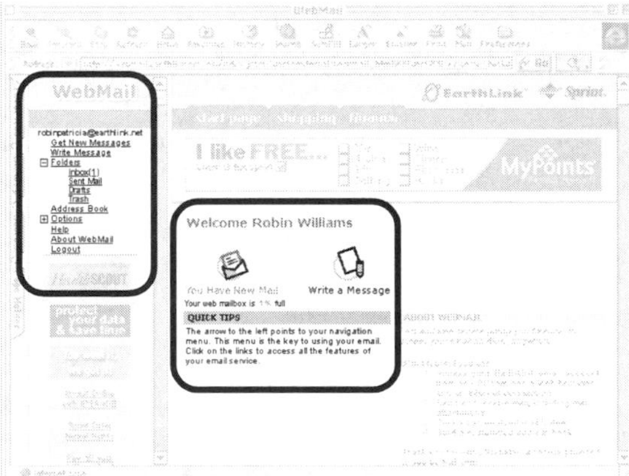

If you prefer, click the link "Open My Mail Program" and your regular email program should open (Outlook Express or Eudora or whatever you use).

10A. If you click "Go to Web Mail," you will get another messy web page (shown to the left) where you can write new messages, check mail, make an address book, etc. You did it.

Skip pages 365–368.

Read page 369 about logging on and off.

Read pages 370–372 about the Internet control panel.

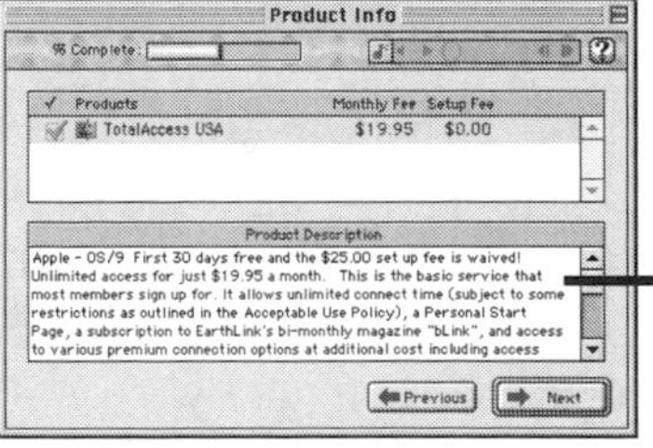

When signing up, this is the information you need to read very carefully. The "International roaming access" at 15¢ a minute ($9 an hour) actually applies to Alaska and Hawaii, so be careful!

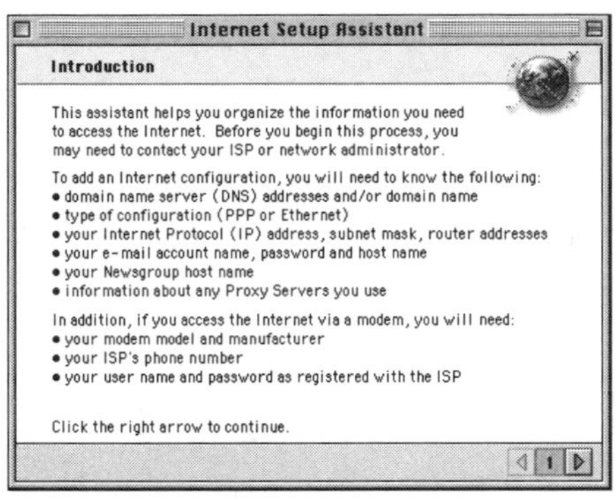

4B. So if you are at this dialog box it means you have the information ready to plug into these dialog boxes. Call your ISP if you need any of this data. If you are **not** on a LAN (local area network, like in a corporation or large office), you won't need to know your IP address, subnet mask, and route addresses. If you **are** on a network or if you have a high-speed connection (DSL, T1, ISDN, cable), make sure you get that information from your installer or network supervisor because you will be asked to enter it.

Important note: The **user name and password as registered with the ISP** is NOT the same as your name and password for your email!! Often the ISP assigns you a user name and password and you might not even know what it is. Be very sure to ask specifically for this information.

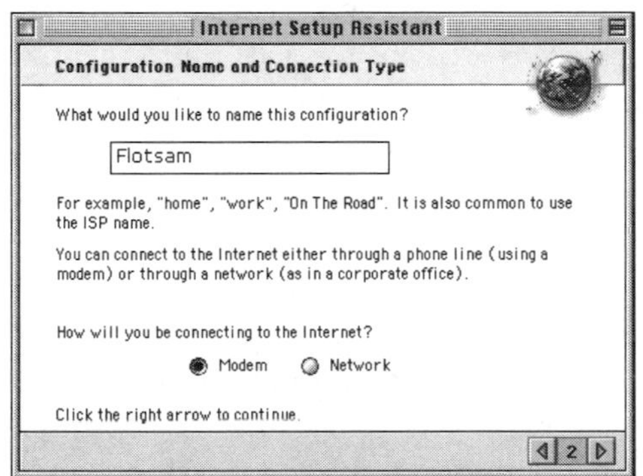

5B. The name of the **configuration** (the connection specifications you are about to set up) should be something you would recognize in a list, such as the name of the person to whom the account belongs, or perhaps the name of the provider.

If you are using the company network, click the "Network" button. Some of the windows you see will look different from the ones shown here because you have to enter other information.

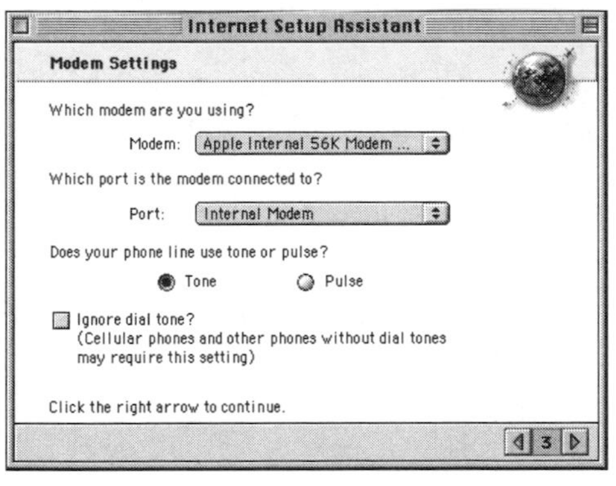

6B. Your **Modem** is probably already selected. If not, choose it from the list; ifyou don't find exactly your modem, choose one by the same manufacturer, or try one of the Hayes models.

If your modem is internal, choose that option for the **Port.** If it's not internal, choose the "Modem port" option unless you specifically know you should choose something else.

Most modern phones use **Tone.** If you have a pushbutton phone, it's tone. If you have an old phone that dials, it's **Pulse** (and it's not great for data transfer over the Internet).

You might want to **Ignore dial tone** if you have a phone answering service that gives you a different dial tone to indicate you have messages waiting.

If you have **call waiting** service, you must enter *70 to turn it off while you are connected because if you are online and someone calls you, your call waiting will disconnect you from the Internet.

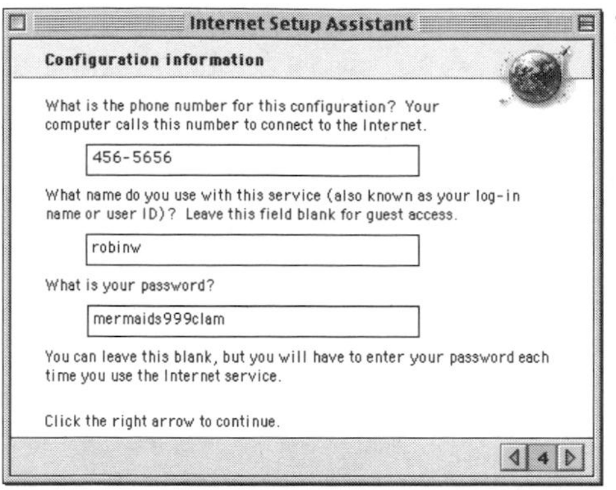

7B. Your service provider gives you the **phone number** you need. This is the number your *computer* will call to connect to the ISP; this is not the number *you* use to call your ISP on the phone!

The **log in name** or **user ID** and the **password,** as I mentioned in Step 4B, might not be the same as your name and password for your email! Be sure to get the specific name and password that the ISP has registered to you for connectivity.

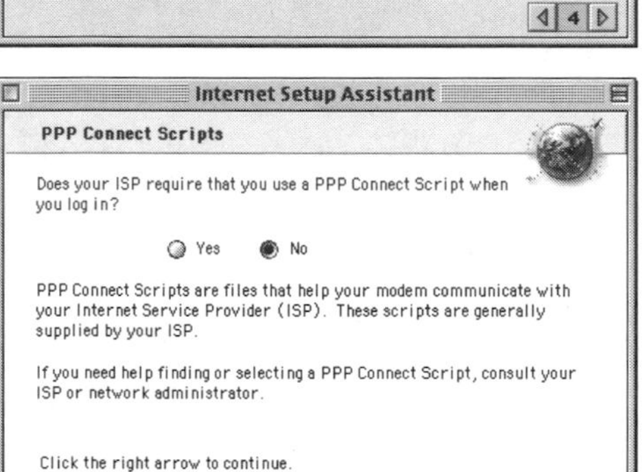

8B. Unless your service provider told you that you need a script and gave you a script file, click "No" here and move on. If your ISP did give you a script file, drop it on top of the closed System Folder; the Mac will put the script into the Modem Scripts folder for you. Ask your ISP how they want you to use it.

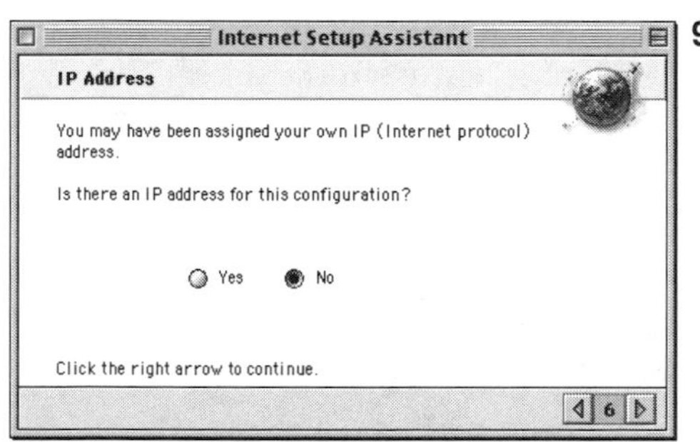

9B. If you are connected to a *dedicated, high-speed line* (DSL, T1, ISDN, cable) that is open all the time, like on a network in an office or school setting, you will have your own **IP address;** ask your network supervisor or installer for the number.

If you use *phone lines* to dial up and connect, you do **not** have a permanent IP address.

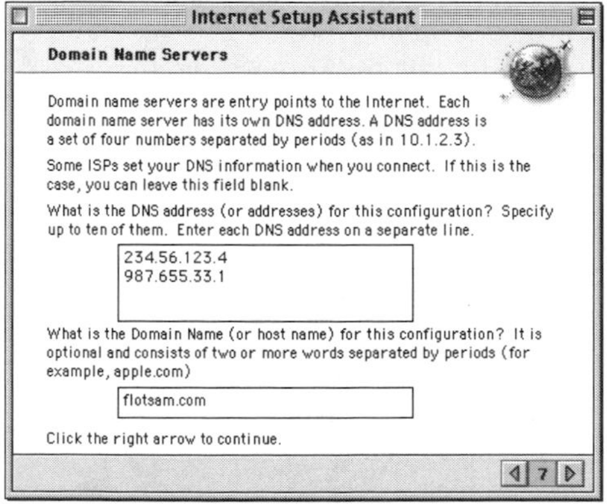

10B. Your ISP will give you this information. They'll probably give you at least two different **DNS addresses.** Type the first one in, then hit a Return to type the second one. It's a good idea to write these numbers down somewhere because I guarantee someday you will have to type them into some other dialog box.

The **domain name** or **host name** is often the same as your email *account* name (see the note in 11B).

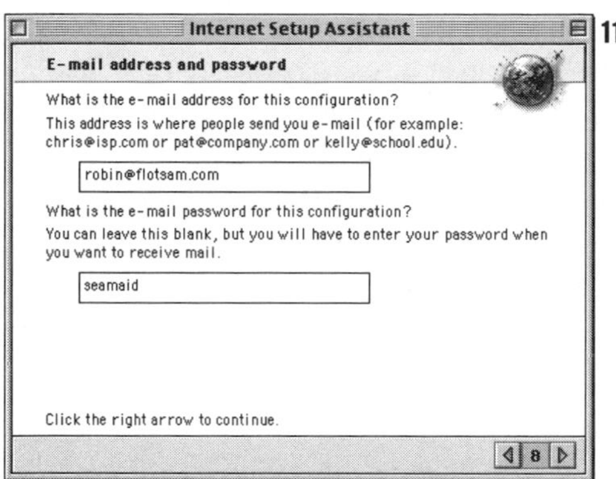

11B. Notice the difference between this window and the next one: this one asks for your **email address** and the next one asks for your **email account.** In many cases these are the same, but often they're not. For instance, my real email **account** is robin@nets.com through a connection with a local ISP called studio x. But I bought the domain ratz.com and I have a web site at ratz.com, so my email **address** that I give out is robin@ratz.com. The ratz *address*, however, actually gets routed through my *account* at nets.com. If you've just set up your account with your ISP and they gave you an email address, then you will enter the same thing in both this window and the next one, unless they tell you differently. Ask if your email address is the same as your email account.

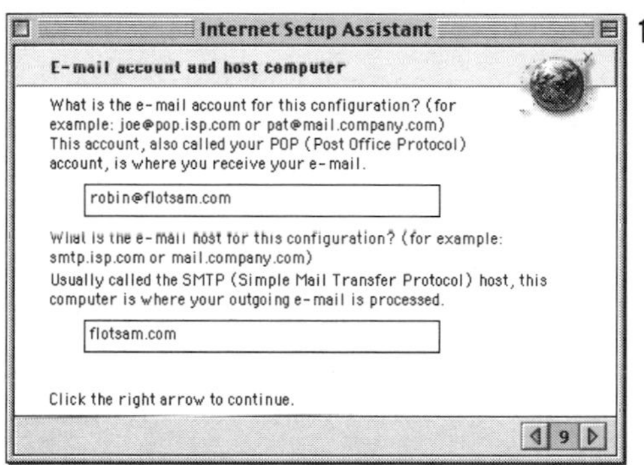

12B. Your ISP will give you the correct information for this window. Take note of the "SMTP" host; you'll run into that term again and it's good to know the name of your SMTP host. It will make you feel powerful and smart, too, to be able to name your SMTP host when you need it.

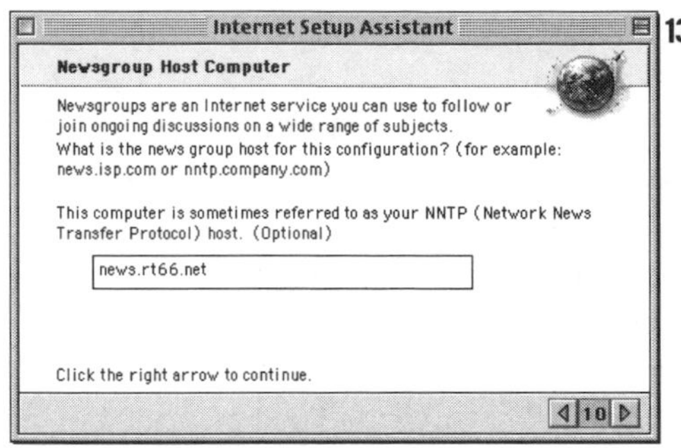

13B. Newsgroups are explained on page 343. Because there are so many thousands of newsgroups, few ISPs can store the information for all of them. Many ISPs have arrangements with another server (a host) to allow their users to access the other servers' newsgroups. Even that host may not have every newsgroup; if they don't have the one you want, you can always ask them to carry a particular one for you. It shouldn't cost anything.

Your ISP will tell you what to enter here. You don't have to enter anything if you think you won't be using newsgroups, and if you change your mind later, you can always add a host name.

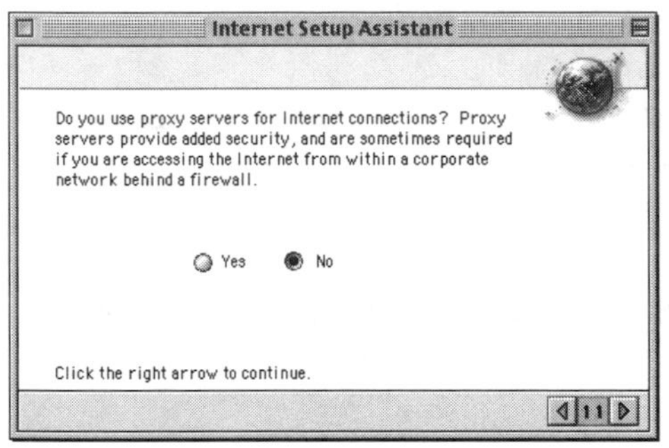

14B. Unless, as it states, you are on something like a corporate or university network, click "No" here. If you *are* on a high-end network, ask your network supervisor which button you should choose.

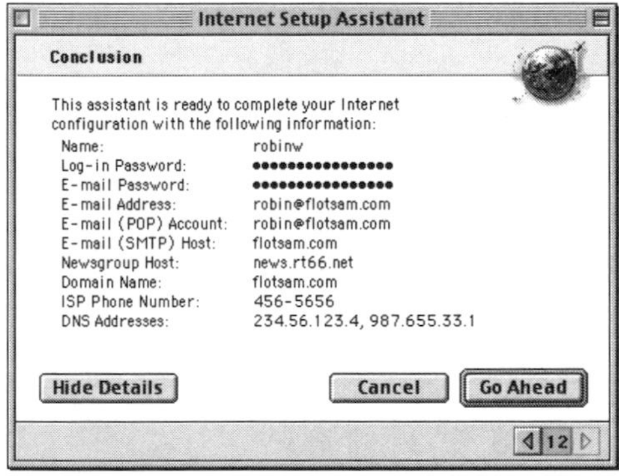

15B. When you get to the next window, click the button **Show Details** (it turns into "Hide Details" after you click it). It's a good idea to keep track of this information. An easy way to capture this info is to make a screen shot of this window and print it up:

1. Press Caps Lock down.
2. Hold the Command and Shift keys down, and tap the number 4. Your pointer will turn into a big, round dot, like this: ●
3. With that big, round dot, click right on the Internet Setup Assistant window. You'll hear a crashing sound, I mean, you'll hear the sound of a picture being taken.

Then go ahead and finish up the connection process: click the "Go Ahead" button (you'll print the window in a minute, after you're done here). The Mac has filled in all the necessary control panels with this information so everything is all set. Read the next page about logging on and logging off.

To print the window with all of that important information: Look in your hard disk window. There's a file called Picture 1. Double-click it and it will open in SimpleText. From the File menu, choose "Print." Click OK. Be sure to fill in the actual passwords before you forget them!!

Logging On to the Internet

There are a number of ways to log on and off of the Internet. You'll find the one that suits you best. It's generally recommended that you establish a connection first, and then open your browser or email software, rather than open the browser or email software and let it make a connection. Here are several options for connecting:

- If you use **America Online,** just double-click the AOL icon. If you want to use a different browser, then after you are logged on with AOL , double-click the alias of your preferred browser (an alias that you previously made and put on the Desktop for this purpose). Skip the rest of these ideas.

OR: If you still have the icon on your Desktop called **Browse the Internet,** just double-click it. It will connect you and also open the browser you have selected in the Internet control panel (see next page), or in Internet Config (if you don't have the Internet control panel; see pages 373–374).

OR: In the Apple menu is a choice called **Remote Access Status.** Choose it and you get the dialog box shown below, left. Click the "Connect" button, and after your connection is established, double-click your browser icon.

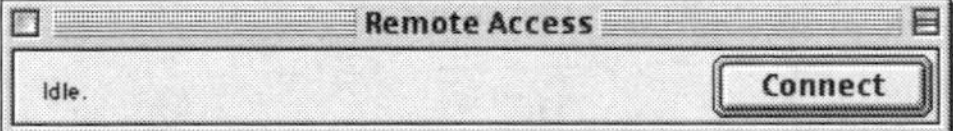

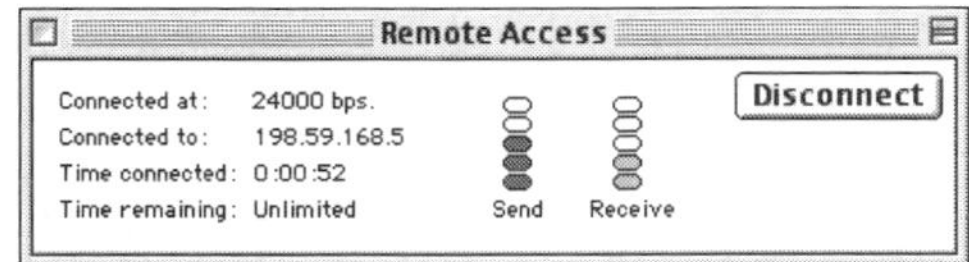

While you are connected, this box provides information to you, and the little bubbles indicate the activity going on. Notice you can disconnect from here.

OR: If your **Control Strip** is showing, use the Remote Access button (below, right). Click it to get the pop-up menu. If you have made more than one configuration, choose the one you want ("Flotsam," in the example). Then click the icon again, and this time click "Connect." If you went throught the EarthLink setup, it created an EarthLink configuration for you.

OR: You might have a **menu item** in the upper-right of your screen for connecting. If you do and you like that, use it.

Logging off

When you quit the browser, that does not automatically disconnect you! Use the Remote Access control panel (pages 376–377) to make your connection automatically disconnect if there's been no activity after a specified amount of time. Manually **disconnect** using the Remote Access Status bar or the Remote Access button on the Control Strip, both shown above.

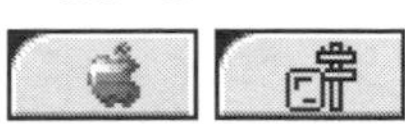

If the Apple icon alternates with the Remote Access icon, you are connected!

Internet Control Panel

This is the greatest invention. This one single control panel will make things so much easier for you. Not only can you set up defaults for your email, browser, etc., but you can make different sets for different situations or people (choose "New Set..." from the File menu), then change sets with the click of a button. You'll become well acquainted with this control panel. If, when you first open it, it's closed up like the one shown below, click on the tiny arrow next to "Edit Sets."

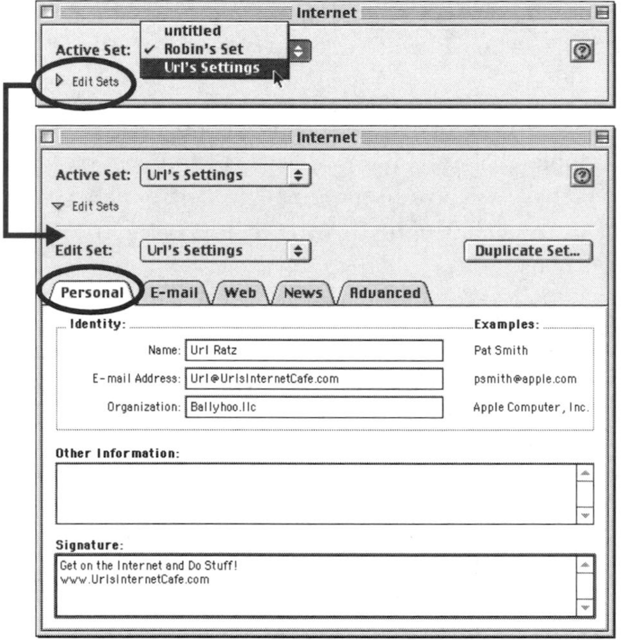

If you went through the Internet Setup Assistant, most of this information was entered for you.

Personal settings

***Finger** is a program that lets anyone see if you're online, how long you've been online, when you were last online, your user ID, your full name, PLUS any information you type into this "Other Information" box. Typically colleges, universities, and corporations have set up a finger facility. You can go to "finger gateways" on the web, type in the email address of anyone, and you might get something back. Many ISPs opt not to supply this information on their servers, and other ISPs might set up information **for** you that someone can finger. Check with your ISP to see what their policy is. America Online does not provide finger information on any of their customers.*

Other Information is where you can type anything you want people to know about you if they "finger" you (see the sidebar explanation).

Anything you type in the **Signature** box will automatically show up at the end of every email you send and every news message you post. You've surely seen signatures in every one else's emails. They can be very elaborate with little pictures made of typed characters, or they might advertise your web site or latest book, provide your postal mail address and phone number, or make a statement about your philosophy of life.

E-mail settings

The "E-Mail" section is pretty self-explanatory. Notice in the example below that I've chosen the endearing AOL "You've Got Mail" as the sound that plays to tell me there's mail, even though I use Eudora (another email application). I found the sound in the AOL folder and put a copy into my System file, and then it shows up in this menu.

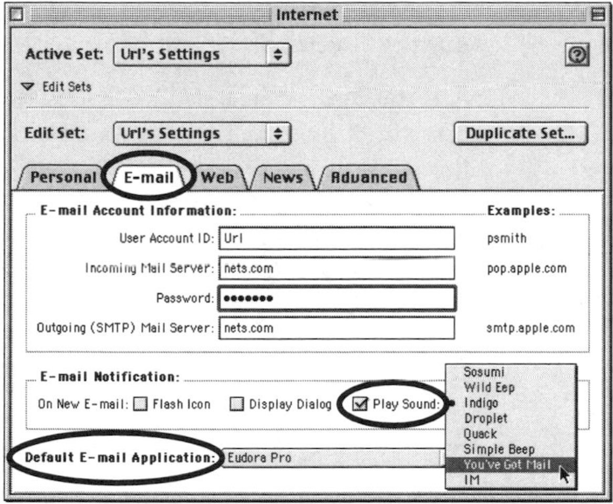

If you went through the Internet Setup Assistant, most of this information was entered for you.

This "Default E-mail Application" is an important option for you to check. Whatever you choose here will open when you double-click the Mail icon (or when you click an email link in the browser Netscape Navigator, but not in Netscape Communicator; see page 372 for the difference between the two applications).

News settings

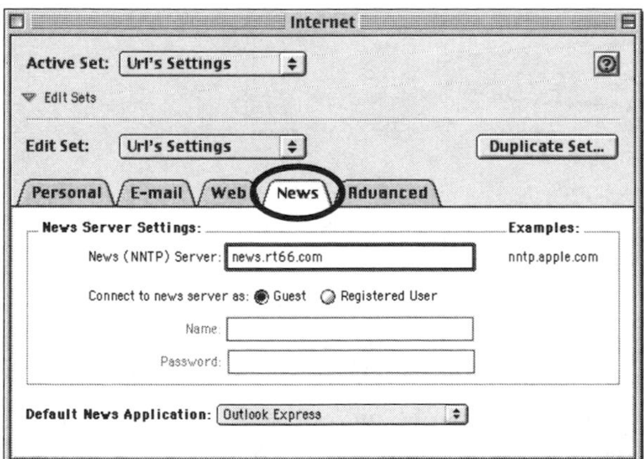

If you went through the Internet Setup Assistant, most of this information was entered for you.

See Step 13B on page 368 about newsgroups. Outlook Express, which is probably on your Mac, is a great application for posting to and viewing newsgroups.

Web settings

The Web settings let you set a **Home Page** and a **Search Page** for when you click the Home or Search buttons in your browser. However, most browsers use their own preferences (which you can also set) rather than these in the Internet control panel. The same goes for **Colors & Links.**

You can create your own folder and have all of your downloaded files go directly into this folder; use the **Download Files To** option. Again, your browser might override your setup here; check and see.

The most important choice for you, though, is the **Default Web Browser.** This one actually works great. On your Mac you probably have both Netscape Communicator and Microsoft Internet Explorer. Whichever one you choose here is what will open when you click the icons "Browse the Internet" or "Connect to...."

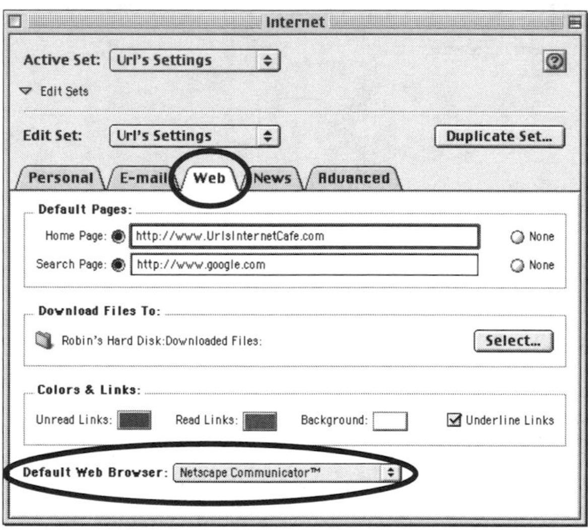

Netscape Navigator vs. Netscape Communicator

Don't bother reading this unless you have a reason to know!

The difference between Navigator and Communicator is that Communicator comes with a suite of integrated programs, most of which the average user doesn't need to use. It includes Navigator as a browser, Collabra for discussion groups, Messenger as an email program, Page Composer for creating web pages, Conference for conferencing, and the AOL instant messenger system. The Communicator folder takes about 20MB of hard disk space and the program wants around 10MB to run. Navigator is simply a browser. It doesn't even do email forms so if you click an email link on a web page, nothing happens. This is because Navigator lets you use your own email program—use Internet Config or the Internet control panel to choose a default email program; then when you click an email link, Navigator will open your email program. The Navigator folder takes about 15MB and the program wants about 5MB to run.

Internet Config is a very useful little utility. The purpose of Internet Config is to prevent you from having to enter the same information into all the different Internet applications you might eventually use. You can create preferences in the Internet Config that will apply to a number of other applications and control panels. Not every Internet application takes advantage of Internet Config, though.

If you are using Mac OS 8.5 and higher, you have the Internet control panel that takes care of some of the things that Internet Config has been taking care of for years (see the previous pages). So if you don't have OS 8.5 and the Internet control panel, poke around in the Internet Config and see what you can do. The most important features you'll need (if you don't have the Internet control panel) are the settings that tell the Mac which browser to open when you double-click **Browse the Internet,** and which email program to open when you double-click **Mail.**

To change the settings to those of your own choosing:

1. Find a copy of Internet Config; double-click it to open its preferences dialog box.

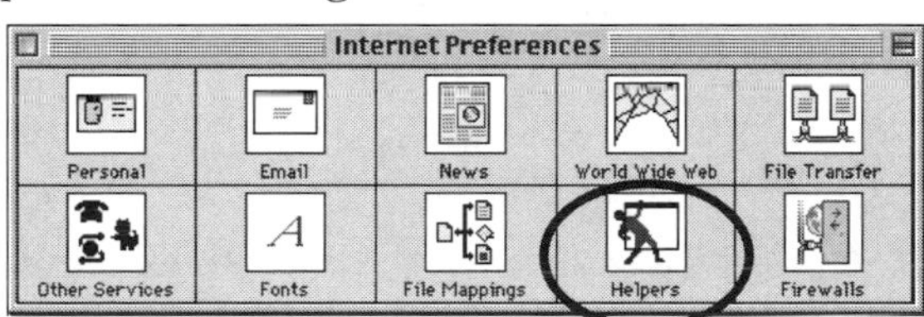

2. Click the box labeled "Helpers." In the resulting dialog box, find and select "mailto," shown below.
3. If it doesn't have an email application listed, or if the one listed is a different program from what you like to use, click the "Change" button. In the little dialog box that comes up, click "Choose Helper...."

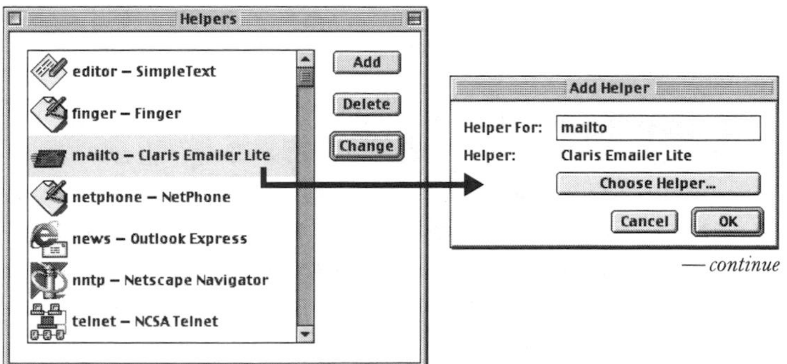

—continue

Internet Config

Use Sherlock to find an Internet Config on your Mac.

Found more than one Config? Don't worry—whatever you enter in one is automatically picked up by every other one on your hard disk.

Note: In Mac OS 9.1 only, many of the specifications in Internet Config are also in the Internet control panel, under the "Advanced" tab.

4. Find your favorite email application and select it; click "Open" (which doesn't really "open" it, but selects it).

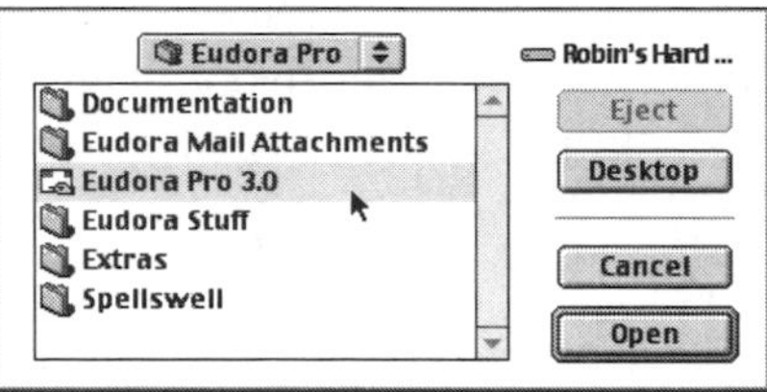

(This process assumes you know how to "navigate." If you don't, please read Chapter 28.)

Don't close the "Helpers" box yet; go to Step 5.

5. Select "http" in the Helpers list. If the browser chosen as the default is not the browser you want to use, click "Change." Find your chosen browser, select its name, then click "Open."

   Now you can close the "Helpers" dialog box—click its close box.

6. Click any of the other options in Internet Config to set the preferences for that item. For instance, to create a signature or a "plan" for fingering, click the "Personal" button.

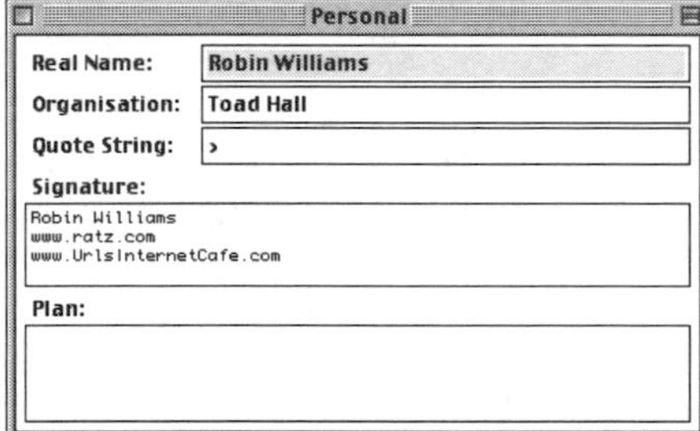

For information about fingering, see the sidebar on page 370.

7. In Netscape, you can choose to let the browser use your Internet Config settings. Open the Preferences and choose "Identity." Check the box, "Use Internet Config." The "Launch" button will open Internet Config for you.

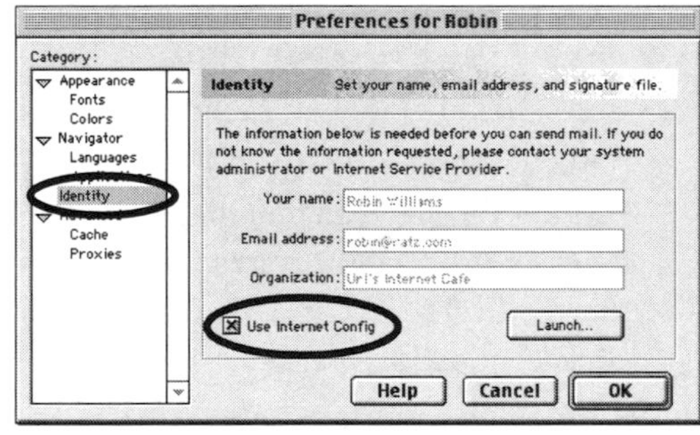

Lots of Internet Configs?

If you do a search on your Mac, you'll probably find half a dozen Internet Config applications. Don't worry—magically, whatever you change in one config appears instantly and automatically in every other one, so you don't have to worry about which one to choose, although it would be best to use the newest version. Use Sherlock (Chapter 26), then click once on the found file and press Command I to get the Get Info box and see what version each one is.

Modem Control Panel

Of course, to connect to the Internet from home, you need a **modem** (unless you have some other kind of connection at home, in which case you can skip this) (you would know if you had some other kind of connection, like cable or ISDN). We talked about modems on page 219, and I hope your modem is at least 28.8, preferably 33.6 or higher. Many Macs now come with modems built-in (which would be an "internal" modem) and all you do is plug a phone cord into the back of the machine and then into the phone jack in the wall. If you need to, you can plug the cord into a phone, and then the phone's cord into the wall, but if you have a wall jack handy, you can go straight in.

The Mac supplies you with a **Modem control panel.** After you install your modem, open the control panel. It's pretty self-explanatory: In the "Connect via" menu, choose the "port," or place on the back of the computer where you plugged the modem in. It's most likely the "Modem Port" because your only other option is the Printer Port and you probably have your printer plugged in there. From the "Modem" list, choose the name of your modem. Make your Sound and Dialing choices, then close the control panel.

If you used the Internet Setup Assistant, it filled in the Modem control panel for you.

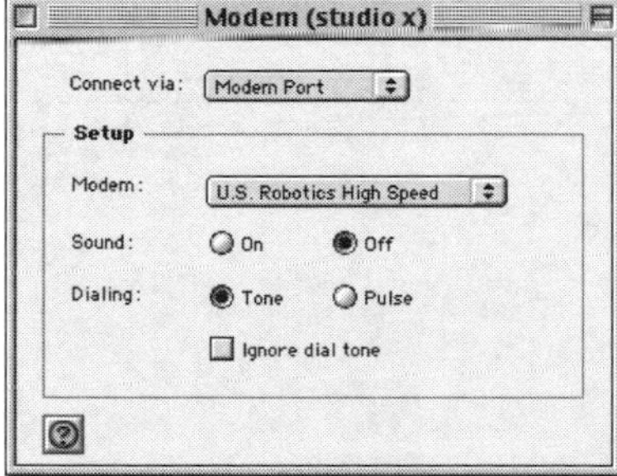

Turn the modem squeal ("Sound") on or off as you like. Sometimes you might like it on so you know it's actually trying to work; other times you might like it off so no one knows you are connecting.

If your phone has push buttons, it's tone. If you have to dial around the numbers, it's pulse (which is not great for connecting).

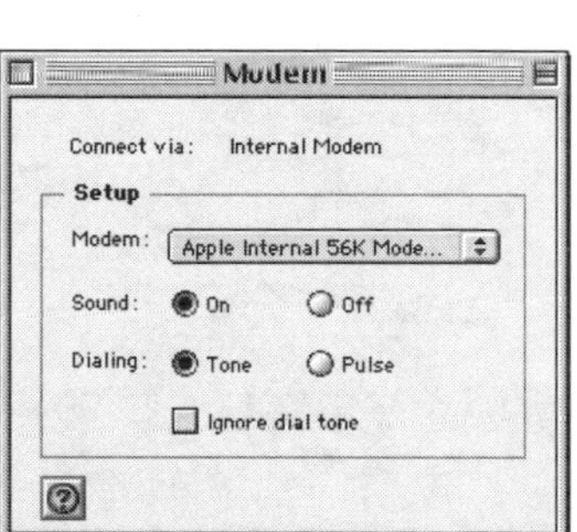

If your modem is internal, your Mac will know it.

Remote Access Control Panel

If America Online is your only Internet access, you don't need to open this control panel because AOL **is** *your telecommunications software!*

You need two things to connect to the Internet: a modem and some sort of telecommunications software. There are software packages you can buy for general telecommunications, but your Mac has provided you with Remote Access, which gets you connected to the Internet quite nicely. The **Remote Access control panel** used to be called PPP (which stands for point-to-point protocol) so if this looks familiar to you, it is.

If you went through the Mac Internet Setup Assistant (pages 361–368), the Remote Access control panel is already filled in with your settings. You only need to open this if you need to make individual changes in your settings, or if you are feeling like an Advanced User and want to make extra "configurations," or collections of settings, that you can apply with the click of a button. For instance, if you are traveling with a PowerBook and want to change the specifications for the hotel you're in, but you don't want to lose your home specs, you can make a new configuration while saving your old one.

You can also use this control panel to connect to the Internet. Generally, though, you'll use one of the other methods mentioned on page 369 to make the connection simply because they're quicker.

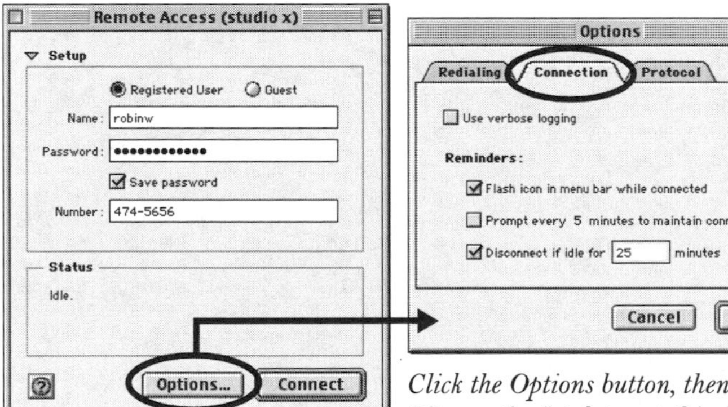

Sometimes your ISP will give you more than one phone number to use, in case one is busy. If so, you can replace the one that's typed in here, then connect to that new number (but keep both numbers written down in a safe place!).

Click the Options button, then click the "Connection" tab to get this dialog box. The default is to flash the icon in the menu bar while connected, which is a good reminder. This is where you can determine the amount of time Remote Access should wait until it automatically disconnects you from the Internet. If you choose a prompt, a dialog box will appear on your screen asking if you want to stay connected. If your voices are turned on, eventually you'll hear a man or lady read the message out loud to you. If that makes you crazy, see page 260.

To make other Remote Access configurations, go to the File menu and choose "Configurations...." To make a new configuration, click "Duplicate...," and name the new one. Its name will appear right in the dialog box you have open. If you click "Done," this dialog box will go away and the previous configuration will still be active. If you want this new one active so you can make changes to the specifications, click "Make Active."

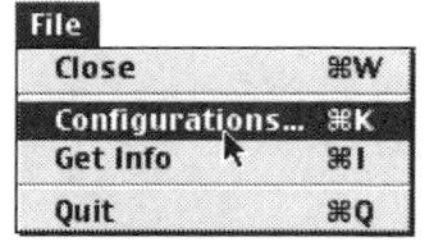

Use the RemoteAccess menu to call up each of the other control panels in which you might want to change specs. You can only get to DialAssist if you first change the User Mode to Advanced (use the Edit menu to do that). DialAssist lets you plug in different numbers for different parts of the world, or perhaps to use a calling card in a hotel room. You'll need it on a laptop, but rarely on your desktop computer.

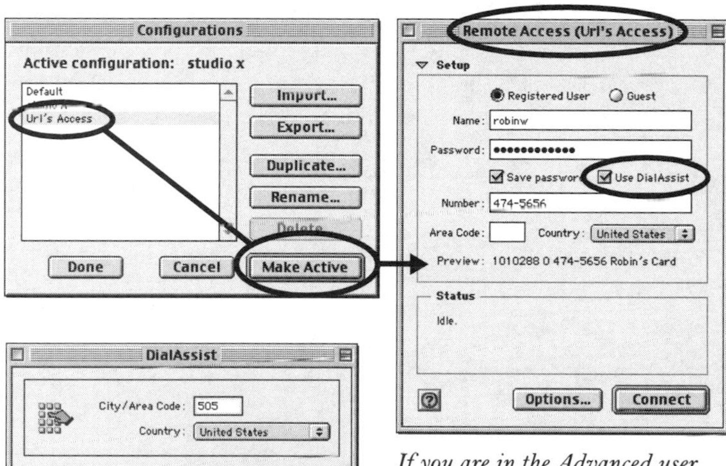

Each of the menus here in DialAssist can be customized if you click on their matching buttons. Check it out—it's quite self-explanatory.

If you are in the Advanced user mode, you'll be able to use DialAssist. Check the "DialAssist" checkbox if you want your connection process to use the numbers you set up in there.

If you travel with your Mac laptop, get The Little iBook Book, *even if you don't have an iBook. With that book you can get any Macintosh laptop connected anywhere in the world.*

TCP/IP Control Panel

The control panel called TCP/IP sounds and looks a little intimidating, but what TCP/IP does is actually quite interesting. You see, when we send an email message, in our minds we picture a little letter going through the phone lines and landing in someone else's computer. What actually happens is that the email message you write gets chopped up into little pieces called packets, all these packets go through the phone lines on different routes, and they're all put back together again at the other end. TCP is the layer of the program that divides the email file into the individual packets and numbers them. TCP then sends the packets to the IP layer of the program. The IP sends the packets on their way, sending each one in a different direction, and the packets stop at all kinds of computers along their paths, asking directions to make sure they're still going the right way. At the other computer, TCP puts all the packets back together again in the right order. Once they're all reassembled correctly, it sends the single file to your mailbox. Amazingly, the same thing happens to web pages coming to you. Once you see how busy and important these little TCP and IP workers are, this dialog box isn't so intimidating.

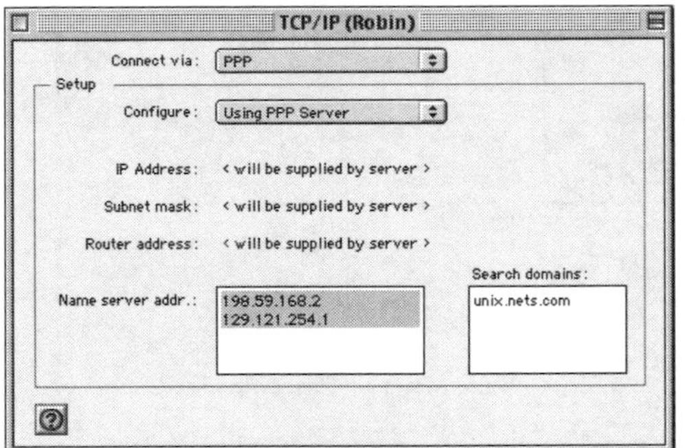

No one expects you to know what the correct choices are for this dialog box. Your ISP has to tell you these things. If you used the Internet Setup Assistant, this dialog box was filled out for you automatically with this information as you supplied it.

Open Transport

While trying to figure out this web sharing and Internet stuff, you may run across references to **Open Transport** or similar. The references sound very important, to the effect that things won't work unless you have this file. But if you try to search for the file, you will find all sorts of "Open Transport Library" and "About Open Transport" files, but no Open Transport itself. That's because there isn't one. Open Transport is the technology that makes TCP/IP work. If you open the TCP/IP control panel, then choose "Get Info" from the File menu, you'll see a version number in the info box. This is the version of Open Transport the documentation refers to.

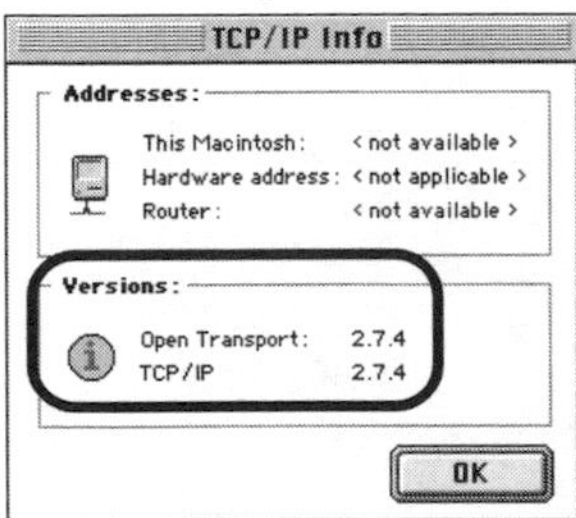

Personal Web Sharing

This is the Web Sharing control panel that enables other people to see your folder through the Internet or intranet.

You may have heard a lot of hoopla about Apple's **Personal Web Sharing.** The concept is that you can put a folder of items, including but not limited to web pages, on your Desktop, and anyone can see the files on *your* Desktop by using *their* browser at *their* computer. If the files are web pages, the other person can look at the web pages just like they look at any web site. If the files are text documents, the other person can read the text. Personal web sharing can go hand in hand with Apple's file sharing (see Chapter 27), with the added advantage that people who are not on your local network can view the files, and people who are using computers other than Macintosh can view the files.

The one most important aspect to understand about this technology is that it is meant for people who are either connected through a LAN (local area network, such as an entire office complex), or people who have a connection that stays on 24 hours a day, such as a DSL or cable connection.

If you use a modem and dial in to an Internet Service Provider, don't bother using Personal Web Sharing. For people to get to your web site through Personal Web Sharing, you have to be connected to the Internet (or your LAN) at the time the person tries to find your web pages, *and* you have to give them a special "IP address" (Internet Protocol, shown below) When you use a modem to dial in to a server, your IP address is different just about every time. The only way someone could get to the web sharing folder on your hard disk is if you connect to your service provider, open the Web Sharing control panel to turn on web sharing and see what the address is for that moment, call the person who wants to get to your folder, tell them the address, and have them connect to the Internet, enter the address, and get to your folder before your dial-up connection drops or you get disconnected for some reason.

A web address, or URL, is the address to a particular web page; an IP address is the address to a particular computer.

—continued

Web Sharing
Web Identity
My Address: http://slip11.nets.com
or http://198.59.168.111
Web Folder: Robin'sHardDisk:Robin's Web Site: Select...
Home Page: default.html Select...
Web Sharing On
Stop
Give everyone read-only access.
Use File Sharing to control user access.
Status
All documents in your shared folder are currently available to all users.

Above you see the IP address you must give someone who wants to connect to share your web folder.

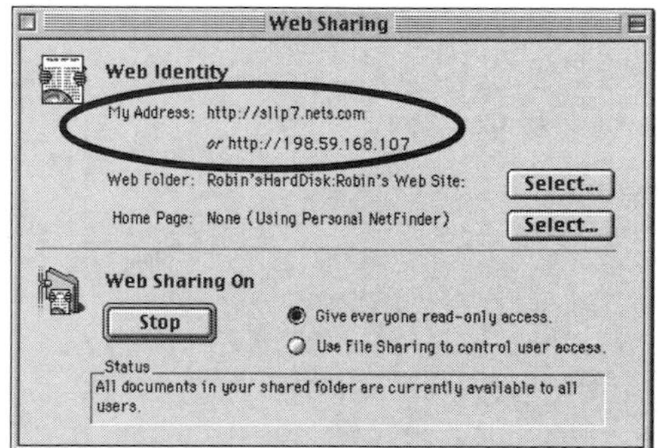

Here you can see that the IP address has changed because I got disconnected and had to log on again.

An intranet vs. the Internet

intra = within
inter = between

You might notice that most of the Apple documentation refers to Personal Web Sharing as "the easiest way to share your information with everyone on your **intranet,**" that you can make your pages "available to everyone in your **organization,**" and that you can "give your address to the people on your **intranet.**" An intranet is different from the Internet. An intranet is a closed network, usually computers within a single office or company that are all connected (networked) and that network is not available to outside viewers. It's possible for companies to have a network that spans states or countries or continents (a WAN, or wide area network), but what is on their intranet is still accessible only to privileged users. The reason Personal Web Sharing is best suited for an intranet is because the network is always on so your computer's IP address never changes.

The basic steps to Personal Web Sharing

Understanding the limitations of Personal Web Sharing, you might still want to do it, either to show a friend or client something over the Internet, or because you are connected to a LAN or a constant high-speed connection. There are many variables to this web sharing stuff, so the best thing to do is read the directions. Read the manual. Read the documentation that's probably installed on your hard disk with the rest of the Personal Web Sharing files (use Sherlock to search for "About Personal WebSharing," with "websharing" as one word). Basically, this is what to do:

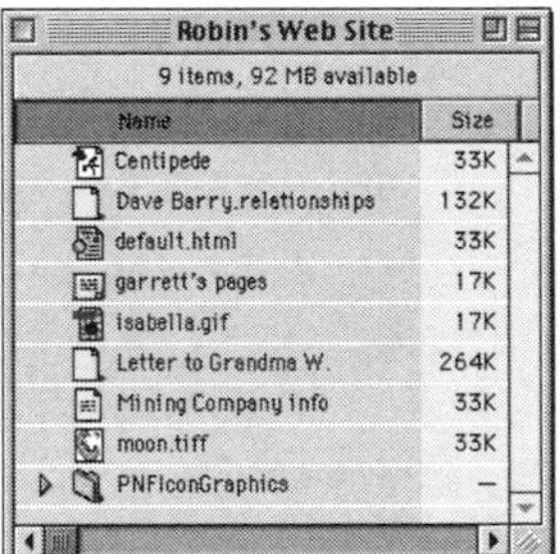

- Make a folder that will store the files (shown to the left).
- In this folder put the files you want to share, the web pages you want to post, or both (shown to the left).
- If your network connection is not already up and running, connect to it now.
- Open the Web Sharing control panel (shown below).
- Click the first "Select" button to tell Web Sharing which folder you want to share.
- Click the second "Select" button to tell Web Sharing the name of the web page you want to appear as the default, the home page. If you choose "None," then the visitor will see a list of the files in the folder (as shown on the next page).
- Click the "Start" button to start the web sharing process.

This is the Web Sharing control panel.

- Notice in the control panel there is a web address in the first line, "My address." Write it down—this is your **IP address,** the address of your computer where your shared file is stored. This is the address you give to anyone who wants to use their browser to surf over to your web site. If you see two addresses, use either one.

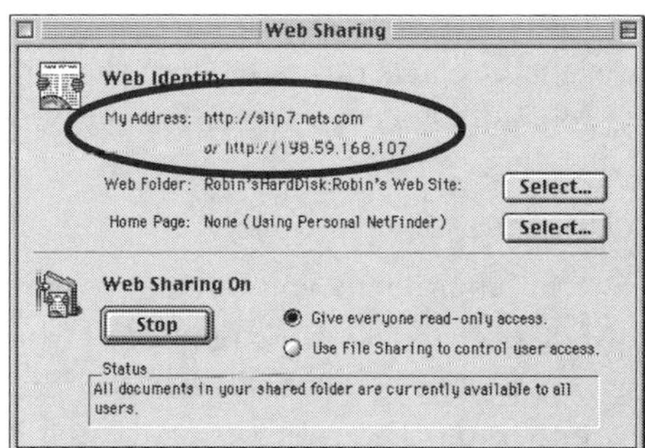

- If you chose a web page as the Home Page, then when a visitor gets to your folder that web page is what they will see in their browser. If you chose "None," they will see something like this:

You have to make a proper web page if you want to use one as a home page. If you are interested in making web pages, read ***The Non-Designer's Web Book,*** *by me and John Tollett.*

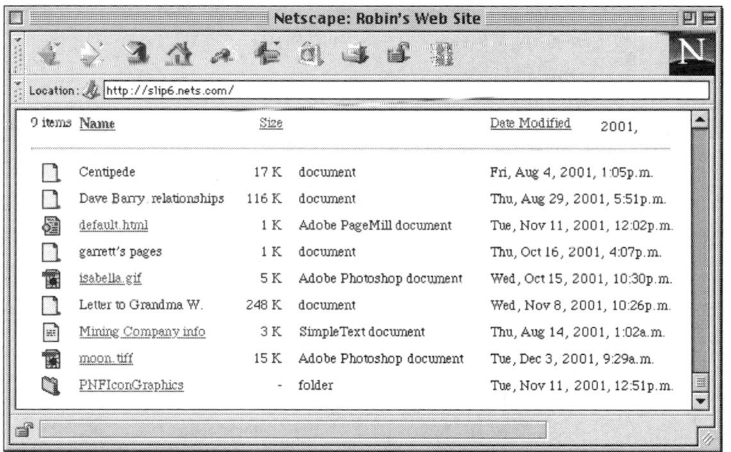

- The files that appear as links in this browser window will open to display the graphic or the text. The files that do not appear as links cannot be opened through the browser.

Important Note

If you experiment with serving a web page from your computer with a dial-up connection, you must remove the alias of the Web Sharing control panel from the Startup Items Folder in the System Folder when you're done. If you don't, every time you turn on your Mac the Web Sharing will try to kick in, causing potential problems. If you have trouble, restart, hold down the Spacebar until the Extensions Manager appears, then uncheck "Web Sharing" from the Startup Items Folder. Click "Continue."

What are These?

The System installs several icons on your Desktop. This is what they do:

If you double-click **Browse the Internet,** your Mac will try to connect to the Internet and open a browser. Don't click this until you have first set up your Internet connection! If you connect in a different way, such as from a menu item or by double-clicking something else, then toss this thing in the garbage (it's just an alias). If you like to use it, you can change the default browser that it opens through either the Internet control panel (page 372) or, if you don't have the Internet control panel, through Internet Config (pages 373–374).

The **Mail** icon represents a "script" that opens your email program for you. Its default is to open Microsoft Outlook Express, but you can change that if you prefer to open something else, such as Eudora. Change the default through either the Internet control panel (page 371) or, if you don't have the Internet control panel, through Internet Config (pages 373–374). Outlook Express is a great program to use if you want to see what newsgroups are all about.

Toss the Mail icon if don't think you'll ever use it. You will still be able to open your email program without it.

The **QuickTime Player** alias on your Desktop lets you play any QuickTime movies you have downloaded or that you find on your Desktop—just drag them on top of this icon and they will play. But first you'll get a stupid commercial that is really annoying, and if you click anything except "Later" you'll log on to the Internet and go to the web site. If you don't use this player alias very often, throw it away—you will still have the actual player in a folder for when you want it.

PictureViewer is great. Drag almost any graphic image onto it, including all the photos you get in your email, and PictureViewer will display them. And no commercials.

Register with Apple automatically disappears after you make an Internet connection with Apple and register your Mac. Because it's just an alias, you can throw it away until you need it, then get the original out of the Apple Extras folder (if you can't find it, use Sherlock).

Oh, this Internet stuff can be so confusing, especially to set it up, and there are so many variables. Don't forget about the Help files. They are often actually helpful. From the Help menu at the Desktop, choose "Mac Help," or press Command ?.

Use the Help Files!

Also, ***read the manual*** *that came with your computer or your new operating system (if you were lucky enough to get one). There is a lot of troubleshooting information in it.*

Click one of the headings in the left panel, and subheadings will appear in the right panel. Or type in a word or phrase at the top of the window, then click "Search."

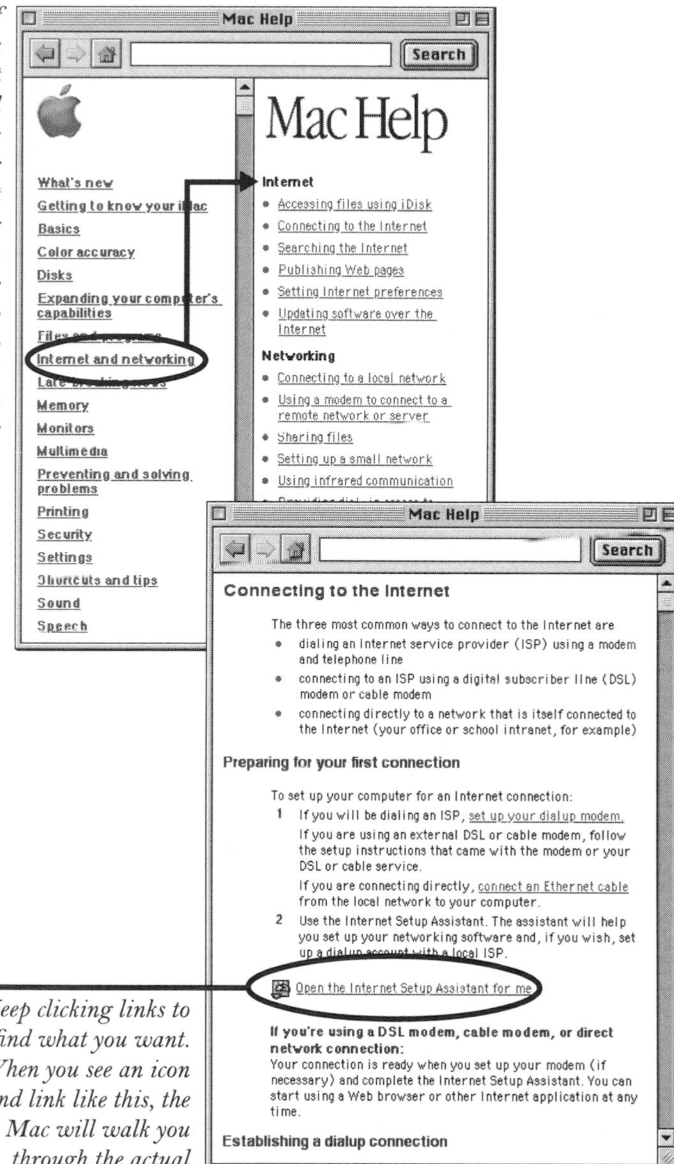

Keep clicking links to find what you want. When you see an icon and link like this, the Mac will walk you through the actual process. It's pretty neat.

Here are a few web addresses you might find handy. Web addresses have a habit of changing as soon as you print them in a book, so I've tried to give you only well-established sites that won't change. If they have changed and any of these addresses don't work, I apologize!

Apple	www.apple.com	
Adobe	www.adobe.com	
Netscape	www.netscape.com	[or click the Netscape icon in the upper-right of the browser]
Macintosh	www.macintouch.com www.maccentral.com www.macfixit.com	
Definitions	www.whatis.com	
Books (retail)	www.borders.com, barnesandnoble.com, www.amazon.com	
For Writers	www.bookwire.com	[inside the book world]
Family	www.parentsoup.com	
	www.family.com	
Movies	www.film.com, us.imdb.com, www.eonline.com	
Television	www.gist.com	
Sports	espn.com	
	www.cnnsi.com	[CNN and Sports Illustrated]
Travel	www.lonelyplanet.com	
	www.city.net	
Weather	www.accuweather.com	
Music	www.tunes.com	
Science	www.discovery.com	
	www.sciam.com	[Scientific American]
Games	www.gamesmania.com	
	www.bezerk.com	
Health	www.vh.org	[The Virtual Hospital]
	www.reutershealth.com	
Money	www.money.com	
Robin & John	www.UrlsInternetCafe.com	

Home Improvements Encyclopedia from Better Homes & Gardens
www.bhglive.com

To download freeware, shareware, and commercial software:
www.download.com
www.shareware.com

Deal with it.
Browser™

PART Four

Extra Stuff

This section contains a variety of useful pieces of information—pictures and descriptions of the ports on the back or side of your Mac, a collection of all the tips in the book (this might be the only chapter you read!), some Help tips, the quiz answers, the index, and some typographic charts.

34 Ports and Peripherals

This chapter describes those places on the back or side of your computer where you plug things in and the things you plug into them. You can spend years on your Mac without knowing the information in this chapter because one of the greatest things about the Mac is that if a cable fits into a port, it's the right match. It's not possible to plug something into the wrong place. So you don't really have to know anything about the back of your computer—it it fits, plug it in and move on. But when you get to the point where you want to know the difference between a SCSI port and a serial port and a USB port, then dive into this short chapter.

What is a Peripheral?

A **peripheral** is any item (or "device") that is outside of the main computer box, but attached to it. Your monitor (except for iMacs) is actually a peripheral device, and so is your mouse, keyboard, and printer. Scanners, CD writers, and external hard disks are peripherals. Devices that are internal (built in) on some machines might be external devices, or peripherals, on another. For instance, I have a little, lightweight PowerBook that has no built-in floppy drive, but it has an external floppy drive that I can attach when I need it, so that floppy drive is a peripheral. If you have a blue-and-white G3, it doesn't have a floppy drive either, but you can always add one as a peripheral. Some computers have built-in modems, others use modems as peripheral devices.

The main computer box is often called a CPU, although the CPU itself is actually a tiny chip in the middle of the main board (the motherboard) inside the box. So a CPU is not a peripheral. You might install a card, or plastic board with circuitry on it, inside of your computer to expand its capabilities, such as a video card or a modem card. Some people consider that the devices on those cards are also peripherals because they are added on, even though they are in the computer box. (But isn't "internal peripheral" an oxymoron?)

What is a Port?

A **port** is a socket, a kind of receptacle, on the back (or side, as on the iMac) of a computer or on the back of peripheral devices. The port is where you connect the peripheral device. A port is very different from a regular socket like the kind in the wall, in that information goes both ways through a port. A wall socket sends power in only one direction—*to* a device. A port sends information *back and forth* between the computer and the device.

There are lots of different kinds of ports, and peripherals are made to match a certain port type. For instance, you might have USB ports, to which you can only connect USB devices, such as USB printers. If you have serial ports instead of USB ports, you'll connect serial printers.

The cables that connect peripherals to the CPU (or to another peripheral) have **connectors** on the ends. The connectors match the ports. On a Mac, if the connector matches the port, it works. You can't plug a connector into the wrong port.

What is a Connector?

Connectors are the parts on the ends of the cables that actually make the connection to the other device. The connector is the part that tells you what kind of cable it is—an Ethernet cable has a very different connector from a serial cable, which is very different from a USB cable (as illustrated on the following pages).

Every connector is either male or female; take one look and you can guess why. The male or female shape is a very important identifying feature. When you start connecting lots of things together (like to project a presentation from the computer to a large wall screen), you will find yourself looking for either a male or female connector.

Another identifying feature of connectors are the pins, or slender metal prongs on the male versions (not all connectors have pins). The number of pins is particularly useful in describing what you need. For instance, I once needed a cable for a video card that I installed in my computer. I didn't know exactly what kind of cable I needed, so I counted the little pin holes and told the guy I needed a 15-pin connector and he thought I knew what I was talking about.

The shape is important. Some connectors are long and skinny, short and fat, rectangular or round, etc. Many connectors have identifying symbols that match the symbol on the port. On the next few pages are illustrations of the most common symbols that identify both the connectors and the ports.

What is an Expansion Slot?

On the back of your computer (not an iMac) you might see some larger, rectangular pieces that look like metal covers to openings. They are. Those are your **expansion slots;** the more slots you have, the more "expandability" your computer has.

You might buy an add-on like a video **card** for a second monitor. The card (also called a **board** or an **adapter**) is a flat, plastic piece with circuitry all over it and a port on one end. You open your computer box, and there are slots in the motherboard (the main board that runs the computer; of course it's a mother) where you stick this card in, usually perpendicular to the motherboard. You pop that rectangular metal piece out of the opening, and the port sticks out that end. Thus when you close the computer box, you have another port to which you can attach another peripheral.

You might get a game card, a video card with extra VRAM (video ram) just for your monitor, a modem card, or other sorts of boards to expand the capability of your Mac.

Note None of the iMac, iBooks, blue-and-white G3s, or G4s have ADB ports or serial ports—Apple switched over to a new system, the Universal Serial Bus, which replaces both ADB and serial (below). Also, there are no SCSI connections on newer Macs. So unless you have an older Mac, skip these two pages.

ADB Ports

This is what an ADB port looks like, and the symbol that identifies it.

ADB stands for Apple Desktop Bus. A *bus* is a system of hardware, software, and wiring that lets all the different parts of your computer communicate with each other. There are different kinds of buses, and the ADB is specifically for *input devices.* An input device includes those items you input information into the computer with, such as a keyboard, mouse, trackball, joystick, or drawing tablet.

So most commonly, the **ADB ports** are where you connect your keyboard and mouse. Many Macs have only one ADB port on the back of the machine, plus one or two ADB ports on the keyboard, so you plug the keyboard into the port on the back of the computer box and then plug the mouse into the keyboard.

Serial Ports

Printer and modem ports

This is what a serial port looks like (above), and the symbols that identify the two on your Mac (below).

A **serial port** is the little round one that looks similar to the ADB port, but it has more holes (to match the pins on the connector). There are two data wires in a serial cable, so the port can send and receive information at the same time.

There are usually two serial ports on the back of the Mac—one labeled with a little picture of a printer, and the other with a picture of a telephone. Although you can use either port for either a printer or a modem cable, the printer port is actually slightly different in that it is the Mac's **LocalTalk network port.** This just means it's faster and more complex than the modem port, and if possible you should plug your serial printer cable into that one and the serial modem into the other one, although either one will work.

Until very recently, almost all printers for the Mac were serial printers, which means they connect to the serial port. As mentioned above, the newer Macs don't have serial ports; they've been replaced with USB (see page 393).

SCSI Ports

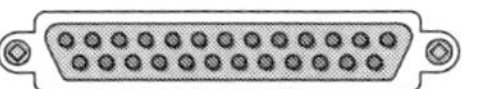

This is what a SCSI port on the back of your Mac looks like (above), and the symbol that identifies it (below), even if your port looks a little different from the one shown above.

SCSI (pronounced *scuzzy*, not *sexy*) stands for Small Computer Systems Interface, which is a standard for connecting personal computers to peripheral devices and having them send information to each other.

There is only one SCSI port on a Mac, but there are two on the back of every SCSI device, which are things like scanners, extra hard disks, or CD drives. The ones on the device itself might look different, much larger, from the one on the back of your computer.

You can *daisy chain* up to seven SCSI devices together; that is, you plug one SCSI device directly into the port on the computer, then hook the others to each other. To daisy chain SCSI devices, you need a cable that has two connectors that match the two connectors you are plugging into. For instance, a Zip drive uses the same connector as the Mac on both ends of its cable, but an older scanner might have two larger SCSI ports that are different from the SCSI port on the back of the Mac. So even though the ports on the two connecting parts are different, you can get cables with a different port on each end.

Each device on the chain has to be pre-set to a different SCSI address. Look on any SCSI device and you'll see a tiny set of changeable numbers —that's the SCSI address. And SCSI devices have to be *terminated;* that is, the last device in the chain has to have a little stopper put in the second port because the data goes in one port and out the other and gets confused if it finds an empty port. Some manufacturers use internal termination, which is great except it can limit the way devices are connected, and you have to *know* that device is internally terminated, which means you have to read the manual and Mac users are famous for not reading manuals (I'm surprised you're even reading this).

SCSI devices are infamous for being unpredictable—sometimes they don't work in one configuration of connections and termination, but they work if you just plug things in differently or if you turn them on in a different order. SCSI devices often refuse to mount, so often that there is a special little utility that most Mac users have called SCSIProbe to force them to mount. If you have SCSI devices, get SCSIProbe from the Internet at www.download.com or www.shareware.com. You can keep it anywhere on your hard disk—it doesn't have to be in any special folder to work.

Ethernet Ports

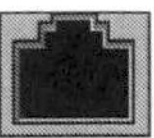

This is what an Ethernet port looks like, and the symbol that identifies it.

Ethernet (pronounced *eether-net*) is the most common networking system for local area networks (LANs), which means the computers that are connected together are close enough to be connected with cables (as opposed to a wide area network, a WAN). All newer Macs have Ethernet ports, which look like large phone jacks. You can use Ethernet even in your home or small office to connect several computers so you can send files back and forth.

This is the port for an internal modem. Don't get it confused with the larger Ethernet port.

You might also have a modem port for your internal modem, which looks exactly like a phone jack (because it is), so don't get it confused with the Ethernet port. The Ethernet port is larger than the internal modem port. (If your modem is external, you'll plug it into the serial modem port.)

Your printer might have an Ethernet port, in which case you can send data to the printer much faster than through the serial port. Even if it doesn't have an actual Ethernet port, you can get adapters for some printers so you can add the printer to your Ethernet network.

AAUI Ports

This is what an AAUI port looks like, and the symbol that identifies it.

The AAUI port (which stands for Apple Adapter Unit Interface) takes a variety of adapters for different networking systems, but the symbol for its port is the same as the symbol for an Ethernet port because Ethernet has become the most commonly used local area network. As explained in Chapter 27 on Sharing Files, you can get an Ethernet adapter for this port so you can connect this computer to one that has an actual Ethernet port.

FireWire Ports

This symbol identifies a FireWire port.

FireWire is Apple's trademarked version of the standard called IEEE 1394. It's a high-performance serial bus (see the description of a bus in the ADB explanation on page 390) for connecting up to 63 devices through one port on your Mac. FireWire is only built into the newer Macs, like the 1999 blue-and-white G3s and up.

You might hear the FireWire ports called IEEE, but IEEE actually stands for the professional society, Institute of Electrical and Electronics Engineers, and the IEEE is a standard they developed. For instance, the Ethernet standard is IEEE 802.3.

The big deal about FireWire is this: It's extremely fast; you can connect 63 devices in any which way you like, such as in a star or tree pattern, and up to 16 in a single chain; you can swap them in and out without having to turn off the computer; they connect with a simple snap-in cable; and there's no termination necessary (see the SCSI explanation for termination). FireWire replaces the serial connection.

You can connect a vast array of consumer electronics to FireWire, such as digital cameras, video tapes, and camcorders, as well as DVD (digital video disk), plus hard disks, optical disks, and printers.

USB Ports

This drawing shows two USB ports, and the symbol that identifies USB.

The **USB ports** are on Macs built since late 1998. USB stands for Universal Serial Bus, which replaces both the Apple Desktop Bus and the serial ports, as described on page 390. With USB, input devices and printers can all connect into the same ports.

You can't daisy chain USB devices, like you can the SCSI devices mentioned on page 391, but you can buy a hub (shown to the right). The hub connects into one of the USB ports on the Mac, and several devices can plug into the hub. You can connect another hub to the first one, and so on, so you can actually connect up to 127 USB devices to one Macintosh. I don't know why you would, but you could.

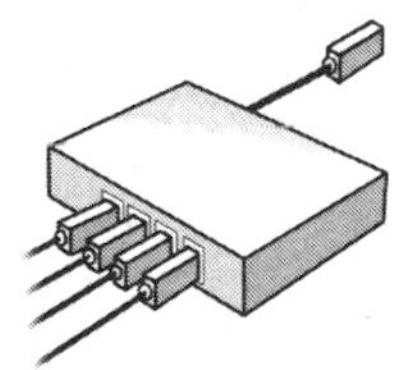

This is a USB hub. The one connector goes into the computer's port, and the other connectors lead to extra devices.

Also check the base of your monitor—you might find USB ports there, which is a great convenience.

One of the most convenient things about USB devices is that you can "hot swap" them; that is, you can connect and disconnect devices such as keyboards, mice, Zip drives, printers, or scanners without having to shut down the computer like you do with SCSI, serial, and even ADB devices.

PCI Bus and Slots

PCI (Peripheral Component Interconnect) is yet another bus system. A bus, as I mentioned earlier, is a system of hardware, software, and wiring that lets different parts of your computer communicate with each other. There are different kinds of buses, and PCI is focused on the expansion slots, which are described on page 389. PCI is now installed on most desktop computers, so if your computer was built in 1998 or later, it has PCI (except if it's an iMac—there is no PCI in an iMac). If your machine doesn't have PCI, it has what's called NUBUS, Apple's previous technology.

When you read the specifications for a computer, it often brags about how many PCI slots it has. The more, the better if you plan to expand.

PC Slots and PC Cards

Most laptop computers, as well as other devices like digital cameras, have **PC slots** into which you slip **PC cards.** You might have heard these slots and cards referred to as PCMCIA, but that term is now limited to the association itself (the Personal Computer Memory Card International Association) and the cards and slots are simply called PC cards and slots.

PC cards are *really* little, as small as credit cards or half a stick of gum. There are a variety of PC cards for a variety of purposes. You can get cards for a cellular phone interface, Ethernet, a global positioning system, a hard drive, joystick, memory, a modem, sound input and output, video capture, and much more. Cards that contain TV tuners, video teleconferencing, AM/FM radio tuners, and even CPUs (the CPU is the powerful chip that runs the entire computer) are available or in the works.

Unlike expansion slots, as explained on page 389, PC slots are accessible from the outside of the computer; like expansion slots, the purpose is to allow expanded capabilities. The slot, or socket, typically has a little flapping door covering the empty space where you slip in the card. Peek inside—you might actually have two sockets for two different cards.

35 Tips and More Tips

This is a collection of some of the tips or important notes that are embedded in the rest of the book, as well as any other hints or fascinating bits of information or shortcuts that haven't been mentioned. Nothing is software-specific; it all relates to the general Mac environment. The page number in the tip indicates where more information on that tip can be found.

Word Processing

To replace highlighted text, just type. p.133

To delete forward while typing, use the del key. p.67

While typing, the insertion point picks up the formatting of the character to its left—font, style, size, alignment, and ruler settings—so load the insertion point *before* you type. p.136

To remove all the styles attached to characters (bold, italic, shadowed, etc.), select the text and choose Plain or Normal. p.136

To place accent marks over letters, use the Option characters. p.140

To use special characters, use Key Caps. pp.141, 216–217

You can still type numbers while Caps Lock is down. p.62

Use the Shift and arrow keys to select text. p.66

Type only one space between sentences! p.132

Type the euro symbol in certain fonts. p.442

Windows

To make a window active, click on any visible part. p.71

To move a window without making it active, hold the Command key while you press-and-drag any edge or the title bar. p.71

To switch the organization of a list view, click another column header. p.78

To resize the column headers, drag their edges. p.81

To rearrange the columns, drag the headers. p.81

To move the contents of the window around, Command-drag inside the window. p.83

To view the list by name yet still see the individual icons, use the View Options from the View menu and choose the middle-sized icon. p.78

To put the application at the top of a window list so it's easy to find, view By Kind. p.80

To close the active window, press Command W. p.72

To close every window, press Command Option W, or press the Option key and click in the active window's close box. p.72
In Mac OS 9.1, hold down the Command and Option keys, go to the Window menu, and choose "Desktop." p. 82

Double-click in the title bar to roll up window, or click in the collapse box. p.72

To collapse every window on the Desktop or in an application, press the Option key and click in the active window's collapse box, or Option–double-click the title bar of any window. p.83

To keep windows open without taking any Desktop space, make pop-up windows. p.77

To make a window close up behind you, hold down the Option key while opening folders. p.72

To make palettes in applications roll up (collapse), be sure to turn on the double-click title bar option in the Appearance control panel. p.83

To make sure all previously left-open windows are closed when you open a disk, hold down the Option key while inserting a disk or just before the Mac gets to your Desktop when starting up. p.83

To open a window as large as possible, press Option while you click the zoom box. p.71

To view the hierarchy of a nested folder, hold the Command key down and press on the title of the window. p.85

To print the contents of the active window, choose "Print Window" from the File menu. p.88

To print a picture of a window, make a screen shot of it and paste it into a document or print it from SimpleText. p.89

To organize icons in a window, from the View menu choose "Arrange." p.78

To organize the icons into the invisible grid, press the Command key as you drag them in window. p.78 If your icons are set to "Always snap to grid," then hold the Command key down when you move them and they *won't* snap to grid. p.78

To sort the items in a list in the opposite direction, click the Sort Order button. p.81

To create default settings you can apply to every window, use the Finder Preferences. p.79

To select a button while in Button view, click once on the name, or drag around the button with the pointer. p.76

Spring open a window, drop a file in, and let the window close automatically. pp.84, 109

To spring open a window even if the spring-loaded feature is turned off, use the Spacebar. pp.84, 109

To burrow down through nested folders, use a click-and-a-half. p.84

Folders and Files

To expand a folder, press Command RightArrow. p.109

To compress a folder, press Command LeftArrow. p.109

To compress all the folders that are expanded, press Command A to select all, then press Command LeftArrow. p.109

To select items from more than one folder at a time, expand the folders. pp.109, 118

To select a file in a window, just type the first letter or several letters of the name of the file. p.117

To select an icon that is alphabetically after the currently selected icon, press Tab. To select the icon that is alphabetically *before* the currently selected icon, press Shift-Tab. p.117

To force the selected file name to appear toward the top of the list window, press the End key before you type the first letter of the file name. p.118

To select files in windows use arrow keys, edit keys, the Tab key, and letters. pp.117–118

To select the name of an icon faster so you can rename it, type the first letter or two of the icon to select it, then press Return. p.107

To spring-open a folder without double-clicking it, hover the file over the folder. pp.84, 109

To spring-open a folder instantly, press the Spacebar while holding a file over the folder. pp.84, 109

To spring-open a folder without a file on the end of your pointer, use a click-and-a-half. pp.84, 107

To undo a file name change, press Command Z. p.97

Use Sherlock to find files you are too lazy to dig for. pp.119, 274

To color your file icons, use the Labels command from the File menu. p.100

To customize your file icons, use Get Info. p.98

To put files back where they came from, press Command Y. pp.96,122

Documents

To open a document, drag the icon and drop it on top of its application icon. pp.94, 128

To open an unknown document, drag the icon over the top of all your applications or aliases of your applications. The application icon that highlights will usually open the document. pp.94, 128

If you change your mind about the changes you just made in a document, close it and don't save those changes; when you reopen it, the document will have reverted to the last-saved version. p.147

To make several versions of a document, use "Save As." p.146

To make a template out of any document, called a stationery pad, use the Get Info box. pp.103, 147

Desktop

To be really mean and change someone's Desktop font to Zapf Dingbats or 36 point Symbol, use the Appearance control panel. p.250

Clean up the Desktop. pp.40, 68

To print everything on the Desktop, choose "Print Desktop" from the File menu. p.76

To make the Desktop level active, press Command Shift UpArrow. p.75

Create your own Desktop patterns and add your own photos. p.229

Disks: floppy and cartridge hard disks

To eject a floppy disk and to unmount CDs and cartridges, press Command Y. p.174

To eject a stuck disk that didn't come out when the computer was turned off, hold the mouse button down while you turn the machine back on. p.177

To eject a disk as a last resort, use a paper clip. p.177

To help organize the content on disks, or to put the contents of a disk in hierarchical menus in your Apple menu, use aliases. p.268

Aliases

To make an alias, select a file and press Command M. p.269

To make an alias without the word "alias" on the end, Command-Option-drag to another folder or to the Desktop. p.269

To find the original of an alias, select the alias and press Command R, or Control-click on it and choose "Show Original." p.269

To make an alias of a file from Sherlock, Command-Option-drag the file to the Desktop. p.275

To put an alias into the Apple menu, use the "Automated Task" from the Apple menu. p.229

Use aliases to keep track of files that you keep stored on removable disks. p.269

Apple Menu

Organize your Apple menu. p.231–233

Organize your Favorites in the Apple menu. p.228

To put an alias of an item in the Apple menu, use an Automated Task. p.229

To eliminate any of the "Recent" items in the Apple menu, use the Apple Menu control panel. p.234–235

Printing

Use Get Info to get information about the printer. p.165

Create a PostScript file of a document. p.162

To print a PICT, EPS, or a JPEG, drag its icon and drop it on top of the printer icon. It will print without opening any application. p.164

To prevent the toner from flaking off of special paper and to make the toner nice and dark, spray the printed page lightly with a spray fixative, available at office supply and art supply stores. Do not put the sprayed paper back through the printer!

Sounds

To make your own sounds, use the Sound control panel and click the Alerts button or tab. p.255

To hear a sound when you reach the Desktop on startup, place a sound into your Startup Items folder. pp.189, 255

To hear a sound when you shut down, place a sound into your Shutdown Items folder. pp.189, 255

Listen to audio CDs through your Macintosh CD drive. p.215

To tell that man or lady to shut up so they'll stop reading (or singing) the alert messages to you, use the Speech control panel. p.260

Trash

To put any file or selection of files in the trash, Control-click on it (or on one of the selection) and choose "Move to Trash." Or press Command Delete. p.122

To throw away a locked file, hold down the Option key when you choose "Empty Trash." p.123

To avoid the trash warning box, hold down the Option key while trashing the item. p.123

To permanently remove the trash warning, uncheck the "Warn before emptying" box in the Get Info window. p.123

To empty the trash, Control-click on the trash can and choose "Empty Trash." p.123

To empty the trash in Mac OS 9.1, press Command Shift Delete; you don't need to select the trash can.

Launcher

Create your own categories on the Launcher, p.249.

Drag-and-drop files onto the Launcher to create new buttons, p.248

To remove items from the Launcher, Option-drag them to the Desktop or trash can. pp.248, 249

Trouble

To unfreeze the screen, try a "force quit." pp.63, 411

To restart after you crash without having to turn off the power, use the Restart button. p.411 On the original bondi-blue iMacs, use a paperclip; on the colorful iMacs, press the restart button. p.411 On some G4 towers, hold down the Power button on the tower for five seconds to turn off the machine; press the Power button again to reboot.

To get rid of the pesky message telling you to insert the missing disk, try typing Command Period. p.175

To open the Extensions Manager on startup so you can turn off certain extensions, hold down the Spacebar when you restart. p.258

A diamond symbol in the Application menu means that program needs to tell you something, something not good. p.167

Allocate more memory to the application if you are always running out of memory in a particular program. p.327

Miscellaneous

Use the Return key to activate default buttons. pp.63

Press Command Period to activate Cancel button. p.58

Use keyboard shortcuts while navigating dialog boxes. p. 64, 318

Use the mouse left-handed. p.47

Shut Down with the Power key or button. p.67, 181

Change the Power button on some Macs so it becomes a Sleep button, and vice versa. p. 262

To open any desk accessory, wherever it is stored, double-click on it. p.223

To see what applications are still running, check the Application menu. pp.171, 325

To create your own puzzle, see p.219

Three dots (the ellipsis, ...) after a menu item indicates that you will get a dialog box when you choose that item. p.58, 332

To connect to a shared computer quickly, use an alias of the file server icon. p.306

To view a PICT graphic, open the Jigsaw Puzzle (from the Apple menu) and drag the PICT icon onto the Jigsaw Puzzle. p.219

To print a PICT, EPS, or JPEG, drag its icon and drop it on the active printer icon (the one with the heavy, black border). p.164

Application Menu

Don't forget you can choose to "Hide Others" from the **Application menu** to hide all the windows from the other programs that are running and that are visible from the Desktop.

If you hold down the Option key as you choose an application from the Application menu, all other windows in the current program will automatically hide. Also, if you hold down the Option key and click on the Desktop, all other application windows will be hidden when you arrive at the Finder.

Tear off the Application menu to create the Application Switcher palette. Press Command Tab or Shift Command Tab to switch between programs. Use the Option trick (above) in the palette.

Tab to Select

In any dialog box that contains boxes for you to fill in, press the **Tab key** to move the selection from box to box. If there is data already in the box, that data will be highlighted and anything you type will replace it (you don't have to delete it first). If there is no data in the box, the Tab key will set the insertion point there, ready for you to type.

Screen Savers

You may have heard about or own a **screen saver** whose job is to help avoid screen burn, where an image gets burned into the screen by being visible for too long. A screen saver usually turns the screen black or colors and has images that constantly move, like shooting stars or geometric shapes or flying toasters. As soon as you move the mouse or touch a key it disappears. Unfortunately, screen savers are one of the biggest culprits of causing things to go wrong on your computer. If you use a screen saver and experience any sort of glitches, the first troubleshooting technique you should try is disabling your screen saver. With today's monitors, there is no longer any risk of screen burn.

Get Info

The **Get Info** box displays different information depending on what you select. These are some of the things you can do in Get Info:

Put comments in a Get Info box for future reference. p.274, 286
Find out the version numbers of software. p.107
Increase the memory allocation for a program. p.327
Change the icon of a file. p.98
Make a stationery pad (template). p.103
Find out what sort of a file an icon represents. p.223
Turn off the trash warning. p.123
Lock a document so no one can change the information in it. p.103

You can also find out this information from the Get Info box:

How large a folder is.
The total numbers of files contained within a folder (including all the files within folders within folders, etc.).
How big your hard disk is and how many files are on it.
What zone a shared printer is in.
Where the original of an alias is stored.

Real Quotation Marks and Apostrophes!

“ and ”
‘ and ’
not " and '

It's easy to make the mistake of using inch and foot marks in place of **real quotation marks** and **apostrophes.** Yes, on the typewriters we grew up with (or that your keyboard teachers grew up with) we used those marks, but we are no longer using typewriters. Also, we are attempting to come close to professional type, and you never see inch and foot marks used as quotation marks in professional type. Unfortunately, these marks are not located in an obvious spot, so you won't know they're there unless somebody tells you. So I'll tell you:

To type this mark:	Press these keys:
“	Option [
”	Option Shift [
‘	Option]
’	Option Shift]

Most software applications now have a checkbox you can check so the real quotation marks and apostrophes appear automatically. Look in your Preferences or Options dialog boxes. It will say something like “Typographer's quotes,” “Smart quotes,” or something similar. It's important to know how to type them manually, however, so you can put them in the proper place in words like ’90s or rock ’n’ roll.

Contextual Menus

Contextual menus are called thus because the context of the menu varies depending on what you click. Experiment. Hold down the Control key (not the Command key!) and click on items. You'll notice these sorts of things when you click on:

- The trash can: Empty the trash (when there's something in it).
- A desktop printer: Start and stop documents in the printing queue, or set the selected file as the default printer.
- A document: Move it to the trash, Get Info on it, color it with a label, make an alias, duplicate it, or open it.
- In a blank spot in a Window: Share the folder whose window this is, make a new folder inside this window, close it, change the view, arrange the items, Get Info, and more.
- An alias: All the expected things, plus Show Original.

This contextual menu from Tools & Toys lets you have contextual menus without having to hold down the Control key—you just click on the item.

Lots of third parties* are making contextual menus that you can add to your system, as shown to the left. You can download these new files from the Internet (try www.shareware.com). Drop them on your System Folder, restart, and they work. There's no telling what they will be able to do!

Apple is the first party; they* ***make* *the computers and the operating system. You are the second party; you* ***use*** *the computer and operating system. Other people who* ***make things for you to use*** *on your computer are the third party.*

Disable Extensions

Occasionally you may find the need to **disable the system extensions** you have installed. You might do this because one of them is causing problems and you have to get it out but you can't take it out while it's working. Or you want them all off because you need to install new software.

To prevent all extensions from loading: Hold the **Shift key** down when you turn on your Mac or restart, and *none of your extensions will start up (load)*. Keep the Shift key down until you see the message, "Extensions Disabled." This is an all-or-nothing deal. If you have lots of extensions, you may want to get one of the utilities that manage these startup documents.

To selectively turn off extensions at startup: Hold down the **Spacebar** instead of the Shift key when you restart; keep it down until you see *Extensions Manager.* You can turn off just the extensions you think may be causing trouble. If in doubt, choose the set "Mac OS 9.x base" to allow just the extensions that enable the system to be fully functional. Close the Extensions Manager to continue booting.

The "x" in "OS 9.x" is just a substitute for whatever number you might see on your System.

Rebuilding Your Desktop

You may start to notice that your hard disk slows down after a few months. One reason for this is there's an invisible file that keeps track of all the icons that have ever been seen on your Desktop, even if you just opened disks to see what was on them! There is a way to **rebuild your Desktop** and remove all the unnecessarily stored information. Follow these steps every couple of weeks:

1. From the Special menu choose "Restart."
   Or you could do this next time you start up.
2. As your Mac starts up, hold down the Command and Option keys.
3. Hold down those keys until you see this dialog box:

4. Click OK (*or* simply hit the Return key).

Rebuild floppy disk and removable cartridge hard disk desktop files the same way: hold the Command and Option keys down while inserting a disk, until you see the above dialog box.

Rebuilding the Desktop fixes an amazing number of problems. I've noticed whenever I have problems printing, I rebuild the Desktop and everything works fine again. Don't ask me why.

Tip: *I usually hold down the Shift key in addition to the Command and Option keys when I rebuild the Desktop. The Shift key prevents the extensions from loading, which makes the process faster and cleaner. Then when I finally get to the Desktop again, I restart once more with no keys down so my extensions can load.*

How Much RAM?

Do you want to know how much RAM any program you are running is actually using from the amount allotted to it?

- At the Desktop, choose "Show Balloons" from the Help menu.
- From the Apple menu, choose "About this Macintosh…."
- Position the pointer over the bar representing the memory allocation and a balloon will appear with the information.

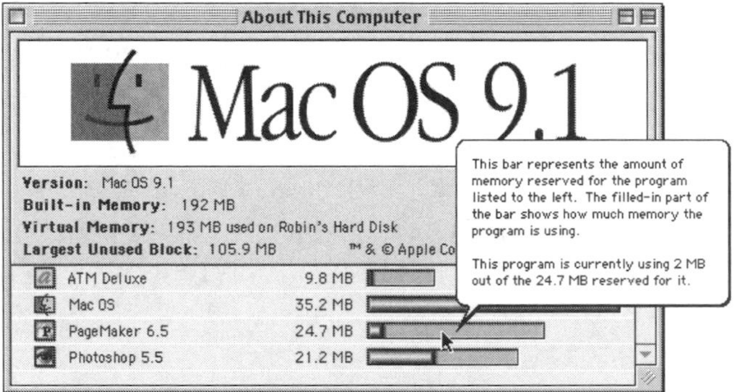

Checking Your Fonts at the Desktop

To see **what fonts are in the System** while you are at your Desktop, from the Apple menu choose "Key Caps." A new menu item will appear in your menu bar: Fonts. Press on it to see your font list. See pages 216–217 for more information about Key Caps.

Easter Eggs!

An **Easter Egg** is a surprise hidden in a program, a surprise created by the programmers. An example is at the Desktop: hold down the Option key and go to the Apple menu. The first item in the menu, the one that usually says, "About This Computer," now says "About The Finder." Choose it and you'll get a lovely image, which was the image for the original Mac (but now it's in color). Wait about ten seconds and you'll see a scrolling list of the developers of the Macintosh.

Lots of programs have Easter Eggs. QuarkXPress has a violent little creature that marches out and blasts objects off your page: select an object, then press Command Option Shift K.

My favorite Easter Egg is an old one, but still my favorite. It's in the word processor called WriteNow, from WordStar. If you have this application, open it. From the Apple menu, choose "About WriteNow." Hold down the Option key and click on the info window. It's the best.

A bunch of little people run all over the place rearranging the letters in the credits.

Aaack!! HELP!

36

This list doesn't pretend to be an all-inclusive reference for every sort of catastrophe that may befall; rather, it is a compilation of the most common, simple problems one may encounter when first beginning to work on a Macintosh, and their most common, simple solutions.

The Help Menu

You've surely noticed by now the Help item in your menu bar. This is actually quite a useful resource for all kinds of questions, not just for your Mac but for many of your applications. The question mark icon you see in many control panels is a direct link to the same Help files you can get from the Help menu. Also in the Help menu you see an option to "Show Balloons," which are sometimes useful (often not). Let's take a look at the ways this Help menu can offer you answers.

Apple's Help Guide

Apple installed a Help guide in your Mac. If you haven't removed it or turned off the Apple Guide extension, then it should be working. You can access it in several ways:

- At the Desktop, choose "Help" from the Help menu.
- At the Desktop, press Command ?
- Whenever you see a question mark icon (shown to the left), click on it.

Wherever you see these icons, click on them to get the help files for that topic.

The guide is very easy to use and quite self-explanatory. Sometimes the information is really great; sometimes it's not so great. Sometimes they leave out steps that are very important. As you use it, watch for the big red circle it draws around the items it wants you to pay attention to or do something with.

Check the Help menu in your applications

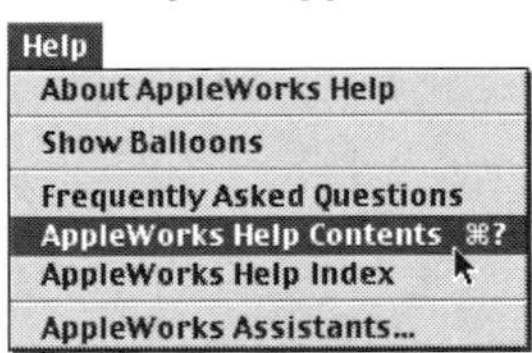

Many applications now have great and extensive help files. Often you can press Command ? and you'll get a big question mark cursor, then use that question mark to click on menu items or dialog boxes and get the specific help section for that item. Try it in your favorite application.

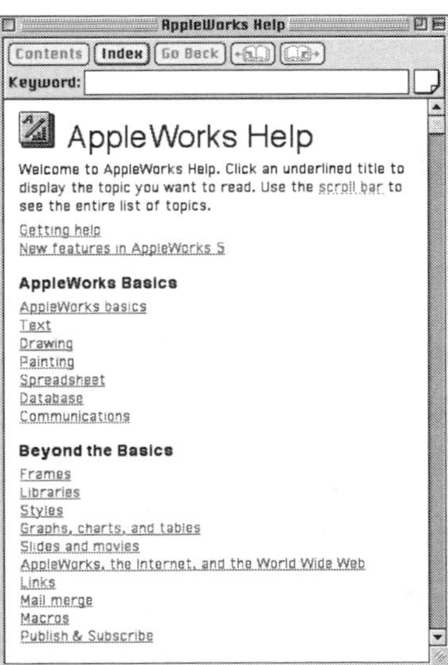

If Command ? doesn't work, try the Help menu (as shown to the far left) to get the application's help files (shown to the left). Anything you see underlined is a link to more information; click the link to go to that information. You'll usually find buttons like "Index," "Contents," or "Topics," and edit boxes where you can enter "Keywords" to find something in particular. Click them, type what you are looking for, click a link, etc., and you'll be amazed at what you can learn.

Balloon Help

Balloon Help is available not only on the Desktop, but in just about any application.

- From the Help menu, choose "Show Balloons."
- Now move your cursor over the screen and see what pops up. Some applications have incorporated Balloon help right in the program so you can slide down menu lists or palettes and get balloons for commands. Not all applications use balloons.
- To turn off the Balloons, from the Help menu choose "Hide Balloons."

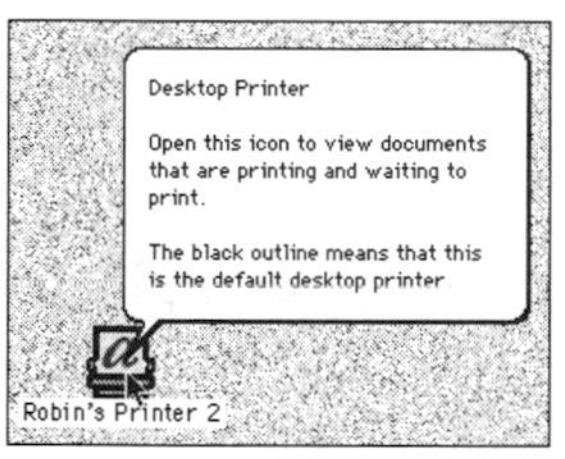

Sometimes the balloons provide useful information.

Huh? Sometimes they are not so helpful.

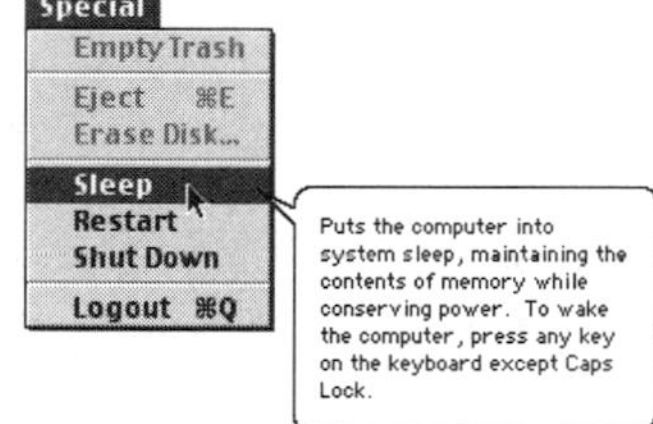

Try balloons in menu items, both at the Desktop and in your favorite application.

Computer Doesn't Turn On

If the **computer doesn't turn on at all**, check *all* your switches and plugs. When a switch is labeled **I** or **O,** the **I** means **On.**

- If you have a floor surge-protector bar with an on-off switch, it may have been kicked to the *off* position—make sure it is *on.*
- If you have any other devices attached to your computer, such as a scanner, hard disk, or CD player, sometimes they must be turned on first or sometimes they need to be turned on in a specific order. Try changing the order.

There used to be other things that could prevent a Mac from turning on, but if you're using Mac OS 9, you don't have one of the older machines or older problems.

You see the Question Mark, the Flashing X, or the Sad Mac on Startup

The Happy Mac. We like this guy.

The flashing question mark.

The flashing X.

The Sad Mac, better than the Dead Mac.

Ideally, when you start the computer you see the **Happy Mac.** This means all is well. Sometimes, though, you may see another icon, like the image of a disk with a flashing **question mark.** This is a visual clue that the Mac cannot find the System Folder. The System Folder *must* contain the System file and Finder file. If you are using an external hard disk, make sure the hard disk unit itself is turned on and is up and running, and make sure any extra switches are also on. If there are any other devices attached to the computer, they sometimes have to be turned on first. When you start attaching a lot of things to a Mac, they start getting fussy about the order they're turned on.

The disk with a **flashing X** means the Mac found the disk you thought was a startup disk, but it really isn't a startup disk. There may even have been a System on it, but the Mac can't use it. Try your other startup disk (next page).

The icon you really don't want to see is the **Sad Mac.** This means there is something really wrong and you probably need your power user friend to help you figure it out. Even more serious is when the Sad Mac shows up on a black screen (rather than gray or colored or patterned) and plays the Chimes of Doom for you. On the black background, it looks like a **Dead Mac.** I, personally, have heard the Chimes of Doom six times in my life, although it has been years since I've heard them.

Startup disk

Always keep the original CD for the operating system because it is made to be used as an emergency startup disk for those times when, for whatever reason, your computer won't boot. You can usually at least boot from this disk (if not, you have a more serious problem), and then take a look at your System Folder and perhaps find something obviously wrong, like a Finder missing. You can trash corrupted fonts or files, remove extensions, and even reinstall your System.

To force the Mac to boot from the CD, put the CD in the drive, restart (see below), and instantly hold down the letter C key and keep it held down. You can tell if the CD is running the machine because its icon will be in the top-right corner instead of your normal hard disk.

Screen Freezes

Occasionally the computer screen just **freezes.** The pointer may move around, but you can't click anything and it doesn't respond to the keys. If you can hear your hard disk chugging away, the Mac might have just gotten hung up on something—wait a minute or two, and don't click on a bunch of stuff because then the computer will try to do those tasks as well. If it lasts more than two or three minutes, it's got a problem. Sometimes static electricity can cause this, or a conflict inside your Mac, or sometimes it happens when the computer runs out of memory. You can try pressing Command Period, but it rarely helps.

Force quit

What is sometimes effective, though, is a **force quit.** Press Command Option Escape (esc). You will get a dialog box asking if you really want to force the application to quit. Well, you have no choice. Anything you had not saved in that application when you force quit is lost.

> If the message warns you that you are quitting the **Finder,** *don't click OK because the Finder is what runs your Desktop—* if you quit the Finder you won't be any better off than before.

If the force quit in your application actually works, it's a good idea to save and quit in all other open applications and then restart. If force quit doesn't work and everything is still frozen, Restart . . .

Restart after a Crash

Restart: hold down the Command and Control keys, and push the Power key (the big one at the top with the triangle on it). This is safer for your computer than turning the power off and on. Some newer towers don't have a Power key: press the Power button and hold it down to the count of five, then push it again to restart.

On older iMacs, there is a tiny hole underneath the triangle symbol. Poke the paperclip in the round hole.

Most **iMacs** cannot restart with the key combination above. To restart an older iMac, straighten a paperclip and poke it into the restart hole, which is inside the side panel; it has a triangle above the tiny hole. Newer iMacs have a little button to push in that same position.

Can't Find Your Document

In the beginning you may very often save a document dutifully, but then when you get to your Desktop you **can't find** it anywhere. This is because when you saved it you weren't paying attention into which disk and/or folder you were saving the document. Be sure to read Chapter 15 on Saving Documents and Chapter 28 on Navigating, and carefully look at the dialog boxes pictured there so you understand how to save files where you can find them again.

Anyway, at the moment you can't find it. Use Sherlock (Chapter 26). When you find your document, put it in a folder you have created (page 106), just as if you would put it in a file folder in the filing cabinet: press-and-drag the document icon over to the folder or disk of your choice. The folder/disk should turn *black;* when it's black, let go and the document will drop right in.

Can't Open a File

Sometimes when you click on an icon you get a message that tells you the **file is locked or in use,** or maybe that **an application can't be found.**

This symbol indicates the disk is locked.

A locked disk is also called "write-protected."

If the **disk is locked,** you'll see a little lock symbol in the upper left of its window. When a disk is locked you can't save to it, although you can read, copy, and print files that are on it. To unlock a floppy disk, first eject it. In one of the corners is a little black tab that covers or uncovers a hole. When the hole is open, the disk is locked (seems backwards, doesn't it?). So to unlock it, switch the tab back so the hole is closed. (More details on page 30.)

A CD-ROM is always locked. "ROM" stands for "read-only memory," meaning you can only read things from the disk, you can't write anything onto it. There are also writable and rewritable CDs.

This is a locked file. I locked it in the Get Info window.

If the **file is locked,** click once on it and choose "Get Info" from the File menu. In the bottom-left corner of the box there is a checkbox labeled, "Locked." If that box is checked, then click in the box to uncheck it and thus unlock the file.

If the **folder is locked,** click once on it and choose "Get Info" from the File menu. In the "Show" menu right there in the Get Info box, choose "Sharing." There is a checkbox labeled, "Can't move, rename, or delete this item (locked)." If that box is checked, then click in the box to uncheck it and thus unlock the file.

This is a locked folder. I locked it through the Get Info box, in the "Sharing" section.

If the **file is in use,** then it's in use. Usually you get this message if you try to open an icon that looks like a Macintosh; Mac icons are part of the System.

Application can't be found

If a messsage tells you an **application can't be found,** then one of two things is happening:

- The software application in which you created the document is not in the computer. Even though your document icon may *look* like FileMaker Pro, to display itself the document has to go *into* the application FileMaker Pro.
- Some files cannot open straight from the Desktop, even if the application is in the computer. In this case, if you know the document was created in a certain application and you know that particular application is in your machine, then go into the *application* itself (double-click on its icon) and open the file you want from inside, choosing "Open" from the File menu.

Try the tip on page 128 to find another application that may open the file besides the one that created it. Most applications can usually open several file formats.

Viewing Clip Art Files

When trying to **view clip art,** often you will get the message that "An application can't be found," even when the program it was generated in is on the disk. It may be in a different version of the software you have. Open *the actual application itself,* then open each individual document through the File menu, choosing "Open." Also see the previous suggestion for "An application can't be found."

Most clip art does not need to be opened—you need to insert it into a document. In your word processor, for instance, check the menus for something like "Insert" or "Place," choose it, then find the clip art. Double-click the name of the clip art and it should appear on your document page.

System Crashes

"Not Enough Memory"

Running out of **RAM** is a primary cause of System crashes. RAM (random access memory) is the area in your computer where all information is temporarily stored while you are working on it. When you Save, you send that information permanently to the disk and thus free up that much space in RAM. If you don't save very often, **RAM gets full** and the Mac just checks out (crashes). If you have a lot of extensions (page 236), remember many of those get loaded into RAM as soon as you turn the computer on. Then your application gets loaded into RAM. Then the fonts you use get loaded into RAM. If you open more than one application at a time, they all take up RAM. Then as you work, there is not a great deal of room left. Read Chapter 29, Very Important Information. Decide whether you *really* need all those extensions and fonts and eliminate any unnecessary ones. If you run out of RAM often, buy more (ask your power user friend or local Mac user group).

Desktop File is full If the invisible **Desktop File gets too large,** you may run out of memory (and your computer will work slowly). At least several times a month you should *rebuild your Desktop* (it's very easy; see page 405).

Extension conflicts If you use **extensions,** keep in mind that it is not unusual for them to be buggy, unstable, corrupted, etc., especially the free ones. It's a well-known fact that they can cause problems, including System crashes. Use the Extensions Manager control panel to help discover the source of the problem (see pages 258–259): If you think one of your extensions might be a problem, turn it off, restart, and see if the problem clears up. Or turn off a number of them at once, then add them back one at a time, using your computer for several days between adding each one.

Text Formatting Unexpectedly Changes

It's not uncommon to open your document on another *System* and find major **formatting changes.** If you created a document on your hard disk using the font Baskerville, then gave a copy of the document on disk to a co-worker who opened it up and found it had transmogrified itself into the font Helvetica and all your formatting was thrown off, that's because Baskerville was not in the coworker's *System.* If the document can't find the font in which it was created, then it has to choose another from what is available. The solution is to make sure both Systems have the same fonts from the same vendors, or make sure you are both using the latest version of ATM from Adobe (see www.adobe.com).

Printing Doesn't Work

Oh dear. There are a number of reasons why printing sometimes doesn't work. Here are a few of the most common.

- One of the most common reasons why **printing won't work** is that the appropriate printer icon wasn't chosen. Go to Chooser from the Apple menu and choose your printer (see page 155).
- Make sure the printer is on, that it has paper, and that the paper tray, if there is one, is firmly attached.
- Make sure any networking cables are connected.
- If the hard disk that the *System Folder is on* is running out of space, the Mac cannot print. It needs some free space (always leave at least 10 percent of your hard disk free!) to send over the messages for printing. You may have to free up some space on that disk by removing a file or two.
- Don't print files that are on removable disks—first copy them to your internal hard disk, then print from there.

- Rebuilding the Desktop (see page 405) solves a lot of inexplicable printing problems. Rebuild your Desktop and turn off the printer for a couple of minutes. Try again. This often works.
- Sometimes gremlins prevent printing properly. If you've checked everything and there really seems to be no logical reason for the file not to print, go away for a while, let someone else print to that printer, shut down, come back later, try again. This sometimes works. One never knows.
- On an ImageWriter, make sure the Select light is on. It *must* be on in order to print.
- Also on an ImageWriter make sure the lever on the hand roller corresponds to the way you are feeding paper—that is, friction-feed for single sheets (that's the symbol with two rollers, towards the back); and pin-feed for pin-fed labels and paper (that's the symbol with one roller and little pins, pulled towards the front).

Netscape page prints tiny

When you **print a web page in Netscape,** the entire thing prints up about one-inch square! In Netscape, go to Page Setup and uncheck the box, "Fit to page if possible." Reprint the page.

There's Garbage Hanging Around Outside the Trash Can

If **garbage piles up around your trash can,** it's because you didn't put it *inside* the can, but set it down *outside,* just like the kids. When the *very tip of the pointer* touches the can and turns it black, that's the time to let go. *It doesn't matter if the icon you are throwing away is positioned over the can*—it's the **pointer tip** that opens the lid.

Gray Disk Icon is Left on the Screen

A **gray disk icon** means either the disk is open or it is in **RAM.**

If the disk itself is still in the drive, then the blank gray shadow only means that you have already double-clicked on it and its window is open somewhere on the screen. If you can't see the disk's window because there are other windows in the way, simply double-click on the gray disk shadow and it will come forth as the active window.

If the disk itself is not in the drive, then you most likely ejected that disk by choosing "Eject Disk" from a dialog box. This procedure does eject the disk, but also leaves its information in the Mac's *memory.* Read page 175 for an explanation of what happened and how to avoid it.

Lost Your Application? Other Windows Popped Up in Front of Your Face?

You **lost your application?** Your menu suddenly changed and you can't find "Font"? Now your window is buried under other windows? Don't worry—you just accidentally switched applications or perhaps you clicked on the Desktop and popped back to the Finder where all your Desktop windows are. Use the Application menu to choose the application you were previously working in: when you press on the Application menu (upper right of your menu bar) you will see a list of programs that are open. Choose the one you want. Then read Chapter 29 on Very Important Information, taking special note of the Application menu. Also use the Application menu to hide the windows of applications you're not using.

Desktop Windows Open Very Slowly

If your **Desktop windows open too slowly** or perhaps everything on the Desktop seems to take longer than it should, check to see if you have told your windows to calculate the folder size: In your window in a list view, under the column "Size," do you see the size of folders? That's what is slowing you down. To fix it, make sure that window is the active window, then from the View menu choose "View Options…" and uncheck the box, "Calculate folder size."

Erratic Typing or Mouse Movement

Is the movement of the **mouse rather erratic?** Does your typing jerk around? Do your menus not show up right away? You are probably trying to do something in the background, like copy a large file or print. While the computer is doing something like printing, it has to split its attention between you and the printer, which results in putting you on hold for seconds at a time. Just relax and it will go away when the printing or copying is done.

Can't Eject a CD or Cartridge

You can't just push a button to **eject a CD or most cartridge hard disks.** You must first *unmount them*—drag the icon to the trash, *or* select the icon and press Command Y. After it has unmounted (its icon will disappear from the screen), the disk will eject. Many CD and removable disk drives have a button you must push to get the disk out of the drive—don't try to push the button until after you have unmounted the disk.

If you get the annoying message that **the disk cannot be ejected because it is being shared,** you have to stop file sharing before the disk will unmount. If you still have the wonderful "Automated Task" option in your Apple menu, then slide down to "Automated Tasks" and out to "Stop File Sharing." To start file sharing again, use the same menu.

The Control Strip, that little bar that shows up in the bottom-left corner of the screen, has a control to start and stop file sharing. If for some reason you don't have it there, just go to the Apple menu, then Control Panels menu, choose "File Sharing," and turn it off there.

This is the Control Strip.

You Don't Have Access Privileges or Something is Locked

If you try to move or rename files in the System Folder or the Applications folder and you get a message telling you that something is **locked** or that you **don't have access privileges,** shoot it. No, that doesn't work. You must be using an operating system older than Mac OS 9: Go to the Control Panels (in the Apple menu) and choose General Controls. Uncheck the boxes that say, "Protect System Folder" or "Protect Application Folder." Close the General Controls control panel and try again.

Reset Switch

When you crash and must restart, sometimes you cannot get to the Desktop to choose "Restart" from the Special menu. (The "Restart" button on the alert box that tells you you've crashed almost never works.) Before you resort to actually turning off the power, try these:

- On most machines you can restart by holding down the Control and Command keys, then pushing the Power key (the key that turns on your Mac if you have the kind of Mac that you turn on by tapping the triangle-marked key on the keyboard). On iMacs, see the tip at the bottom of page 411.
- If that doesn't work, press the Reset Button on your Mac, if you have one. It's a little button somewhere on the front, side, or back of most Macintoshes. There are usually two buttons or tabs—the Reset one has a tiny triangle on it.
- If that doesn't work, turn off the computer by pressing the little button on the back (oh, sometimes it's on the front) of the computer box (not the the monitor). On some machines it isn't even a button, but a little plastic tab that presses in. It might look like this: ◐ or: ⏻

  After you turn it off, wait at least ten seconds before you turn it back on.
- Some computers don't have a separate little button for resetting the machine—you have to use the Power button. For instance, on some G4s, to turn off the computer when it crashes you must hold the Power button in for five seconds, then push it again to turn the machine back on. On some G3s, the little light that glows on the front of the box to tell you the machine is on is actually a Power button—push it to turn the machine off when all else fails.

Addendum

These are a few extra features that are new and specific to Mac OS 9 and 9.1. I apologize for relegating them to an addendum.

Software Update control panel

The **Software Update control panel** will go online for you, to the Internet, and find any available software updates for the applications you have on your Mac, download them for you, and install them. Be sure to check the box "Ask me before installing new software" because the files, as you can see in the example below, can be huge (the message says to ask before "installing," but it actually asks before downloading). On our pathetic QWest phone connectivity in New Mexico, downloading the updates would take about three days and even then it wouldn't work because we'd be disconnected long before that.

As you can see below, you can set up a schedule so the control panel will go online regularly (once a week is often enough) and check for you. If you have a fast, always-on connection, like a DSL, T1, ISDN, or cable, this can be a convenience that your Mac will implement while you are having your coffee.

Click the "Schedule..." button to arrange a schedule.

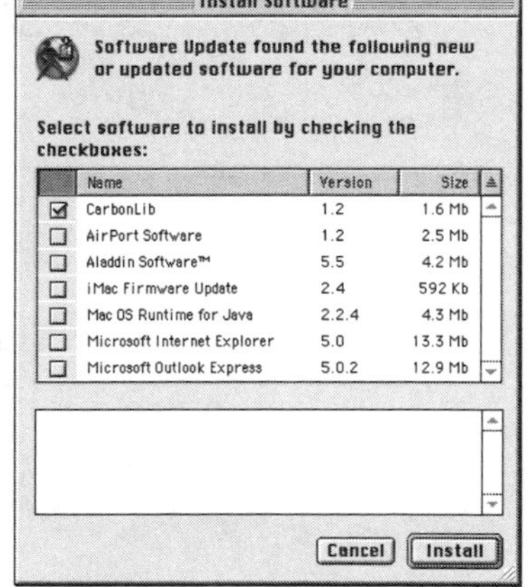

Put checkmarks in the boxes for the software you want updated. Then click "Install."

Multiple Users

The **Multiple Users control panel** is a wonderful solution for families who are sharing a computer, or even for small offices that have multiple users for one Mac. Once the users are set up, the computer opens to a welcome screen before it gets to the Desktop, as shown below, and the current user double-clicks their name. They log on (sign in) with a password, and the Mac is customized for them. There are three levels: **Normal,** which gives access to the entire computer; **Limited,** so you can limit the applications and uses a person has, but the Mac looks the same; and **Panels,** which is a great place for kids—it creates a very simplified, single-click environment with big buttons (shown below), and the user, a child, for instance, can only access what you allow. You're not stuck with anything—the system is entirely flexible and you can add or delete applications or access at any time.

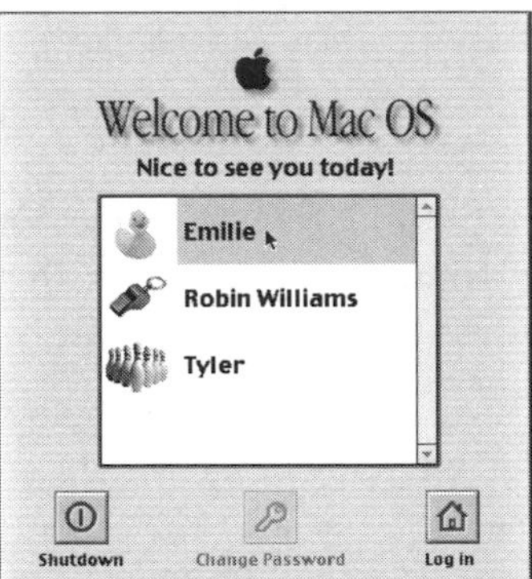

This is the welcome screen that you see once you turn on Multiple Users (see opposite page). A user just double-clicks their name, or selects their name and then clicks the "Log in" button.

The little message, "Nice to see you today!" is customizable (see opposite page), and so are the graphic icons for each name.

You do not need to shut down between users. Once Multiple User Accounts is on, your Special menu has this added item, "Logout," or Command Q.

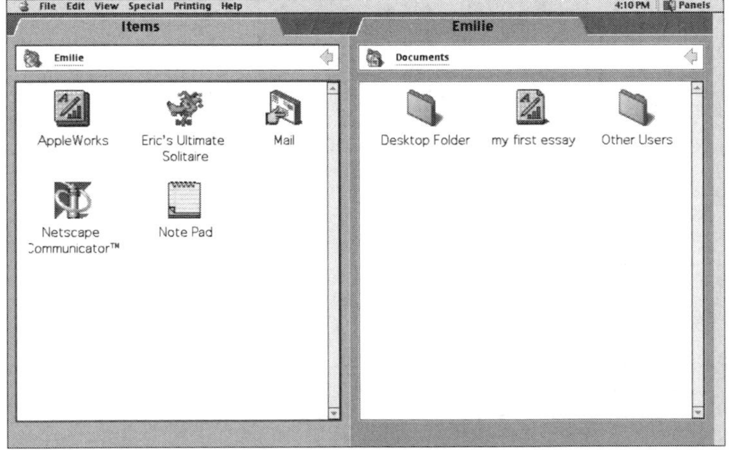

This is an example of what 8-year-old Emilie would see. If you have young children, put all of their educational software and games in a panel like this. Each child can log in to their own, customized Desktop.

To set up a new user:

1. From the Apple menu, slide down to Control Panels, then out to the side and choose "Multiple Users."
2. Make sure the button at the bottom is clicked "On," then click the "New User" button.
3. You'll see the dialog box shown below. If you don't see the bottom portion, as shown here, click the tiny triangle next to "Show Setup Details."

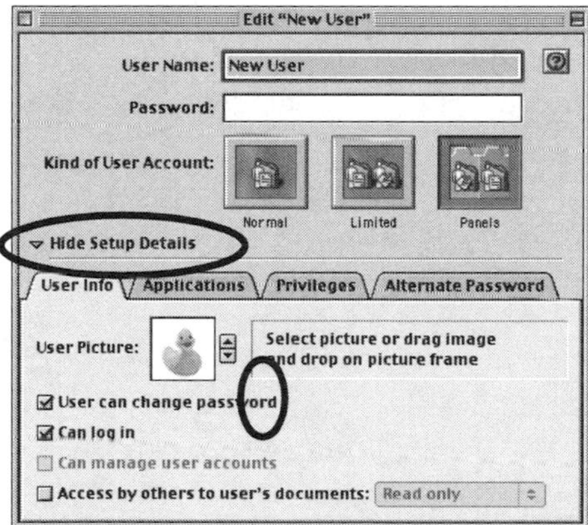

Click the arrows to cycle through icons to identify the new user. If you have photos on your Mac, simply drag the photo to this control panel and drop it right on top of the duck.

Set up a new user

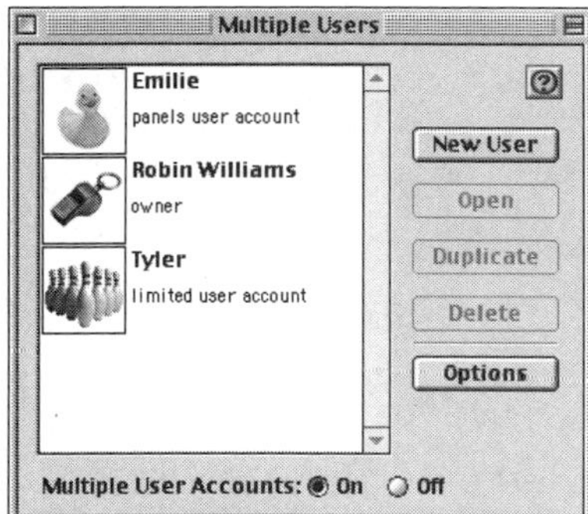

Tip: *If you decide **not** to make a new user, the control panel will yell at you because it wants a name and password. Go ahead and make one, then in the control panel, select the useless name and click the "Delete" button.*

4. Choose the "Kind of User Account" as described on the previous page, fill in the name and password, then click each available tab and make your choices (not all tabs are available for all account types). Close the dialog box. From the Special menu, choose "Logout," and then you can log back in again as the new user.

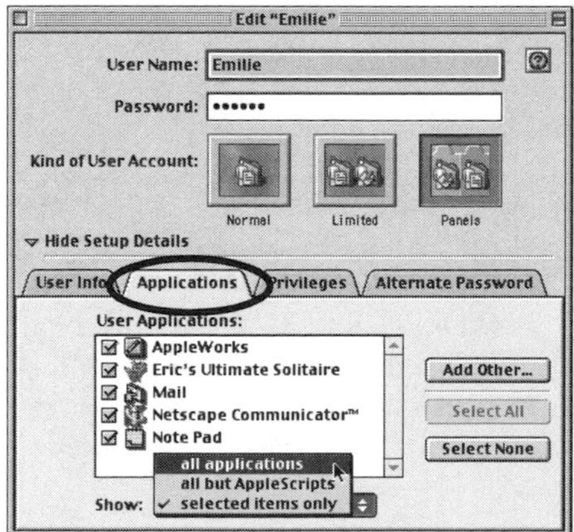

When you first click the "Applications" tab, you'll see every application on the hard disk. Choose the ones you want to appear in a panel.

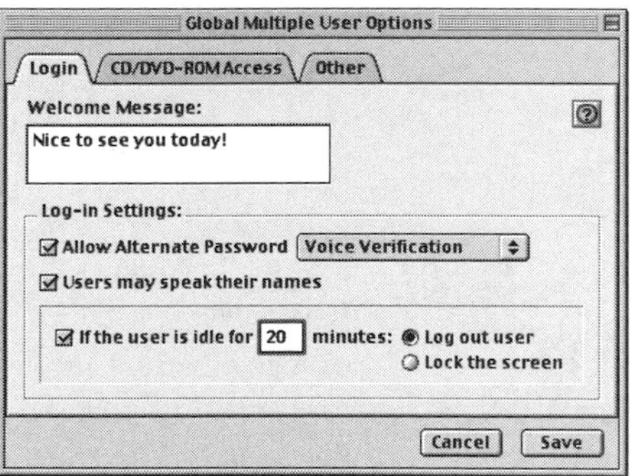

Click the "Options" button in the control panel to get this dialog box. Voice verification, where the user can create a spoken password instead of typing it (great for small children), is only available if your Speech control panel has the "Speakable Items" choice, which is not available on all Macs.

Apple File Security

Your Mac has several security features for you. The Keychain Access control panel is one, but for the few number of readers who will want to struggle through learning how to use and manage it, I must refer you to the Mac Help files, where everything is explained: at the Desktop, go to the Help menu, choose "Mac Help," then type in "Keychain access" and hit Return.

This is the file security program.

For readers who want a quick and easy way to password-protect files and applications, use **Apple File Security,** which should be in your Applications folder. When you double-click this icon, it opens a dialog box where you select the file you want to *encrypt* (which means to encode in such a way that no one can use it; they need a password to *decrypt* the file to make it usable). You are then asked to provide a passphrase (more than one word; use a memorable phrase and don't forget it!!). The icon of the file changes, as shown below. When someone double-clicks it, they'll get a dialog box asking for the passphrase.

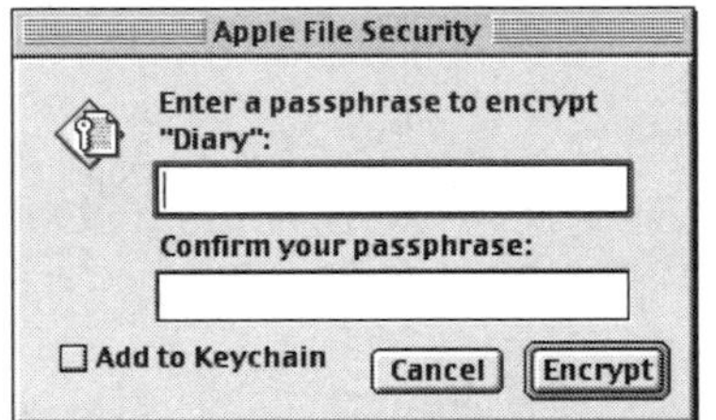

Create a passphrase to encrypt a document or application file. Encrypting an alias actually encrypts the original file. (You cannot encrypt entire folders or disks.)

Unless you know how to use Keychain Access, do not check the box to "Add to Keychain"!

These are examples of files that are encrypted. Notice the ***visual clue!***

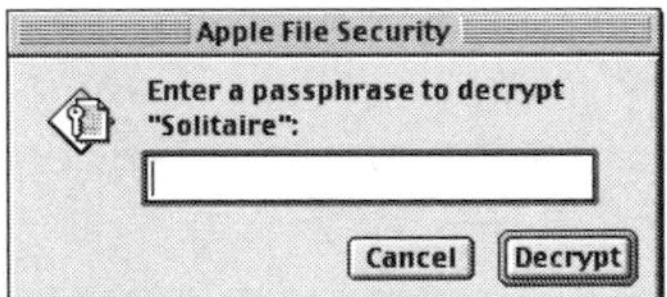

When you double-click an encrypted file, you will have to enter the passphrase.

Make an alias for easy security

Once a file has been decrypted, you must encrypt it again if you want it password-protected once more. If you do this often, make an alias of the Apple File Security application and leave the alias on your Desktop. Just drag a file to this alias, drop it on top, and you'll get the little dialog box asking for the passphrase.

Quiz Answers

1. Ks, Megs, Gigs, and Disks

1. Bit.
2. Bits, bytes, kilobytes, megabytes, gigabtyes.
3. 1.4 megabytes.
4. A magnet.
5. Locked.
6. Kilobytes.
7. Megabytes.
8. Megahertz, speed of the computer.
9. Speed of the computer.
10. Of course.

2. Starting Up

1. The disk that has the System Folder on it and is running the computer.
2. It is always in upper right corner.
3. System file, Finder file.
4. Nothing, unless you *know* it's supposed to be there.
5. Into the floppy disk drive.
6. Read The Manual.
7. Read them.
8. Nine point one point two.
9. Love letters dot sit.
10. One.

3. The Mouse

1. Single-click.
2. Double-click.
3. Single-click.
4. Double-click.
5. Double-click.
6. Press or single-click.
7. Press-and-drag, or single-click/single-click.
8. Control-click.
9. Shift-click.
10. Shift-click.

4. Desktop and Finder

1. a, home base.
2. The Finder is the software that runs the Desktop.
3. Folder icons.
4. Yes.
5. Select the Desktop by clicking on the trash can or hard disk icon; from the View menu, choose "Clean Up."
6. Desktop Pictures control panel.
7. The menu has "File Edit View Special Help" (particularly look for "Special") and the icon on the far right of the menu bar is the happy Mac OS face. Mac OS 9.1 also has a menu item called "Windows."
8. From the Application menu, choose "Hide Others."
9. Hold the Option key down while you click on any visible part of the Desktop, or while you choose "Finder" from the Application menu.
10. Of course.

5. Menus

1. "Close."
2. Three (Acquire, Export, and Preferences).
3. Eight (New, Open, Place, Save As, Save a Copy, File Info, Page Setup, Print).
4. Two.
5. Six (New, Open, Close, Save, Print, Quit).
6. Command N.
7. You'll get a dialog box.
8. Four menus (Font, Size, Underline, Color).
9. Two edit boxes (Position By and Spacing By).
10. Command Period.

6. Important Keys

1. Return or Enter.
2. Tab.
3. *Check grammar:* Command Shift G
   Word count: Option F15
   Renumber: Command F15
   Commands: Command Shift Option C
   Page break: Shift Enter
   Section break: Command Enter
4. Escape key: c
   Option key: k
   Control key: f
   Command key: h
   Tilde key: d
   Asterisk: i
   Shift key: b
   Forward slash: e
   Backslash: j
   Tab key: a
   Enter key: g

7. All Windows

1. Check labels with illustration on page 70.
2. Typo Class.
3. "Little Mac Book" is open.
4. 24 items in this folder (check information bar, top).
5. The scroll bar on the right is gray (in addition to the number of items in information bar).
6. It's off, no double arrows at bottom.

8. Desktop Windows

1. View by Size.
2. View by Name.
3. Click on the column header.
4. Select the window; from the File menu, choose "Print Window…."
5. Hold down the Command key and drag any visible window edge.
6. Hold down the Option key and click in the zoom box (upper right corner).
7. View as Icons, then Arrange by Name.
8. Command Option W.
9. Hold down Command key and press on the title bar of a window.
10. Gray folder means it is already open; if you double-click on it, its window will come forward as the active window.
11. Use the Spacebar.
12. To dig deep into folders and have them all close automatically.

9. Icons and Files

Match description with icon:

Application:	Nisus Writer
Hard disk:	Projects
Folder:	Charlie
Document:	TidBITS #862
Open file:	PageMill
Zip disk:	Research on Mary
Stationery pad:	Fax cover sheet
Unknown doc:	Buttons
Selected icon:	Blip
Trash can:	Trash
Control panel:	Keyboard
Picture file:	Picture 6
System file:	System
Ready to rename:	Online

Match application with document:

Acrobat Reader:	Jargon
Adobe PageMill:	sources.html
Adobe PageMaker:	Layout 1
MS Excel:	Planner
Nisus Writer:	Grocery List
SimpleText:	Letters

10. Folders

1. To organize.
2. It appears in the active window.
3. Command N.
4. Select the folder, wait until you see the border (visual clue) around the name, then type.
5. Double-click on it.
6. Folder opens to a window and you see the files that are stored inside.
7. *To expand:* select folder(s), press Command RightArrow.
   To compress: select folder(s), press Command LeftArrow.
8. Press Command A to select all; press Command LeftArrow.
9. You don't have folders all over the screen, and you can select items from more than one folder simultaneously.
10. Of course.

11. Copying and Selecting

1. a
2. c
3. b
4. c
5. c
6. False; always check to make sure you're not copying unnecessary or duplicate files.
7. False; it's the Shift key.
8. True (assuming they are in the same window).
9. True of course.
10. False; Tab will select files alphabetically.

12. Trash Can

1. A bulging can has something in it.
2. When you choose "Empty Trash" from Special menu.
3. It opens to a window, displaying its contents.
4. Drag the file to the trash can; select the file, from the File menu choose "Move to Trash"; select item, press Command Delete; hold down Control key and click on item, then select "Move to Trash."
5. Double-click trash can, drag item out of the window. Or select item, press Command Y.
6. No. Not unless you have disk recovery software or you take your hard disk to someone who does.
7. Hold down the Option key as you choose "Empty Trash" from the Special menu.
8. Option.
9. Select trash can; press Command I to Get Info (or choose "Get Info" from the File menu); uncheck the warning box.
10. No, it can be anywhere. You can also put aliases of the trash can anywhere.

13. Opening Files

1. Application; it's fancy, and there is no turned-down corner.
2. It will open the application, giving you a blank, new document or a choice of what kind of blank new document you want.
3. A document—it has the top-right corner turned down.
4. It will open the application it was created in and put itself on the screen.
5. Click on the column header "Kind."
6. "New" opens a new, blank page to create a document; "Open" opens a document you previously created and saved.
7. a: The directory, or list, is the box full of file names.
   b: "Book list," "Essay on Arab politics," or "Letter to Mom"
   c: Charlie.
   d: "Charlie" is a menu.

14. Word Processing

1. Select first, then do it to it.
2. I-beam: I
   Insertion point: |
   Pointer: ↖
3. I-beam.
4. Insertion point.
5. Either the character to its left, or the specifications you choose from the menu while the insertion point is flashing.
6. Usually Command B for Bold, Command I for Italic, Command U for Underline. Some applications also use a Shift key in combination (for instance, Command Shift B to change to Bold).
7. Press Command B (or whatever the command is), type the bold word(s), then press Command B again to toggle off the command.
8. 1) Select the paragraph (press-and-drag over it with the text tool, or try triple-clicking on it). 2) Cut the paragraph (from the Edit menu, choose "Cut," or press Command X). 3) Position the I-beam where you want to insert the paragraph, then click to set the insertion point at that spot. 4) Paste (from the Edit menu, choose "Paste," or press Command V).
9. *Cut:* Command X.
   Copy: Command C.
   Paste: Command V.
10. "Cut" removes the item and places it on the Clipboard. "Clear" removes the item and does *not* place it on the Clipboard—it's just gone.

15. Saving Documents

1. A (There is a border around the directory/list.)
2. B (There is an insertion point flashing in the edit box.)
3. You would select (highlight) the folder named "Figures 1 to 4" because it starts with the letter F.
4. It would open the folder "Notes" and the files in that folder would be listed in the directory.
5. Tab.
6. Press on the "My Stuff" label at the top.
7. You would view the files stored on the hard disk named "Power HD."
8. If the File menu has a command to "Revert," use it. Or close the document and when asked if you want to save changes, click "No."
9. In RAM, also known as "memory."
10. "Save as..."

16. Printing Documents

1. D/E: Open the document or turn on the printer.
   D/E: Turn on the printer or open the document.
   I: From the File menu, choose "Chooser."
   F. Choose the printer driver.
   B: Choose name of printer.
   J: Click the Setup button, if there is one, choose "Auto Setup," click OK.
   H: Close the Chooser.
   A: Choose "Page Setup," click OK.
   G: From File menu, choose "Print."
   C: Customize specs; click OK.
2. Because the computer is trying to do two things at once.
3. PostScript printer is a computer.
4. 11 x 13 inches.
5. The active window.
6. Double-click on the active Desktop Printer icon (the active one has a dark border).
7. "Hold" puts the **selected** print job on hold; "Stop Print Queue" puts **all** the print jobs in the list on hold.

17. Closing and Quitting

1. Close.
2. Quit.
3. Close.
4. Quit.
5. Close.
6. Quit.
7. Application menu, far-right of menu bar.
8. Three (Photoshop, InDesign, and AppleWorks).
9. AppleWorks—you can tell by the checkmark.
10. Choose Photoshop from the Application menu. Press Command Q to quit (or choose "Quit" from the File menu).

18. Ejecting Disks

1. The disk ejects.
2. Drag the disk to the trash can; select the disk and choose "Eject" from the Special menu (or press Command E); hold down the Control key and click on the disk, then choose "Eject" from the contextual menu.
3. From the Application menu, choose "TeachText" or "SimpleText," or whichever word processing program opened the ReadMe file. Then press Command Q to quit that program.
4. The computer cannot "read" the disk; its icon does not show up on the Desktop.
5. Command Y or Command E (after you select the disk icon).
6. The disk ejects, but leaves a gray icon of itself on the screen.
7. *First:* Insert the disk again.
   Then: If you don't have the disk, drag the icon to the trash.
   Then: Press Command Period (perhaps several times).
   Then: Restart the Mac.

19. Shut Down

1. Three (Appleworks, InDesign, Photoshop).
2. Choose the application from the menu, then press Command Q. Go back to the Application menu and choose another open application, then press Command Q. Continue until nothing is left in Application menu except Finder.
3. The Mac will ask if you want to save any open documents and quit any open applications before it shuts down the computer.
4. Command Option W.
5. The Mac will shut down, closing any open documents, quitting any applications, and asking if you're sure you want to shut down.

20. System Folder

1. Nothing.
2. Nothing.
3. No.
4. System and Finder.
5. No.
6. Drop the files onto the closed System Folder.
7. Apple Menu Items, Startup Items, Shut Down Items, Launcher Items.
8. Startup Items folder.
9. Apple Menu Items folder.
10. Of course not.

21. Fonts

1. PostScript.
2. Both PostScript and TrueType.
3. No. The screen fonts can hang around anywhere.
4. ATM (Adobe Type Manager).
5. *Cresci:* PostScript printer font.
   Pontif 18: bitmapped screen fonts
   Charcoal: TrueType
6. PostScript.
7. Drop the files (or a folder containing the files) onto the icon of the System Folder.
8. ATM cannot find the printer font for Avant Garde because its printer font lies in the PostScript printer's ROMs.

9/10 *Arial, Arial (italic), Arial (bold),* and *Arial (bold italic)* are one group because they are all members of one TrueType font family.
Florens Regular 18 is the screen font for *FloreReg* printer font, and *Florens Flourished 18* is the screen font for *FloreFlo* printer font—they are all part of one PostScript font family.

22. Desk Accessories

1. AppleCD Audio Player
2. Key Caps
3. Scrapbook
4. Stickies
5. Chooser
6. Calculator
7. Key Caps
8. Note Pad
9. Graphing Calculator
10. Jigsaw Puzzle

23. Apple Menu

1. Aliases (unless it is a true desk accessory).
2. A substitute for the real thing.
3. Into the Apple Menu Items folder, which is in the System Folder.
4. All of the items listed.
5. Type a blank space before each of their names.
6. Use the "Automated Task" in the Apple menu to "Add Alias to Apple Menu."
7. Go to the Apple Menu Options control panel and type a 0 (zero) for the number of recent servers you want the Mac to remember.
8. No.
9. Its name is in italic.
10. This is up to you!

24. Control Panels

1. Mouse control panel; set to fastest speed.
2. Desktop Pictures.
3. File Sharing; set File Sharing to Start.
4. Keyboard control panel.
5. Monitors control panel; click Monitors and change the "Resolution."
6. Date & Time; set to correct time.
7. General Controls; uncheck "Show Desktop when in background."
8. Monitors control panel; click Monitors; choose 256 or 16.
9. Sound control panel; click "Alerts," then click "Add" to record.
10. Apple Menu Options; type 0 (zero) in "Servers" edit box.

25. Aliases

1. A representation of the real file. An alias goes and gets the real file.
2. 2 to 3 K.
3. Select a file, then from the File menu choose "Make Alias." Or select a file, then press Command M. Or hold down the Control key, click on the file, choose "Make Alias." Or hold down Command and Option, drag the file to another window or to the Desktop. Or select a file, from the Apple menu choose "Add Alias to Apple Menu" from Automated Tasks.
4. Select the original file, from the Apple menu, slide down to "Automated Tasks" and choose "Add Alias to Apple Menu."
5. Nothing.
6. Nothing; they stay, now useless, right where you left them.

7. Click once on the alias. From the File menu, choose "Show Original" (or press Command R).
8. On the Desktop.
9. In the Startup Items folder found in the System folder.
10. The file is actually put into the **real** folder.
11. Nothing. The alias can still find it.

26. Sherlock

1. No. The more characters you give the computer, however, the faster it can find your file.
2. No. It is "case independent," meaning it does not check for caps and lowercase letters.
3. Yes. A space is a character to the computer.
4. a) Press Command F *or* click the hard disk channel ("Files"); make sure the "File Names" button is checked. b) First index the hard disk, then click the "Contents" button. c) Press Command H *or* click one of the Internet channels.
5. Click the "Edit..." button. Search for "name contains budget." Also search for "date created is within 2 weeks of 1/15/01."
6. Choose "Sherlock 2" from the Apple menu.
7. Double-click on the site name right there in the list of results.
8. Select the file in the top portion of the window, then press Command E.
9. Drag its icon right out of the top portion of the results list and into the trash can.
10. Click on the header name (Name, Size, Kind, Date) of the view you want them sorted (organized) by. Or choose a view from the View menu while the Sherlock results window is active.

28. Navigating and Saving

1. "Navigating" refers to finding your way around dialog boxes such as Open, Save As, import, export, etc.
2. The filing cabinet.
3. The folders on the hard disk or other disk. Or you could say it is another way of looking at the Desktop.
4. The disk name is displayed in the upper-right corner of the dialog box.
5. The folder name is displayed right above the list, or directory.
6. On the Desktop, right under the hard disk icon on the right (well, the Mac will put it in the next available spot under the hard disk icon).
7. On the Desktop, open that folder. If you forgot which folder you saved it into, you can always use Find File.
8. This is a "Save as" dialog box. You see the names of all the other files that are also saved into this folder so you don't name the new one the same as an old one—these are just gray because their only purpose is to let you know they are there. The folder names are black because you can open one of them to store a file within.
9. You will select the folder, "Adobe Magazine," because the **directory** is selected—it has a border around it.
10. Tab.

29. Very Important Information

1. Hard disk (storage, like your filing cabinet).
2. RAM (temporary, like your work on your desk).
3. RAM (System is stored on the hard disk, but goes into RAM to run).
4. Hard disk (System is stored on the hard disk, but goes into RAM to run).
5. RAM (memory is full and the computer can't work on that file anymore).
6. Hard disk (no more room left on your hard disk).
7. Hard disk (permanent, that is, until your hard disk dies).
8. Hard disk (the document is permanently stored onto the hard disk when you save).
9. RAM (document is stored in RAM until you save it to the disk).
10. RAM (analogy to your office—where you work and where the computer works).
11. RAM (which applications are still open in memory).
12. RAM (how much memory is allocated to the application).
13. Hard disk (how much storage space it takes up on your disk).
14. Both (using hard disk as memory).

30. Visual Clues

1. Five (Font, Size, Size Arrow, Underline, Color).
2. Into the Spacing edit box.
3. Two (Position, Spacing). (Actually, Size is also an edit box, but Microsoft doesn't follow guidelines, thus confusing people).
4. None to eight (checkboxes indicate you can choose any, all, or none of them).
5. One (you can only choose one radio button).
6. Three (OK, Cancel, Apply).
7. It would activate the OK button, as indicated by the dark border around it.
8. Yes, you can move it. You can tell by the lines in the title bar.
9. Command Period activates the Cancel button.
10. Ryan, as indicated by the border around the name.

31. What is the Internet?

1. Email, newsgroups, mailing lists, World Wide Web.
2. 28.8 (28,800)
3. Listserv
4. A Web site.
5. The "table of contents" page, often the first page you come to.
6. So you can see the web pages.
7. You can access the Internet by going through America Online.
8. No.
9. Log on to AOL, the double-click your Netscape icon.
10. The Macintosh!

32. Using the World Wide Web

1. b
2. d
3. a
4. c
5. a
6. d
7. a
8. b
9. c
10. d
11. c
12. b

Good Job!

Index

Symbols

b

g

h

I

j

k

l

m

n

O

P

u

W

Special Characters

Here is a handy chart for finding some of the special characters available that will make your work look more professional.

“	Option [	Opening double quote
”	Option Shift [	Closing double quote
‘	Option]	Opening single quote
’	Option Shift]	Closing single quote; Apostrophe
-	Hyphen	Hyphen
–	Option Hyphen	En dash
—	Option Shift Hyphen	Em dash
…	Option ;	Ellipsis *(this character cannot be separated at the end of a line as the three periods can)*
•	Option 8	Bullet
❏	o	(in font Zapf Dingbats)
■	n	(in font Zapf Dingbats)
□	n (outlined)	(in font Zapf Dingbats)
©	Option g	Copyright symbol
™	Option 2	Trademark symbol
®	Option r	Registration symbol
°	Option Shift 8	Degree symbol: 105° F
¢	Option $	Cents symbol
⁄	Option Shift !	Fraction bar *(doesn't allow fractions to break; doesn't descend below the baseline as the slash does)*
ﬁ	Option Shift 5	Ligature for **f** and **i**
ﬂ	Option Shift 6	Ligature for **f** and **l**
£	Option 3	English pound sign
¿	Option Shift ?	Spanish symbol
ç	Option c	Cedilla, lowercase
Ç	Option Shift c	Cedilla, capital
⌘	Control Q	(only in the Chicago font)
¤	Option Shift 2	Euro currency symbol (only in new fonts)

Accent Marks

Refer to page 140 to learn how to type these in; this page is merely a quick reference.

´	Option e
`	Option ~
¨	Option u
~	Option n
^	Option i

Text	Zapf	Shift	Option	Shift & Option
1	✑	✁	②	➚
2	✒	✠	♥	➢
3	✓	✃	❣	➜
4	✔	✄	❢	→
5	✕	☎	⑤	➞
6	✖	✾	❤	➟
7	✗	✆	❦	➠
8	✘	☛	❥	❡
9	✙	✈	❻	➡
0	✐	✉	❼	➣
-	✍	✿	❼	❽
=	✝	☞	②	⑥
q	❑	✱	❻	❺
w	◗	✶	❷	➢
e	❅	✥	♠	♠
r	❒	✲	♣	➤
t	▼	✴		
y	❙	✹	⑨	➧
u	◆	✺	①	①
i	❉	✩	①	➩
o	❏	✯	❿	④
p	❐	✰	❹	❸
[	✻	❛	❾	❿
]	✽	❝	➔	→
a	❁	✡	❴	❫
s	▲	✳	❧	➪
d	❄	✤	❶	➫
f	❆	✦	⑤	➬
g	❇	✧	♦	➼
h	❈	★	➛	➯
j	❊	✪	⑦	➩
k	❋	✫	➻	
l	●	✬	③	➩
;	✛	✚	⑩	➲
'	✇	✂	❾	③
z	❚	✷	❽	➽
x	❘	✸	⑥	➾
c	✳	✣	❵	❨
v	❖	✵	④	↕
b	❂	✢	❺	➺
n	■	✮	❞	➘
m	❍	✭	⑩	➥
,	✌	✜	⑦	➸
.	✎	✞	⑧	➶
/	✏	✟	↔	①
`	❀	❞	❀	❀
spacebar			❶	❶
\	✼	❜	⑧	⑨

In the chart to the left, find the **Zapf Dingbat** you wish to type. Hold down the Shift, the Option, or the Shift-and-Option keys while pressing the text character. The dingbat in the Zapf column needs no extra keys.

Sh]	❝	n (outlined)	□
Sh `	❞	l (outlined)	○
Sh [	❛	t (outlined)	▽
Sh \	❜	s (outlined)	△
		u (outlined)	◇
		Opt 6 (outlined)	♡

Opt Sh /	①	Opt u space	①
Opt 1	②	Opt =	②
Opt l	③	Opt Sh '	③
Opt v	④	Opt Sh o	④
Opt f	⑤	Opt 5	⑤
Opt x	⑥	Opt Sh =	⑥
Opt j	⑦	Opt ,	⑦
Opt \	⑧	Opt .	⑧
Opt Sh \	⑨	Opt y	⑨
Opt ;	⑩	Opt m	⑩

Opt d	❶	Opt Spcbar	❶
Opt w	❷	Opt ` then Sh a	❷
Opt Sh p	❸	Opt n then Sh a	❸
Opt p	❹	Opt n then Sh o	❹
Opt b	❺	Opt Sh q	❺
Opt q	❻	Opt q	❻
Opt 0	❼	Opt -	❼
Opt z	❽		
Opt '	❾		
Opt o	❿		

Just in case you wanna know

I live on 2.5 acres of high desert just south of Santa Fe, New Mexico. I helped found the Santa Fe Mac User Group and the New Mexico Internet Professionals Association. I have columns in several magazines, and I wrote a bunch of other books relating to the Mac, design, typography, and the web. I run around the country teaching and doing workshops, and I hang around online. I have three incredible kids who are growing up. I quite enjoy my life. But then, my sister Shannon says I can have fun in a paper bag.

What do I want to do for the *next* 45 years of my life? Learn a new language every two years, carve wood, write novels and screenplays, ride horses, play the steel drums, lay tile, create mosaics, have dinner parties, work with clay, dance, study literature and world history, play chess, pull weeds, travel, watch my family grow, wear hats, and make no one unhappy. So mote it be.

Colophon

I created this book entirely within PageMaker 6.5—the writing, editing, page layout, table of contents, and indexing. PageMaker's table of contents and indexing features are incredible. Today I'm working on a G4 with a 20-inch ViewSonic monitor. I used Captivate Select from Mainstay to create the screen shots and cleaned them up in Adobe Photoshop. I use Adobe Type Manager Deluxe to manage my fonts. I proofed pages on a LaserWriter Select 360.

The main fonts in this book are Bell for the body copy, Trade Gothic for the paragraph heads, and ITC Tapioca for the chapter openers. All are available at www.eyewire.com.